HISTORICAL THEOLOGY

HISTORICAL THEOLOGY

An Introduction to the History of Christian Thought

Alister E. McGrath

BLACKWELL *Publishers*

First published 1998
Reprinted 1998 (twice)

Blackwell Publishers Ltd
108 Cowley Road
Oxford OX4 1JF
UK

Blackwell Publishers Inc.
350 Main Street
Malden, Massachusetts 02148
USA

British Library Cataloguing in Publication Data
A CIP catalogue record for this book is available from the British Library.

Library of Congress Cataloging-in-Publication Data
McGrath, Alister E., 1953–
        Historical theology: an introduction to the history of Christian
thought / Alister E. McGrath.
        p.   cm.
        Includes bibliographical references and index.
        ISBN 0–631–20843–7 (hardcover : alk. paper). — ISBN 0–631–20844–5
(pbk. : alk. paper)
        1.   Theology—History. I. Title.
BT21.2.M17   1998
230'.09—dc21   97-37183
                                                                              CIP

Typeset in 10.5 on 13 pt Galliard
by Ace Filmsetting Ltd, Frome, Somerset
Printed in Great Britain by T J International Ltd, Padstow, Cornwall

This book is printed on acid-free paper

BRIEF CONTENTS

FULL CONTENTS

How to Use this Book

This book aims to introduce you to historical theology as an important and interesting subject. It is also a very large subject; to do justice to the subject, at least five substantial volumes would be required. This book aims to pack as much useful information into a single volume as is realistically possible, using approaches which have been tried and tested in classrooms in Europe, North America, and Australasia. The book makes use of some material already presented in the best-selling work *Christian Theology: An Introduction*, which has been reconfigured for the specific purpose of introducing students to the discipline of historical theology. Although much new material has been added, the basic approach and some contents of this earlier work have been retained.

It will help you to use this book if you understand the guiding principle which lies behind it. This principle is *selective attention*. It works on the assumption that you do not have the time to become familiar with every aspect of the history of Christian thought, but want a general familiarity with its most important aspects. The approach adopted is to begin by painting a scene using some very broad brush strokes, and then filling in the fine detail in selected areas of importance. This will allow you to come away from reading this book with a good general understanding of the development of Christian theology. Despite its brevity, however, the work includes a lot of material – considerably more than is included in most introductions of this kind.

The book opens with an Introduction which tries to explain what historical theology is, how it fits into the study of theology as a whole, and why it is a subject worth studying. You are strongly recommended to read this Introduction before proceeding further.

The history of Christian thought has been divided into four broad periods, as follows:

Chapter 1 The Patristic Period, *c*.100–451
Chapter 2 The Middle Ages and the Renaissance, *c*.500–1500

Chapter 3   The Reformation and Post-Reformation Periods, 1500–1750
Chapter 4   The Modern Period, 1750 – the present day

These divisions are a little arbitrary; however, they have proved useful in a teaching context, and have therefore been retained. Each chapter contains two major sections, as follows:

1   A general *overview* of the period in question, which identifies the historical background to the period, and its main theological developments, individual theologians, and schools of thought or theological movements which you need to know about. It also introduces the basic theological vocabulary which you will need to know to make sense of other theological works. You should read this overview before exploring the individual case studies which follow. If you need a very brief overview of the history of Christian thought, you are recommended to read only the four historical overviews, and leave the individual case studies for study at a later date.
2   A series of individual *case studies* which examine some of the themes of the period in question in much greater detail. This allows you to supplement a general understanding of the period with a specific knowledge of some of its significant themes. In some cases, the case studies are text-intensive, allowing you to engage with primary texts of importance. Here, you will be given guidance as to how to read the texts, and gain the most from them. Other case studies may take the form of general surveys, aiming to pack as much information as possible into a limited space.

If you are using the book to teach yourself historical theology, it is recommended that you read the chapters in the order in which they are presented. This volume works on the basis of "explain it the first time round." Thus the material on the medieval period assumes that you know about the patristic period, the material on the sixteenth century assumes that you know about the medieval period, and so forth. However, if you are using the book in conjunction with a taught course, you can easily work out which sections of the book relate to the ordering of material used by your teacher. If in doubt, ask for guidance. A substantial section entitled "For Further Reading" will allow you to identify books or articles which will be helpful to you if you want to follow up on anything that interested you, and which you would like to explore in great depth.

If you come across terms which you don't understand, you have two options. First, try the glossary at the end of the work, which may give you a brief definition of the term, and refer you to a discussion of the relevant material in the text. Second, try the index, which will provide you with a more extensive analysis of key discussion locations within the volume.

Finally, be assured that everything in this book – including the contents and the arrangement of the material – has been checked out at first hand with student audiences and readers in Australia, Canada, the United Kingdom, and the United States. The work is probably about as user-friendly as you can get. But both the author and publisher welcome suggestions from teachers and students for further improvement, which will be included in later editions of the work.

INTRODUCTION

This volume aims to serve as an introduction to historical theology. It is therefore important to have a sense of the place and importance of this discipline within theology as a whole. We may begin by considering the origins of theology as a distinct academic discipline in its own right, and gain an understanding of its main components.

THE CONCEPT OF "THEOLOGY": A BRIEF INTRODUCTION

The word "theology" is easily broken down into two Greek words: *theos* (God), and *logos* (word). Theology is thus "discourse about God," in much the same way as "biology" is discourse about life (Greek: *bios*). If there is only one God, and if that God happens to be the "God of the Christians" (to borrow a phrase from the second-century writer Tertullian), then the nature and scope of theology is relatively well defined: theology is reflection upon the God whom Christians worship and adore.

The word "theology" is not biblical, but came to be used occasionally in the early patristic period to refer to at least some aspects of Christian beliefs. Thus Clement of Alexandria, writing in the late second century, contrasted Christian *theologia* with the *mythologia* of pagan writers, clearly understanding "theology" to refer to "Christian truth claims about God," which could be compared with the spurious stories of pagan mythology. Other writers of the patristic period, such as Eusebius of Caesarea, also use the term to refer to something like "the Christian understanding of God." However, it seems that the word was not used to refer to the entire body of Christian thought, but only to those aspects relating directly to God.

Yet Christianity came into existence in a polytheistic world, where belief in the existence of many gods was a commonplace. Part of the task of the earliest Christian writers appears to have been to distinguish the Christian god from other gods in the religious marketplace. At some point, it had to be asked which god Christians were talking about, and how this god related to the "God of Abraham, Isaac, and Jacob," who figures so prominently in the Old Testament. The doctrine of the Trinity appears to have been, in part, a response to the pressure to identify the god that Christian theologians were speaking about.

As time passed, polytheism began to be regarded as outdated and rather primitive. The assumption that there was only one god, and that this god was identical to the Christian god, became so widespread that, by the early Middle Ages in Europe, it seemed self-evident. Thus Thomas Aquinas, in developing arguments for the existence of God, did not think it worth demonstrating that the god whose existence he had proved was the "god of the Christians": after all, what other god was there? To prove the existence of god was, by definition, to prove the existence of the Christian god.

Theology was thus understood as systematic analysis of the nature, purposes and activity of God. At its heart lay the belief that it was an attempt, however inadequate, to speak about a divine being, distinct from humans. Although "theology" was initially understood to mean "the doctrine of God," the term developed a subtly new meaning in the twelfth and thirteenth centuries, as the University of Paris began to develop. A name had to be found for the systematic study of the Christian faith at university level. Under the influence of Parisian writers such as Peter Abelard and Gilbert de la Porrée, the Latin word *theologia* came to mean "the discipline of sacred learning," embracing the totality of Christian doctrine, not merely the doctrine of God.

There is no doubt that the introduction of theology into university circles in the twelfth and thirteenth centuries gave a new stimulus to the systematization of the subject. Medieval universities – such as Paris, Bologna, and Oxford – generally had four faculties: arts, medicine, law, and theology. The faculty of arts was seen as entry level, qualifying students to go on to more advanced studies in the three "higher faculties." This general pattern continued into the sixteenth century, as can be seen from the educational backgrounds of two leading theologians of this period. Martin Luther initially studied arts at the University of Erfurt, before going on to study within the higher faculty of theology. John Calvin began his university life by studying arts at the University of Paris, before going on to study law at the University of Orléans. The result of this development was that theology became established as a significant component of advanced study at European universities. As more and more universities were established in western Europe, so the academic study of theology became more widespread.

Initially, the study of Christianity in western Europe was focused on schools attached to cathedrals and monasteries. Theology was generally understood to be concerned with practical matters, such as issues of prayer and spirituality, rather than as a theoretical subject. However, with the founding of the universities, the academic study of the Christian faith gradually moved out of monasteries and cathedrals into the public arena. The word "theology" came to be used extensively at the University of Paris during the thirteenth century to refer to the systematic discussion of Christian beliefs in general, and not simply beliefs about God. The use of the word in this sense can be seen to a limited extent in earlier works, such as the writings of Peter Abelard. However, the work which is widely regarded as being of decisive importance in establishing the general use of the term appeared in the thirteenth century – Thomas Aquinas' *Summa Theologiae*. Increasingly, theology came to be seen as a theoretical rather than a practical subject, despite reservations about this development.

Many early thirteenth-century theologians, such as Bonaventure and Alexander of Hales, were concerned about the implications of neglecting the practical side of theology. However, Thomas Aquinas' argument that theology was a speculative and theoretical discipline gained increasing favor among theologians. This alarmed many medieval spiritual writers, such as Thomas à Kempis, who felt that this encouraged speculation about God rather than obedience to God. At the time of the Reformation, writers such as Martin Luther attempted to rediscover the practical aspects of theology. The Genevan Academy, founded by Calvin in 1559, was initially concerned with the theological education of pastors, oriented toward the practical needs of ministry in the church. This tradition of treating theology as concerned with the practical concerns of Christian ministry would continue in many Protestant seminaries and colleges. However, later Protestant writers operating in a university context generally returned to the medieval understanding of theology as a theoretical subject, even if they made it clear that it had certain definite practical implications in the areas of spirituality and ethics.

The rise of the Enlightenment during the eighteenth century, particularly in Germany, called the place of theology in the university into question. Enlightenment writers argued that academic inquiry should be free from any kind of external authority. Theology was regarded with suspicion, in that it was seen to be based on "articles of faith," such as those contained in the Christian creeds or in the Bible. Theology came increasingly to be seen as outmoded. Kant argued that university faculties of philosophy were concerned with the pursuit of truth, while other faculties (such as theology, medicine or law) were concerned with more practical matters, such as ethics and good health. Increasingly, philosophy came to be seen as the discipline which was concerned with issues of truth; the continuing existence of a university faculty of theology would have to be justified on other grounds.

One of the most robust justifications of the need for university faculties of theology was provided in the early nineteenth century by F. D. E. Schleiermacher, who argued that it was essential for the good of both the church and state to have a well-educated clergy. In his *Brief Outline of the Study of Theology* (1811),

Schleiermacher argued that theology had three major components: philosophical theology (which identifies the "essence of Christianity"); historical theology (which deals with the history of the church, in order to understand its present situation and needs); and practical theology (which is concerned with "techniques" of church leadership and practice). This approach to theology had the result of linking its academic credentials with public agreement that it was important for society to have a well-educated clergy. This assumption was fine in early nineteenth-century Berlin, where Schleiermacher was based. But with the rise of secularism and pluralism in the west, its validity has come increasingly to be questioned.

In countries in which a strongly secular approach came to be adopted, Christian theology was virtually excluded from the university curriculum. The French Revolution of 1789 led to a series of measures designed to eliminate Christian theology from public education at every level. Most of the older universities in Australia (such as the Universities of Sydney and Melbourne) were founded on the basis of strongly secular assumptions, with theology being excluded as a matter of principle. These strongly secular ideologies are now being relaxed, so that undergraduate degrees in theology, or with significant theological components, are now available in Australia.

However, it is a pluralist rather than a secular approach which is now more widespread in the west, particularly in North America. Here, the distinctive position of Christian theology in public education has been called into question, in that it is held to privilege one religion over others. One result of this trend has been the formation of "faculties of religion" in state universities, in which a variety of religious positions are tolerated. Christian theology can therefore be taught in such a context, but only as one aspect of religious studies as a whole. For this reason, the most important centers of Christian theological education and research now tend to be in seminaries, in which a more committed approach to the issues can be adopted.

In the last decades, a new debate has opened up in North America and beyond over the proper function of theology. The original stimulus to this debate was a volume published by Edward Farley in 1983, entitled *Theologia: The Fragmentation and Unity of Theological Education*. Farley argued that theology has changed its meaning from its classic sense of "a heartfelt knowledge of divine things" to the mastery of different and unconnected techniques. Theology has become fragmented into a collection of unrelated theoretical and practical disciplines, and lost any sense of coherence. No longer is theology a unitary discipline; it has become an aggregate of unrelated specialities. The debate now ranges more widely than this, and has raised questions about the "architecture of theology" – for example, the relationship between biblical studies and systematic theology, or systematic and pastoral theology.

With this point in mind, we may now turn to explore the architecture of theology, as we consider its various components, before considering the discipline of historical theology as a subject in its own right.

THE ARCHITECTURE OF THEOLOGY

The great medieval scholar Etienne Gilson liked to compare the great systems of scholastic theology to "cathedrals of the mind." It is a powerful image, which suggests permanence, solidity, organization, and structure – qualities which were highly prized by the writers of the period. Perhaps the image of a great medieval cathedral, evoking gasps of admiration from parties of camera-laden tourists, seems out of place today; the most that many university teachers of theology can expect these days, it seems, is a patient tolerance. But the idea of theology possessing a structure remains important. For theology is a complex discipline, bringing together a number of related fields in an uneasy alliance. Our attention in this volume will focus on historical theology, which we shall explore in the following section. However, it will be helpful to introduce some of the other components of the discipline of theology at this stage in the work.

Biblical Studies

The ultimate source of Christian theology is the Bible, which bears witness to the historical grounding of Christianity in both the history of Israel and the life, death, and resurrection of Jesus Christ. (Note that the word-pairs "Scripture" and "the Bible," and "scriptural" and "biblical," are synonymous for the purposes of theology.) As is often pointed out, Christianity is about belief in a person (Jesus Christ), rather than belief in a text (the Bible). Nevertheless, the two are closely interlocked. Historically, we know virtually nothing about Jesus Christ, except what we learn from the New Testament. In trying to wrestle with the identity and significance of Jesus Christ, Christian theology is thus obliged to wrestle with the text which transmits knowledge of him. This has the result that Christian theology is intimately linked with the science of biblical criticism and interpretation – in other words, with the attempt to appreciate the distinctive literary and historical nature of the biblical texts, and to make sense of them.

The importance of biblical studies to theology is easily demonstrated. The rise of humanist biblical scholarship in the early 1500s demonstrated a series of translation errors in existing Latin versions of the Bible. As a result, pressure grew for the revision of some existing Christian doctrines, which were grounded in biblical passages which were once held to support them, but which now turned out to say something rather different. The sixteenth-century Reformation may plausibly be argued to represent an attempt to bring theology back into line with Scripture, after a period in which it had departed considerably from it.

The discipline of systematic theology (to which we shall turn in a moment) is thus dependent upon biblical scholarship, although the extent of that dependence is controverted. The reader must therefore expect to find reference to modern scholarly debates over the historical and theological role of the Bible in the present volume. To give an example, it is impossible to understand the development of modern Christologies without coming to terms with at least some of the developments in biblical scholarship over the last two centuries. Rudolf Bultmann's kerygmatic approach to theology can be argued to bring together contemporary New Testament scholarship, systematic theology, and philosophical theology (specifically, existentialism). This illustrates a vitally important point: systematic theology does not operate in a watertight compartment, isolated from other intellectual developments. It responds to developments in other disciplines (especially New Testament scholarship and philosophy).

Systematic Theology

The term "systematic theology" has come to be understood as "the systematic organization of theology." But what does "systematic" mean? Two main understandings of the term have emerged. First, the term is understood to mean "organized on the basis of educational or presentational concerns." In other words, the prime concern is to present a clear and ordered overview of the main themes of the Christian faith, often following the pattern of the Apostles' Creed. In the second place, it can mean "organized on the basis of presuppositions about method." In other words, philosophical ideas about how knowledge is gained determine the way in which material is arranged. This approach is of particular importance in the modern period, when a concern about theological method has become more pronounced.

In the classic period of theology, the subject matter of theology was generally organized along lines suggested by the Apostles' Creed or Nicene Creed, beginning with the doctrine of God, and ending with eschatology. Classic models for the systematization of theology are provided by a number of writings. The first major theological textbook of western theology is Peter Lombard's *Four Books of the Sentences*, compiled at the University of Paris during the twelfth century, probably during the years 1155–8. In essence, the work is a collection of quotations (or "sentences"), drawn from patristic writers in general, and Augustine in particular. These quotations were arranged topically. The first of the four books deals with the Trinity, the second with creation and sin, the third with incarnation and Christian life, and the fourth and final book with the sacraments and the last things. Commenting on these sentences became a standard practice for medieval theologians, such as Thomas Aquinas, Bonaventure, and Duns Scotus, although Thomas Aquinas's *Summa Theologiae*, dating from a century later, surveyed the totality of Christian theology in three parts, using principles similar to those adopted by Peter Lombard, while placing greater emphasis on philosophical questions (particularly those raised by Aristotle) and the need to reconcile the different opinions of patristic writers.

Two different models were provided at the time of the Reformation. On the Lutheran side, Philip Melanchthon produced the *Loci Communes* ("Commonplaces") in 1521. This work provided a survey of the main aspects of Christian theology, arranged topically. John Calvin's *Institutes of the Christian Religion* is widely regarded as the most influential work of Protestant theology. The first edition of this work appeared in 1536, and its definitive edition in 1559. The work is arranged in four books, the first of which deals with the doctrine of God, the second with Christ as mediator between God and humanity, the third with the appropriation of redemption, and the final book with the life of the church. Other more recent major works of systematic theology to follow similar lines include Karl Barth's massive *Church Dogmatics*.

In the modern period, issues of method have become of greater importance, with the result that the issue of "prolegomena" (see p. 333) has become significant. An example of a modern work of systematic theology which is heavily influenced by such concerns is F. D. E. Schleiermacher's *Christian Faith*, the first edition of which appeared in 1821–2. The organization of material within this work is governed by the presupposition that theology concerns the analysis of human experience. Thus Schleiermacher famously places the doctrine of the Trinity at the *end* of his systematic theology, whereas Aquinas placed it toward the beginning.

Philosophical Theology

Theology is an intellectual discipline in its own right, concerned with many of the questions that have intrigued humanity from the dawn of history. Is there a god? What is god like? Why are we here? Questions such as this are asked outside the Christian community, as well as within it. So how do these conversations relate to one another? How do Christian discussions of the nature of God relate to those within the western philosophical tradition? Is there a common ground? Philosophical theology is concerned with what might be called "finding the common ground" between Christian faith and other areas of intellectual activity. Thomas Aquinas' Five Ways (that is, five arguments for the existence of God) are often cited as an example of philosophical theology, in which non-religious arguments or considerations are seen to lead to religious conclusions.

In the course of this work, we shall explore some of the areas in which philosophical considerations have made a considerable impact upon Christian theology. Examples include the patristic analysis of the nature of God, which shows a marked influence from classical Greek philosophy; Thomas Aquinas' arguments for the existence of God, which are influenced by Aristotelian physics; the Christology of nineteenth-century writers such as D. F. Strauss, which draws upon a Hegelian understanding of the historical process; or the existential approach to Christology, developed by Rudolf Bultmann. In each case, a philosophical system is treated as resource or dialogue partner in the development of a theology. Many theologians have worked on the basis of the assumption that a philosophy provides a secure foundation on which theology may build.

Nevertheless, it must be noted that there exists a trend within Christian theology which has been severely critical of attempts to use secular philosophies in matters of theology. Tertullian raised the question in the second century: "What has Athens to do with Jerusalem? or the Academy with the church?" More recently, the same critical reaction may be seen in the writings of Karl Barth, who argued that the use of philosophy in this way ultimately made God's self-revelation dependent upon a particular philosophy, and compromised the freedom of God. The reader can therefore expect to encounter, both in the past and in the present, a continuing debate concerning the scope and limits of philosophy within theology.

Pastoral Theology

It cannot be emphasized too strongly that Christianity does not occupy its present position as a global faith on account of university faculties of theology or departments of religion. There is a strongly pastoral dimension to Christianity, which is generally inadequately reflected in the academic discussion of theology. Indeed, many scholars have argued that Latin American liberation theology represents an overdue correction of the excessively academic bias of western theology, with a healthy correction in the direction of social applicability. Theology is here seen as offering models for transformative action, rather than purely theoretical reflection.

This academic bias is, however, a recent development. Puritanism is an excellent instance of a movement which placed theological integrity alongside pastoral applicability, believing that each was incomplete without the other. The writings of individuals such as Richard Baxter and Jonathan Edwards are saturated with the belief that theology finds its true expression in pastoral care and the nurture of souls. In more recent years, this concern to ensure that theology finds its expression in pastoral care has led to a resurgence of interest in pastoral theology. This development is reflected in the present volume, which is written on the basis of the assumption that many of its readers, like its writer, are concerned to bring the full critical resources of Christian theology to the sphere of pastoral ministry.

Church History

An understanding of the development of the history of Christianity, especially its institutional elements, is widely regarded as an integral part of the discipline of theology. Students who intend to minister in a particular Christian tradition, or who are interested in deepening their understanding and appreciation of their own tradition, will find the history of that tradition to be of particular importance. Many church history courses include elements of historical theology. For example, it is very difficult to understand the origins and development of the European Reformation without some understanding of Luther's doctrine of justification by faith alone, just as a lack of knowledge of the issues surrounding the Donatist controversy will make it hard to make sense of the history of the church in North Africa during the fourth century.

Nevertheless, church history must be considered as a discipline with its own integrity, despite this clear overlap of interest with historical theology. The Toleration Edict of Valerius (April 311) is of enormous importance in church history, in that it established Christianity as a legitimate religion within the Roman Empire, and opened the way to numerical growth and institutional advancement. Yet the Edict has little importance to historical theology, in that it does not contribute *directly* to the development of theological reflection. To deal with the history of the church is to study cultural, social, political, and institutional factors which have shaped the development of the church down the ages. It is to study the emergence of institutions (such as the papacy, the episcopacy, and lay fraternities) and movements (such as Methodism, Pentecostalism, and the Cathars). Christianity is set within the flux of history, and church history aims to explore the particular place of Christian ideas, individuals and institutions within that flux. That influence is two-way: Christianity both influences and is influenced by culture. The study of church history allows insights into history in general, as well as into theology in particular.

HISTORICAL THEOLOGY: ITS PURPOSE AND PLACE

Historical theology is the branch of theological inquiry which aims to explore the historical development of Christian doctrines, and identify the factors which were influential in their formulation. It will be clear that historical theology therefore has direct and close links with the disciplines of church history and systematic theology, despite differing from them both. The relationship may be clarified as follows:

1 *Church History* is of major importance to historical theology, in that it identifies factors within the history of the Christian church which are of

importance to understanding the development of aspects of Christian theology. Historical theology is the branch of theology which aims to explore the historical situations within which ideas developed or were specifically formulated. It aims to lay bare the connection between context and theology. For example, it demonstrates that it was no accident that the doctrine of justification by faith first became of foundational significance in the late Renaissance. It shows how, for example, the concept of salvation, found in Latin American liberation theology, is closely linked with the socio-economic situation of the region. It illustrates how secular cultural trends – such as liberalism or conservatism – find their corresponding expression in theology. Church history and historical theology thus relate to each other in a positive and symbiotic manner.

2 *Systematic theology* aims to provide a contemporary statement of the leading themes of the Christian faith. A full understanding of the historical develop-ment of that doctrine is essential to its comtemporary restatement. Yet historical theology does more than simply provide the background material to modern theological statements. It indicates the extent to which theologi-cal formulations are conditioned by the environment in which they emerge. Contemporary theological statements are no exception to this rule. Histori-cal theology indicates the way in which ideas which were actively appropriated by one generation are often abandoned as an embarrassment by another. Historical theology thus has both a *pedagogic* and a *critical* role, aiming to inform systematic theologians about what has been thought in the past (and why!), while identifying the factors which make some form of restatement necessary.

Theology has a history. This insight is too easily overlooked, especially by those of a more philosophical inclination. Christian theology can be regarded as an attempt to make sense of the foundational resources of faith in the light of what each day and age regards as first-rate methods. This means that local circumstances have a major impact upon theological formulations. Christian theology regards itself as universal, in that it is concerned with the application of God's saving action toward every period in history. Yet it is also characterized by its particularity as an experience of God's saving work in particular cultures, and is shaped by the insights and limitations of persons who were themselves seeking to live the gospel within a particular context. The universality of Christianity is thus complemented with – rather than contradicted by – its particular application.

The Development of Historical Theology

The origins of historical theology are generally agreed to lie in the sixteenth century. The Reformation witnessed an intense debate over Christian authenticity, in which the continuity between both the Protestant and Catholic reformations and the early church came to be seen as critically important. As a result, writers on both sides of the debate found that they had to become familiar with both patristic theology and the modification of these ideas in the Middle Ages. Although this study was undertaken primarily for polemical reasons, it led to the production of a large number of works of reference in this field, including editions of the works of patristic writers.

A perhaps more important development took place during the eighteenth century, with the rise of the movement known as "the history of dogma," usually known in its German form, *Dogmengeschichte*. The basic assumption of this movement was that the doctrinal formulations of the church ("dogmas"), especially during the patristic period, were heavily conditioned by the social and cultural conditions of the era. This conditioning, which could be uncovered and subjected to critical scrutiny and evaluation by historical methods, made such doctrinal formulations inappropriate for the modern church, which was obliged to develop restatements of these doctrines appropriate to the modern period.

This program can be seen in the writings of G. S. Steinbart, who argued that the Augustinian doctrine of original sin – foundational to traditional understandings of baptism and the work of Christ – was basically little more than a hangover from Augustine's Manichaean period. It represented the intrusion of pagan ideas into Christianity, and had no place in a proper Christian theology. Steinbart's analysis, which extended to include Anselm of Canterbury's doctrine of the satisfaction of Christ, represents a classic instance of the criticism of dogma by a critical study of its origins.

This program, extended by writers such as F. C. Baur and A. B. Ritschl, reached its climax in the work of Adolf von Harnack. In his *History of Dogma* (which occupies seven volumes in English translation), Harnack argued that dogma was not itself a Christian notion. Rather, it arose through the expansion of Christianity from its original Palestinian context to a Hellenistic milieu. As a result, Christian writers absorbed the Hellenistic tendency to conceptualize, and use a metaphysical framework to articulate the gospel. Harnack saw the doctrine of the incarnation as perhaps the most obvious instance of the influence of Hellenism upon Christianity, and argued that historical analysis opened the way for its elimination. For Harnack, the gospel was about Jesus himself, and the impact which he had upon people. The shift from soteriology to the abstract metaphysical speculation of Christology is, for Harnack, an insidious yet reversible theological development. Harnack singled out Martin Luther as one who attempted to eliminate metaphysics from theology, and commended him as an example to posterity.

Although Harnack's emphasis upon the "Hellenization" of the gospel is now regarded as overstated, the general principles which he developed are still regarded as valid. The historian of dogma can still discern areas of Christian theology in which a number of central conditioning assumptions appear to derive from Greek metaphysics. The modern debate about whether God can suffer (which we shall explore further below) has drawn attention to the manner in which the classical notion of the *apatheia* of God appears to rest upon the assumptions of Greek metaphysics, rather than the Old and New Testament witness to the acts of God in history.

Harnack's particular interest in historical theology rested on his belief that history provided a means for the correction or elimination of dogma. This "critical" function of historical theology remains important, and we shall explore it in more detail presently. Yet Harnack's massive amount of writing in this field also caused growing interest in the field of historical theology as a subject worthy of interest in its own right.

Historical Theology as a Pedagogic Tool

Many students of church history neglect the role of ideas, in order to focus on the sociological, economic, and institutional aspect of this fascinating subject. Yet one can never hope to understand some of the most important episodes in that history without at least some understanding of the ideas which so influenced the course of church history. Just as a historian of the Russian Revolution cannot ignore the ideas of Marx, Engels, Lenin, and Trotsky, so the church historian needs to understand the ideas of Athanasius, Augustine, and Luther (to name but three). Historical theology acts as a major resource to those studying church history, allowing them to understand the specific nature of the ideas which affected the church at critical periods in that history.

Historical theology does not, however, merely help us to understand the past; it is a resource for theology in the present. Many critics of modern theology have argued that the discipline behaves as if it were the first to deal with the issue in question, or that all previous attempts to wrestle with the issue could be disregarded completely. It is virtually impossible to do theology as if it had never been done before. There is always an element of looking over one's shoulder, to see how things were done in the past, and what answers were then given. Part of the notion of "tradition" is a willingness to take seriously the theological heritage of the past. The Swiss Protestant theologian Karl Barth expresses this idea in a pointed form:

> We cannot be in the church without taking as much responsibility for the theology of the past as for the theology of the present. Augustine, Thomas Aquinas, Luther, Schleiermacher and all the rest are not dead but living. They still speak and demand a hearing as living voices, as surely as we know that they and we belong together in the church.

It is therefore of importance that the reader becomes familiar with the rich legacy of the Christian past, which provides vital reference points for the modern debate.

Historical theology thus provides an essential pedagogical resource for the contemporary statement of theology. The following points are of especial importance in this respect:

1   Historical theology provides us with a "state of the question" report on major theological themes, allowing us to identify what has already been discussed.
2   By studying the discussion of theological issues in the past, an understanding may be gained of both the strengths and weaknesses of existing approaches to questions.
3   Historical theology allows us to identify "landmarks" in the development of Christian thinking, which remain relevant and important today. Such "landmarks" include writers (such as Athanasius, Augustine, and Aquinas), debates (such as the Donatist and Arian controversies), and documents (such as the Nicene Creed).

In these ways and others, historical theology acts as an important pedagogical resource for systematic theology.

Historical Theology as a Critical Tool

It may seem to be little more than a self-evident fact to state that Christianity often unconsciously absorbs ideas and values from its cultural backdrop. Yet that observation is enormously important. It points to the fact that there is a provisional or conditional element to Christian theology, which is not necessitated by or implied in its foundational resources. In other words, certain ideas which have often been regarded as Christian ideas sometimes turn out to be ideas imported from a secular context. A classic example is the notion of the "impassibility of God" – that is, the idea that God cannot suffer. This idea was well established in Greek philosophical circles. Early Christian theologians, anxious to gain respect and credibility in such circles, did not challenge this idea. As a result, it became deeply embedded in the Christian theological tradition. We shall explore this matter further below.

The study of the history of Christianity provides a powerful corrective to static views of theology. It allows us to see:

1   That certain doctrines assume particular importance at various points in Christian history (for example, the doctrine of justification by faith during the sixteenth century).
2   That certain ideas came into being under very definite circumstances; and that, occasionally, mistakes are made.

3   That theological development is not irreversible; the mistakes of the past may be corrected.

A specific example, already noted above, will illustrate the importance of this point, and help identify some of the factors which impact on the development of theology. The question is whether God suffers. Writers of the first major era of Christian history (the patristic period) tended to answer this question in the negative. The answer that has tended to become the "new orthodoxy" since about 1945 has been affirmative. So how is this difference to be explained? The answer lies in a series of cultural and philosophical influences. To understand this, we will explore the issue in a little more depth, before drawing some conclusions.

The patristic discussion of this question is deeply influenced by the idea that God is perfect. So how is "perfection" to be defined? Greek patristic writers felt that contemporary classical philosophy offered a reliable answer: to be perfect is to be unchanging and self-sufficient. It is therefore impossible for a perfect being to be affected or changed by anything outside itself. Furthermore, perfection was understood in very static terms within classical philosophy. If God is perfect, change in any direction is an impossibility. If God changes, it is either a move *away from* perfection (in which case God is no longer perfect), or *toward* perfection (in which case, God was not perfect in the past). Aristotle, echoing such ideas, declared that "change would be change for the worse," and thus excluded his divine being from change and suffering.

This understanding passed into Christian theology at an early stage. Philo, a Hellenistic Jew whose writings were much admired by early Christian writers, wrote a treatise entitled *Quod Deus immutabilis sit*, "That God is unchangeable," which vigorously defended the impassibility of God. Biblical passages which seemed to speak of God suffering were, he argued, to be treated as metaphors, and not to be allowed their full literal weight. To allow that God changes was to deny the divine perfection. "What greater impiety could there be than to suppose that the Unchangeable changes?" asked Philo. It seemed to be an unanswerable question. For Philo, God could not be allowed to suffer, or undergo anything which could be spoken of as "passion." Anselm of Canterbury, influenced by this idea, argued that God was compassionate in terms of our experience, but not in terms of the divine being itself. The language of love and compassion is treated as purely figurative when used in relation to God.

However, this consensus has been challenged in the modern period. In part, the challenge results from a realization of the extent to which patristic thinking on this question has been influenced by Greek philosophical notions; in part, it also results from a realization that the Old Testament appears to speak of the suffering of God more than was appreciated. There are thus solid theological foundations to this tendency to affirm that God is able to suffer. But it must be appreciated that there are other factors at work, helping to dispose Christian theologians to giving a positive answer to that question: Does God suffer?

One pressure is cultural, and relates directly to the new cultural awareness of suffering in the world. The sheer horror of the First World War made a deep impact upon western theological reflection. The suffering of the period led to a widespread perception that liberal Protestantism was fatally compromised by its optimistic views of human nature. It is no accident that dialectical theology, a movement which was vigorously critical of liberal Protestantism, arose in the aftermath of this trauma. Another significant response was the movement known as Protest Atheism, which raised a serious moral protest against belief in God. How could anyone believe in a God who was above such suffering and pain in the world?

Traces of such ideas can be found in Fyodor Dostoyevsky's nineteenth-century novel *The Brothers Karamazov*. The ideas were developed more fully in the twentieth century, often using Dostoyevsky's character Ivan Karamazov as a model. Karamazov's rebellion against God (or, perhaps more accurately, against the *idea* of God) has its origins in his refusal to accept that the suffering of an innocent child could ever be justified. Albert Camus developed such ideas in *The Rebel*, which expressed Karamazov's protest in terms of a "metaphysical rebellion." This intensely moral form of atheism seemed to many theologians to demand a credible theological response – a theology of a suffering God.

A second pressure arises from a shifting understanding of a central idea – in this case, the idea of "love." Theologians rooted in the classical tradition – such as Anselm and Aquinas – defined love in terms of expressions and demonstrations of care and goodwill towards others. It is thus perfectly possible to speak of God "loving impassibly" – that is, loving someone without being emotionally affected by that person's situation. Yet the new interest in the psychology of human emotions has raised questions over this notion of love. Can one really speak of "love," unless there is some mutual sharing of suffering and feelings? Surely "love" implies the lover's intense awareness of the suffering of the beloved, and thus some form of sharing in its distress? Such considerations have undermined the intuitive plausibility (yet not, interestingly, the intellectual credibility) of an impassible God.

This very brief analysis shows how theology can be influenced by philosophical trends, cultural shifts, and changes in psychology. Theological reflection always takes place against a complex background, and – whether this is appreciated or not! – incorporates aspects of that background into that reflection. Patristic reflection on whether God could suffer were significantly influenced by the prevailing philosophical consensus that a perfect being could not change, or be affected by outside influences. Modern discussion of that same question is influenced by a cultural pressure to respond to the human experience of suffering, and a growing sympathy for the philosophical idea of God as a "fellow-sufferer"

(Alfred North Whitehead). Whatever the "right" answer to this question may be – and that debate continues in modern theology – it is essential to appreciate the factors which exercise a significant (and sometimes unacknowledged) influence over theology.

Historical theology both documents the answers given to the great questions of Christian theology, and attempts also to account for the factors which have been significant in formulating those answers – whether those factors were noticed or evaluated by those formulating the answers or not. The study of historical theology is thus subversive, as it indicates how easily theologians are led astray by the "self-images of the age" (Alasdair MacIntyre). Nor is this something that is restricted to the past! Too often, modern trends in theology are little more than knee jerk reactions to short-term cultural trends. The study of history makes us alert to both the mistakes of the past, and the alarming way in which they are repeated in the present. "History repeats itself. It has to. Nobody listens the first time round" (Woody Allen).

It is for such reasons that the present volume aims to provide its readers with the maximum amount of historical background to theological debates, within the limits of the space available. All too often, theological issues are conducted as if the debate began yesterday. An understanding of how we got to be where we are is essential to an informed debate of such issues.

But we have spent enough time introducing our subject. It is time to plunge into the complex world of patristic theology, as we begin to explore the emergence of the Christian theological tradition.

Chapter 1

THE PATRISTIC PERIOD, c.100–451

AN OVERVIEW OF THE PATRISTIC PERIOD

The patristic period is one of the most exciting and creative periods in the history of Christian thought. This feature alone is enough to ensure that it will continue to be the subject of study for many years to come. The period is also of importance for theological reasons. Every mainstream Christian body – including the Anglican, Eastern Orthodox, Lutheran, Reformed and Roman Catholic churches – regards the patristic period as a definitive landmark in the development of Christian doctrine. Each of these churches regards themselves as continuing, extending and, where necessary, criticizing the views of the early-church writers. For example, the leading seventeenth-century Anglican writer Lancelot Andrewes (1555–1626) declared that orthodox Christianity was based upon two testaments, three creeds, four gospels, and the first five centuries of Christian history. In what follows, we shall explore the basic features of this important period in the history of Christian thought.

The patristic period was of major importance in clarifying a number of issues. A task of initial importance was sorting out the relationship between Christianity and Judaism. The letters of Paul in the New Testament bear witness to the importance of this issue in the first century of Christian history, as a series of doctrinal and practical issues came to the fore. Should Gentile (that is, non-Jewish) Christians be obliged to be circumcised? And how was the Old Testament to be correctly interpreted?

However, other issues soon came to the fore. One which was of especial importance in the second century is that of *apologetics* – the reasoned defense and justification of the Christian faith against its critics. During the first period of Christian history, the church was often persecuted by the state. Its agenda was that of survival; there was limited place for theological disputes when the very existence of the Christian church could not be taken for granted. This observation helps us understand why apologetics came to be of such importance to the early church, through writers such as Justin Martyr (*c*.100–*c*.165), concerned to explain and defend the beliefs and practices of Christianity to a hostile pagan public. Although this early period produced some outstanding theologians – such as Irenaeus of Lyons (*c*.130–*c*.200) in the west, and Origen (*c*.185–*c*.254) in the east – theological debate could only begin in earnest once the church had ceased to be persecuted.

In view of the importance of the changing status of Christianity within the Roman Empire during the patristic period, we may consider the matter in more detail. Christianity had its origins in Palestine – more specifically, the region of Judea, especially the city of Jerusalem. Christianity regarded itself as a continuation and development of Judaism, and initially flourished in regions with which Judaism was traditionally associated, supremely Palestine. However, it rapidly spread to neighboring regions in which Judaism had a presence, partially through the efforts of early Christian evangelists such as Paul of Tarsus. By the end of the first century, Christianity appears to have become established throughout the eastern Mediterranean world, and even to have gained a significant presence in the city of Rome, the capital of the Roman Empire.

Rome was the administrative center of an empire which embraced the whole Mediterranean region. Indeed, the Romans tended to refer to the Mediterranean as "Mare Nostrum" – "our sea." The region of Judea, in which Christianity had its origins, was part of this vast empire – and a rather insignificant part at that. Although the languages spoken in this region of the empire were Aramaic (a language closely related to Hebrew) and Greek, Latin was used for administrative purposes. John's gospel makes reference to the charge against Jesus to the effect that he claimed to be "king of the Jews" being written in all three languages (John 19: 19–20). In many paintings and representations of the crucifixion of Jesus, this inscription is represented by four letters: INRI – the initial letters of the Latin phrase *Iesus Nazarenus Rex Iudaeorum*, meaning "Jesus of Nazareth, King of the Jews."

It is not clear when Christianity gained a presence in Rome, although it is generally thought that it dates form the 40s. Paul's letter to the Romans, dating from around 57, refers to a number of individuals with Latin names, such as Urbanus, Aquila, Rufus, and Julia. This suggests that a number of Romans may have converted to the religion by this stage. The bulk of the names mentioned are Greek, reflecting the fact that Christianity seems initially to have been the religion of a Greek-speaking minority. There is evidence that Mark's gospel may have been written in Rome at some point around 64, on the eve of Nero's persecution of Christians in the city. For example, Mark 12: 42 notes that two Greek copper coins make one *quadrans*, a Roman coin not in circulation in the eastern part of the empire. Similarly, Mark 15: 16 explains that a Greek word corresponds to the Latin *praetorium*. These explanations suggest that Mark is explaining unfamiliar ideas or terms to a Roman audience.

Since becoming established in Rome in the 40s, Christianity had an ambiguous legal status. On the one hand, it was not legally recognized, and so did not enjoy any special rights; on the other, it was not forbidden. However, its growing numerical strength led to periodic attempts to suppress it by force. Sometimes these persecutions were local, restricted to regions such as North Africa; sometimes, they were sanctioned throughout the Roman Empire as a whole. A particularly significant period of persecution dates from the accession of the Emperor Decius in 249. His first major act of hostility toward Christianity was the execution of Fabian, bishop of Rome, in January 250. The Decian persecution resulted from the Edict of Decius, issued in June 250, which commanded provincial governors and magistrates to ensure that there was universal observance of the requirement to offer sacrifices to the Roman gods, and to the emperor. A certificate (*libellus pacis*) was issued to those who offered such sacrifices. The Edict seems to have been widely ignored, but was nevertheless enforced in some regions. Thousands of Christians were martyred during this difficult period. Some offered sacrifices to the gods in order to get hold of the required certificates; some were able to obtain the certificates without actually offering sacrifices.

The Decian persecution ended in June 251, when Decius was killed on a military expedition. The persecution led to many Christians lapsing or abandoning their faith in the face of persecution. Division arose immediately within the church over how these individuals should be treated: did such a lapse mark the end of their faith, or could they be reconciled to the church by penance? Opinions differed sharply, and serious disagreement and tension resulted. Very different views were promoted by Cyprian of Carthage and Novatian. Both of these writers were martyred during the persecution instigated by the Emperor Valerian in 257–258.

One of the most severe outbursts of persecution came about in February 303, under the Emperor Diocletian. An edict was issued ordering the destruction of all Christian places of worship, the surrender and destruction of all their books, and the cessation of all acts of Christian worship. Christian civil servants were to lose all privileges of rank or status and to be reduced to the status of slaves. Prominent Christians were forced to offer sacrifice according to traditional Roman practices. It is an indication of how influential Christianity had become that Diocletian forced both his wife and daughter, who were known to be Christians, to comply with this order. The persecution continued under successive emperors, including Galerius, who ruled the eastern region of the empire.

In 311, Galerius ordered the cessation of the persecution. It had been a failure, and had merely hardened Christians in their resolve to resist the reimposition of classical Roman pagan religion. Galerius issued an edict which permitted Christians to live normally again and "hold their religious assemblies, provided that they do nothing which would disturb public order." The edict explicitly identified Christianity as a religion, and offered it the full protection of the law.

19

The legal status of Christianity, which had been ambiguous up to this point, was now resolved. The church no longer existed under a siege mentality.

Christianity was now a legal religion; it was, however, merely one among many such religions. The conversion of the Emperor Constantine changed this irreversibly, and brought about a complete change in the situation of Christianity throughout the Roman Empire. Constantine was born to pagan parents in 285. (His mother would eventually become a Christian, apparently through her son's influence.) Although he showed no particular attraction to Christianity in his early period, Constantine certainly seems to have regarded toleration as an essential virtue. Following Maxentius' seizure of power in Italy and North Africa, Constantine led a body of troops from western Europe in an attempt to gain authority in the region. The decisive battle took place on October 28, 312 at the Milvian Bridge, to the north of Rome. Constantine defeated Maxentius, and was proclaimed emperor. Shortly afterwards, he declared himself to be a Christian.

This point is affirmed by both Christian and pagan writers. What is not clear is precisely why or when this conversion took place. Some Christian writers (such as Lactantius and Eusebius) suggest that the conversion may have taken place before the decisive battle, with Constantine seeing a heavenly vision ordering him to place the sign of the cross on his soldiers' shields. Whatever the reasons for the conversion, and whether it dates from before or after the battle of Milvian Bridge, the reality and consequences of this conversion are not in doubt. Gradually, Rome became Christianized. On his own instructions, the statue of the emperor erected in the Forum depicts Constantine bearing a cross – "the sign of suffering that brought salvation," according to the inscription provided by Constantine. In 321, Constantine decreed that Sundays should become public holidays. Christian symbols began to appear on Roman coins. Christianity was now more than just legitimate; it was on its way to becoming the established religion of the empire.

As a result, constructive theological debate became a public affair. Apart from a brief period of uncertainty during the reign of Julian the Apostate (361–363), the church could now count upon the support of the state. Theology thus emerged from the hidden world of secret church meetings, to become a matter of public interest and concern throughout the Roman Empire. Increasingly, doctrinal debates became a matter of both political and theological importance. Constantine wished to have a united church throughout his empire, and was thus concerned that doctrinal differences should be debated and settled as a matter of priority.

As the church at Rome became increasingly powerful, tensions began to develop between the Christian leadership at Rome and at Constantinople, foreshadowing the later schism between the western and eastern churches arising out of these respective centers of power. In addition to Rome and Constantinople, a number of regions emerged as significant centers of theological debate.

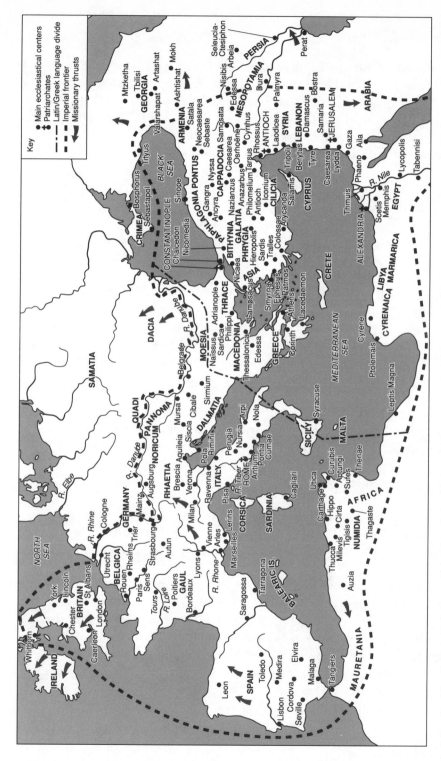

Map 1   *The Roman Empire and the church in the fourth century (note that modern rather than ancient place names are used)*

21

Three may be singled out as having especial importance, the first two of which were Greek-speaking, and the third Latin-speaking.

1   The city of Alexandria, in modern-day Egypt, which emerged as a center of Christian theological education. A distinctive style of theology came to be associated with this city, reflecting its long-standing association with the Platonic tradition. The student will find reference to "Alexandrian" approaches in areas such as Christology and biblical interpretation (see pp. 51–5) reflecting both the importance and distinctiveness of the style of Christianity associated with the area.

2   The city of Antioch in ancient Syria, and the region of Cappadocia, in modern-day Turkey. A strong Christian presence came to be established in this northern region of the eastern Mediterranean at an early stage. Some of Paul's missionary journeys related to this region, and Antioch features significantly at several points in the history of the very early church, as recorded in the Acts of the Apostles. Antioch itself soon became a leading center of Christian thought. Like Alexandria, it became associated with particular approaches to Christology and biblical interpretation. The term "Antiochene" is often used to designate this distinct theological style (see pp. 55–61). The "Cappadocian fathers" were also an important theological presence in this region in the fourth century, notable especially for their contribution to the doctrine of the Trinity.

3   Western North Africa, especially the area of modern-day Algeria. In the late classical period, this was the site of Carthage, a major Mediterranean city and at one time a political rival to Rome for dominance in the region. During the period when Christianity expanded in this region, it was a Roman colony. Major writers of the region include Tertullian, Cyprian of Carthage, and Augustine of Hippo.

This is not to say that other cities in the Mediterranean were devoid of significance. Milan and Jerusalem were also centers of Christian theological reflection, even if neither was destined to achieve quite the significance of their rivals.

As Christianity became an established presence in the Mediterranean world, the stable conditions needed for serious theological reflection emerged. As a result, the later patristic period (from about 310 to 451) may be regarded as a high water mark in the history of Christian theology. Theologians now enjoyed the freedom to work without the threat of persecution, and were able to address a series of issues of major importance to the consolidation of the emerging theological consensus within the churches. That consensus involved extensive debate, and a painful learning process in which the church discovered that it had to come to terms with disagreements and continuing tensions. Nonetheless, a significant degree of consensus, eventually to be enshrined in the ecumenical creeds, can be discerned as emerging within this formative period.

The patristic period is obviously of considerable importance to Christian theology. It is, however, found to be very difficult to understand by many modern students of theology. Four main reasons can be given for this situation:

1   Some of the debates of the period seem hopelessly irrelevant to the modern world. Although they were viewed as intensely important at the time, it is often very difficult for the modern reader to empathize with the issues, and understand why they attracted such attention. It is interesting to contrast the patristic period with the Reformation era, which addressed many issues which are a continuing concern for the modern church; many teachers of theology find that their students are able to relate to the concerns of this later period much more easily.

2   Many of the patristic debates hinge upon philosophical issues, and only make sense if the reader has some familiarity with the philosophical debates of the period. Whereas at least some students of Christian theology have some familiarity with the ideas found in Plato's dialogues, these ideas were subject to considerable development and criticism in the Mediterranean world during the patristic period. Middle Platonism and Neo-Platonism differ significantly from one another, and from Plato's original ideas. The strangeness of many of the philosophical ideas of the period acts as another barrier to its study, making it difficult for students beginning the study of theology to fully appreciate what is going on in some of the patristic debates.

3   The patristic period is characterized by immense doctrinal diversity. It was an age of flux, during which landmarks and standards – including documents such as the Nicene Creed and dogmas such as the two natures of Christ – emerged gradually. Students familiar with the relative stability of other periods in Christian doctrine (such as the Reformation, in which the person of Christ was not a major issue) often find this feature of the patristic period disconcerting.

4   The period saw a major division arise, for both political and linguistic reasons, between the eastern Greek-speaking and the western Latin-speaking church. Many scholars discern a marked difference in theological temperament between theologians of the east and west: the former are often philosophically inclined and given to theological speculation, whereas the latter are often hostile to the intrusion of philosophy into theology, and regard theology as the exploration of the doctrines set out in Scripture. The famous rhetorical question of the western theologian Tertullian (*c*.160–*c*.225), "What has Athens to do with Jerusalem? or the Academy with the church?" illustrates this point.

A Clarification of Terms

The term "patristic" comes from the Latin word *pater*, "father," and designates both the period of the church fathers, and the distinctive ideas which came to develop within this period. The term is non-inclusive; no generally acceptable inclusive term has yet to emerge in the literature. The following related terms are frequently encountered, and should be noted.

The Patristic Period

This is a vaguely defined entity, which is often taken to designate the period from the closing of the New Testament writings (*c.*100) to the definitive Council of Chalcedon (451).

Patristics

This term is usually understood to mean the branch of theological study which deals with the study of "the fathers (*patres*)."

Patrology

This term once literally meant "the study of the fathers" (in much the same way as "theology" meant "the study of God (*theos*)." In recent years, however, the word has shifted its meaning. It now refers to a manual of patristic literature, such as that of the noted German scholar Johannes Quasten, which allows its readers easy access to the leading ideas of patristic writers, and some of the problems of interpretation associated with them.

Key Theologians

During the course of this work, reference will be made to a significant number of theologians from the patristic period. The following six writers, however, are of especial importance, and deserve to be singled out for special mention.

Justin Martyr (*c.*100–*c.*165)

Justin is perhaps the greatest of the Apologists – the Christian writers of the second century who were concerned to defend Christianity in the face of intense criticism from pagan sources. In his "First Apology," Justin argued that traces of Christian truth were to be found in the great pagan writers. His doctrine of the *logos spermatikos* ("seed-bearing word") allowed him to affirm that God had prepared the way for his final revelation in Christ through hints of its truth in classical philosophy. Justin provides us with an important early example of a theologian who attempts to relate the gospel to the outlook of Greek philosophy, a trend especially associated with the eastern church.

Irenaeus of Lyons (*c.*130–*c.*200)

Irenaeus is believed to have been born in Smyrna (in modern-day Turkey), although he subsequently settled in Rome. He became Bishop of Lyons around 178, a position which he held until his death two decades later. Irenaeus is noted especially for his vigorous defense of Christian orthodoxy in the face of a challenge from Gnosticism (see p. 40). His most significant work, "Against all Heresies" (*Adversus omnes Haereses*), represents a major defense of the Christian understanding of salvation, and especially of the role of tradition in remaining faithful to the apostolic witness in the face of non-Christian interpretations.

Origen (*c.*185–*c.*254)

One of the most important defenders of Christianity in the third century, Origen provided an important foundation for the development of eastern Christian thought. His major contributions to the development of Christian theology can be seen in two general areas. In the field of biblical interpretation, Origen developed the notion of allegorical interpretation, arguing that the surface meaning of Scripture was to be distinguished from its deeper spiritual meaning. In the field of Christology, Origen established a tradition of distinguishing between the full divinity of the Father, and a lesser divinity of the Son. Some scholars see Arianism as a natural consequence of this approach. Origen also adopted with some enthusiasm the idea of *apocatastasis* or universal restoration, according to which every creature – including both humanity and Satan – will be saved.

Tertullian (*c.*160–*c.*225)

Tertullian was originally a pagan from the North African city of Carthage, who converted to Christianity in his thirties. He is often regarded as the father of Latin theology, on account of the major impact which he had upon the western church. He defended the unity of the Old and New Testaments against Marcion, who had argued that they related to different gods. In doing so, he laid the foundations for a doctrine of the Trinity. Tertullian was strongly opposed to making Christian theology or apologetics dependent upon extra-scriptural sources. He is amongst the most forceful early exponents of the principle of the sufficiency of Scripture, denouncing those who appeal to secular philosophies (such as those of the Athenian Academy) for a true knowledge of God.

Athanasius (*c*.296–*c*.373)

Athanasius' significance relates primarily to Christological issues, which became of major importance during the fourth century. Possibly while still in his twenties, Athanasius wrote the treatise *De incarnatione* ("On the incarnation"), a powerful defense of the idea that God assumed human nature in the person of Jesus Christ. This issue proved to be of central importance in the Arian controversy (see pp. 45–51), to which Athanasius made a major contribution. Athanasius pointed out that if, as Arius argued, Christ was not fully God, a series of devastating implications followed. First, it was impossible for God to redeem humanity, as no creature could redeem another creature. And second, it followed that the Christian church was guilty of idolatry, as Christians regularly worshipped and prayed to Christ. As "idolatry" can be defined as "worship of a human construction or creation," it followed that this worship was idolatrous. Such arguments eventually carried the day, and led to the rejection of Arianism.

Augustine of Hippo (354–430)

In turning to deal with Aurelius Augustinus, usually known as "Augustine of Hippo" – or just plain "Augustine" – we encounter what is probably the greatest and most influential mind of the Christian church throughout its long history. Attracted to the Christian faith by the preaching of Bishop Ambrose of Milan, Augustine underwent a dramatic conversion experience. Having reached the age of 32 without satisfying his burning wish to know the truth, Augustine was agonizing over the great questions of human nature and destiny in a garden in Milan. He thought he heard some children singing *Tolle, lege* ("take up and read") nearby. Feeling that this was divine guidance, he found the New Testament document nearest to hand – Paul's letter to the Romans, as it happened – and read the fateful words "clothe yourselves with the Lord Jesus Christ" (Romans 13: 14). This was the final straw for Augustine, whose paganism had become increasingly difficult to maintain. As he later recalled, "a light of certainty entered my heart, and every shadow of doubt vanished." From that moment onward, Augustine dedicated his enormous intellectual abilities to the defense and consolidation of the Christian faith, writing in a style which was both passionate and intelligent, appealing to both heart and mind.

Possibly suffering from some form of asthma, Augustine left Italy to return to North Africa, and was made bishop of Hippo (in modern Algeria) in 395. The remaining thirty-five years of his life witnessed numerous controversies of major importance to the future of the Christian church in the west, and Augustine's contribution to the resolution of each of these was decisive. His careful exposition of the New Testament, particularly the letters of Paul, gained him a reputation which continues today, as the "second founder of the Christian faith" (Jerome). When the Dark Ages finally lifted over western Europe, Augustine's substantial body of theological writings would form the basis of a major program of theological renewal and development, consolidating his influence over the western church.

A major part of Augustine's contribution lies in the development of theology as an academic discipline. The early church cannot really be said to have developed any "systematic theology." Its primary concern was to defend Christianity against its critics (as in the apologetic works of Justin Martyr), and to clarify central aspects of its thinking against heresy (as in the anti-Gnostic writings of Irenaeus). Nevertheless, major doctrinal development took place during the first four centuries, especially in relation to the doctrine of the person of Christ and the doctrine of the Trinity.

Augustine's contribution was to achieve a synthesis of Christian thought, supremely in his major treatise *De civitate Dei*, "On the City of God." Like Charles Dickens's famous novel, Augustine's "City of God" is a tale of two cities – the city of the world, and the city of God. The work is apologetic in tone: Augustine is sensitive to the charge that the fall of Rome was due to its having abandoned classic paganism in favor of Christianity. Yet as he defended Christianity against such charges, he inevitably ended up by giving a systematic presentation and exposition of the main lines of Christian belief.

However, in addition, Augustine may also be argued to have made key contributions to three major areas of Christian theology: the doctrine of the church and sacraments, arising from the Donatist controversy (see pp. 72–9); the doctrine of grace, arising from the Pelagian controversy (see pp. 79–86); and the doctrine of the Trinity (see pp. 61–72). Interestingly, Augustine never really explored the area of Christology (that is, the doctrine of the person of Christ), which would unquestionably have benefited from his considerable wisdom and acumen.

KEY THEOLOGICAL DEVELOPMENTS

The following areas of theology were explored with particular vigor during the patristic period.

The Extent of the New Testament Canon

From its outset, Christian theology recognized itself to be grounded in Scripture. There was, however, some uncertainty as to what the term "Scripture" actually designated. The patristic period witnessed a process of decision-making, in which limits were laid down to the New Testament – a process usually known as "the fixing of the canon." The word "canon" needs explanation. It derives from the Greek word *kanon* meaning "a rule" or "a fixed reference point." The "canon of Scripture" refers to a limited and defined group of writings, which are accepted as authoritative within the Christian church. The term "canonical" is used to refer to scriptural writings accepted to be within the canon. Thus the Gospel of Luke is referred to as "canonical," whereas the Gospel of Thomas is "extra-canonical" (that is, lying outside the canon of Scripture).

For the writers of the New Testament, the term "Scripture" meant primarily *a writing of the Old Testament*. However, within a short period, early Christian writers (such as Justin Martyr) were referring to the "New Testament" (to be contrasted with the "Old Testament"), and insisting that both were to be treated with equal authority. By the time of Irenaeus, it was generally accepted that there were four gospels; by the late second century, there was a consensus that the gospels, Acts, and letters had the status of inspired Scripture. Thus Clement of Alexandria recognized four gospels, the Acts, fourteen letters of Paul (the letter to the Hebrews being regarded as Pauline), and Revelation. Tertullian declared that alongside the "law and the prophets" were the "evangelical and apostolic writings" (*evangelicae et apostolicae litterae*), which were both to be regarded as authoritative within the church. Gradually, agreement was reached on the list of books which were recognized as inspired Scripture, and the order in which they were to be arranged. In 367, Athanasius circulated his thirty-ninth Festal Letter, which identifies the twenty-seven books of the New Testament, as we now know it, as being canonical.

Debate centered especially on a number of books. The western church had hesitations about including Hebrews, in that it was not specifically attributed to an apostle; the eastern church had reservations about Revelation. Four of the smaller books (2 Peter, 2 and 3 John, and Jude) were often omitted from early lists of New Testament writings. Some writings now outside the canon were regarded with favor in parts of the church, although they ultimately failed to gain universal acceptance as canonical. Examples of this include the first letter of Clement (an early bishop of Rome, who wrote around 96) and the *Didache*, a short early Christian manual on morals and church practices, probably dating from the first quarter of the second century.

The arrangement of the material was also subject to considerable variation. Agreement was reached at an early stage that the gospels should have the place of honor within the canon, followed by the Acts of the Apostles. The eastern church tended to place the seven "Catholic letters" (that is, James, 1 and 2 Peter, 1, 2 and 3 John, and Jude) before the fourteen Pauline letters (Hebrews being accepted as Pauline), whereas the western church placed Paul's letters immediately after Acts, and followed them with the Catholic letters. Revelation ended the canon in both east and west, although its status was subject to debate for some time within the eastern church.

What criteria were used in drawing up the canon? The basic principle appears to have been that of the *recognition* rather than the *imposition* of authority. In other words, the works in question were recognized as already possessing authority, rather than having an arbitrary authority imposed upon them. For Irenaeus, the church does not *create* the canon; it *acknowledges*, *conserves*, and *receives* canonical Scripture on the basis of the authority which is already inherent to it. Some early Christians appear to have regarded apostolic authorship as of decisive importance; others were prepared to accept books which did not appear to have apostolic credentials. However, although the precise details of how the selection was made remain unclear, it is certain that the canon was closed within the western church by the beginning of the fifth century. The issue of the canon would not be raised again until the time of the Reformation.

The Role of Tradition

The early church was confronted with a major challenge from a movement known as Gnosticism. This diverse and complex movement, not dissimilar to the modern New Age phenomenon, achieved considerable influence in the late Roman Empire. The basic ideas of Gnosticism do not concern us at this point; what is of relevance here is that Gnosticism appeared very similar to Christianity at many points. For this reason, it was viewed as a major challenge by many early Christian writers, especially Irenaeus. Furthermore, Gnostic writers had a tendency to interpret New Testament passages in a manner which dismayed Christian leaders, and prompted questions about the correct manner of interpretation of Scripture.

In such a context, an appeal to tradition became of major importance. The word "tradition" literally means "that which has been handed down or over," although it can also refer to "the act of handing down or over." Irenaeus insisted that the "rule of faith" (*regula fidei*) was faithfully preserved by the apostolic church, and that it had found its expression in the canonical books of Scripture. The church had faithfully proclaimed the same gospel from the time of the Apostles until the present day. The Gnostics had no such claim to continuity with the early church. They had merely invented new ideas, and were improperly suggesting that these were "Christian." Irenaeus thus emphasized the continuity of the teaching and preaching office of the church and its officials (especially its bishops). Tradition came to mean "a traditional interpretation of Scripture" or "a traditional presentation of the Christian faith," which is reflected in the creeds of the church and its public doctrinal pronouncements. This fixing of the creeds as a public expression of the teaching of the church is of major importance, as will become clear in the following section.

29

Tertullian adopted a related approach. Scripture, he argued, is capable of being understood clearly, provided that it is read as a whole. However, he conceded that controversy over the interpretation of certain passages was inevitable. Heretics, he observed gloomily, can make Scripture say more or less anything that they like. For this reason, the tradition of the church was of considerable importance, as it indicated the manner in which Scripture had been received and interpreted within the church. The right interpretation of Scripture was thus to be found where true Christian faith and discipline had been maintained. A similar view was taken by Athanasius, who argued that Arius' Christological mistakes would never have arisen if he had remained faithful to the church's interpretation of Scripture.

Tradition was thus seen as a legacy from the Apostles, by which the church was guided and directed toward a correct interpretation of Scripture. It was not seen as a "secret source of revelation" in addition to Scripture, an idea which Irenaeus dismissed as "Gnostic." Rather, it was seen as a means of ensuring that the church remained faithful to the teaching of the Apostles, instead of adopting idiosyncratic interpretations of Scripture.

The Fixing of the Ecumenical Creeds

The English word "creed" derives from the Latin word *credo*, "I believe," with which the Apostles' Creed – probably the most familiar of all the creeds – begins: "I believe in God. . . ." It has come to refer to a statement of faith, summarizing the main points of Christian belief, which is common to all Christians. For this reason, the term "creed" is never applied to statements of faith associated with specific denominations. These latter are often referred to as "confessions" (such as the Lutheran *Augsburg Confession* or the Reformed *Westminster Confession of Faith*). A "confession" pertains to a denomination, and includes specific beliefs and emphases relating to that denomination; a "creed" pertains to the entire Christian church, and includes nothing more and nothing less than a statement of beliefs which every Christian ought to be able to accept and be bound by. A "creed" has come to be recognized as a concise, formal, and universally accepted and authorized statement of the main points of Christian faith.

The patristic period saw two creeds coming to be treated with authority and respect throughout the church. The stimulus to their development appears to have been the felt need to provide a convenient summary of Christian faith suitable for public occasions, of which perhaps the most important was baptism. The early church tended to baptize its converts on Easter Day, using the period of Lent as a time of preparation and instruction for this moment of public declaration of faith and commitment. An essential requirement was that each convert who wished to be baptized should declare his or her faith in public. It seems that creeds began to emerge as a uniform declaration of faith which converts could use on such occasions.

The Apostles' Creed

The document known as the "Apostles' Creed" is widely used in the western church as a succinct summary of the leading themes of the Christian faith. Its historical evolution is complex, with its origins lying in declarations of faith which were required of those who wanted to be baptized. The 12 individual statements of this creed, which seems to have assumed its final form in the eighth century, are traditionally ascribed to individual apostles, although there is no historical justification for this belief. During the twentieth century, the Apostle's Creed has become widely accepted by most churches, eastern and western, as a binding statement of Christian faith despite the fact that its statements concerning the "descent into hell" and the "communion of saints" (here printed within square brackets) are not found in eastern versions of the work.

1. I believe in God, the Father almighty, creator of the heavens and earth;
2. and in Jesus Christ, his only Son, our Lord;
3. who was conceived by the Holy Spirit and born of the Virgin Mary;
4. suffered under Pontius Pilate, was crucified, dead and buried; [he descended to hell;]
5. on the third day he was raised from the dead;
6. he ascended into the heavens, and sits at the right hand of God the Father almighty;
7. from where he will come to judge the living and the dead.
8. I believe in the Holy Spirit;
9. in the holy Catholic church; [the communion of saints;]
10. the forgiveness of sins;
11. the resurrection of the flesh;
12. and eternal life.

The *Apostles' Creed* is probably the most familiar form of the creed known to western Christians. It falls into three main sections, dealing with God, Jesus Christ, and the Holy Spirit. There is also material relating to the church, judgment, and resurrection.

The *Nicene Creed* is the longer version of the creed (more strictly known as the "Niceno-Constantinopolitan creed") which includes additional material relating to the person of Christ and the work of the Holy Spirit. In response to the controversies concerning the divinity of Christ, this creed includes strong affirmations of his unity with God, including the expressions "God from God" and "being of one substance with the Father."

The development of the creeds was an important element in the move toward achieving a doctrinal consensus within the early church. One area of doctrine which witnessed considerable development and controversy related to the person of Christ, to which we may now turn.

The Two Natures of Jesus Christ

The two doctrines to which the patristic period may be argued to have made a decisive contribution relate to the person of Christ (an area of theology which, as we noted, is generally designated "Christology") and the nature of the Godhead. These two developments are organically related to one another. By 325, the early church had come to the conclusion that Jesus was "of one substance" (*homoousios*) with God. (The term *homoousios* can also be translated as "one in being" or "consubstantial".) The implications of this Christological statement were twofold: in the first place, it consolidated at the intellectual level the spiritual importance of Jesus Christ to Christians; in the second, however, it posed a powerful challenge to simplistic conceptions of God. For if Jesus *is* recognized as "being of the same substance" as God, then the entire doctrine of God has to be reconsidered in the light of this belief. For this reason, the historical development of the doctrine of the Trinity dates from after the emergence of a Christological consensus within the church. Only when the divinity of Christ could be treated as an agreed and assured starting point could theological speculation on the nature of God begin.

It may be noted that the Christological debates of the early church took place largely in the eastern Mediterranean world, and were conducted in the Greek language, and often in the light of the presuppositions of major Greek schools of philosophy. In practical terms, this means that many of the central terms of the Christological debates of the early church are Greek, often with a history of use within the Greek philosophical tradition.

The main features of patristic Christology will be considered in some detail at pp. 51–61, to which the reader is referred. At this early stage, however, we may summarize the main landmarks of the patristic Christological debate in terms of two schools, two debates, and two councils, as follows.

1   *Schools* The *Alexandrian school* tended to place emphasis upon the divinity of Christ, and interpret that divinity in terms of "the word becoming incarnate." A scriptural text which was of central importance to this school is John 1:14, "the word became flesh, and dwelt among us." This emphasis upon the idea of incarnation led to the festival of Christmas being seen as especially important. The *Antiochene school*, however, placed a corresponding emphasis upon the humanity of Christ, and attached especial importance to his moral example (see pp. 55–61).

2 *Debates* The *Arian* controversy of the fourth century is widely regarded as one of the most significant in the history of the Christian church. Arius (*c*.250–*c*.336) argued that the scriptural titles for Christ, which appeared to point to his being of equal status with God, were merely courtesy titles. Christ was to be regarded as a creature, although nevertheless as pre-eminent amongst other creatures. This provoked a hostile response from Athanasius, who argued that the divinity of Christ was of central importance to the Christian understanding of salvation (an area of theology known as "soteriology"). Arius' Christology was, he declared, inadequate soteriologically. Arius' Christ could not redeem fallen humanity. In the end, Arianism (the movement associated with Arius) was declared to be heretical. This was followed by the *Apollinarian* debate, which centered on Apollinaris of Laodicea (*c*.310–*c*.390). A vigorous opponent of Arius, Apollinaris argued that Christ could not be regarded as being totally human. In Christ's case, the human spirit was replaced by the divine *logos*. As a result, Christ did not possess full humanity. This position was regarded as severely deficient by writers such as Gregory of Nazianzus, in that it implied that Christ could not fully redeem human nature (see pp. 55–61).

3 *Councils* The *Council of Nicea* (325) was convened by Constantine, the first Christian emperor, with a view to sorting out the destabilizing Christological disagreements within his empire. This was the first "ecumenical council" (that is, an assembly of Christians drawn from the entire Christian world, whose decisions are regarded as normative for the churches). Nicea (now the city of Iznik in modern-day Turkey) settled the Arian controversy by affirming that Jesus was *homoousios* ("one in being" or "of one substance") with the Father, thus rejecting the Arian position in favor of a vigorous assertion of the divinity of Christ. The *Council of Chalcedon* (451), the fourth ecumenical council, confirmed the decisions of Nicea, and responded to new debates which had subsequently erupted over the humanity of Christ.

The Doctrine of the Trinity

Once the Christological debates of the early church had been settled, the consequences of those decisions were explored. In this intensely creative and interesting period of Christian theology, the doctrine of the Trinity began to emerge in a recognizable form. The basic feature of this doctrine is that there are three persons within the Godhead – Father, Son, and Holy Spirit – and that these are to be regarded as equally divine and of equal status. The co-equality of Father and Son was established through the Christological debates leading up to the Council of Nicea; the divinity of the Spirit was established in the aftermath of this, especially through the writings of Athanasius and Basil of Caesarea.

The main thrust of the Trinitarian debates increasingly came to concern the

33

manner in which the Trinity was to be understood, rather than its fundamental validity. Two quite distinct approaches gradually emerged, one associated with the eastern, and the other with the western, churches.

The *eastern* position, which continues to be of major importance within the Greek and Russian Orthodox churches of today, was developed especially by a group of three writers, based in modern-day Turkey. Basil of Caesarea (*c.*330–79), Gregory of Nazianzus (329–89), and Gregory of Nyssa (*c.*330–*c.*395), known as the *Cappadocian fathers*, began their reflections on the Trinity by considering the different ways in which the Father, Son, and Spirit are experienced. The *western* position, especially associated with Augustine of Hippo, began from the unity of God, and proceeded to explore the implications of the love of God for our understanding of the nature of the Godhead. These positions will be explored in greater detail at the appropriate point in this work (see pp. 61–72).

The doctrine of the Trinity represents a rare instance of a theological issue of concern to both the eastern and western churches. Our attention now shifts to two theological debates which were specifically linked with the western church, and have both come to be particularly associated with Augustine of Hippo.

The Doctrine of the Church

A major controversy within the western church centered on the question of the holiness of the church. The Donatists were a group of native African Christians, based in modern-day Algeria, who resented the growing influence of the Roman church in northern Africa. The Donatists argued that the church was a body of saints, within which sinners had no place. The issue became of especial importance on account of the persecution undertaken by the emperor Diocletian in 303, which persisted until the conversion of Constantine in 313. During this persecution, in which the possession of Scripture was illegal, a number of Christians handed their copies of Scripture in to the authorities. These were immediately condemned by others who had refused to cave in under such pressure. After the persecution died down, many of these *traditores* – literally, "those who handed over [their Scriptures]" – rejoined the church. The Donatists argued for their exclusion.

Augustine argued otherwise, declaring that the church must expect to remain a "mixed body" of saints and sinners, refusing to weed out those who had lapsed under persecution or for other reasons. The validity of the church's ministry and preaching did not depend upon the holiness of its ministers, but upon the person of Jesus Christ. The personal unworthiness of a minister did not compromise the validity of the sacraments. This view, which rapidly became normative within the church, has had a deep impact upon Christian thinking about the nature of the church and its ministers.

The Donatist debate, which will be explored in greater detail elsewhere, was the first to center on the question of the doctrine of the church (known as "ecclesiology"), and related questions, such as the way in which sacraments function. Many of the issues raised by the controversy would surface again at the time of the Reformation, when ecclesiological issues would once more come to the fore (see pp. 200–7). The same may be said of the doctrine of grace, to which we now turn.

The Doctrine of Grace

The doctrine of grace had not been an issue of significance in the development of theology in the Greek-speaking eastern church. However, an intense controversy broke out over this question in the second decade of the fifth century. Pelagius, a British ascetic monk based at Rome, argued forcefully for the need for human moral responsibility. Alarmed at the moral laxity of the Roman church, he insisted upon the need for constant self-improvement, in the light of the Old Testament law and the example of Christ. In doing so, he seemed to his opponents – chief among whom was Augustine – to deny any real place to divine grace in the beginning or continuation of the Christian life. Pelagianism came to be seen as a religion of human autonomy, which held that human beings are able to take the initiative in their own salvation.

Augustine reacted forcefully against Pelagianism, insisting upon the priority of the grace of God at every stage in the Christian life, from its beginning to its end. Human beings did not, according to Augustine, possess the necessary freedom to take the initial steps toward salvation. Far from possessing "freedom of the will," humans were in possession of a will that was corrupted and tainted by sin, and which biased them toward evil and away from God. Only the grace of God could counteract this bias toward sin. So forceful was Augustine's defense of grace that he later became known as "the doctor of grace" (*doctor gratiae*).

A central theme of Augustine's thought is the *fallenness* of human nature. The imagery of "the Fall" derives from Genesis 3, and expresses the idea that human nature has "fallen" from its original pristine state. The present state of human nature is thus not what it is intended to be by God. The created order no longer directly corresponds to the "goodness" of its original integrity. It has lapsed. It has been spoiled and ruined – but not irredeemably, as the doctrines of salvation and justification affirm. The image of a "Fall" conveys the idea that creation now exists at a lower level than that intended for it by God.

According to Augustine, it follows that all human beings are now contaminated by sin from the moment of their birth. In contrast to many twentieth-century existentialist philosophies (such as that of Martin Heidegger), which affirm that "fallenness" (*Verfallenheit*) is an option which we choose (rather than something which is chosen for us), Augustine portrays sin as inherent to human nature. It is an integral, not an optional, aspect of our being. This insight, which is given more rigorous expression in Augustine's doctrine of original sin, is of central importance to his doctrines of sin and salvation. In that all are sinners, all require redemption. In that all have fallen short of the glory of God, all require to be redeemed.

For Augustine, humanity, left to its own devices and resources, could never enter into a relationship with God. Nothing that a man or woman could do was sufficient to break the stranglehold of sin. To use an image which Augustine was fortunate enough never to have encountered, it is like a narcotic addict trying to break free from the grip of heroin or cocaine. The situation cannot be transformed from within – and so, if transformation is to take place, it must come from outside the human situation. According to Augustine, God intervenes in the human dilemma. He need not have done so, but out of his love for fallen humanity, he entered into the human situation in the person of Jesus Christ in order to redeem it.

Augustine held "grace" to be the unmerited or undeserved gift of God, by which God voluntarily breaks the hold of sin upon humanity. Redemption is possible only as a divine gift. It is not something which we can achieve ourselves, but is something which has to be done for us. Augustine thus emphasizes that the resources of salvation are located outside of humanity, in God himself. It is God who initiates the process of salvation, not men or women.

For Pelagius, however, the situation looked very different. Pelagius taught that the resources of salvation are located within humanity. Individual human beings have the capacity to save themselves. They are not trapped by sin, but have the ability to do all that is necessary to be saved. Salvation is something which is earned through good works, which place God under an obligation to humanity. Pelagius marginalizes the idea of grace, understanding it in terms of demands made of humanity by God in order that salvation may be achieved – such as the Ten Commandments, or the moral example of Christ. The ethos of Pelagianism could be summed up as "salvation by merit," whereas Augustine taught "salvation by grace."

It will be obvious that these two different theologies involve very different understandings of human nature. For Augustine, human nature is weak, fallen, and powerless; for Pelagius, it is autonomous and self-sufficient. For Augustine, humanity must depend upon God for salvation; for Pelagius, God merely indicates what has to be done if salvation is to be attained, and then leaves men and women to meet those conditions unaided. For Augustine, salvation is an unmerited gift; for Pelagius, salvation is a justly earned reward.

One aspect of Augustine's understanding of grace needs further comment. As human beings were incapable of saving themselves, and as God gave his gift of grace to some (but not all), it followed that God had "preselected" those who would be saved. Developing hints of this idea to be found in the New Testament,

Augustine developed a doctrine of predestination. The term "predestination" refers to God's original or eternal decision to save some, and not others. It was this aspect of Augustine's thought which many of his contemporaries, not to mention his successors, found unacceptable. It need hardly be said that there is no direct equivalent in Pelagius' thought.

The Council of Carthage (418) decided for Augustine's views on grace and sin, and condemned Pelagianism in uncompromising terms. However, Pelagianism, in various forms, continued to be a point of contention for some time to come. As the patristic era came to its close, with the Dark Ages settling over western Europe, many of the issues remained unresolved. They would be taken up again during the Middle Ages, and supremely at the time of the Reformation (see pp. 156–76).

KEY NAMES, WORDS, AND PHRASES

By the end of this chapter you will have encountered the following terms, which will recur during the work. Ensure that you are familiar with them! They have been capitalized as you are likely to encounter them in normal use.

Apollinarianism
Arianism
Augustinianism
canon
canonical
Cappadocian fathers
Christological
Christology
creed
Donatist
Donatism
ecclesiological

ecclesiology
ecumenical council
extra-canonical
incarnation
patristic
patrology
Pelagian
Pelagianism
soteriology
Trinity
Trinitarian

QUESTIONS 1

1 Locate the following cities or regions on map 1 (p. 21): Alexandria; Antioch; Cappadocia; Constantinople; Hippo; Jerusalem; Rome.
2 Now find the Latin/Greek dividing line on the same map. Latin was the main language west of that line, and Greek east of it. Identify the predominant language in each of the cities mentioned in question 1.

3   Which language would you associate with the following writers: Athanasius; Augustine of Hippo; Origen; Tertullian?

4   The following movements were of major importance during the patristic period: Arianism; Donatism; Gnosticism; Pelagianism. Associate the controversies centering on each of these movements with one of the following theologians: Athanasius; Augustine of Hippo; Irenaeus of Lyons. (Note that one of these theologians is associated with more than one controversy.)

5   Why was there relatively little interest in the doctrine of the church in this early period?

CASE STUDIES

Case Study 1.1   The Bible and Tradition

A major issue of theological debate throughout Christian history concerns the way in which the Bible is interpreted. There have always been those who believed that an issue of Christian doctrine could be settled simply by an appeal to the Bible. However, the great theological debates of the patristic period showed that this approach was seriously flawed. Arianism and Pelagianism – both of which would be condemned as heretical, although for very different reasons – appealed to an impressive array of biblical texts in support of their teachings. Their opponents, however, argued that their interpretation of these texts was incorrect. It was not enough simply to quote the Bible; it was necessary to interpret it in an orthodox manner. But who decides what is an orthodox interpretation, and what is not? What resources can be appealed to in an attempt to establish the correct interpretation of a biblical passage?

Such debates have taken place throughout the history of Christian thought, but were of particular importance at the time of the Reformation. However, the patristic period saw an especially important answer to such questions being formulated. For many patristic writers, an appeal to tradition was of major importance in challenging unorthodox interpretations of Scripture or teachings. In what follows, we shall explore the contributions of three writers to this debate: Irenaeus (second century), Tertullian (third century) and Vincent of Lérins (fifth century). We begin, however, by noting the way in which the idea of "tradition" is embedded in the New Testament itself.

In its earliest period, Christianity was spread through the oral transmission of a more or less fixed body of teaching. The term "tradition" derives from the Latin word *traditio*, which literally means "handing down" or "handing over." The study of early Christianity indicates that the basic elements of the Christian faith were "handed over" from one teacher to another. Paul, writing to the church at Corinth, makes reference to "passing on" certain key themes to his audience (1 Corinthians 15: 1–4), a clear reference to the verbal transmission of central elements of the Christian message, especially the death and resurrection of Christ.

It is also known that the gospels of Matthew, Mark, and Luke are based on collections of material which were transmitted orally, before they were finally committed to writing in what are now known as the "synoptic gospels". Thus the opening of Luke's gospel makes reference to using reports "just as they were handed over to us by those who were eyewitnesses and ministers of the word from the beginning" (Luke 1: 1–2). The general consensus within New Testament scholarship is that four sources can be discerned for the synoptic gospels:

1   Mark's gospel itself, which seems to be used as a source by Matthew and Mark. Thus 90 percent of the contents of Mark's gospel are included in Matthew; 53 percent of Mark can be found in Luke. Mark's material is written in a style which suggests that it is older than the style found in the corresponding passages in Matthew or Luke, using many semitic phrases. It is very difficult to explain this observation on the basis of any hypothesis other than that Matthew and Luke both based themselves on Mark, and "tidied up" his style.
2   Material common to both Matthew and Luke. This section of material, which is about 200 verses in length, is generally referred to as "Q." There is no evidence that Q was a complete gospel in itself, or that it existed as an independent written source.
3   Material found only in Matthew (usually known as "M").
4   Material found only in Luke (usually known as "L").

The most widely accepted explanation of the way in which the three synoptic gospels were compiled was developed in detail in its current form at the University of Oxford in the opening decade of the twentieth century. Its most celebrated statements can be found in B. H. Streeter's *Four Gospels* (1924) and W. Sanday's *Studies in the Synoptic Problem* (1911). Streeter's work represents a collection of papers reflecting the work of the Oxford gospel seminar, which met nine times a year over a period of 15 years. Although this theory is sometimes known as "the Oxford hypothesis," it is more commonly referred to as "the two-source theory." Its basic features can be set out as follows.

Mark was the first gospel to be written down. It was available to both Matthew and Luke, who used it as a source, altering the style of the language as appropriate, but retaining Mark's ordering of the material. Matthew was written after Mark, but before Luke. Both Matthew and Luke had access to the source known as Q. In addition, Matthew had access to another source known as M; Luke had access to a different source, known as L. Although this theory acknowledges four sources (Mark, Q, M, and L), it is known as the "two-source" theory on account of the importance of Mark and Q in relation to its approach.

This theory has found much support in modern New Testament scholarship. However, it is by no means the only theory to command support. For example, some scholars deny the existence of Q, and argue that Luke simply used Matthew as a source. J. J. Griesbach developed an influential hypothesis, according to which Matthew was written first, followed by Luke (who used Matthew). Finally, Mark was written, making use of both Matthew and Luke. It must also be stressed that the "synoptic problem" concerns our understanding of the way in which the oral traditions concerning Jesus were passed down to us. It does not call their historical accuracy or theological reliability into question, but allows a deeper understanding of the formative period of the gospel traditions, in which the words and deeds of Jesus were passed down and handed over during the period *c.*30–60.

Our concern in this case study, however, relates to a slightly different issue concerning the idea of "tradition," which became of major importance during the second century. A movement known as "Gnosticism" emerged as a major threat to the Christian church during this period, partly on account of the fact that its teachings were at least superficially similar to those of Christianity itself. Many Gnostic writers argued that salvation was achieved through access to a secret teaching, which alone ensured that believers would be saved. The "secret knowledge" in question, for some Gnostic writers, was almost like a form of "cosmic password." When someone died, their spirit was liberated from its physical prison, and it was free to begin its long and complex journey to its final and glorious destination. To get there, it needed to get past a series of potential obstacles, for which the "secret knowledge" was required.

Some Gnostic writers argued that this secret oral teaching had been passed down from the apostles, and that it was to be found in a "veiled" form in the Bible. Only those who knew how to read the Bible in a certain way could gain access to this knowledge, which was not publicly available. Only those who were initiated into the mysteries of Gnosticism could therefore hope to benefit from the salvation which the New Testament offered.

It was clearly of major importance for the Christian church to rebut this teaching. It implied that, while the church had access to the Bible, it did not have access to the special way of reading and interpreting the Bible which was required if its true meaning was to be understood. Perhaps more importantly, the salvation which the New Testament promised was only available to those who had access to the secret traditions of Gnosticism. In response to the threat from Gnosticism, a "traditional" method of understanding certain passages of Scripture began to develop. Second-century patristic theologians such as Irenaeus of Lyons began to develop the idea of an authorized way of interpreting certain texts of Scripture, which he argued went back to the time of the apostles themselves. Scripture could not be allowed to be interpreted in any arbitrary or random way: it had to be interpreted within the context of the historical continuity of the Christian church. The parameters of its interpretation were historically fixed and given. "Tradition" here means simply "a traditional way of interpreting Scripture within the community of faith." This is what is known as a *single-source* theory of tradition.

Irenaeus of Lyons (*c.*130–*c.*200). Probably a native of Asia Minor, who was elected bishop of the southern French city of Lyons around 178. He is chiefly noted for his major writing *adversus haereses* ("Against the heresies"), which defended the Christian faith against Gnostic misrepresentations and criticisms.

To understand Irenaeus at this point, we shall examine a passage from his major work *Against Heresies*, in which he engages with the Gnostic threat through an appeal to tradition. Irenaeus here argues that the living Christian community possessed a tradition of interpreting Scripture which was denied to heretics. By their historical succession from the apostles, the bishops ensure that their congregations remain faithful to their teachings and interpretations.

1.1.1   Irenaeus of Lyons on Scripture and Tradition

When [the heretics] are refuted out of the Scriptures, they turn to accusing the Scriptures themselves, as if they were not right or did not possess authority, because the Scriptures contain a variety of statements, and because it is not possible for those who do not know the tradition to find the truth in them. For this has not
5   been handed down by means of writings, but by the "living voice". . . . Everyone who wishes to perceive the truth should consider the apostolic tradition, which has been made known in every church in the entire world. We are able to number those who are bishops appointed by the apostles, and their successors in the churches to the present day, who taught and knew nothing of such things as these people
10   imagine. For if the apostles had known secret mysteries which they taught privately and secretly to the perfect, they would have passed them down to those to whom they entrusted the churches. For they would have wanted those who they left as their successors, and to whom they handed over their own office of authority, to be perfect and blameless. . . . Therefore, as there are so many demonstrations of
15   this fact, there is no need to look anywhere else for the truth which we can easily obtain from the church. The apostles have, as it were, deposited this truth in all its fullness in this depository, so that whoever wants to may draw from this water of life. This is the gate of life; all others are thieves and robbers.

Note the following points:

1 Irenaeus begins by identifying one of the key Gnostic arguments (lines 2–5). Only those who "know the tradition" are able to interpret the Bible correctly. When the Bible seems to contradict Gnostic teachings, the Gnostic response is therefore to the effect that this is only a superficial or apparent contradiction. When the Bible is read properly, in the light of the secret oral tradition to which they alone have access, it is seen to support, rather than challenge, their teachings. Note particularly that this tradition is *oral*, not written. The phrase "the living voice" was used by some Gnostic writers to refer to this secret unwritten tradition.

2 Irenaeus contrasts this with the *publicly accessible* Christian tradition, which is "made known in every church in the entire world" (lines 5–10). If this tradition is so important, why has it been kept secret? Irenaeus argues that the teachings of the apostles, which secure salvation for those who accept them, are made known through the public teaching of the church. The apostolic teaching "in all its fullness" (line 17) has been "deposited" – that is, made available and accessible – through the church.

3 Note how Irenaeus points out a problem with the Gnostic position. If the Gnostics are dependent on a "secret tradition," deriving from the apostles, how can they be sure that it has been passed down *correctly*? To whom was it entrusted? And who did these people pass it on to subsequently? Irenaeus stresses that, in the case of the Christian church, the immediate and subsequent successors to the apostles are known and can be named (lines 7–14). Irenaeus sees the bishops as visible embodiments of the institutional and doctrinal continuity between the apostles and the contemporary church. The apostles chose to entrust their teaching to named successors within the church.

Tertullian (*c*.160–*c*.225). A major figure in early Latin theology, who produced a series of significant controversial and apologetic writings. He is particularly noted for his ability to coin new Latin terms to translate the emerging theological vocabulary of the Greek-speaking eastern church.

A similar point is made by Tertullian, in an early third-century analysis of the sources of theology dedicated to demonstrating the weaknesses of the heretical positions. Tertullian here lays considerable emphasis upon the role of tradition and apostolic succession in the defining of Christian theology. Orthodoxy depends upon remaining historically continuous with and theologically dependent upon the apostles. The heretics, in contrast, cannot demonstrate any such continuity.

1.1.2 Tertullian on the Role of Tradition

[The apostles] first bore witness to faith in Jesus Christ throughout Judea, and established churches there, after which they went out into the world and proclaimed the same doctrine of the same faith to the nations. And they likewise established churches in every city, from which the other churches subsequently
5   derived the origins of faith and the seeds of doctrine, and are still deriving them in order that they may become churches. It is through this that these churches are counted as "apostolic," in that they are the offspring of apostolic churches. . . . It is so for this reason that we lay down this ruling: if the Lord Jesus Christ sent out the apostles to preach, no preachers other than those which are appointed by
10   Christ are to be received, since "no one knows the Father except the Son and those to whom the Son has revealed him," and the Son appears to have revealed him to no one except the apostles who he sent to preach what he had revealed to them. What they preached – that is, what Christ revealed to them – ought, by this ruling, to be established only by those churches which those apostles founded by their
15   preaching and, as they say, by the living voice, and subsequently through their letters. If this is true, all doctrine which is in agreement with those apostolic churches, the sources and originals of the faith, must be accounted as the truth, since it indubitably preserves what the churches received from the apostles, the apostles from Christ, and Christ from God. . . . If any of these [heresies] dares to
20   trace their origins back to the apostolic era, so that it might appear that they had been handed down by the apostles because they existed under the apostles, we are able to say: let them therefore show the origins of their churches; let them unfold the order of their bishops, showing that there is a succession from the beginning, so that their first bishop had as his precursor and predecessor an apostle or some
25   apostolic man who was associated with the apostles.

Tertullian's argument lays considerable emphasis on the importance of historical continuity. Note how he stresses the importance of the link between apostles and bishops, and especially the way in which he demands that those who claim to represent "apostolic" teaching must be able to verify their historical links with the apostles.

The debate over authentic Christian teaching continued well into the fifth century. One major concern focused on the idea of doctrinal innovation. What was the church to make of teachings which claimed to be based on Scripture, but which seemed to represent new teachings? The controversies within the early church often seemed to end up introducing new teachings, rather than simply defending older teachings.

> **Vincent of Lérins (died before 450).** A French theologian who settled on the island of Lérins. He is particularly noted for his emphasis on the role of tradition in guarding against innovations in the doctrine of the church, and is credited with the formulation of the so-called "Vincentian canon."

A major contribution to this question was made in 434 by Vincent of Lérins, based in the south of France, and sometimes known by the pseudonym "Peregrinus." Writing in the aftermath of the Pelagian controversy, Vincent of Lérins expressed his belief that the controversies of that time had given rise to theological innovations, such as new ways of interpreting certain biblical passages. It is clear that he regarded Augustine's doctrine of double predestination (which arose as a response to Pelagius' views on grace) as a case in point. But how could such doctrinal innovations be identified? In response to this question, he argues for a triple criterion by which authentic Christian teaching may be established: ecumenicity (being believed everywhere), antiquity (being believed always), and consent (being believed by all people). This triple criterion is often described as the "Vincentian canon," the word "canon" here having the sense of "rule" or "norm."

1.1.3   Vincent of Lérins on Tradition and Orthodoxy

I have devoted considerable study and much attention to inquiring, from men of outstanding holiness and doctrinal correctness, in what way it might be possible for me to establish a kind of fixed and, as it were, general and guiding principle for distinguishing the truth of the Catholic faith from the depraved falsehoods of the
5   heretics.... Holy Scripture, on account of its depth, is not accepted in a universal sense. The same statements are interpreted in one way by one person, in another by someone else, with the result that there seem to be as many opinions as there are people.... Therefore, on account of the number and variety of errors, there is a need for someone to lay down a rule for the interpretation of the prophets and
10   the apostles in such a way that is directed by the rule of the Catholic church. Now in the Catholic church itself the greatest care is taken that we hold that which has been believed everywhere, always, and by all people (*quod ubique, quod semper, quod ab omnibus creditum est*).

Note how Vincent identifies the problem: how are authentically Christian teachings to be distinguished from those of heretics? An initial answer to this question might seem to be that these teachings can be identified on account of their faithfulness to Scripture. However, Vincent makes the point that Scripture is interpreted in different ways by different people (lines 5–8). A simple appeal to the Bible is therefore not good enough; something additional is needed. For this reason, Vincent argues for the need for a "rule for the interpretation of the prophets and the apostles" (lines 9–10). He finds this "rule" in what has since come to be known as the *consensus fidelium* – "the consensus of the faithful," which has, according to Vincent, three elements. A belief or way of interpreting Scripture must have been accepted "everywhere, always, and by all people." In other words, it must not be limited to a certain geographical region, a specific period of time, or a small group of people.

Vincent's definition proved highly influential, and is often reflected in later writings dealing with this theme. By the end of the patristic period, the idea of interpreting the Bible within the living tradition of the Christian church was seen as an essential antidote to heresy, and had become part of the accepted way of doing theology.

Case Study 1.2   The Arian Controversy: The Divinity of Christ

The patristic period saw considerable attention being paid to the doctrine of the person of Christ. The debate was conducted primarily within the eastern church; interestingly, Augustine of Hippo never wrote anything of consequence on Christology. The period proved to be definitive, laying down guidelines for the discussion of the person of Christ which remained normative until the dawn of the Enlightenment debates on the relation of faith and history, to be considered in a later case study (see case study 4.1).

The task confronting the patristic writers was basically the development of a unified Christological scheme, which would bring together and integrate the various Christological hints and statements, images and models, found within the New Testament – some of which have been considered briefly above. That task proved complex. The first period of the development of Christology centered on the question of the divinity of Christ, and may be regarded as focusing on the question of whether Jesus Christ may legitimately be described as "God." That Jesus Christ was human appeared to be something of a truism to most early patristic writers. It was self-evidently true, and did not require justification. What required explanation about Christ concerned the manner in which he differed from, rather than approximated to, other human beings.

Two early viewpoints were quickly rejected as heretical. *Ebionitism*, a primarily Jewish sect which flourished in the early first centuries of the Christian era, regarded Jesus as an ordinary human being, the human son of Mary and Joseph. This reduced Christology was regarded as totally inadequate by its opponents, and soon passed into oblivion. More significant was the diametrically opposed view, which came to be known as *Docetism*, from the Greek verb *dokein* (to seem or appear). This approach – which is probably best regarded as a tendency within

45

theology rather than a definite theological position – argued that Christ was totally divine, and that his humanity was merely an appearance. The sufferings of Christ are thus treated as apparent rather than real. Docetism held a particular attraction for the Gnostic writers of the second century, during which period it reached its zenith. By this time, however, other viewpoints were in the process of emerging, which would eventually eclipse this tendency.

Justin Martyr represents one such viewpoint. Justin Martyr, amongst the most important of the second-century Apologists, was especially concerned to demonstrate that the Christian faith brought to fruition the insights of both classical Greek philosophy and Judaism. Adolf von Harnack summarized the manner in which Justin achieved this objective: he argued that "Christ is the Logos and Nomos." Of particular interest is the Logos-Christology which Justin develops, in which he exploits the apologetic potential of the idea of the "Logos," current in both Stoicism and the Middle Platonism of the period. The Logos (a Greek term which is usually translated as "word" – e.g., as it occurs at John 1: 14) is to be thought of as the ultimate source of all human knowledge. The one and the same Logos is known by both Christian believers and pagan philosophers; the latter, however, only have partial access to it, whereas Christians have full access to it, on account of its manifestation in Christ. Justin allows that pre-Christian secular philosophers, such as Heraclitus or Socrates, thus had partial access to the truth, on account of the manner in which the Logos is present in the world.

Justin Martyr (*c*.100–*c*.165). One of the most noted of the Christian apologists of the second century, with a concern to demonstrate the moral and intellectual credibility of Christianity in a pagan world. His *First Apology* stresses the manner in which Christianity brings to fulfillment the insights of classical philosophy.

An idea of especial importance in this context is that of the *logos spermatikos*, which appears to derive from Middle Platonism. The divine Logos sowed seeds throughout human history; it is therefore to be expected that this "seed-bearing Logos" will be known, even if only in part, by non-Christians. Justin is therefore able to argue that Christianity builds upon and fulfills the hints and anticipations of God's revelation which is to be had through pagan philosophy. The Logos was known temporarily through the theophanies (that is, appearances or manifestations of God) in the Old Testament; Christ brings the Logos to its fullest revelation. The world of Greek philosophy is thus set firmly in the context of Christianity: it is a prelude to the coming of Christ, who brings to fulfillment what it had hitherto known only in part.

It is in the writings of Origen that the Logos-Christology appears to find its fullest development. It must be made clear that Origen's Christology is complex, and that its interpretation at points is highly problematical. What follows is a simplification of his approach. In the incarnation, the human soul of Christ is united with the Logos. On account of the closeness of this union, Christ's human soul comes to share in the properties of the Logos. Origen illustrates this idea with an often-quoted analogy:

> If a lump of iron is constantly kept in a fire, it will absorb its heat through all its pores and veins. If the fire is continuous, and the iron is not removed, it becomes totally converted to the other. . . . In the same way, the soul which has been constantly placed in the Logos and Wisdom of God, is God in all that it does, feels and understands.

Nevertheless, Origen insists that the Logos must be regarded as subordinate to the Father. Although both the Logos and Father are co-eternal, the Logos is subordinate to the Father.

Origen (*c.*185–*c.*254). Leading representative of the Alexandrian school of theology, especially noted for his allegorical exposition of Scripture, and his use of Platonic ideas in theology, particularly Christology. The originals of many of his works, which were written in Greek, have been lost, with the result that some are known only in Latin translations of questionable reliability.

We noted above that Justin Martyr argued that the Logos was accessible to all, even if only in a fragmentary manner. Its full disclosure only came in Christ. Related ideas can be found in other writers to adopt the Logos-Christology, including Origen. Origen adopts an illuminationist approach to revelation, in which God's act of revelation is compared to being enlightened by the "rays of God," which are caused by "the light which is the divine Logos." For Origen, both truth and salvation are to be had outside the Christian faith.

What has been said thus far is intended to be an introduction to one of the most important landmark theological debates of the patristic period – the Arian controversy of the fourth century. The Arian controversy remains a landmark in the development of classical Christology, and therefore demands extensive discussion. It must be noted that certain aspects of the history of the controversy remain obscure, and are likely to remain so, despite the best efforts of historians to clarify them. What concern us here are the theological aspects of the debate, which are comparatively well understood. However, it must be stressed that we know Arius' views mainly in the form in which they have been mediated to us by his opponents, which raises questions about the potential bias of their presentations. What follows is an attempt to present Arius' distinctive Christological ideas as fairly as possible, on the basis of the relatively few reliable sources now available to us.

Arius emphasizes the self-subsistence of God. God is the one and only source of all created things; nothing exists which does not ultimately derive from God. This view of God, which many commentators have suggested is due more to Hellenistic philosophy than to Christian theology, clearly raises the question of the relation of the Father to the Son. In his *Against the Arians*, Arius' critic Athanasius represents him as making the following statements on this point:

> God was not always a father. There was a time when God was all alone, and was not yet a father; only later did he become a father. The Son did not always exist. Everything created is out of nothing . . . so the Logos of God came into existence out of nothing. There was a time when he was not. Before he was brought into being, he did not exist. He also had a beginning to his created existence.

These statements are of considerable importance, and bring us to the heart of Arianism. The following points are of especial significance.

Arius (*c.*250–*c.*336). The originator of Arianism, a form of Christology which refused to concede the full divinity of Christ. Little is known of his life, and little has survived of his writings. With the exception of a letter to Eusebius of Nicomedia, his views are known mainly through the writings of his opponents.

1   The Father is regarded as existing before the Son. "There was when he was not." This decisive affirmation places Father and Son on different levels, and is consistent with Arius' rigorous insistence that the Son is a creature. Only the Father is "unbegotten"; the Son, like all other creatures, derives from this one source of being. However, Arius is careful to emphasize that the Son is like every other creature. There is a distinction of rank between the Son and other creatures, including human beings. Arius has some difficulty in identifying the precise nature of this distinction. The Son, he argued, is "a perfect creature, yet not as one among other creatures; a begotten being, yet not as one among other begotten beings." The implication seems to be that the Son outranks other creatures, while sharing their essentially created and begotten nature.

2   Arius stresses the unknowability of God to creatures, with the result that the Father must be unknown to the Son (who is, as we have noted, a creature). Arius emphasizes the utter transcendence and inaccessibility of God. God cannot be known by any other creature. Yet, as we noted above, the Son is to be regarded as a creature, however elevated above all other creatures. Arius presses home his logic, arguing that the Son cannot know the Father. "The one who has a beginning is in no position to comprehend or lay hold of the one who has no beginning." This important affirmation rests upon the radical distinction

between Father and Son. Such is the gulf fixed between them, that the latter cannot know the former unaided. In common with all other creatures, the Son is dependent upon the grace of God if the Son is to perform whatever function has been ascribed to him. It is considerations such as these which have led Arius' critics to argue that, at the levels of revelation and salvation, the Son is in precisely the same position as other creatures.

3   Arius argued that the biblical passages which seemed to speak of Christ's status in terms of divinity were merely using language in an honorific manner. (The technical term for this way of using language is "catachrestic.") Arius' opponents were easily able to bring forward a series of biblical passages pointing to the fundamental unity between Father and Son. On the basis of the controversial literature of the period, it is clear that the Fourth Gospel was of major importance to this controversy, with John 3: 35, 10: 30, 12: 27, 14: 10, 17: 3 and 17: 11 being discussed frequently. Arius' response to such texts is significant: the language of "sonship" is variegated in character, and metaphorical in nature. To refer to the "Son" is an honorific, rather than theologically precise, way of speaking. Although Jesus Christ is referred to as "Son" in Scripture, this metaphorical (more accurately, catachrestic) way of speaking is subject to the controlling principle of a God who is totally different in essence from all created beings – including the Son.

Arius' position can therefore be summarized in the following manner:

1   The Son is a creature, who, like all other creatures, derives from the will of God.
2   The term "Son" is thus a metaphor, an honorific term intended to underscore the rank of the Son among other creatures. It does not imply that Father and Son share the same being or status.
3   The status of the Son is itself a consequence of the will of the Father; it is not a consequence of the nature of the Son, but of the will of the Father.

Athanasius had little time for Arius' subtle distinctions. If the Son is a creature, then the Son is a creature like any other creature, including human beings. After all, what other kind of creaturehood is there? For Athanasius, the affirmation of the creaturehood of the Son had two decisive consequences, each of which had uniformly negative implications for Arianism.

First, Athanasius makes the point that it is only God who can save. God, and God alone, can break the power of sin, and bring us to eternal life. An essential feature of being a creature is that one requires to be redeemed. No creature can save another creature. Only the creator can redeem the creation. Having emphasized that it is God alone who can save, Athanasius then makes the logical move which the Arians found difficult to counter. The New Testament and the

Christian liturgical tradition alike regard Jesus Christ as Saviour. Yet, as Athanasius emphasized, only God can save. So how are we to make sense of this?

> **Athanasius (*c.*296–373).** One of the most significant defenders of orthodox Christology during the period of the Arian controversy. Elected as bishop of Alexandria in 328, he was deposed on account of his opposition to Arianism. Although he was widely supported in the west, his views were only finally recognized at the Council of Constantinople (381) after his death.

The only possible solution, Athanasius argues, is to accept that Jesus is God incarnate. The logic of his argument at times goes something like this:

1   No creature can redeem another creature.
2   According to Arius, Jesus Christ is a creature.
3   Therefore, according to Arius, Jesus Christ cannot redeem humanity.

At times, a slightly different style of argument can be discerned, resting upon the statements of Scripture and the Christian liturgical tradition.

1   Only God can save.
2   Jesus Christ saves.
3   Therefore Jesus Christ is God.

Salvation, for Athanasius, involves divine intervention. Athanasius thus draws out the meaning of John 1: 14 by arguing that the "word became flesh": in other words, God entered into our human situation, in order to change it.

The second point that Athanasius makes is that Christians worship and pray to Jesus Christ. This represents an excellent case study of the importance of Christian practices of worship and prayer for Christian theology. By the fourth century, prayer to and adoration of Christ were standard features of the way in which public worship took place. Athanasius argues that if Jesus Christ is a creature, then Christians are guilty of worshiping a creature instead of God – in other words, they had lapsed into idolatry. Christians, Athanasius stresses, are totally forbidden to worship anyone or anything except God himself. Athanasius thus argued that Arius seemed to be guilty of making nonsense of the way in which Christians prayed and worshiped. Athanasius argued that Christians were right to worship and adore Jesus Christ, because by doing so, they were recognizing him for what he was – God incarnate.

The Arian controversy had to be settled somehow, if peace was to be established within the church. Debate came to center upon two terms as possible descriptions of the relation of the Father to the Son. The term *homoiousios*, "of like substance" or "of like being," was seen by many as representing a judicious compromise, allowing the proximity between Father and Son to be asserted without requiring any further speculation on the precise nature of their relation. However, the rival term *homoousios*, "of the same substance" or "of the same being," eventually gained the upper hand. Though differing by only one letter from the alternative term, it embodied a very different understanding of the relationship between Father and Son. The fury of the debate prompted the British historian Edward Gibbon to comment in his *Decline and Fall of the Roman Empire* that never had there been so much energy spent over a single vowel. The Nicene Creed – or, more accurately, the Niceno-Constantinopolitan Creed – of 381 declared that Christ was "of the same substance" with the Father. This affirmation has since widely become regarded as a benchmark of Christological orthodoxy within all the mainstream Christian churches, whether Protestant, Catholic or Orthodox.

The present case study has explored a controversy that arose concerning the issue of Christology. The following case study explores a debate which arose specifically within the Alexandrian Christological school, centering on the teachings of Apollinaris of Laodicea.

Case Study 1.3   The Alexandrian Christological School: The Apollinarian Controversy

In an earlier case study (case study 1.2), we considered Athanasius' response to Arius. In doing so, we began to touch on some of the features of the Alexandrian school of Christology. It is therefore appropriate to explore these in more detail, and one debate which illustrated the tensions within the school. In a later case study (case study 1.4), we shall explore the views of the rival Antiochene school.

The outlook of the Alexandrian school, of which Athanasius is a representative, is strongly soteriological in character. Jesus Christ is the redeemer of humanity, where "redemption" means "being taken up into the life of God" or "being made divine," a notion traditionally expressed in terms of deification. Christology gives expression to what this soteriological insight implies. We could summarize the trajectory of Alexandrian Christology along the following lines: if human nature is to be deified, it must be united with the divine nature. God must become united with human nature in such a manner that the latter is enabled to share in the life of God. This, the Alexandrians argued, was precisely what happened in and through the incarnation of the Son of God in Jesus Christ. The Second Person of the Trinity assumed human nature, and by doing so, ensured its divinization. God became human, in order that humanity might become divine.

Alexandrian writers thus placed considerable emphasis upon the idea of the Logos assuming human nature. The term "assuming" is important; a distinction is drawn between the Logos "dwelling within humanity" (as in the case of the

Old Testament prophets), and the Logos taking human nature upon itself (as in the incarnation of the Son of God). Particular emphasis came to be placed upon John 1: 14 ("the word became flesh"), which came to embody the fundamental insights of the school, and the liturgical celebration of Christmas. To celebrate the birth of Christ was to celebrate the coming of the Logos to the world, and its taking human nature upon itself in order to redeem it.

This clearly raised the question of the relation of the divinity and humanity of Christ. Cyril of Alexandria is one of many writers within the school to emphasize the reality of their union in the incarnation. The Logos existed "without flesh" before its union with human nature; after that union, there is only one nature, in that the Logos united human nature to itself. This emphasis upon the one nature of Christ distinguishes the Alexandrian from the Antiochene school, which was more receptive to the idea of two natures within Christ. Cyril, writing in the fifth century, states this point as follows:

> We do not affirm that the nature of the Logos underwent a change and became flesh, or that it was transformed into a whole or perfect human consisting of flesh and body; rather, we say that the Logos . . . personally united itself to human nature with a living soul, became a human being, and was called the Son of Man, but not of mere will or favour.

Cyril of Alexandria (died 444). A significant writer, who was appointed patriarch of Alexandria in 412. He became involved in the controversy over the Christological views of Nestorius, and produced major statements and defenses of the orthodox position on the two natures of Christ.

This raised the question of what kind of human nature had been assumed. We may return to the fourth century to explore this point further. Apollinaris of Laodicea had anxieties about the increasingly widespread belief that the Logos assumed human nature in its entirety. It seemed to him that this implied that the Logos was contaminated by the weaknesses of human nature. How could the Son of God be allowed to be tainted by purely human directive principles? The sinlessness of Christ would be compromised, in Apollinaris' view, if he were to possess a purely human mind; was not the human mind the source of sin and rebellion against God? Only if the human mind were to be replaced by a purely divine motivating and directing force could the sinlessness of Christ be maintained. For this reason, Apollinaris argued that, in Christ, a purely human mind and soul were replaced by a divine mind and soul: "the divine energy fulfills the role of the animating soul and of the human mind" in Christ. The human nature of Christ is thus incomplete.

Apollinaris of Laodicea (*c.*310–*c.*390). A vigorous defender of orthodoxy against the Arian heresy, who was appointed bishop of Laodicea at some point around 360. He is chiefly remembered for his Christological views, which were regarded as an overreaction to Arianism, and widely criticized at the Council of Constantinople (381).

This can be seen clearly from a letter written by Apollinaris to the bishops at Diocaesarea, which sets out the leading features of his Christology. The most important is the unequivocal assertion that the Word did not assume a "change-able" human mind in the incarnation, which would have led to the Word being trapped in human sin. Rather, it assumed "an immutable and heavenly divine mind." As a result, Christ cannot be said to be totally human.

1.3.1 Apollinaris of Laodicea on the Mind of Christ

We confess that the Word of God has not descended upon a holy man, which was what happened in the case of the prophets. Rather, the Word himself has become flesh without having assumed a human mind – that is, a changeable mind, which is enslaved to filthy thoughts – but which exists as an immutable and heavenly
5   divine mind.

This idea appalled many of Apollinaris' colleagues. The Apollinarian view of Christ may have had its attractions for some; others, however, were shocked by its soteriological implications. It was pointed out above (p. 51) that soteriological considerations are of central importance to the Alexandrian approach. How could human nature be redeemed, it was asked, if only part of human nature had been assumed by the Logos? Perhaps the most famous statement of this position is set out by Gregory of Nazianzus in his *Letter 101*, in which he stressed the redemptive importance of the assumption of human nature in its totality at the incarnation.

Gregory of Nazianzus (329–389), also known as "Gregory Nazianzen." He is particularly remembered for his "Five Theological Orations," written around 380, and a compilation of extracts from the writings of Origen, which he entitled the *Philokalia.*

In this letter, written in Greek at some point in 380 or 381, Gregory mounts a frontal assault on the central thesis of Apollinarianism: that Christ was not fully human, in that he possessed "an immutable and heavenly divine mind," rather than a human mind. For Gregory, this amounts to a denial of the possibility of redemption. Only what is assumed by the Word in the incarnation can be redeemed. If Christ did not possess a human mind, humanity is not redeemed.

1.3.2   Gregory of Nazianzus on the Incarnation

Do not let people deceive themselves and others by saying that the "Man of the Lord," which is the title they give to him who is rather "Our Lord and God," is without a human mind. We do not separate the humanity from the divinity; in fact, we assert the dogma of the unity and identity of the Person, who previously was
5   not just human but God, the only Son before all ages, who in these last days has assumed human nature also for our salvation; in his flesh possible, in his Deity impassible; in the body subject to limitation, yet unlimited in the Spirit; at one and the same time earthly and heavenly, tangible and intangible, comprehensible and incomprehensible; that by one and the same person, a perfect human being and
10   perfect God, the whole humanity, fallen through sin, might be recreated.

If anyone does not believe that holy Mary is *Theotokos*, they will be cut off from the Deity. . . . If anyone asserts that humanity was created and only afterwards endued with divinity, they also are to be condemned. . . . If anyone brings in the idea of two sons, one of God the Father, the other of the mother, may they lose
15   their share in the adoption. . . . For the Godhead and the humanity are two natures, as are soul and body, but there are not two Sons or two Gods. . . . For both natures are one by the combination, the Godhead made man or the manhood deified, or whatever be the right expression. . . .

If anyone has put their trust in him as a human being lacking a human mind, they
20   are themselves mindless and not worthy of salvation. For what has not been assumed has not been healed; it is what is united to his divinity that is saved. . . . Let them not grudge us our total salvation, or endue the Saviour with only the bones and nerves and mere appearance of humanity.

The following points are of especial importance in this passage, and should be noted carefully:

1   Gregory stresses that Jesus Christ is both perfect God and a perfect human person (lines 9–10). Even though human nature has fallen, through the impact of sin, it remains capable of being redeemed. And if the whole of human nature is to be redeemed, it follows that the whole of that human nature must be assumed.

2   Note the use of the term *Theotokos* (lines 11–12) to refer to Mary. For

Gregory, the use of this title (which can be translated literally as "bearer of God," but is often translated in a more popular form as "Mother of God") is a necessary consequence of the incarnation. To deny this title is to deny the reality of the incarnation – a point which is of especial importance in relation to the controversy which broke out within the Antiochene school over the teaching of Nestorius on this matter, which we shall consider in a later case study (case study 1.4).

3   Note the argument of the final paragraph (lines 20–21), and especially the assertion: "what has not been assumed has not been healed." For Gregory, only those aspects of human nature which have been united to the divinity in the incarnation are saved. If we are to be saved in the totality of our human nature, that totality must be brought into contact with the divinity. If Christ is only partly or apparently human, then salvation is not possible.

In the present case study, we have explored a major controversy within one of the two dominant patristic schools of Christology. In the following case study, we shall examine a highly significant debate which broke out within the Antiochene school.

Case Study 1.4   The Antiochene Christological School: The Nestorian Controversy

In an earlier case study (case study 1.3), we noted the development of the Alexandrian school of Christology, and traced the trajectory of a major controversy within it. In the present case study, we shall repeat this exercise, focusing on the rival school of Antioch.

The school of Christology which arose in ancient Syria (modern-day Turkey) differed considerably from its Egyptian rival at Alexandria. One of the most significant points of difference concerns the context in which Christological speculation was set. The Alexandrian writers were motivated primarily by soteriological considerations. Concerned that deficient understandings of the person of Christ were linked with inadequate conceptions of salvation, they used ideas derived from secular Greek philosophy to ensure a picture of Christ which was consistent with the full redemption of humanity. The idea of the "Logos" was of particular importance here, especially when linked with the notion of incarnation.

The Antiochene writers differed at this point. Their concerns were moral, rather than purely soteriological, and they drew much less significantly on the ideas of Greek philosophy. The basic trajectory of much Antiochene thinking on the identity of Christ can be traced along the following lines. On account of their disobedience, human beings exist in a state of corruption, from which they are unable to extricate themselves. If redemption is to take place, it must be on the basis of a new obedience on the part of humanity. In that humanity is unable to break free from the bonds of sin, God is obliged to intervene. This leads to the coming of the redeemer as one who unites humanity and divinity, and thus to the re-establishment of an obedient people of God.

The two natures of Christ are vigorously defended. Christ is at one and the same time both God and a human being. Against the Alexandrian criticism that this was to deny the unity of Christ, the Antiochenes responded that they upheld that unity, while simultaneously recognizing that the one redeemer possessed both a perfect human and perfect divine nature. There is a "perfect conjunction" between the human and divine natures in Christ. The complete unity of Christ is thus not inconsistent with his possessing two natures, divine and human. Theodore of Mopsuestia stressed this, in asserting that the glory of Jesus Christ "comes from God the Logos, who assumed him and united him to himself. . . . And because of this exact conjunction which this human being has with God the Son, the whole creation honors and worships him."

So how did the Antiochene theologians envisage the mode of union of divine and human natures in Christ? We have already seen the "assumption" model which had gained the ascendency at Alexandria, by which the Logos assumed human flesh. What model was employed at Antioch? The answer could be summarized as follows:

Alexandria: Logos assumes a general human nature.
Antioch: Logos assumes a specific human being.

Theodore of Mopsuestia often implies that the Logos did not assume "human nature" in general, but a specific human being. Instead of assuming a general or abstract human nature, Theodore appears to suggest that the Logos assumed a specific concrete human individual. This seems to be the case in his work *On the Incarnation*: "In coming to indwell, the Logos united the assumed (human being) as a whole to itself, and made him to share with it in all the dignity which the one who indwells, being the Son of God by nature, possesses."

So how are the human and divine natures related? Antiochene writers were convinced that the Alexandrian position led to the "mingling" or "confusion" of the divine and human natures of Christ. Instead, they devised a manner of conceptualizing the relationship between the two natures which maintained their distinct identities. This "union according to good pleasure" involves the human and divine natures of Christ being understood to be rather like watertight compartments within Christ. They never interact, or mingle with one another. They remain distinct, being held together by the good pleasure of God. The "hypostatic union" – that is, the union of the divine and human natures in Christ – rests in the will of God.

Theodore of Mopsuestia (*c.*350–428). A leading representative of the Antiochene school, noted especially for his biblical exegesis. He became bishop of Mopsuestia in 392. His views on Christology were criticized at the time by Alexandrian writers, and were subsequently condemned at the Councils of Ephesus (431) and Constantinople (553).

This might seem to suggest that Theodore of Mopsuestia regards the union of the divine and human natures as being a purely moral union, like that of a husband and wife. It also leads to a suspicion that the Logos merely puts on human nature, as one would put on a coat: the action involved is temporary and reversible, and involves no fundamental change to anyone involved. However, the Antiochene writers do not seem to have intended these conclusions to be drawn. Perhaps the most reliable way of approaching their position is to suggest that their desire to avoid confusing the divine and human natures within Christ led them to stress their distinctiveness – yet in so doing, to inadvertently weaken their link in the hypostatic union.

This became a matter of controversy on account of the way in which Nestorius chose to express his Christological views, which seemed to his critics to amount to a doctrine of "two sons" – that is, that Jesus Christ was not a single person, but two, one human and one divine. Yet this is explicitly excluded by the leading writers of the school, such as Nestorius. Christ is, according to Nestorius, "the common name of the two natures."

> Christ is indivisible in that he is Christ, but he is twofold in that he is both God and a human being. He is one in his sonship, but is twofold in that which takes and that which is taken. . . . For we do not acknowledge two Christs or two sons or "only-begottens" or Lords; not one son and another son, not a first "only-begotten" and a new "only-begotten," not a first and second Christ, but one and the same.

Nestorius (died *c.*451). A major representative of the Antiochene school of theology, who became patriarch of Constantinople in 428. His vigorous emphasis upon the humanity of Christ seemed to his critics to amount to a denial of his divinity. Nestorius' failure to endorse the term *Theotokos* led to him being openly charged with heresy. Although far more orthodox than his opponents allowed, the extent of Nestorius' orthodoxy remains unclear and disputed.

Nestorius' views created something of a scandal, as contemporary reports indicate. What follows is an extract from a history of the church compiled around this time by Socrates, also known as "Scholasticus." While there is probably a degree of bias in the reporting of Nestorius' actions and words, what is found in this passage corresponds well with what is known of the situation at this time. Notice how the controversy focuses on whether Mary, the mother of Jesus Christ, may properly be referred to as *Theotokos* (God-bearer). Nestorius is here depicted as confused about whether to use the term or not, hesitant as to what its use affirms, yet fearful as to what its denial might imply.

1.4.1   A Contemporary Account of Nestorius' Views

Now [Nestorius] had as a colleague the presbyter Anastasius, who he had brought from Antioch. He had high regard for him, and consulted him over many matters. Anastasius was preaching one day in church, and said, "Let no one call Mary the Mother of God (*Theotokos*): for Mary was only a human being, and it is impossible
5   that God should be born of a human being." This caused a great scandal, and caused distress to both the clergy and the laity, as they had been taught to this point to acknowledge Christ as God, and not to separate his humanity from his divinity on account of the economy [of salvation]. . . . While great offence was taken in the church at what was proclaimed in this way, Nestorius, who was eager to establish
10   Anastasius' proposition – for he did not wish to have someone who he so highly esteemed found guilty of blasphemy – continually kept on giving instruction in church on this subject. He adopted a controversial attitude, and totally rejected the term *Theotokos*. The controversy on the matter was taken one way by some and another way by others, with the result that the ensuing discussion divided the
15   church, and began to look like people fighting in the dark, with everyone coming out with the most confused and contradictory assertions. Nestorius acquired the popular reputation of asserting that the Lord was nothing more than a human being, and attempting to impose the teaching of Paul of Samosata and Photinus on the church. This led to such a great outcry that it was thought necessary to
20   convene a general council to rule on the matter in dispute. Having myself studied the writings of Nestorius, I have found him to be an unlearned man and shall express quite frankly my own views about him. . . . I cannot concede that he was a follower of either Paul of Samosata or Photinus, or that he ever said that the Lord was nothing more than a human being. However, he seemed scared of the term
25   *Theotokos*, as though it were some terrible phantom. The fact is, the groundless alarm he showed on this subject just showed up his extreme ignorance: for being a man of natural ability as a speaker, he was considered well educated, but in reality he was disgracefully illiterate. In fact he had no time for the hard work which an accurate examination of the ancient expositors would have involved and, made
30   arrogant on account of his readiness of expression, he did not give his attention to the ancients, but thought himself above them.

To understand the point at issue here, we need to explore an aspect of Christology known as the doctrine of the "communication of attributes," a notion often discussed in terms of the Latin phrase *communicatio idiomatum*. The issue involved can be explored as follows. By the end of the fourth century, the following propositions had gained widespread acceptance within the church:

1   Jesus is fully human.
2   Jesus is fully divine.

If both these statements are simultaneously true, it was argued, then what was true of the humanity of Jesus must also be true of his divinity – and vice versa. An example might be the following:

> Jesus Christ is God;
> Mary gave birth to Jesus;
> Therefore Mary is the Mother of God.

This kind of argument became increasingly commonplace within the late fourth-century church; indeed, it often served as a means of testing the orthodoxy of a theologian. A failure to agree that Mary was the "Mother of God" became seen as tantamount to a refusal to accept the divinity of Christ. This can be seen, for example, in Gregory of Nyssa's response to Apollinaris, noted in case study 1.3.

But how far can this principle be pressed? For example, consider the following line of argument:

> Jesus suffered on the cross;
> Jesus is God;
> Therefore God suffered on the cross.

The first two statements are orthodox, and commanded widespread assent within the church. But the conclusion drawn from them was widely regarded as unacceptable. It was axiomatic to most patristic writers that God could not suffer. The patristic period witnessed theologians agonizing over the limits that could be set to this approach. Thus Gregory of Nazianzus insisted that God must be considered to suffer; otherwise the reality of the incarnation of the Son of God was called into question. However, it was the Nestorian controversy which highlighted the importance of the issues.

By the time of Nestorius, the title *Theotokos* had become widely accepted within both popular piety and academic theology. Nestorius was, however, alarmed at its implications. It seemed to deny the humanity of Christ. Why not call Mary *anthropotokos* (bearer of humanity) or even *Christotokos* (bearer of the Christ)? His suggestions were met with outrage and indignation, on account of the enormous theological investment which had come to be associated with the term *theotokos*. Nestorius may be regarded as making an entirely legitimate point; however, the manner in which he made it caused considerable offence. The controversy was unquestionably heightened by a simmering political controversy over the status of the patriarchate of Constantinople. Those hostile to its growing status within the Christian world (especially those linked with the rival city of Alexandria) seized on Nestorius' comments, and exploited their potentially controversial nature to challenge the status of the patriarchate. This kind of hostility can be seen in the response of Cyril of Alexandria to Nestorius, to which we now turn.

In an important section of his *Letter 17*, written around 430, Cyril condemns 12 propositions associated with the Antiochene school of Christology. Although Cyril regards these views as heretical, there are points at which it seems that his primary concern is to establish the supremacy of the Alexandrian over the Antiochene position. Of the 12 propositions, the first three are particularly significant.

1.4.2   Cyril of Alexandria on the Antiochene Christology

1   If any one does not acknowledge that Emmanuel is truly God, and that the holy Virgin is, in consequence, "Theotokos," for she gave birth in the flesh to the Word of God who has become flesh, let them be condemned.
2   If any one does not acknowledge that the Word of God the Father was substantially united with flesh, and with his own flesh is one Christ, that is, one and the same God and human being together, let them be condemned.
3   If any one divides the persons in the one Christ after their union, joining them together in a mere conjunction in accordance with their rank, or a conjunction effected by authority or power, instead of a combination according to a union of natures, let them be condemned.

The following points are of especial interest.

1   The first point focuses on the use of the term *Theotokos*, in effect making a willingness to use this term a litmus test for orthodoxy in relation to the doctrine of the incarnation. For Cyril, anyone who refuses to use this term is, in effect, denying the reality of the divinity of Christ, and is therefore heretical.
2   The second point insists upon a physical union of some kind between humanity and divinity in Christ. Cyril is here critiquing the Antiochene model of incarnation, in which the humanity and divinity were understood to be fully present in Christ, yet in a non-interactive mode. For Cyril, only the

model of "assumption," in which the divine nature "assumes" the human, can do justice to the orthodox teaching.

3   Cyril therefore condemns, in his third point, the idea of a "union according to god's pleasure," which was characteristic of the Antiochene school. Dismissing this as a mere "conjunction" rather than a genuine union, Cyril argues that this is totally ineffective in safeguarding the vital theological and spiritual principles at stake in the doctrine of the incarnation.

> **Cyril of Alexandria (died 444).** A significant writer, who was appointed patriarch of Alexandria in 412. He became involved in the controversy over the Christological views of Nestorius, and produced major statements and defenses of the orthodox position on the two natures of Christ.

It will be clear that Christology was an issue of major importance during the patristic period. As a result of the debates of the period, the contours of the Christian consensus on the matter began to emerge, and advance the agenda of theological debate. It is widely agreed that, once the Christological issue had been settled, the next issue to be debated was the distinctive Christian doctrine of God. This naturally brings us to the doctrine of the Trinity, which is the subject of the following case study.

Case Study 1.5   The Trinity

The development of the doctrine of the Trinity is best seen as organically related to the evolution of Christology. It became increasingly clear that there was a consensus to the effect that Jesus was "of the same substance (*homoousios*)" as God, rather than just "of similar substance (*homoiousios*)." But if Jesus was God, in any meaningful sense of the word, what did this imply about God? If Jesus was God, were there now two Gods? Or was a radical reconsideration of the nature of God appropriate? Historically, it is possible to argue that the doctrine of the Trinity is closely linked with the development of the doctrine of the divinity of Christ. The more emphatic the church became that Christ was God, the more it came under pressure to clarify how Christ related to God.

The starting point for Christian reflections on the Trinity is the New Testament witness to the presence and activity of God in Christ and through the Spirit. For Irenaeus, the whole process of salvation, from its beginning to its end, bore witness to the action of Father, Son, and Holy Spirit. Irenaeus made use of a term which featured prominently in future discussion of the Trinity: "the economy of salvation." That word "economy" needs clarification. The Greek word *oikonomia* basically means "the way in which one's affairs are ordered" (the relation to the modern sense of the word will thus be clear). For Irenaeus, the "economy of salvation" means "the way in which God has ordered the salvation of humanity in history."

At the time, Irenaeus was under considerable pressure from Gnostic critics, who argued that the creator god was quite distinct from (and inferior to) the redeemer god. In the form favoured by Marcion, this idea took the following form: the Old Testament god is a creator god, and totally different from the redeemer god of the New Testament. As a result, the Old Testament should be shunned by Christians, who should concentrate their attention upon the New Testament. Irenaeus vigorously rejected this idea. He insisted that the entire process of salvation, from the first moment of creation to the last moment of history, was the work of the one and the same God. There was a single economy of salvation, in which the one God – who was both creator and redeemer – was at work to redeem his creation.

In his *Demonstration of the Preaching of the Apostles*, Irenaeus insisted upon the distinct yet related roles of Father, Son, and Spirit within the economy of salvation. He affirmed his faith in:

> God the Father uncreated, who is uncontained, invisible one God, creator of the universe . . . and the Word of God, the Son of God, our Lord Jesus Christ, who . . . in the fulness of time, to gather all things to himself, became a human among humans, to . . . destroy death, bring life, and achieve fellowship between God and humanity. . . . And the Holy Spirit . . . was poured out in a new way on our humanity to make us new throughout the world in the sight of God.

This passage brings out clearly the idea of an economic Trinity – that is to say, an understanding of the nature of the Godhead in which each person is responsible for an aspect of the economy of salvation. Far from being a rather pointless piece of theological speculation, the doctrine of the Trinity is grounded directly in the complex human experience of redemption in Christ, and is concerned with the explanation of this experience.

Tertullian gave the theology of the Trinity its distinctive vocabulary; he also shaped its distinctive form. God is one; nevertheless, God cannot be regarded as something or someone who is totally isolated from the created order. The economy of salvation demonstrates that God is active in his creation. This activity is complex; on analysis, this divine action reveals both a *unity* and a *distinctiveness*. Tertullian argues that *substance* is what unites the three aspects of the economy of salvation; *person* is what distinguishes them. The three persons of the Trinity are distinct, yet not divided, different yet not separate or independent of each other. The complexity of the human experience of redemption is thus the result of the three persons of the Godhead acting in distinct yet coordinated manners in human history, without any loss of the total unity of the Godhead.

By the second half of the fourth century, the debate concerning the relation of the Father and Son gave every indication of having been settled. The recognition that Father and Son were "of one being" settled the Arian controversy, and established a consensus within the church over the divinity of the Son. But further theological construction was necessary. What was the relation of the Spirit to the Father? and to the Son? There was a growing consensus that the Spirit could not be omitted from the Godhead. The Cappadocian fathers, especially Basil of Caesarea, defended the divinity of the Spirit in such persuasive terms that the foundation was laid for the final element of Trinitarian theology to be put in its place. The divinity and co-equality of Father, Son, and Spirit had been agreed; it now remained to develop Trinitarian models to allow this understanding of the Godhead to be visualized.

Basil of Caesarea (c.330–379). Also known as "Basil the Great," this fourth-century writer was based in the region of Cappadocia, in modern Turkey. He is particularly remembered for his writings on the Trinity, especially the distinctive role of the Holy Spirit. He was elected bishop of Caesarea in 370.

In general, eastern theology tended to emphasize the distinct individuality of the three persons or *hypostases*, and safeguard their unity by stressing the fact that both the Son and the Spirit derived from the Father. The relation between the persons or *hypostases* is ontological, grounded in what those persons are. Thus the relation of the Son to the Father is defined in terms of "being begotten" and "sonship." As we shall see, Augustine moves away from this approach, preferring to treat the persons in relational terms. We shall return to these points presently, in discussing the *filioque* controversy.

The western approach, however, was more marked by its tendency to begin from the unity of God, especially in the work of revelation and redemption, and to interpret the relation of the three persons in terms of their mutual fellowship. It is this position which is characteristic of Augustine, and which we shall explore later in this case study.

The eastern approach might seem to suggest that the Trinity consists of three independent agents, doing quite different things. This possibility was excluded by two later developments, which are usually referred to by the terms "mutual interpenetration (*perichoresis*)" and "appropriation." Although these ideas find their full development at a later stage in the development of the doctrine, they are unquestionably hinted at in both Irenaeus and Tertullian, and find more substantial expression in the writings of Gregory of Nyssa. We may usefully consider both these ideas at this stage.

> **Gregory of Nyssa (*c.*330–*c.*395).** One of the Cappadocian fathers, noted especially for his vigorous defense of the doctrine of the Trinity and the incarnation during the fourth century.

The Greek term *perichoresis* – which is often found in either its Latin (*circumincessio*) or English (mutual interpenetration) forms – came into general use in the sixth century. It refers to the manner in which the three persons of the Trinity relate to one another. The concept of *perichoresis* allows the individuality of the persons to be maintained, while insisting that each person shares in the life of the other two. An image often used to express this idea is that of "a community of being," in which each person, while maintaining its distinctive identity, penetrates the others and is penetrated by them.

The idea of "appropriation" is related to *perichoresis*, and follows on from it. The modalist heresy (to be discussed presently) argued that God could be considered as existing in different "modes of being" at different points in the economy of salvation, so that, at one point, God existed as Father and created the world; at another, God existed as Son and redeemed it. The doctrine of appropriation insists that the works of the Trinity are a unity; every person of the Trinity is involved in every outward action of the Godhead. Thus Father, Son, and Spirit are all involved in the work of creation, which is not to be viewed as the work of the Father alone. For example, Augustine of Hippo pointed out that the Genesis creation account speaks of God, the Word, and the Spirit (Genesis 1: 1–3), thus indicating that all three persons of the Trinity were present and active at this decisive moment in salvation history. Yet it is *appropriate* to think of creation as the work of the Father. Despite the fact that all three persons of the Trinity are implicated in creation, it is properly seen as the distinctive action of the Father. Similarly, the entire Trinity is involved in the work of redemption. It is, however, appropriate to speak of redemption as being the distinctive work of the Son.

> **Augustine of Hippo (354–430).** Widely regarded as the most influential Latin patristic writer, Augustine was converted to Christianity at the northern Italian city of Milan in the summer of 386. He returned to North Africa, and was made bishop of Hippo in 395. He was involved in two major controversies – the Donatist controversy, focusing on the church and sacraments, and the Pelagian controversy, focusing on grace and sin. He also made substantial contributions to the development of the doctrine of the Trinity, and the Christian understanding of history.

Taken together, the concepts of *perichoresis* and appropriation allow us to think of the Godhead as a "community of being," in which all is shared, united, and mutually exchanged. Father, Son, and Spirit are not three isolated and diverging compartments of a Godhead, like three subsidiary components of an international corporation. Rather, they are differentiations within the Godhead, which become evident within the economy of salvation and the human experience of redemption and grace. The doctrine of the Trinity affirms that beneath the surface of the complexities of the history of salvation and our experience of God lies one God, and one God only.

Modalism

The term "modalism" was introduced by the German historian of dogma, Adolf von Harnack, to describe the common element of a group of Trinitarian heresies, associated with Noetus and Praxeas in the late second century, and Sabellius in the third. Each of these writers was concerned to safeguard the unity of the godhead, fearing a lapse into some form of tritheism as a result of the doctrine of the Trinity. (As will become clear, this fear was amply justified.) This vigorous defense of the absolute unity of God (often referred to as "monarchianism," from the Greek words meaning "single principle of authority") led these writers to insist that the one and only God revealed himself in different ways at different times. The divinity of Christ and the Holy Spirit is to be explained in terms of three different ways or modes of divine revelation (hence the term "modalism"). The following Trinitarian sequence is thus proposed:

1 The one God is revealed in the manner of creator and lawgiver. This aspect of God is referred to as "the Father."
2 The same God is then revealed in the manner of a savior, in the person of Jesus Christ. This aspect of God is referred to as "the Son."
3 The same God is then revealed in the manner of the one who sanctifies and gives eternal life. This aspect of God is referred to as "the Spirit."

There is thus no difference, save that of appearance and chronological location, between the three entities in question.

The Cappadocian approach to the Trinity

The Cappadocians played a pivotal role in establishing the full divinity of the Holy Spirit, a decision which was formally endorsed by the Council of Constantinople in 381. Once this decisive theological step had been taken, the way was open to a full statement of the doctrine of the Trinity. With the recognition of the identity of substance of Father, Son, and Holy Spirit, the door was opened to exploring their mutual relationship within the Trinity. Once more, the Cappadocians played a decisive role in this major theological development.

The Cappadocian approach to the Trinity is best understood as a defense of the divine unity, coupled with a recognition that the one Godhead exists in three different "modes of being." The formula which expresses this approach best is "one substance (*ousia*) in three persons (*hypostaseis*)." The one indivisible Godhead is common to all three persons of the Trinity. This one Godhead exists simultaneously in three different "modes of being" – Father, Son, and Holy Spirit.

One of the most distinctive features of this approach to the Trinity is the priority assigned to the Father. Although the Cappadocian writers stress that they do not accept that either the Son or Spirit is subordinate to the Father, they nevertheless explicitly state that the Father is to be regarded as the source or fountainhead of the Trinity. The being of the Father is imparted to both the Son and the Spirit, although in different ways: the Son is "begotten" of the Father, and the Spirit "proceeds" from the Father. Gregory of Nyssa thus writes of "the one person of the Father, from whom the Son is begotten and the Spirit proceeds."

So how can the one substance be present in three persons? The Cappadocians answered this question by appealing to the relation between a universal and its particulars – for example, humanity and individual human beings. Thus Basil of Caesarea argues that the one substance within the Trinity can be conceived as analogous to a universal, and the three persons to particulars. A common human nature, shared by all people, does not mean that all human beings are identical; it means that they retain their individuality, even though they share this common nature. Gregory of Nyssa states this as follows:

> Peter, James and John are called three humans, even though they share a single common humanity. . . . So how do we compromise our belief, by saying on the one hand that the Father, Son and the Holy Spirit have a single godhead, while on the other hand denying that we are talking about three gods?

Gregory of Nazianzus (329–89), also known as "Gregory Nazianzen." He is particularly remembered for his "Five Theological Orations," written around 380, and a compilation of extracts from the writings of Origen, which he entitled the *Philokalia*.

Thus each of the three persons within the Trinity has a distinctive characteristic. According to Basil of Caesarea, the distinctives of each of the persons are as follows: the Father is distinguished by fatherhood, the Son by sonship, and the Spirit by the ability to sanctify. For Gregory of Nazianzus, the Father is distinguished by "being ingenerate" (*agennesis*, a difficult word which conveys the idea of "not being begotten" or "not deriving from any other source"), the Son by "being generate" (*gennesis*, which could also be translated as "being begotten" or "deriving one's origins from someone else"), and the Spirit by "being sent" or "proceeding." The difficulty with this analogy for modern readers is that it seems to hint at tritheism. While Gregory's Platonism allows him to think of "Peter, James, and John" as different instances of the same human nature, the more natural way of interpreting the illustration today is in terms of three distinct and independent individuals.

Augustine's model of the Trinity

Augustine takes up many elements of the emerging consensus on the Trinity. This can be seen in his vigorous rejection of any form of subordinationism (that is, treating the Son and Spirit as inferior to the Father within the Godhead). Augustine insists that the action of the entire Trinity is to be discerned behind the actions of each of its persons. Thus humanity is not merely created in the image of God; it is created in the image of the Trinity. An important distinction is drawn between the eternal Godhead of the Son and the Spirit, and their place in the economy of salvation. Although the Son and Spirit may appear to be posterior to the Father, this judgment only applies to their role within the process of salvation. Although the Son and Spirit may appear to be subordinate to the Father in history, in eternity all are co-equal. This is an important anticipation of the later distinction between the essential Trinity, grounded in God's eternal nature, and the economic Trinity, grounded in God's self-revelation within history.

Perhaps the most distinctive element of Augustine's approach to the Trinity concerns his understanding of the person and place of the Holy Spirit; we shall consider specific aspects of this in a later section, as part of our discussion of the *filioque* controversy. However, Augustine's conception of the Spirit as the love which unites the Father and Son together demands attention at this early stage.

Having identified the Son with "wisdom," Augustine proceeds to identify the Spirit with "love." He concedes that he had no explicit biblical grounds for this identification; nevertheless, he regards it as a reasonable inference from the biblical material. The Spirit "makes us dwell in God, and God in us." This explicit identification of the Spirit as the basis of union between God and believers is important, as it points to Augustine's idea of the Spirit as the giver of community. The Spirit is the gift of God which binds us to him. There is, Augustine argues, therefore a corresponding relation within the Trinity itself. God already exists in the kind of relation to which he wishes to bring us. And just as the Spirit is the bond of union between God and the believer, so the Spirit exercises a comparable role within the Trinity, binding the persons together. "The Holy Spirit . . . makes us dwell in God, and God in us. But that is the effect of love. So the Holy Spirit is God who is love."

This argument is supplemented by a general analysis of the importance of love within the Christian life. Augustine, basing himself loosely on 1 Corinthians 13: 13 ("These three remain: faith, hope, and love. But the greatest of these is love"), argues along the following lines:

1   God's greatest gift is love;
2   God's greatest gift is the Holy Spirit;
3   Therefore the Holy Spirit is love.

Both these lines of argument are brought together in the following passage:

> Love is of God, and its effect in us is that we dwell in God, and he in us. This we know, because he has given us his Spirit. Now the Spirit is God who is love. If, among God's gifts there is none greater than love, and if there is no greater gift than the Holy Spirit, we naturally conclude that the one who is said to be both God and of God is love.

This style of analysis has been criticized for its obvious weaknesses, not least in leading to a curiously depersonalized notion of the Spirit. The Spirit appears as a sort of glue, binding Father and Son together, and binding both to believers. The idea of "being bound to God" is a central feature of Augustine's spirituality, and it is perhaps inevitable that this concern will appear prominently in his discussion of the Trinity.

One of the most distinctive features of Augustine's approach to the Trinity is his development of "psychological analogies." The reasoning which lies behind the appeal to the human mind in this respect can be summarized as follows. It is not unreasonable to expect that, in creating the world, God has left a characteristic imprint upon that creation. But where is that imprint (*vestigium*) to be found? It is reasonable to expect that God would plant this distinctive imprint upon the height of his creation. Now the Genesis creation accounts allow us to conclude that humanity is the height of God's creation. Therefore, Augustine argues, we should look to humanity in our search for the image of God.

However, Augustine then takes a step which many observers feel to have been unfortunate. On the basis of his neo-Platonic worldview, Augustine argues that the human mind is to be regarded as the apex of humanity. It is therefore to the individual human mind that the theologian should turn, in looking for "traces of the Trinity" in creation. The radical individualism of this approach, coupled with its obvious intellectualism, means that he chooses to find the Trinity in the inner mental world of individuals, rather than – for example – in personal relationships (an approach favored by medieval writers, such as Richard of St

Victor). Furthermore, a first reading of *On the Trinity* suggests that Augustine seems to regard the inner workings of the human mind as telling us as much about God as the economy of salvation. Although Augustine stresses the limited value of such analogies, he himself appears to make more use of them than this critical appraisal would warrant.

Augustine discerns a triadic structure to human thought, and argues that this structure of thought is grounded in the being of God. He himself argues that the most important such triad is that of mind, knowledge, and love, although the related triad of memory, understanding, and will is also given considerable prominence. The human mind is "an image" – inadequate, to be sure, but still an image – of God. So just as there are three such faculties in the human mind, which are not ultimately totally separate and independent entities, so there can be three "persons" in God.

There are some obvious weaknesses here, possibly even some fatal weaknesses. As has often been pointed out, the human mind cannot be reduced to three entities in quite this neat and simplistic manner. In the end, however, it must be pointed out that Augustine's appeal to such "psychological analogies" is actually illustrative, rather than constitutive. They are intended to be visual aids (although visual aids that are grounded in the doctrine of creation) to insights that may be obtained from Scripture and reflection on the economy of salvation. Augustine's doctrine of the Trinity is not ultimately grounded in his analysis of the human mind, but in his reading of Scripture, especially of the Fourth Gospel.

The filioque controversy

One of the most significant events in the early history of the church was agreement throughout the Roman Empire, both east and west, on the Nicene Creed. The Nicene Creed was intended to bring doctrinal stability to the church in a period of considerable importance in its history. Part of that agreed text referred to the Holy Spirit "proceeding from the Father." By the ninth century, however, the western church routinely altered this phrase, speaking of the Holy Spirit "proceeding from the Father and the Son." The Latin term *filioque* ("and from the Son") has since come to refer to this addition, now normative within the western churches, and the theology which it expresses. This idea of a "double procession" of the Holy Spirit was a source of intense irritation to Greek writers: not only did it raise serious theological difficulties for them; it also involved tampering with the supposedly inviolable text of the creeds. Many scholars see this bad feeling as contributing to the split between the eastern and western churches, which took place around 1054. Although this development (and the resulting controversy) took place after 451, the resulting debate was the inevitable outcome of the ideas documented in this case study, making it entirely proper to discuss this debate at this point.

The *filioque* debate is of importance, both as a theological issue in itself, and also as a matter of some importance in the contemporary relations between the eastern and western churches. We therefore propose to explore the issues in some detail. The basic issue at stake is whether the Spirit may be said to proceed from the Father alone, or from the Father and the Son. The former is associated with the eastern church, and is given its most weighty exposition in the writings of the Cappadocian fathers; the latter is associated with the western church, and is developed with particular clarity in Augustine's treatise *On the Trinity*.

The Greek patristic writers insisted that there was only one source of being within the Trinity. The Father alone was the sole and supreme cause of all things, including the Son and the Spirit within the Trinity. The Son and the Spirit derive from the Father, but in different manners. In searching for suitable terms to express this relationship, theologians eventually fixed on two quite distinct images: the Son is begotten of the Father, while the Spirit proceeds from the Father. These two terms are intended to express the idea that both Son and Spirit derive from the Father, but are derived in different ways. The vocabulary is clumsy, reflecting the fact that the Greek words involved are difficult to translate into modern English.

To assist in understanding this complex process, the Greek fathers used two images. The Father pronounces his word; at the same time as he utters this word, he breathes out in order to make this word capable of being heard and received. The imagery used here, which is strongly grounded in the biblical tradition, is that of the Son as the Word of God, and the Spirit as the breath of God. An obvious question arises here: why should the Cappadocian fathers, and other Greek writers, spend so much time and effort on distinguishing Son and Spirit in this way? The answer is important. A failure to distinguish the ways in which Son and Spirit derive from the one and the same Father would lead to God having two sons, which would have raised insurmountable problems.

Within this context, it is unthinkable that the Holy Spirit should proceed from the Father and the Son. Why? Because it would totally compromise the principle of the Father as the sole origin and source of all divinity. It would amount to affirming that there were two sources of divinity within the one Godhead, with all the internal contradictions and tensions that this would generate. If the Son were to share in the exclusive ability of the Father to be the source of all divinity, this ability would no longer be exclusive. For this reason, the Greek church regarded the western idea of a "double procession" of the Spirit with something approaching stark disbelief. The Greek tradition, however, was not entirely unanimous on this point. Cyril of Alexandria had no hesitation in speaking of the Spirit as "belonging to the Son," and related ideas were not slow to develop within the western church.

This understatement of the procession of the Spirit from Father and Son was developed and given its classic statement by Augustine. Possibly building upon the position hinted at by Hilary, Augustine argued that the Spirit had to be thought of as proceeding from the Son. One of his main proof texts was John 20: 22, in which the risen Christ is reported as having breathed upon his disciples, and said: "Receive the Holy Spirit." Augustine explains this as follows:

> Nor can we say that the Holy Spirit does not also proceed from the Son. After all, the Spirit is said to be the Spirit of both the Father and the Son [John 20: 22 is then cited]. . . . The Holy Spirit proceeds not only from the Father, but also from the Son.

In making this statement, Augustine thought that he was summarizing a general consensus within both the eastern and western churches. Unfortunately, his knowledge of Greek does not appear to have been good enough to allow him to appreciate that the Greek-speaking Cappadocian writers adopted a rather different position. Nevertheless, there are points at which Augustine is obviously concerned to defend the distinctive role of the Father within the Godhead:

> God the Father alone is the one from whom the Word is born, and from whom the Spirit principally proceeds. Now I have added the word "principally," because we find that the Holy Spirit also proceeds from the Son. Nevertheless, the Father gave the Spirit to the Son. It was not as if the Son already existed and possessed the Spirit. Whatever the Father gave to the only-begotten Word, he gave by begetting him. Therefore he begot him in such a way that the common gift should be the Spirit of both.

So what did Augustine think he was doing, in understanding the role of the Spirit in this way? The answer lies in his distinctive understanding of the Spirit as the "bond of love" between Father and Son. Augustine developed the idea of relation within the Godhead, arguing that the persons of the Trinity are defined by their relations to one another. The Spirit is thus to be seen as the relation of love and fellowship between the Father and Son, a relation which Augustine believed to be foundational to the Fourth Gospel's presentation of the unity of will and purpose of Father and Son.

We can summarize the root differences between the two approaches as follows:

1   The *Greek* intention was to safeguard the unique position of the Father as the sole source of divinity. In that both the Son and Spirit derive from him, although in different but equally valid manners, their divinity is in turn safe-guarded. To the Greeks, the Latin approach seemed to introduce two separate sources of divinity into the Godhead, and to weaken the vital distinction between Son and Spirit. The Son and Spirit are understood to have distinct, yet complementary roles; whereas the western tradition sees the Spirit as the Spirit of Christ.

2   The *Latin* intention was to ensure that the Son and Spirit were adequately distinguished from one another, yet shown to be mutually related to one another. The strongly relational approach adopted to the idea of "person" made it inevitable that the Spirit would be treated in this way. Sensitive to the Greek position, later Latin writers stressed that they did not regard their approach as presupposing two sources of divinity in the Godhead. The Council of Lyons stated that "the Holy Spirit proceeds from the Father and the Son, yet not as from two origins but as from one origin." However, the doctrine remained a source of contention, and continues to be an issue of dispute today.

Case Study 1.6   The Donatist Controversy

As we noted in our introductory historical overview of the patristic period, under the Roman Emperor Diocletian (284–313) the Christian church was subject to various degrees of persecution. The origins of the persecution date from 303; it finally ended with the victory of Constantine, and the issuing of the Edict of Milan in 313. Under an edict of February 303, Christian books were ordered to be burned and churches demolished. Those Christian leaders who handed over their books to be burned came to be known as *traditores* – "those who handed over." The modern English word "traitor" derives from the same root. Once such *traditor* or "traitor" was Felix of Aptunga, who later consecrated Caecilian as bishop of Carthage in 311.

Many local Christians were outraged that such a person should have been allowed to be involved in this consecration, and declared that they could not accept the authority of Caecilian as a result. The hierarchy of the catholic church was tainted, as a result of this development. The church ought to be pure, and should not be permitted to include such people. By the time Augustine returned to Africa in 388, a breakaway faction had established itself as the leading Christian body in the region, with especially strong support from the local African population. Sociological issues clouded theological debate; the Donatists tended to draw their support from the indigenous population, whereas the Catholics drew theirs from Roman colonists.

The theological issues involved are of considerable importance, and relate directly to a serious tension within the theology of a leading figure of the African church in the third century – Cyprian of Carthage. In his *Unity of the Catholic Church* (251), Cyprian had defended two major related beliefs.

1   Schism (that is, the deliberate breaking away from the church) is totally and absolutely unjustified. The unity of the church cannot be broken, for any pretext whatsoever. To step outside the bounds of the church is to forfeit any possibility of salvation.
2   It therefore follows that a lapsed or schismatic bishop is deprived of all ability

to administer the sacraments or act as a minister of the Christian church. By passing outside the sphere of the church, they have lost their spiritual gifts and authority. They should therefore not be permitted to ordain priests or bishops. Any whom they have ordained must be regarded as invalidly ordained; any whom they have baptized must be regarded as invalidly baptized.

Cyprian of Carthage (died 258). A Roman rhetorician of considerable skill who was converted to Christianity around 246, and elected bishop of the North African city of Carthage in 248. He was martyred in that city in 258. His writings focus particularly on the unity of the church, and the role of its bishops in maintaining orthodoxy and order.

Cyprian's arguments against schism are set out with particular clarity, and are worth noting in a little detail.

1.6.1   Cyprian of Carthage on the Impossibility of Schism

The bride of Christ cannot be made an adulteress; she is undefiled and chaste. She has one home, and guards with virtuous chastity the sanctity of one chamber. She serves us for God, who enrolls into his Kingdom the children to whom she gives birth. Anyone who cuts themselves off from the Church and is joined to an
5 adulteress is separated from the promises of the Church, and anyone who leaves the Church of Christ behind cannot benefit from the rewards of Christ. Such people are strangers, outcasts, and enemies. You cannot have God as father unless you have the Church as mother. . . . This sacrament of unity, this inseparable bond of peace, is shown in the gospel when the robe of the Lord Jesus Christ was neither
10 divided at all or torn, but they cast lots for the clothing of Christ . . . so the clothing was received whole and the robe was taken unspoilt and undivided. . . . That garment signifies the unity which comes "from the part above," that is, from heaven and from the Father, a unity which could not be torn at all by those who received and possessed it, but it was taken undivided in its unbreakable entirety.
15 Anyone who rends and divides the Church of Christ cannot possess the clothing of Christ.

The following points should be noted:

1   Cyprian argues that there is only one church. Anyone who chooses to leave the church in schism therefore moves outside the boundaries of the church,

and ceases to have any connection with it (lines 4–6). It is impossible to benefit from Christ's salvation without being a member of the church. This is summed up in the famous slogan: "You cannot have God as father unless you have the Church as mother" (lines 7–8).

2 Note the image that Cyprian uses to stress the indivisibility of the church. The church is like the seamless robe in which Christ was clothed as he walked to his crucifixion. Cyprian here alludes to the incident in the gospels, in which those who crucified Jesus threw lots for his robe, in that they did not wish to tear it (see John 19: 23–4). Cyprian argues that the church is analogous to that robe: it cannot be torn or divided (lines 8–16).

It will be clear, then, that Cyprian rigorously excludes schism. But what happens if a bishop lapses under persecution, and subsequently repents? Cyprian's theory is profoundly ambiguous, and is open to two lines of interpretation:

1 By lapsing, the bishop has committed the sin of apostasy (literally, "falling away"). He has therefore placed himself outside the bounds of the church, and can no longer be regarded as administering the sacraments validly.
2 By his repentance, the bishop has been restored to grace, and is able to continue administering the sacraments validly.

The Donatists adopted the first such position, the catholics (as their opponents came to be universally known) the second.

As a result, the Donatists believed that the entire sacramental system of the Catholic church had become corrupted. It was therefore necessary to replace *traditores* with people who had remained firm in their faith under persecution. It was also necessary to rebaptize and reordain all those who had been baptized and ordained by *traditores*. Inevitably, this resulted in the formation of a breakaway faction. By the time of Augustine, the breakaway faction was larger than the church which it had originally broken away from.

Yet Cyprian had totally forbidden schism of any kind. One of the greatest paradoxes of the Donatist schism is that the schism resulted from principles which were due to Cyprian – yet contradicted those very same principles. As a result, both the Donatists and Catholics appealed to Cyprian as an authority – but to very different aspects of his teaching. The Donatists stressed the outrageous character of apostasy; the catholics equally emphasized the impossibility of schism. A stalemate resulted. That is, until Augustine of Hippo arrived, and became bishop of Hippo in the region. Augustine was able to resolve the tensions within the legacy of Cyprian, and put forward an "Augustinian" view of the church, which has remained enormously influential ever since. In what follows, we shall outline the main features of this distinctive approach.

Augustine of Hippo (354–430). Widely regarded as the most influential
Latin patristic writer, Augustine was converted to Christianity at the northern
Italian city of Milan in the summer of 386. He returned to North Africa, and
was made bishop of Hippo in 395. He was involved in two major controversies
– the Donatist controversy, focusing on the church and sacraments, and the
Pelagian controversy, focusing on grace and sin. He also made substantial
contributions to the development of the doctrine of the Trinity, and the
Christian understanding of history.

First, Augustine emphasizes the sinfulness of Christians. The church is not
meant to be a society of saints, but a "mixed body" of saints and sinners.
Augustine finds this image in two biblical parables: the parable of the net which
catches many fishes, and the parable of the wheat and the tares (note that "tares"
is the traditional older English word for "weeds"; we shall use the two terms
interchangeably in the following discussion). It is this latter parable (Matthew 13:
24–31) which is of especial importance, and requires further discussion.

The parable tells of a farmer who sowed seed, and discovered that the resulting
crop included both wheat and tares – grain and weeds. What could be done about
it? To attempt to separate the wheat and the weeds while both were still growing
would be to court disaster, probably involving damaging the wheat while trying
to get rid of the weeds. But at the harvest, all the plants – wheat and tares – are cut
down, and sorted out without any danger of damaging the wheat. The separation
of the good and the evil thus takes place at the end of time, not in history.

For Augustine, this parable refers to the church in the world. It must expect
to find itself including both saints and sinners. But to attempt a separation in this
world is premature and improper. That separation will take place in God's own
time, at the end of history. No human can make that judgment or separation in
God's place. So in what sense is the church holy? For Augustine, the holiness in
question is not that of its members, but of Christ. The church cannot be a
congregation of saints in this world, in that its members are contaminated with
original sin. However, the church is sanctified and made holy by Christ – a
holiness which will be perfected and finally realized at the last judgment. In
addition to this theological analysis, Augustine makes the practical observation
that the Donatists failed to live up to their own high standards of morality. The
Donatists, Augustine suggests, were just as capable as catholics of getting drunk
or beating people up.

Second, Augustine argues that schism and *traditio* (the handing over of
Christian books, or any form of lapse from faith) are indeed both sinful – but
that, for Cyprian, schism is by far the more serious sin. The Donatists are thus
guilty of serious misrepresentation of the teaching of the great North African
martyr bishop.

On the basis of these considerations, Augustine argues that Donatism is fatally flawed. The church is, and is meant to be, a mixed body. Sin is an inevitable aspect of the life of the church in the present age, and is neither the occasion nor the justification for schism.

Yet the Donatist controversy concerned more than a theoretical understanding of the nature of the church. It affected aspects of everyday Christian ministry, on account of the Donatist insistence that only certain untainted persons could administer the sacraments properly. The Donatists refused to recognize that a *traditor* could administer the sacraments properly. Accordingly, they argued that baptisms, ordinations, and eucharists administered by such ministers were invalid.

This attitude rested in part upon the authority of Cyprian of Carthage. Cyprian had argued that no true sacraments exist outside the church. Heretical baptism was thus not valid, as heretics did not accept the faith of the church, and were thus outside its bounds. Logically unassailable though Cyprian's views may have been, they failed to allow for the situation which arose during the Donatist controversy – that is, ministers who are of orthodox faith, but whose personal conduct is held to be unworthy of their calling. Were doctrinally orthodox yet morally inferior ministers entitled to administer the sacraments? And were such sacraments valid or not?

Pressing Cyprian's views beyond their apparent intended limits, the Donatists argued that ecclesiastical actions could be regarded as invalid on account of subjective imperfections on the part of the person administering them. The Donatists thus held that those who were baptized or ordained by Catholic priests or bishops who had not joined the Donatist movement required to be rebaptized and reordained at the hands of Donatist ministers. The sacraments derive their validity from the personal qualities of the person who administers them.

Responding to this approach, Augustine argued that Donatism laid excessive emphasis upon the qualities of the human agent, and gave insufficient weight to the grace of Jesus Christ. It is, he argued, impossible for fallen human beings to make distinctions concerning who is pure and impure, worthy or unworthy. This view, which is totally consistent with his understanding of the church as a "mixed body" of saints and sinners, holds that the efficacy of a sacrament rests, not upon the merits of the individual administering it, but upon the merits of the one who instituted them in the first place – Jesus Christ. The validity of sacraments is independent of the merits of those who administer them.

Having said this, Augustine qualifies it in an important context. A distinction must be drawn, he argues, between "baptism" and "the right to baptize." Although baptism is valid, even when administered by those who are heretics or schismatics, this does not mean that the right to baptize is indiscriminately distributed among all peoples. The right to confer baptism exists only within the church, and supremely on the part of those ministers which it has chosen and authorized to administer the sacraments. The authority to administer the sacraments of Christ was committed by him to the apostles, and through them and their successors, the bishops, to the ministers of the Catholic church.

The theological issue at stake has come to be represented by two Latin slogans, each reflecting a different understanding of the grounds of the efficacy of the sacraments.

1   Sacraments are efficacious *ex opere operantis* – literally, "on account of the work of the one who works." Here, the efficacy of the sacrament is understood to be dependent upon the personal qualities of the minister.
2   Sacraments are efficacious *ex opere operato* – literally, "on account of the work which is worked." Here, the efficacy of the sacrament is understood to be dependent upon the grace of Christ, which the sacraments represent and convey.

The Donatist position is consistent with an *ex opere operantis*, and Augustine's with an *ex opere operato*, understanding of sacramental causality. The latter view became normative within the western church, and was maintained by the mainstream reformers during the sixteenth century. The former was upheld by more radical sections of the Reformation, and continues to be significant within some sections of Protestantism, especially those stressing the importance of holiness or charismatic gifts.

Augustine sets out his position in the following passage, taken from his treatise "On Baptism." As we noted earlier, Augustine's view of the church accepts that congregations and priests will include sinners as well as saints. So does this invalidate the sacraments? Against the Donatist view, which declared that only the righteous can administer and profitably receive the sacraments (an *ex opere operantis* view of sacramental efficacy), Augustine argues that the efficacy of the sacraments rests on Christ himself, not the merits of either the administrator or recipient (which, as noted above, is an *ex opere operato* view of sacramental efficacy).

1.6.2   Augustine on the Efficacy of Sacraments

To my mind it is abundantly clear that in the matter of baptism we have to consider not who he is that gives it, but what it is that he gives; not who he is that receives, but what it is that he receives. . . . Wherefore, any one who is on the side of the devil cannot defile the sacrament, which is of Christ. . . . When baptism is administered
5   by the words of the gospel, however great the evil of either minister or recipient may be, the sacrament itself is holy on account of the one whose sacrament it is.

> In the case of people who receive baptism from an evil person, if they do not receive
> the perverseness of the minister but the holiness of the mystery, being united to
> the church in good faith and hope and charity, they will receive the forgiveness of
> 10 their sins.

Note the following points in particular:

1 Augustine draws a fundamental distinction (lines 2–3) between the one who
   gives the gift, and the gift that is given. The personal qualities of the "giver"
   (in this case, the minister of the sacrament) have no bearing on the quality of
   what is given (that is, the sacrament itself).
2 Sacraments derive their efficacy from "the one whose sacrament it is" (line 6).
   In other words, whatever a sacrament does results from the holiness of God,
   not from the holiness (or lack of it) on the part of the minister.

This can be contrasted with the views of Petilian, a noted Donatist writer who
was active at the beginning of the fifth century. Petilian, the Donatist bishop of
Cirta (a city in North Africa), circulated a letter to his priests warning against the
moral impurity and doctrinal errors of the Catholic church. Augustine's reply,
dated 401, led Petilian to write against Augustine in more detail. In this letter,
dating from 402, from which Augustine quotes extracts, Petilian sets out fully the
Donatist insistence that the validity of the sacraments is totally dependent upon
the moral worthiness of those who administer them. Petilian's words are included
within citation marks within Augustine's text.

1.6.3. A Donatist View of the Efficacy of the Sacraments

"What we look for is the conscience" [Petilian] says, "of the one who gives [the
sacraments], giving in holiness, to cleanse the conscience of the one who receives.
For anyone who knowingly receives 'faith' from the faithless does not receive faith,
but guilt." And he will then go on to say: "So how do you test this? For everything
5 consists of an origin" he says, "and a root; if it does not possess something as its
head, it is nothing. Nor can anything truly receive a second birth, unless it is born
again from good seed."

Note that Petilian argues that the holiness or guilt of the minister affects
the person who receives the sacraments from that minister (lines 1–2). It is
therefore essential that ministers should be holy and unblemished if their

ministries are not to be compromised through the contaminating effect of sin.

The Donatist controversy was of major importance to the development of the western church during the fourth century. A second controversy to break out in this region of the church – also centering on Augustine of Hippo – concerned the whole issue of the interaction of divine grace and human freedom. It is to the Pelagian controversy that we now turn.

Case Study 1.7   The Pelagian Controversy

The Pelagian controversy, which erupted in the early fifth century, brought a cluster of questions concerning human nature, sin, and grace into sharp focus. Up to this point, there had been relatively little controversy within the church over human nature. The Pelagian controversy changed that, and ensured that the issues associated with human nature were placed firmly on the agenda of the western church. The controversy centered upon two individuals: Augustine of Hippo and Pelagius. The controversy is complex, at both the historical and theological levels, and, given its impact upon western Christian theology, needs to be discussed at some length. We shall summarize the main points of the controversy under four heads: (1) the understanding of the "freedom of the will"; (2) the understanding of sin; (3) the understanding of grace; (4) the understanding of the grounds of justification.

The "freedom of the will"

For Augustine, the total sovereignty of God and genuine human responsibility and freedom must be upheld at one and the same time, if justice is to be done to the richness and complexity of the biblical statements on the matter. To simplify the matter, by denying either the sovereignty of God or human freedom, is to seriously compromise the Christian understanding of the way in which God justifies man. In Augustine's own lifetime, he was obliged to deal with two heresies which simplified and compromised the gospel in this way. Manichaeanism was a form of fatalism (to which Augustine himself was initially attracted) which

Augustine of Hippo (354–430). Widely regarded as the most influential Latin patristic writer, Augustine was converted to Christianity at the northern Italian city of Milan in the summer of 386. He returned to North Africa, and was made bishop of Hippo in 395. He was involved in two major controversies – the Donatist controversy, focusing on the church and sacraments, and the Pelagian controversy, focusing on grace and sin. He also made substantial contributions to the development of the doctrine of the Trinity, and the Christian understanding of history.

upheld the total sovereignty of God but denied human freedom, while Pelagianism upheld the total freedom of the human will while denying the sovereignty of God. Before developing these points, it is necessary to make some observations concerning the term "free will."

The term "free will" (translating the Latin term *liberum arbitrium*) is not itself biblical, but derives from Greek philosophical movements, especially Stoicism. It was introduced into western Christianity by the second century theologian Tertullian. Augustine retained the term, but attempted to restore a more Pauline meaning to it by emphasizing the limitations placed upon the human free will by sin. Augustine's basic ideas can be summarized as follows. First, natural human freedom is affirmed: we do not do things out of any necessity, but as a matter of freedom. Second, Augustine argues that human free will has been weakened and incapacitated – but not eliminated or destroyed – through sin. In order for that free will to be restored and healed, it requires the operation of divine grace. Free will really does exist; it is, however, distorted by sin.

In order to explain this point, Augustine deploys a significant analogy. Consider a pair of scales, with two balance pans. One balance pan represents good, and the other evil. If the pans are properly balanced, the arguments in favor of doing good or doing evil could be weighed, and a proper conclusion drawn. The parallel with the human free will is obvious: we weigh up the arguments in favor of doing good and evil, and act accordingly. But what, asks Augustine, if the balance pans are loaded? What happens if someone puts several heavy weights in the balance pan on the side of evil? The scales will still work, but they are seriously biased towards making an evil decision. Augustine argues that this is exactly what has happened to humanity through sin. The human free will is biased towards evil. It really exists, and really can make decisions – just as the loaded scales still work. But instead of giving a balanced judgment, a serious bias exists towards evil. Using this and related analogies Augustine argues that the human free will really exists in sinners, but that it is compromised by sin.

For Pelagius and his followers (such as Julian of Eclanum), however, humanity possessed total freedom of the will, and was totally responsible for its own sins. Human nature was essentially free and well created, and was not compromised or incapacitated by some mysterious weakness. According to Pelagius, any imperfection in man would reflect negatively upon the goodness of God. For God to intervene in any direct way to influence human decisions was equivalent to compromising human integrity. Going back to the analogy of the scales, the Pelagians argued that the human free will was like a pair of balance pans in perfect equilibrium, and not subject to any bias whatsoever. There was no need for divine grace in the sense understood by Augustine (although Pelagius did have a quite distinct concept of grace, as we shall see later).

In 413, Pelagius wrote a lengthy letter to Demetrias, who had recently decided to turn her back on wealth in order to become a nun. In this letter, Pelagius

Pelagius. A British theologian who was active at Rome in the final decade of the fourth and first decade of the fifth centuries. No reliable information exists concerning the date of his birth or death. Pelagius was a moral reformer, whose theology of grace and sin brought him into sharp conflict with Augustine, leading to the Pelagian controversy. Pelagius' ideas are known mostly through the writings of his opponents, especially Augustine.

spelled out with remorseless logic the consequences of his views on human free will. God has made humanity, and knows precisely what it is capable of doing. Hence all the commands given to us are capable of being obeyed, and are meant to be obeyed. It is no excuse to argue that human frailty prevents these commands from being fulfilled. God has made human nature, and only demands of it what it can endure. Pelagius thus makes the uncompromising assertion that since perfection is possible for humanity, it is obligatory.

1.7.1 Pelagius on Divine Commands

[Instead of regarding God's commands as a privilege] . . . we cry out at God and say, "This is too hard! This is too difficult! We cannot do it! We are only human, and hindered by the weakness of the flesh!" What blind madness! What blatant presumption! By doing this, we accuse the God of knowledge of a twofold
5 ignorance – ignorance of God's own creation and of God's own commands. It would be as if, forgetting the weakness of humanity – his own creation – God had laid upon us commands which we were unable to bear. And at the same time – may God forgive us! – we ascribe to the righteous One unrighteousness, and cruelty to the Holy One; first, by complaining that God has commanded the impossible,
10 second, by imagining that some will be condemned by God for what they could not help; so that – the blasphemy of it! – God is thought of as seeking our punishment rather than our salvation. . . . No one knows the extent of our strength better than the God who gave us that strength. . . . God has not willed to command anything impossible, for God is righteous; and will not condemn anyone for what
15 they could not help, for God is holy.

Note especially the argument (lines 4–7) which runs as follows. God knows our weakness, and therefore asks nothing of us which we cannot achieve. A demand on the part of God therefore corresponds to a human ability to fulfill that demand.

The nature of sin

For Augustine, humanity is universally affected by sin as a consequence of the Fall. The human mind has become darkened and weakened by sin. Sin makes it impossible for the sinner to think clearly, and especially to understand higher spiritual truths and ideas. Similarly, as we have seen, the human will has been weakened (but not eliminated) by sin. For Augustine, the simple fact that we are sinners means that we are in the position of being seriously ill, and unable to diagnose our own illness adequately, let alone cure it. It is through the grace of God alone that our illness is diagnosed (sin), and a cure made available (grace).

The essential point which Augustine makes is that we have no control over our sinfulness. It is something which contaminates our lives from birth, and dominates our lives thereafter. It is a state over which we have no decisive control. We could say that Augustine understands humanity to be born with a sinful disposition as part of human nature, with an inherent bias towards acts of sinning. In other words, sin causes sins: the state of sinfulness causes individual acts of sin. Augustine develops this point with reference to three important analogies: original sin as a "disease," as a "power," and as "guilt."

1   The first analogy treats sin as a hereditary disease, which is passed down from one generation to another. As we saw above, this disease weakens humanity, and cannot be cured by human agency. Christ is thus the divine physician, by whose "wounds we are healed" (Isaiah 53: 5), and salvation is understood in essentially sanative or medical terms. We are healed by the grace of God, so that our minds may recognize God and our wills may respond to the divine offer of grace.

2   The second analogy treats sin as a power which holds us captive, and from whose grip we are unable to break free by ourselves. The human free will is captivated by the power of sin, and may only be liberated by grace. Christ is thus seen as the liberator, the source of the grace which breaks the power of sin.

3   The third analogy treats sin as an essentially judicial or forensic concept – guilt – which is passed down from one generation to another. In a society which placed a high value on law, such as the later Roman Empire, in which Augustine lived and worked, this was regarded as a particularly helpful way of understanding sin. Christ thus comes to bring forgiveness and pardon.

For Pelagius, however, sin is to be understood in a very different light. The idea of a human disposition toward sin has no place in Pelagius' thought. For Pelagius, the human power of self-improvement could not be thought of as being compromised. It was always possible for humans to discharge their obligations towards God and their neighbors. Failure to do so could not be excused on any grounds. Sin was to be understood as an act committed willfully against God. Pelagianism thus seems to be a rigid form of moral authoritarianism – an insistence that humanity is under obligation to be sinless, and an absolute rejection of any excuse for failure. Humanity is born sinless, and only sins through deliberate actions. Pelagius insisted that many Old Testament figures actually remained sinless. Only those who were morally upright could be allowed to enter the church – whereas Augustine, with his concept of fallen human nature, was happy to regard the church as a hospital where fallen humanity could recover and grow gradually in holiness through grace.

The nature of grace

One of Augustine's favorite biblical texts is John 15: 5, "apart from me you can do nothing." For Augustine, we are totally dependent upon God for our salvation, from the beginning to the end of our lives. Augustine draws a careful distinction between the natural human faculties – given to humanity as its natural endowment – and additional and special gifts of grace. God does not leave us where we are naturally, incapacitated by sin and unable to redeem ourselves, but gives us grace in order that we may be healed, forgiven and restored. Augustine's view of human nature is that it is frail, weak, and lost, and needs divine assistance and care if it is to be restored and renewed. Grace, according to Augustine, is God's generous and quite unmerited attention to humanity, by which this process of healing may begin. Human nature requires transformation through the grace of God, so generously given.

Pelagius uses the term "grace" in a very different way. First, grace is to be understood as the natural human faculties. For Pelagius, these are not corrupted or incapacitated or compromised in any way. They have been given to humanity by God, and they are meant to be used. When Pelagius asserts that humanity can, through grace, choose to be sinless, what he means is that the natural human faculties of reason and will should enable humanity to choose to avoid sin. As Augustine was quick to point out, this does not seem to be what the New Testament understands by the term.

Second, Pelagius understands grace to be external enlightenment provided for humanity by God. Pelagius gives several examples of such enlightenment – for example, the Ten Commandments, and the moral example of Jesus Christ. Grace informs us what our moral duties are (otherwise, we would not know what they were); it does not, however, assist us to perform them. We are enabled to avoid sin through the teaching and example of Christ. Augustine argued that this was "to locate the grace of God in the law and in teaching." The New Testament, according to Augustine, envisaged grace as divine assistance to humanity, rather than just moral guidance. For Pelagius, grace was something external and passive, something outside us. Augustine understood grace as the real and redeeming presence of God in Christ within us, transforming us; something that was internal and active.

The basis of salvation

For Augustine, humanity is justified as an act of grace: even human good works are the result of God working within fallen human nature. Everything leading up to salvation is the free and unmerited gift of God, given out of love for sinners. Through the death and resurrection of Jesus Christ, God is enabled to deal with fallen humanity in this remarkable and generous manner, giving us that which we do not deserve (salvation), and withholding from us that which we do deserve (condemnation).

Augustine's exposition of the Parable of the laborers in the vineyard (Matthew 20: 1–10) is of considerable importance in this respect. As we shall see, Pelagius argued that God rewarded each individual strictly on the basis of merit. Augustine, however, points out that this parable indicates that the basis of the reward given to the individual is the promise made to that individual. Augustine emphasizes that the laborers did not work for equal periods in the vineyard, yet the same wage (a denarius) was given to all. The owner of the vineyard had promised to pay each individual a denarius, providing he worked from the time when he was called to sundown – even though this meant that some worked all day, and others only for an hour.

Augustine thus draws the theologically important conclusion that the basis of our justification is the divine promise of grace made to us. God is faithful to that promise, and thus justifies sinners. Just as the laborers who began work in the vineyard so late in the day had no claim to a full day's wages, except through the generous promise of the owner, so sinners have no claim to justification and eternal life, except through the gracious promises of God, received through faith.

For Pelagius, however, humanity is justified on the basis of its merits: human good works are the result of the exercise of the totally autonomous human free will, in fulfillment of an obligation laid down by God. A failure to meet this obligation opens the individual to the threat of eternal punishment. Jesus Christ is involved in salvation only to the extent that he reveals, by his actions and teaching, exactly what God requires of the individual. If Pelagius can speak of "salvation in Christ," it is only in the sense of "salvation through imitating the example of Christ."

It will thus be clear that Pelagianism and Augustinianism represent two radically different outlooks, with very divergent understandings of the manner in which God and humanity relate to one another. Augustinianism would eventually gain the upper hand within the western theological tradition; nevertheless, Pelagianism continues to exercise influence over many Christian writers down the ages, not least those who felt that an emphasis upon the doctrine of grace could too easily lead to a devaluation of human freedom and moral responsibility.

The general lines of Augustine's position can be studied from the following extract from his treatise "On Nature and Grace," originally written in 415.

Augustine here identifies the consequences of the Fall for human nature. Originally created without any fault, human nature is now contaminated by sin, and can only be redeemed through grace.

1.7.2 Augustine on Nature and Grace

Human nature was certainly originally created blameless and without any fault (*vitium*); but the human nature by which each one of us is now born of Adam requires a physician, because it is not healthy. All the good things, which it has by its conception, life, senses, and mind, it has from God, its creator and maker. But
5 the weakness which darkens and disables these good natural qualities, as a result of which that nature needs enlightenment and healing, did not come from the blameless maker but from original sin (*ex originali peccato*), which was committed by free will (*liberum arbitrium*). For this reason our guilty nature is liable to a just penalty. For if we are now a new creature in Christ, we were still children of wrath
10 by nature, like everyone else. But God, who is rich in mercy, on account of the great love with which He loved us, even when we were dead through our sins, raised us up to life with Christ, by whose grace we are saved. But this grace of Christ, without which neither infants nor grown persons can be saved, is not bestowed as a reward for merits, but is given freely (*gratis*), which is why it is called grace (*gratia*).

Note especially the following points:

1 In the first part of the passage, Augustine uses primarily medical imagery to describe the impact of sin on human nature. Note especially his use of the terms "physician," "healthy," "healing" (lines 3–6). He then follows this with more legal or penal models – note his use of such terms as "guilty" and "penalty" (lines 8–9).
2 Note the emphasis on the original integrity of creation (line 1). Augustine's concern here is to defend God against any charge that God is somehow responsible for sin or evil within the world. The present imperfection of the world does not result from God's creation, but from original sin and the abuse of human free will (lines 7–8).
3 Augustine establishes a connection between the Latin words *gratis* ("freely" or "without cost") and *gratia* ("grace" see lines 13–14). He then uses this point to reinforce his argument that salvation cannot be considered to be a reward, somehow earned through human merit, status or achievement; rather, it is a gift.

Case Study 1.8   Faith and Philosophy

Christianity had its origins in Palestine. However, it soon spread rapidly. Within decades, Christianity began to expand along the borders of the Mediterranean Sea. The Acts of the Apostles documents the rapid expansion of Christianity throughout the Roman Empire. Its first 12 chapters focus on a series of events which led to the Christian gospel becoming firmly rooted in Jerusalem and the surrounding regions. The remainder of the work explores the manner in which Christianity gradually became established in much of the Roman Empire. This later section of the work focuses on Paul, and pays particular attention to the role which he played in the expansion of the Christian church from Palestine into the regions of modern Turkey and Greece. It gives details of the three missionary journeys he undertook in the eastern Mediterranean, and ends with a description of his final voyage, as a prisoner, to Rome itself. The implication is that by about AD 64, Christianity had become a permanent presence in much of the eastern section of the Mediterranean world.

The Christian expansion into regions such as Egypt, Asia Minor, and Greece raised important issues for Christian writers. One of the most significant concerned the relationship of Christianity and classical philosophy. Much of the civilized world in this region spoke Greek, and had at least some degree of familiarity with the ideas of classical Greek philosophy, whether this took the form of classical Platonism, Middle Platonism, or occasionally revived versions of classical paganism. The question therefore arose: how does the Christian gospel relate to these ways of thinking? Does it totally contradict them? Or were these classical ways of thinking in some way a form of preparation for the Christian gospel, which built on their foundations? To anticipate a question raised by Tertullian: what does Jerusalem have to do with Athens?

It is widely thought that one of the most important descriptions of the early confrontation between Christianity and classical paganism is found in Paul's Areopagus address at Athens, documented in Acts 17. In view of the importance of this encounter to subsequent Christian thinking on this issue during the patristic period, we may explore it in a little more detail.

According to Acts, Paul arrived at Athens after a voyage from Macedonia, clearly aware of the reputation of the city and its potential importance in relation to the spread of Christianity. (In what follows, we shall accept the widely prevailing consensus that Acts was written by Luke, and that it forms the second part of a work, of which the first part is the gospel which bears Luke's name.) Luke comments that Athens was a city which was "full of idols," by which he probably intends us to understand that, in addition to a large number of idols inside buildings, others were displayed publicly at points of strategic import- ance. A large number of temples had been built in the general area of the Acropolis, whether in the time of Pericles, or the more recent edifices erected under Augustus, which included a number of temples or statues dedicated to the imperial cult. It is entirely possible that these impressive buildings may have promoted Paul's comment concerning man-made temples (Acts 17: 24). The term "Areopagus" can refer both to a body of people, and to a physical location. As a group of people, it was the most important administrative body within Athens. As a physical location, it referred to "the Hill of Mars." Although the exact location of Paul's "Areopagus sermon" is not specified, it is possible that the specific reference (Acts 17: 18) to Epicurean and Stoic philosophers might suggest that the encounter took place in the *agora*, an open space surrounded by colonnades (the "*stoa*" from which the "*Stoics*" took their name).

In his address, Paul appears to argue that the Christian gospel resonates with and builds upon central Stoic philosophical beliefs. What the Greeks held to be unknown, possibly unknowable, Paul argues to have been made known through Christ. This is made especially clear in his references to an altar dedicated "to an unknown god" (Acts 17: 23). There are classical precedents for such dedications, especially according to the writings of Diogenes Laertius. Numerous Christian writers of the early patristic period explained Paul's meaning at this point by appealing to the "anonymous altars" which were scattered throughout the region at that time.

The fundamental point being made is that a deity of whom Greek philosophy had some implicit or intuitive awareness is being made known to them by name and in full. The god who is known indirectly through the creation can be known directly and more fully in redemption. Paul seems to use the theme of creation as a *praeparatio evangelica*, a way of introducing the theme of redemption in Christ. Classical philosophy can thus be seen as, in some way and to some degree, preparing the way for the coming of the Christian revelation, in much the same way (as some early Christian writers would argue) the Old Testament prepared the Jewish people for the coming of their Messiah.

Approaches along these lines can be found in the writings of patristic theologians active in cultural situations in which various forms of classic Greek philosophy were a significant presence. In what follows, we shall explore the approaches associated with Justin Martyr and Clement of Alexandria, both of whom were concerned to demonstrate that Christianity was consistent with certain forms of Platonism

Justin Martyr (*c.*100–*c.*165). One of the most noted of the Christian apologists of the second century, with a concern to demonstrate the moral and intellectual credibility of Christianity in a pagan world. His *First Apology* stresses the manner in which Christianity brings to fulfillment the insights of classical philosophy, especially Middle Platonism.

In his two apologies for the Christian faith, written in Greek at Rome at some point during the period 148–61, Justin sets out a vigorous defense of Christianity, in which he seeks to relate the gospel to secular wisdom. The idea of the "Logos" is of major importance to Justin, and needs to be considered. The Greek term "Logos" (best translated as "Word") was used within Middle Platonism to refer to the mediating principle between the world of ideas and the everyday world. The term is applied to Jesus Christ in John's gospel (see John 1: 14, which declares that "the *Logos* became flesh, and dwelled among us"). Justin uses this statement to argue that all wisdom derives from the Logos, which is fully revealed in Jesus Christ, although it is not restricted to him.

A central theme in Justin's argument is the idea that God has scattered "the seeds (*spermata*) of his Logos" throughout the world before the coming of Christ, so that secular wisdom and truth can point, however imperfectly, to Christ. It follows that those who tried to live according to this "Logos" before the coming of Christ can be thought of as Christians, even though they would not have thought of themselves in this way. This aspect of Justin's teaching would be repudiated by most other writers of the patristic period, who felt that he had gone too far in his attempts to relate faith and philosophy.

1.8.1 Justin Martyr on Faith and Philosophy

We have been taught that Christ is the firstborn of God, and we have proclaimed that he is the Logos, in whom every race of people have shared. And those who live according to the Logos are Christians, even though they may have been counted as atheists – such as Socrates and Heraclitus, and others like them, among
5 the Greeks. . . . Whatever either lawyers or philosophers have said well, was articulated by finding and reflecting upon some aspect of the Logos. However, since they did not know the Logos – which is Christ – in its entirety, they often contradicted themselves. . . . Whatever all people have said well belongs to us Christians. For we worship and love, next to God, the Logos, who comes from the
10 unbegotten and ineffable God, since it was for our sake that he became a human being, in order that he might share in our sufferings and bring us healing. For all writers were able to see the truth darkly, on account of the implanted seed of the Logos which was grafted into them.

Note especially the following points:

1 Justin argues that Jesus Christ is the Logos. All true human wisdom derives from this Logos, whether this is explicitly recognized or not. Philosophical

tensions and contradictions arise through incomplete access to the Logos – but such full access is now possible through Jesus Christ (lines 6–9).

2   Anyone who tries to act according to this Logos can be thought of as a Christian – including Socrates (lines 1–5). This aspect of Justin's teaching proved controversial.

3   Anything that is good and true in secular philosophy may therefore be accepted and honored by Christians (lines 5–6), in that it derives from the Logos.

> **Clement of Alexandria (*c.*150–*c.*215).** A leading Alexandrian writer, with a particular concern to explore the relation between Christian thought and Greek philosophy.

A related approach is adopted a little later by Clement of Alexandria, who aims to bring out the way in which classical philosophy can be thought of as preparing the way for the gospel. The eight books of Clement's *Stromata* (the word literally means "carpets") deal at length with the relation of the Christian faith to Greek philosophy. In this extract from the *Stromata*, originally written in Greek in the early third century, Clement argues that God gave philosophy to the Greeks as a way of preparing them for the coming of Christ, in more or less exactly the same way as he gave the Jews the law of Moses. While not allowing that philosophy has the status of revelation, Clement goes beyond Justin Martyr's suggestion that the mere seeds of the Logos are to be found in Greek philosophy.

1.8.2   Clement of Alexandria on Faith and Philosophy

Until the coming of the Lord, philosophy was necessary to the Greeks for righteousness. And now it assists those who come to faith by way of demonstration, as a kind of preparatory training for true religion. For "you will not stumble" (Proverbs 3: 23) if you attribute all good things to providence, whether it belongs
5   to the Greeks or to us. For God is the source of all good things, some directly (as with the Old and the New Testaments), and some indirectly (as with philosophy). But it might be that philosophy was given to the Greeks immediately and directly, until such time as the Lord should also call the Greeks. For philosophy acted as a "schoolmaster" to bring the Greeks to Christ, just as the law brought the Hebrews.
10 Thus philosophy was by way of a preparation, which prepared the way for its perfection in Christ.

Note especially the following points:

1   Classical philosophy is seen as having a definite place in the "economy of salvation." In other words, Clement argues that, in the providence of God, philosophy had a place in preparing the way for the coming of Christ.
2   After the coming of Christ, philosophy retains an important role as a "kind of preparatory training" (lines 1–3). Clement clearly regards philosophy in a positive light, and sees it as a route leading to, rather than a rival worldview leading away from, Christianity.
3   Note the analogy between philosophy and the Old Testament (lines 8–9). Clement's argument seems to be that, just as God provided the Old Testament law to prepare Israel for the coming of Christ, so God provided philosophy to prepare the Greeks for his coming.
4   Christ is seen as the perfection and fulfillment of philosophy, just as he is also seen as the fulfillment and culmination of the Old Testament law. For Clement (as for Justin Martyr), Christ can be said to be "Logos and Nomos."

> **Tertullian (*c*.160–*c*.225).** A major figure in early Latin theology, who produced a series of significant controversial and apologetic writings. He is particularly noted for his ability to coin new Latin terms to translate the emerging theological vocabulary of the Greek-speaking Eastern church.

Yet not all early Christian writers shared such a positive attitude to classical philosophy. Tertullian is an example of a patristic writer who had serious misgivings concerning the place of philosophy within Christian thought, arguing that it could be profoundly misleading at points. Philosophy, he argued, was pagan in its outlook, and its use in theology could only lead to heresy within the church. In his "On the Rule of the Heretics," written in Latin in the first years of the third century, Tertullian sets up a celebrated contrast between Athens and Jerusalem, symbolizing the tension between pagan philosophy and the revelation of the Christian faith. Note that reference to the "Academy" is not a general reference to the academic world, but specifically to the Platonic Academy at Athens. For Tertullian, the pagan ideas of "the Academy" have no place within Christianity.

1.8.3   Tertullian on Faith and Philosophy

For philosophy provides the material of worldly wisdom, in boldly asserting itself to be the interpreter of the divine nature and dispensation. The heresies themselves receive their weapons from philosophy. It was from this source, that

Valentinus, who was a disciple of Plato, got his ideas about the "aeons" and the
5 "trinity of humanity." And it was from there that the god of Marcion (much to be
preferred, on account of his tranquility) came; Marcion came from the Stoics. To
say that the soul is subject to death is to go the way of Epicurus. And the denial
of the resurrection of the body is found throughout the writings of all the
philosophers. To say that matter is equal with God is to follow the doctrine of
10 Zeno; to speak of a god of fire is to draw on Heraclitus. It is the same subjects which
preoccupy both the heretics and the philosophers. Where does evil come from, and
why? Where does human nature come from, and how? … What is there in
common between Athens and Jerusalem? between the Academy and the church?
Our system of beliefs comes from the Porch of Solomon, who himself taught that
15 it was necessary to seek God in the simplicity of the heart. So much the worse for
those who talk of a "stoic," "platonic" or "dialectic" Christianity! We have no need
for curiosity after Jesus Christ, nor for inquiry after the gospel. When we believe,
we desire to believe nothing further. For we need believe nothing more than "there
is nothing else which we are obliged to believe."

Note especially the following points:

1 Tertullian argues that, as a matter of historical fact, heresies seem to derive
   many of their leading ideas from secular philosophy (1–10). This, in his view,
   is enough to raise very serious questions concerning the use of such
   philosophies in theology.
2 Some of the particular heresies which Tertullian lists (4–6) are all forms of
   Gnosticism. It is, in fact, a matter of debate as to whether Gnosticism can be
   regarded as drawing upon the ideas of secular Greek philosophy; some
   scholars have argued that Gnosticism was actually quite anti-intellectual.
3 Tertullian argues that many classical philosophical systems contain core ideas
   (such as the denial of the resurrection) which are inconsistent with Christianity. How, he asks, can aspects of such systems be used by Christians, when
   they reflect such anti-Christian ideas at their heart?

Tertullian's points could, of course, be met by arguing for the need to *critically
appropriate* the ideas of philosophy. It could be argued that Justin and Clement
were perhaps unduly optimistic in their attitude towards secular philosophy,
while Tertullian was too negative. Not every idea found in Greek philosophy was
right, just as not every idea was wrong. It is this kind of approach that we find in
the early writings of Augustine, to which we now turn.

In his work "On Christian doctrine," originally written in Latin around 397,
Augustine deals at some length with the relation between Christianity and pagan

> **Augustine of Hippo (354–430).** Widely regarded as the most influential
> Latin patristic writer, Augustine was converted to Christianity at the northern
> Italian city of Milan in the summer of 386. He returned to North Africa, and
> was made bishop of Hippo in 395. He was involved in two major controversies
> – the Donatist controversy, focusing on the church and sacraments, and the
> Pelagian controversy, focusing on grace and sin. He also made substantial
> contributions to the development of the doctrine of the Trinity, and the
> Christian understanding of history.

philosophy. Using the exodus from Egypt as a model, Augustine argues that
there is no reason why Christians should not extract all that is good in philosophy,
and put it to the service of preaching the gospel. The analogy which he uses to
justify this approach is found in the Book of Exodus in the Old Testament, which
tells of the circumstances under which Israel left Egypt – an event which is
universally known as "the Exodus." Israel was oppressed while in Egypt; on
escaping, the people left behind those burdens, yet carried off the treasures of
their former oppressors. So, Augustine argues, just as Israel left behind the
burdens of Egypt, while carrying off its treasures, so theology can discard what
is useless in philosophy, and exploit what is good and useful.

1.8.4   Augustine on Faith and Philosophy

If those who are called philosophers, particularly the Platonists, have said anything
which is true and consistent with our faith, we must not reject it, but claim it for
our own use, in the knowledge that they possess it unlawfully. The Egyptians
possessed idols and heavy burdens, which the children of Israel hated and from
5   which they fled; however, they also possessed vessels of gold and silver and clothes
which our forebears, in leaving Egypt, took for themselves in secret, intending to
use them in a better manner (Exodus 3: 21–2; 12: 35–6). . . . In the same way,
pagan learning is not entirely made up of false teachings and superstitions. It
contains also some excellent teachings, well suited to be used by truth, and
10   excellent moral values. Indeed, some truths are even found among them which
relate to the worship of the one God. Now these are, so to speak, their gold and
their silver, which they did not invent themselves, but which they dug out of the
mines of the providence of God, which are scattered throughout the world, yet
which are improperly and unlawfully prostituted to the worship of demons. The
15   Christian, therefore, can separate these truths from their unfortunate associations,
take them away, and put them to their proper use for the proclamation of the
gospel. . . . What else have many good and faithful people from amongst us done?
Look at the wealth of gold and silver and clothes which Cyprian – that eloquent

> 20 teacher and blessed martyr – brought with him when he left Egypt! And think of all that Lactantius brought with him, not to mention Marius Victorinus, Optatus and Hilary of Poitiers, and others who are still living! And look at how much the Greeks have borrowed! And before all of these, we find that Moses, that most faithful servant of God, had done the same thing: after all, it is written of him that "he was learned in all the wisdom of the Egyptians" (Acts 7: 22).

This is a very rich passage, and it will be helpful to focus on the following points:

1   Note how Augustine explicitly states that philosophy asserts some things that are true (lines 1–3) and some which are false (lines 7–8). The task for Christian theology is therefore to ascertain what is true, and make use of it. Augustine refuses to adopt an uncritically positive or uncritically negative approach. Christians can therefore separate true beliefs and values from their pagan associations (lines 14–17).

2   The analogy of the Exodus is used to justify this critical appropriation, as noted above (see lines 3–7). But it is also used to develop a related idea, which is explored by considering the imagery of "gold and silver" (lines 5–6). Augustine argues that these riches were not invented by the Egyptians; they were mined. The fact that they were available was due to the good providence of God (lines 11–13).

3   Augustine provides two kind of illustration for the way in which secular wisdom can be put to the service of the Christian church. The first is Moses himself, who is referred to in the New Testament as being "learned in all the wisdom of the Egyptians" (Acts 7: 22 – see lines 22–24). Augustine clearly regarded this as equipping Moses to serve God more effectively. Secondly, Augustine appeals to a series of recent distinguished Christian writers (including Cyprian), who were converted to Christianity from paganism, and who were able to put their secular learning to good use in the service of the church (20–21).

It is widely agreed that the movement within Christianity which explored the relation between Christian faith and philosophy to greatest effect was "scholasticism," a movement which flowered during the Middle Ages. We shall explore this rich intellectual tradition in case study 2.1. Before that, however, we turn to the general exploration of the next major period in the history of Christian thought.

Chapter 2

THE MIDDLE AGES AND THE RENAISSANCE, C.500–1500

THE BIRTH OF THE MIDDLE AGES

The fall of Rome sent shock waves throughout the Mediterranean region, and was of major significance to the development of Christian theology. The northern frontier of the Roman Empire, more or less defined by the River Rhine, collapsed in 404 in the face of assault by "barbarians." Huge areas of the Roman Empire were now under the control of the Franks, Goths, and Vandals. Rome itself was sacked twice, most notably by the forces of Alaric the Goth in 410. By 476, the western regions of the Roman Empire were in ruins. The political stability of the region was eroded, with the result that Christianity found itself facing a period of considerable uncertainty.

Further uncertainty arose through the Arab invasions of the seventh century. Islam first became a significant religious movement amongst the Arab people at this time, and led to a program of conquest being initiated, which eventually led to Arab forces taking control of the entire coastal region of North Africa by about 750. Islamic forces also moved north, posing a serious threat to Constantinople itself. Arab forces laid siege to the city during the period 711–78, eventually being forced to withdraw. The enforcement of Islam in the conquered regions of the Holy Land led to intense concern in the western church, and was one of the factors which led to the crusades during the period 1095–1204.

A further complication arose within the Christian world itself, with growing tensions arising between the Greek-speaking Christians of the eastern Mediter-ranean, centered at Constantinople, and the Latin-speaking Christians of the west, centered on Rome, during the ninth and tenth centuries. Growing disagreement over the wording of the Nicene Creed (see pp. 61–72) was of no small importance to this increasingly sour atmosphere. However, other factors contributed, including the political rivalry between Latin-speaking Rome and Greek-speaking Constantinople, and the increasing claims to authority of the

Roman pope. The final break between the Catholic west and Orthodox east is usually dated to 1054; however, this date is slightly arbitrary.

It is against this background of uncertainty that the development of Christian theology during this period is to be seen. However, we may begin our exploration of this period by considering the emergence of one of the most significant catalysts to Christian theology and spirituality – the rise of the monasteries.

THE ORIGINS OF MONASTICISM

One of the most important developments to take place in the history of early Christianity was the development of monasticism. In view of the importance of monasteries for the development of Christian theology during the Middle Ages, we may explore this development in a little detail. The origins of the movement are generally thought to lie in remote hilly areas of Egypt and parts of eastern Syria during the third century. Significant numbers of Christians began to make their homes in these regions, in order to get away from the population centers, with all the distractions that these offered. An example is Anthony of Egypt, who left his parents' home in 273 to seek out a life of discipline and solitude in the desert.

The theme of withdrawal from a sinful and distracting world became of central importance to these communities. While some lone figures insisted on the need for individual isolation, the concept of a communal life in isolation from the world gained ascendancy. One important early monastery was founded by Pachomius during the years 320–5. This monastery developed an ethos which would become normative in later monasticism. Members of the community agreed to submit themselves to a common life which was regulated by a Rule, under the direction of a superior. The physical structure of the monastery was significant: the complex was surrounded by a wall, highlighting the idea of separation and withdrawal from the world. The Greek word *koinonia* (often translated as "fellowship"), frequently used in the New Testament, now came to refer to the idea of a common corporate life, characterized by common clothing, meals, furnishing of cells (as the monks' rooms were known), and manual labor for the good of the community.

The monastic ideal proved to have a deep attraction for many. By the fourth century, monasteries had been established in many locations in the Christian east, especially in the regions of Syria and Asia Minor. It was not long before the movement was taken up in the western church. By the fifth century, monastic communities had come into existence in Italy (especially along the western coastline), Spain, and Gaul. Augustine of Hippo established two monasteries in North Africa at some point during the period 400–425. For Augustine, the common life (now designated by the Latin phrase *vita communis*) was essential to the realization of the Christian ideal of love. He supplemented this emphasis on community life with an appreciation of the importance of intellectual activity and spiritual study.

During the sixth century, the number of monasteries in the region grew considerably. It was during this period that one of the most comprehensive monastic "Rules" – the "Rule of Benedict" – made its appearance. Benedict of Nursia (*c*.480–*c*.550) established his monastery at Monte Cassino at some point around 525. The Benedictine community followed a rule which was dominated by the notion of the unconditional following of Christ, sustained by regular corporate and private prayer, and the reading of Scripture.

The rise of the monasteries is of considerable importance for the history of Christian theology. Monasteries were frequently centers of theological and spiritual activity. During the patristic and medieval periods, most Christian theologians of importance were either members of monastic communities, or had close links with them. Anselm of Canterbury, Hugh of St Victor, Thomas Aquinas and Bonaventure are all examples of significant western medieval theological writers with monastic connections. The importance of monasteries for eastern Orthodoxy (in both Greek and Russian forms) and for Celtic Christianity should also be noted.

One form of Christianity with monastic roots developed in the regions of western Europe associated with the Celtic peoples. In what follows, we shall explore the rise and gradual eclipse of this distinctive type of Christianity, with its particularly high regard for the natural order.

THE RISE OF CELTIC CHRISTIANITY

The rise of Christianity in the Celtic regions of Europe – more specifically, Ireland, Scotland, Cornwall, Brittany, and Wales – is of considerable interest, not least in that this form of Christianity found itself in opposition to the more Romanized forms which rapidly gained the ascendancy in England. Although the origins of Celtic Christianity seem to lie in Wales, it is Ireland which established itself as a missionary center of distinction in the fifth and sixth centuries. Other centers of missionary activity in the Celtic sphere of influence are known from this period, most notably Candida Casa (modern-day Whithorn, in the Galloway region of Scotland), which was established by bishop Ninian in the fifth century. The significance of this missionary station was that it lay outside the borders of Roman Britain, and was thus able to operate without the restrictions then associated with Roman forms of Christianity.

The person who is traditionally held to be responsible for the evangelization of Ireland was a Romanized Briton by the name of Magonus Sucatus Patricius, more usually known by his Celtic name "Patrick" (*c*.390–*c*.460). Born into a wealthy family, Patrick was taken captive by a raiding party at the age of sixteen, and sold into slavery in Ireland, probably in the region of Connaught. Here, he appears to have discovered the basics of the Christian faith, before escaping and making his way back to his family. He had been in captivity for six years. It is not clear precisely what happened between Patrick's escape from captivity and his subsequent return to Ireland as a missionary. A tradition, dating back to the seventh or eighth century, refers to Patrick spending time in Gaul before his return to Ireland. It is possible that some of Patrick's views on church organization and structures may reflect first-hand acquaintance with the monasticism of certain regions of southern France. There is excellent historical evidence for trading links between Ireland and the Loire Valley around this time.

Patrick returned to Ireland, and established Christianity in the region. It is clear that some form of Christianity already existed; not only does Patrick's conversion account presuppose that others in the region knew about the gospel; contemporary records dating from as early as 429 speak of one Palladius as the bishop of Ireland, indicating that at least some form of rudimentary ecclesiastical structures existed in the region. Irish representatives are also known to have been present at the Synod of Arles (314). Patrick's achievement is perhaps best understood in terms of the consolidation and advancement of Christianity, rather than its establishment in the first place.

The monastic idea took hold very quickly in Ireland. Historical sources indicate that Ireland was largely a nomadic and tribal society at this time, without any permanent settlements of any importance. The monastic quest for solitude and isolation was ideally suited to the Irish way of life. Whereas in western Europe as a whole, monasticism was marginalized within the life of the church, in Ireland it rapidly became its dominant form. It is no exaggeration to say that the Irish church was monastic, with the abbot rather than the bishop being seen as pre-eminent.

The authority structures which emerged within Celtic Christianity were thus rather different from those which came to dominate the Roman–British church at this time. The Irish monastic model came to be seen as a threat to the Roman model of the episcopate, in which the government of the church resided firmly in the hands of the bishops. None of the abbots of Iona ever allowed bishops to formally ordain them, rejecting the need for any such "official" recognition. In Ireland, some of the older bishoprics (including Armagh) were reorganized on a monastic basis, with others being absorbed by monasteries. Abbeys were responsible for the pastoral care of the churches which grew up in their vicinity. The Roman episcopal system was thus marginalized. The Celtic church leaders were openly critical of worldly wealth and status, including the use of horses as a mode of transport, and any form of luxury. Theologically, Celtic Christianity also stressed the importance of the world of nature as a means of knowing God. This is especially clear from the ancient Irish hymn traditionally ascribed to Patrick, and known as "St Patrick's Breastplate." The theme of a "breastplate" was common in Celtic Christian spirituality. It is based upon Paul's references to the "armor of God" (Ephesians 6: 10–18), and develops the theme of the believer being protected by the presence of God and a whole range of associated powers. Although strongly trinitarian in its structure, it shows a fascination with the natural world as a means of knowing God. The God who made the world is the same God who will protect Christians from all dangers.

The Irish monasteries acted as centers for missionary activity, often using sea lanes as channels for the transmission of Christianity. Brendan (died *c.*580) and Columba (died *c.*597) are excellent examples of this type of missionary. In a poem entitled "The Navigation of St Brendan" (*c.*1050), Brendan is praised for his journeys to the "northern and western isles" (usually assumed to be the Orkneys and Hebrides, off the coast of Scotland). Columba brought Christianity from the north of Ireland to the Western Isles of Scotland, and established the abbey of Iona as a missionary outpost. From there, Christianity spread southwards and eastwards. Aidan (died 651) is an excellent example of a monk from Iona who acted as a missionary in this way. At the invitation of the king of the region of Northumbria, he established a missionary monastery on the island of Lindisfarne, off the east coast of northern England. Celtic Christianity began to penetrate into France, and become increasingly influential in the region.

The tensions between Celtic Christianity and its Roman rivals could not be ignored. Celtic Christianity threatened to undermine the episcopate, reduce the power of Rome, make it more difficult for Christianity to become culturally acceptable, and to make monasticism the norm for Christian living. By 597, the year of Columba's death, the ascendancy of the Celtic vision seemed inevitable. However, the following century saw a series of developments which led to its gradual eclipse outside its heartlands in Ireland. By a coincidence of history, the event which led to its eclipse took place in the very year of Columba's death. In 597, Augustine was sent to England by Pope Gregory to evangelize the English. As Roman forms of Christianity became established in England, tensions arose between northern and southern English Christians, the former remaining faithful to Celtic traditions, and the latter to Roman. The Synod of Whitby (664) is widely seen as establishing the dominance of Roman Christianity in England. Although the Synod focused on the question of when Easter should be celebrated (Celtic and Roman traditions differing on the issue), the real issue concerned the growing influence of the see of Canterbury. The Saxon invasions of England in the previous century had resulted in major cultural changes in the region, making inevitable the gradual erosion of Celtic culture, including its distinctive approach to Christianity.

The year 700 may be seen as marking the end of the growth of Celtic Christianity. Yet it is also widely regarded as marking the dawn of a new period of cultural and intellectual consolidation, as what is now known as "the Middle Ages" began in Europe. By the eleventh century, a significant degree of political and social stability had emerged within this region, with three major power groupings having emerged to take the place of the former Roman Empire.

1   Byzantium, centered on the city of Constantinople (located in modern Turkey, and now known as "Istanbul"). The form of Christianity which predominated in this region was based on the Greek language, and was deeply rooted in the writings of patristic scholars of the eastern Mediterranean region, such as Athanasius, the Cappadocians, and John of Damascus. A brief discussion of Byzantine theology may be found at pp. 123–7.

2   Western Europe, mainly regions such as France, Germany, the Low Countries, and northern Italy. The form of Christianity which came to dominate this region was centered on the city of Rome, and its bishop, known as "the Pope." (However, for the period known as the "Great Schism," some confusion developed: there were two rival claimants for the papacy, one based at Rome, the other at the southern French city of Avignon.) Here, theology came to be concentrated in the great cathedral and university schools of Paris and elsewhere, based largely on the Latin writings of Augustine, Ambrose, and Hilary of Poitiers.

3   The Caliphate, an Islamic region embracing much of the extreme eastern and southern parts of the Mediterranean. The expansion of Islam continued, with the fall of Constantinople in 1453 sending shock waves throughout much of Europe. By the end of the fifteenth century, Islam had established a significant presence in two regions of the continent of Europe: Spain and the Balkans. This advance was eventually halted by the defeat of the Moors in Spain in the final decade of the fifteenth century, and the defeat of Islamic armies outside Vienna in 1523.

An event of fundamental importance to the history of the church took place during this period. For a variety of reasons, relations between the eastern church, based at Constantinople, and the western, based at Rome, became increasingly strained during the ninth and tenth centuries. Growing disagreement over the *filioque* clause in the Nicene Creed (see pp. 61–72) was of no small importance to this increasingly sour atmosphere. Other factors also contributed, including the political rivalry between Latin-speaking Rome and Greek-speaking Constantinople, and the increasing claims to authority of the Roman Pope. The final break between the Catholic west and Orthodox east is usually dated to 1054, although this date is slightly arbitrary.

One major result of this tension was that there was little theological interaction between east and west. Although western theologians such as Thomas Aquinas felt free to draw on the writings of Greek fathers, these works tended to antedate this period. The works of later Orthodox theologians, such as the noted writer Gregory Palamas, attracted little attention in the west. It is only in the twentieth

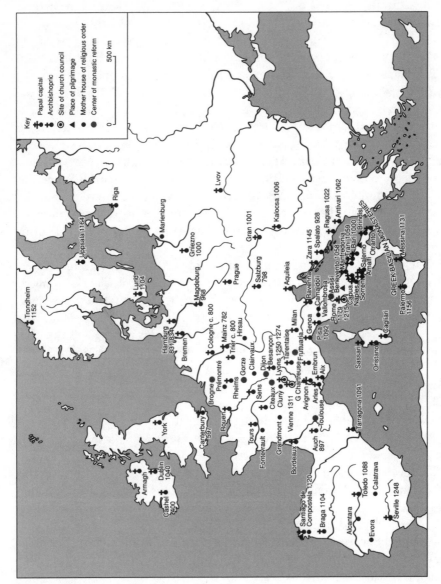

Map 2   Main theological and ecclesiastical centers in western Europe during the Middle Ages

century that western theology may really be said to have begun to rediscover the riches of the Orthodox tradition.

Our concern in this chapter is primarily with western European theology, which has had a deep impact upon modern Christian thought. The term "medieval theology" is often used to refer to western theology during this era, whereas the term "Byzantine theology" is used to refer to the theology of the eastern church over roughly the same period, prior to the fall of Constantinople in 1453. During this period in western European history, the centers of Christian theology gradually moved northward, to central France and Germany. Although Rome remained a center of Christian power in the region, intellectual activity gradually came to migrate to the monasteries of France, such as Chartres, Reims, and Bec. With the foundation of the medieval universities, theology rapidly established itself as a central area of academic study. A typical medieval university possessed four faculties: the lower faculty of arts, and the three higher faculties of theology, medicine, and law.

A Clarification of Terms

Defining periods in history is notoriously difficult. Part of the problem lies in the absence of universal agreement on the defining characteristics of eras. This is especially the case with the "Middle Ages," the "Renaissance," and the "modern period." There are also major difficulties in defining some of the intellectual movements of the period, especially humanism.

The period under consideration in this chapter gave rise to two of the most important intellectual movements in the history of thought: *scholasticism* and *humanism*. Scholasticism and humanism dominated the intellectual world – including the theological world – between 1300 and 1500. Although it could be argued that scholasticism was on the wane by the year 1500, it still exerted immense influence in many European universities, such as the University of Paris. An understanding of the nature of both these movements is essential to any attempt to make sense of the development of Christian theology during the period, or to understand the religious and intellectual pressures which eventually gave rise to the Reformation. The two movements are related, in that the latter is generally regarded as being a response to the cultural poverty and theological overprecision of the former. In what follows, we shall attempt to clarify some of the terms used in the literature relating to this major period of Christian theology.

The Middle Ages

The term "the Middle Ages" was invented by writers of the Renaissance, and seems to have come into general use toward the end of the sixteenth century. The writers of the Renaissance were anxious to discredit the period intervening between the glories of classical antiquity and their own time. They thus invented the term "the Middle Ages" to refer to an uninteresting and stagnant phase separating two important and creative periods. The adjective "medieval" means "relating to the Middle Ages." The term "medieval theology" has passed into general use, and can generally be interpreted to mean "western European theology in the period between the end of the Dark Ages and the sixteenth century." It must, however, be appreciated that the term is imprecise, disputed, and open to various interpretations.

When the so-called Dark Ages finally lifted from western Europe, giving birth to the Middle Ages, the scene was set for revival in every field of academic work. The restoration of some degree of political stability in France in the late eleventh century encouraged the re-emergence of the University of Paris, which rapidly became recognized as the intellectual center of Europe. A number of theological "schools" were established on the Left Bank of the Seine, and on the Île de la Cité, in the shadow of the newly-built cathedral of Notre Dame de Paris.

One such school was the Collège de la Sorbonne, which eventually achieved such fame that "the Sorbonne" came to be a short-hand way of referring to the University of Paris. Even in the sixteenth century, Paris was widely recognized as a leading center for theological and philosophical study, including amongst its students such prominent individuals as Erasmus of Rotterdam and John Calvin. Other such centers of study were soon established elsewhere in Europe. A new program of theological development began, concerned with consolidating the intellectual, legal, and spiritual aspects of the life of the Christian church.

The early part of the medieval period is dominated by developments in France. Several monasteries produced outstanding Christian writers and thinkers, for example, Lanfranc (*c.*1010–89) and Anselm (*c.*1033–1109), both from the monastery at Bec, in Normandy. The University of Paris soon established itself as a leading center of theological speculation, with such scholars as Peter Abelard (1079–1142), Albert the Great (*c.*1200–80), Thomas Aquinas (*c.*1225–74), and Bonaventure (*c.*1217–74). The fourteenth and fifteenth centuries witnessed a considerable expansion of the university sector in western Europe, with major new universities being founded in Germany and elsewhere.

A central resource to the new medieval interest in theology is also linked with Paris. At some point shortly before 1140, Peter Lombard arrived at the university to teach. One of his primary concerns was to get his students to wrestle with the thorny issues of theology. His contribution was a textbook – perhaps one of the most boring books that has ever been written. The *Sententiarum libri quattuor* or *Four Books of the Sentences* bring together quotations from Scripture and the patristic writers, arranged topically. The task Peter set his students was simple: Make sense of the quotes. The book proved to be of major importance in developing the Augustinian heritage, in that students were obliged to wrestle with the ideas of Augustine, and reconcile apparently contradictory texts by devising suitable theological explanations of the inconsistencies (see p. 6).

Some writers attempted to have the book banned, noting its occasional incautious statements (such as the opinion that Christ did not exist as a person, a view which came to be known as "Christological nihilism"). However, by 1215 the work was firmly established as the most important textbook of the age. It became obligatory for theologians to comment on Lombard's work. The resulting writings, known as *Commentaries on the Sentences*, became one of the most familiar theological genres of the Middle Ages. Outstanding examples include those of Thomas Aquinas, Bonaventure, and Duns Scotus.

The Renaissance

The French term "Renaissance" is now universally used to designate the literary and artistic revival in fourteenth- and fifteenth-century Italy. In 1546 Paolo Giovio referred to the fourteenth century as "that happy century in which Latin letters are conceived to have been reborn" (*renatae*), anticipating this nomenclature. Certain historians, most notably Jacob Burckhardt, argued that the Renaissance gave birth to the modern era. It was in this era, Burckhardt claimed, that human beings first began to think of themselves as *individuals*. In many ways, Burckhardt's definition of the Renaissance in purely individualist terms is highly questionable. But in one sense, he is unquestionably correct: *something* novel and exciting developed in Renaissance Italy, which proved capable of exercising a fascination over generations of thinkers.

It is not entirely clear why Italy became the cradle of this brilliant new movement in the history of ideas. A number of factors have been identified as having some bearing on the question:

1. Scholastic theology – the major intellectual force of the medieval period – was never particularly influential in Italy. Although many Italians achieved fame as theologians (including Thomas Aquinas and Gregory of Rimini), they generally lived and worked in northern Europe. There was thus an intellectual vacuum in Italy during the fourteenth century. Vacuums tend to be filled – and Renaissance humanism filled this particular gap.

2. Italy was saturated with visible and tangible reminders of the greatness of antiquity. The ruins of ancient Roman buildings and monuments were scattered throughout the land, and appear to have aroused interest in the civilization of ancient Rome at the time of the Renaissance, acting as a stimulus to its thinkers to recover the vitality of classical Roman culture at a time which was culturally arid and barren.

3. As Byzantium began to crumble – Constantinople finally fell in 1453 – there was an exodus of Greek-speaking intellectuals westward. Italy happened to

be conveniently close to Constantinople, with the result that many such émigrés settled in Italian cities. A revival of the Greek language was thus inevitable, and with it a revival of interest in the Greek classics.

It will be clear that a central component of the worldview of the Italian Renaissance is a return to the cultural glories of antiquity, and a marginalization of the intellectual achievements of the Middle Ages. Renaissance writers had scant regard for the latter, regarding them as outweighed by the greater achievements of antiquity. What was true of culture in general was also true of theology: They regarded the late classical period as totally overshadowing the theological writings of the Middle Ages, both in substance and in style. Indeed, the Renaissance may partly be seen as a reaction against the type of approach increasingly associated with the faculties of arts and theology of northern European universities. Irritated by the technical nature of the language and discussions of the scholastics, the writers of the Renaissance by-passed them altogether. In the case of Christian theology, the key to the future lay in a direct engagement with the text of Scripture and the writings of the patristic period. We shall explore this matter further shortly (see pp. 146–50).

Scholasticism

Scholasticism is probably one of the most despised intellectual movements in human history. Thus the English word "dunce" (fool) derives from the name of one of the greatest scholastic writers, Duns Scotus. Scholastic thinkers – the "schoolmen" – are often represented as debating earnestly, if pointlessly, over how many angels could dance on the head of a pin. Although this particular debate never actually took place, intriguing though its outcome would unquestionably have been, it summarizes precisely the way in which scholasticism was regarded by most people, especially the humanists, at the beginning of the sixteenth century: it was futile, arid intellectual speculation over trivia. Erasmus of Rotterdam, a gentleman whom we shall consider in more detail shortly, spent a few semesters toward the end of the fifteenth century at the scholasticism-dominated University of Paris. He wrote at length of the many things he detested about Paris: the lice, the poor food, the stinking latrines, and the utterly tedious debates which vexed the schoolmen. Could God have become a cucumber instead of a human being? Could he undo the past, by making a prostitute into a virgin? Although serious questions lay behind these debates, Erasmus' waspish wit diverted attention from those questions themselves to the frivolous and ridiculous way in which they were debated.

The very word "scholasticism" could be argued to be the invention of humanist writers, anxious to discredit the movement which it represented. We have already noted that the phrase "the Middle Ages" was largely a humanist invention, coined by sixteenth-century humanist writers to refer disparagingly to an uninteresting period of stagnation between antiquity (the classical period) and modernity (the Renaissance). The "Middle Ages" were seen as little more than an intermezzo between the cultural magnificence of antiquity and its revival during the Renaissance. Similarly, the term "scholastics" (*scholastici*) was used by humanists to refer, equally disparagingly, to the ideas of the Middle Ages. In their concern to discredit the ideas of the medieval period, in order to enhance the attractions of the classical period, the humanists had little interest in drawing distinctions between the various types of "scholastics" – such as Thomists and Scotists. The word "scholasticism" is thus both pejorative and imprecise – yet the historian cannot avoid using it.

How may scholasticism be defined? Like many other significant cultural terms, such as "humanism" and "Enlightenment", it is difficult to offer a precise definition, capable of doing justice to all the distinctive positions of the major schools within the Middle Ages. Perhaps the following working definition may be helpful: Scholasticism is best regarded as the medieval movement, flourishing in the period 1200–1500, which placed emphasis upon the rational justification of religious belief, and the systematic presentation of those beliefs. "Scholasticism" thus does not refer to a *specific system of beliefs*, but to a *particular way of organizing theology* – a highly developed method of presenting material, making fine distinctions, and attempting to achieve a comprehensive view of theology. It is perhaps understandable why, to its humanist critics, scholasticism seemed to degenerate into little more than logical nit-picking.

However, scholasticism may be argued to have produced vitally important work in a number of key areas of Christian theology, especially in relation to the role of reason and logic in theology. The writings of Thomas Aquinas, Duns Scotus, and William of Ockham – often singled out as the three most influential of all scholastic writers – make massive contributions to this area of theology, which have served as landmarks ever since.

So what types of scholasticism were there? Like "humanism," the term "scholasticism" defines an approach or method, rather than a specific set of doctrines which result from the application of this method. There are thus several different types of scholasticism. This section will explore briefly some of the main types, or "schools," paying particular attention to those of relevance to the development of theology during the medieval period. We begin by drawing a distinction between "realism" and "nominalism," two very different theories of knowledge which both had a major impact upon the development of scholasticism.

Realism and nominalism

The distinction between "realism" and "nominalism" is of considerable importance to an understanding of medieval theology, thus obliging us to explore it in a little detail. The early part of the scholastic period (*c.*1200–*c.*1350) was dominated by realism, whereas the later part (*c.*1350–*c.*1500) was dominated by nominalism. The difference between the two systems may be described as follows. Consider two white stones. Realism affirms that there is a universal concept of "whiteness" which these two stones embody. These particular stones possess the universal characteristic of "whiteness." While the white stones exist in time and space, the universal of "whiteness" exists on a different metaphysical plane. Nominalism, however, asserts that the universal concept of "whiteness" is unnecessary, and instead argues that we should concentrate on particulars. There are these two white stones – and there is no need to start talking about "a universal concept of whiteness."

The idea of a "universal," used here without definition, needs to be explored further. Consider Socrates. He is a human being, and is an example of humanity. Now consider Plato and Aristotle. They are also human beings, and examples of humanity. We could go on doing this for some time, naming as many individuals as we liked, but the same basic pattern emerges: Individual named people are examples of humanity. Realism argues that the abstract idea of "humanity" has a real existence of its own. It is the universal; particular people – such as Socrates, Plato, and Aristotle – are individual examples of this universal. The common feature of humanity which unites these three individuals has a real existence of its own.

Two major scholastic "schools" influenced by realism dominate the earlier medieval period. These are *Thomism* and *Scotism*, derived from the writings of Thomas Aquinas and Duns Scotus respectively. Late scholasticism, however, came to be dominated by two other schools, both committed to nominalism, rather than realism. These are generally known as the "modern way" (*via moderna*) and the "modern Augustinian school" (*schola Augustiniana moderna*).

The modern way

The term *via moderna* – "the modern way" – is now becoming generally accepted as the best way of referring to the movement once known as "nominalism," including amongst its adherents such fourteenth- and fifteenth-century thinkers as William of Ockham, Pierre d'Ailly, Robert Holcot, and Gabriel Biel. During the fifteenth century, the "modern way" began to make significant inroads into many northern European universities – for example, at Paris, Heidelberg, and Erfurt. In addition to its philosophical nominalism, the movement adopted a doctrine of justification which many of its critics branded as "Pelagian." It is against this background that Luther's theology is set.

The modern Augustinian school

One of the strongholds of the "modern way" in the early fourteenth century was the University of Oxford. It was here also that the first major negative reaction against the movement occurred. The individual responsible for this backlash was Thomas Bradwardine, later to become Archbishop of Canterbury. Bradwardine wrote a furious attack on the ideas of the Oxford "modern way," entitled *The Case of God against Pelagius*. In this book, he developed a theory of justification which represents a return to the views of Augustine, as they are found in the latter's anti-Pelagian writings.

Important though Oxford was as a theological center, the Hundred Years War of 1337–1453 led to its becoming increasingly isolated from the continent of Europe. Whereas Bradwardine's ideas would be developed in England by John Wycliffe, they were taken up on the mainland of Europe by Gregory of Rimini at the University of Paris. Gregory had one particularly significant advantage over Bradwardine: he was a member of a religious order (the Order of the Hermits of St Augustine, generally referred to as the "Augustinian order"). And just as the Dominicans propagated the views of Thomas Aquinas, and the Franciscans those of Duns Scotus, so the Augustinians would promote the ideas of Gregory of Rimini. It is this transmission of an Augustinian tradition, deriving from Gregory of Rimini, within the Augustinian order which is increasingly referred to as the *schola Augustiniana moderna*, the "modern Augustinian school." What were these views?

First, Gregory adopted a nominalist view on the question of universals. Like many thinkers of his time, he had little use for the realism of Thomas Aquinas or Duns Scotus. In this respect, he has much in common with thinkers of the "modern way," such as Robert Holcot or Gabriel Biel. Second, Gregory developed a soteriology, or doctrine of salvation, which reflects the influence of Augustine. We find an emphasis upon the need for grace, upon the fallenness and sinfulness of humanity, upon the divine initiative in justification, and upon divine predestination. Salvation is understood to be *totally* a work of God, from its beginning to its end. Where the proponents of the "modern way" held that humans could initiate their justification by "doing their best," Gregory insisted that only God could initiate justification.

The "modern way" held that most (but not all) necessary soteriological resources were located *within* human nature. The merits of Christ are an example of a resource lying *outside* humanity; the ability to desist from sin and turn to righteousness is, for a writer such as Biel, an example of a vital soteriological resource located within humanity. In marked contrast, Gregory of Rimini argued that these resources were located exclusively outside human nature. Even the ability to desist from sin and turn to righteousness arose through the action of God, not through human action.

It is obvious that these two approaches represent two totally different ways of understanding the human and divine roles in justification. Although Gregory's academic Augustinianism was particularly associated with the Augustinian order, not every Augustinian monastery or university school seems to have adopted its ideas. Nevertheless, it seems that a school of thought which was strongly Augustinian in cast was in existence in the late Middle Ages on the eve of the Reformation. In many ways, the Wittenberg reformers, with their particular emphasis upon the anti-Pelagian writings of Augustine, may be regarded as having rediscovered and revitalized this tradition.

Humanism

The term "humanism" has now come to mean a worldview which denies the existence or relevance of God, or which is committed to a purely secular outlook. This is not what the word meant at the time of the Renaissance. Most humanists of the period were religious, and concerned to purify and renew Christianity, rather than eliminate it. The term "humanism" actually turns out to be quite difficult to define. In the recent past, two major lines of interpretation of the movement were predominant. According to the first, humanism was a movement devoted to the study of classical languages and literature; according to the second, humanism was basically a set of ideas, comprising the new philosophy of the Renaissance.

As will become clear, both these interpretations of humanism have serious shortcomings. For example, it is beyond doubt that the Renaissance witnessed the rise of classical scholarship. The Greek and Latin classics were widely studied in their original languages. It might therefore seem that humanism was essentially a scholarly movement devoted to the study of the classical period. This is to overlook, however, the question of *why* the humanists wished to study the classics in the first place. The evidence available unquestionably indicates that such study was regarded as a means to an end, rather than an end in itself. That end was the promotion of contemporary written and spoken eloquence. In other words, the humanists studied the classics as models of written eloquence, in order to gain inspiration and instruction. Classical learning and philological competence were simply the tools used to exploit the resources of antiquity. As has often been pointed out, the humanist writings devoted to the promotion of eloquence, written or spoken, far exceed those devoted to classical scholarship or philology.

According to several other recent interpreters of humanism, the movement embodied the new philosophy of the Renaissance, which arose as a reaction to scholasticism. Thus it was argued that the Renaissance was an age of Platonism, whereas scholasticism was a period of Aristotelianism. Others argued that the Renaissance was essentially an anti-religious phenomenon, foreshadowing the secularism of the eighteenth-century Enlightenment.

Two major difficulties confronted this rather ambitious interpretation of humanism. First, as we have seen, humanists appear to have been primarily concerned with the promotion of eloquence. While it is not true to say that humanists made no significant contribution to philosophy, the fact remains that they were primarily interested in the world of letters. Thus, in comparison with those devoted to the "pursuit of eloquence," there are remarkably few humanist writings devoted to philosophy and these are generally somewhat amateurish.

Second, intensive study of humanist writings uncovered the disquieting fact that "humanism" was remarkably heterogeneous. For example, many humanist writers did indeed favor Platonism – but others favored Aristotelianism. Some Italian humanists did indeed display what seemed to be anti-religious attitudes – but most Italian humanists were profoundly religious. Some humanists were indeed republicans – but others adopted different political attitudes. Recent studies have also drawn attention to a less attractive side of humanism – the obsession of some humanists with magic and superstition – which is difficult to harmonize with the conventional view of the movement. In short, it became increasingly clear that "humanism" seemed to lack any coherent philosophy. No single philosophical or political idea dominated or characterized the movement. It seemed to many that the term "humanism" would have to be dropped from the vocabulary of historians, because it had no meaningful content. Designating a writer as a "humanist" actually conveys little hard information concerning his or her philosophical, political, or religious views.

A more realistic approach, which has gained widespread acceptance in scholarly circles, is to view humanism as a cultural and educational movement, primarily concerned with the promotion of eloquence in its various forms. Its interests in morals, philosophy, and politics are of secondary importance. To be a humanist is to be concerned with eloquence first and foremost, and with other matters incidentally. Humanism was essentially a cultural program, which appealed to classical antiquity as a model of eloquence. In art and architecture, as in the written and spoken word, antiquity was seen as a cultural resource, which could be appropriated by the Renaissance. Humanism was thus concerned with *how ideas were obtained and expressed,* rather than with *the actual substance of those ideas.* A humanist might be a Platonist or an Aristotelian – but in both cases, the ideas involved derived from antiquity. A humanist might be a skeptic or a believer – but both attitudes could be defended from antiquity.

Northern European humanism

The form of "humanism" which proved to be of especial importance theologically is primarily northern European humanism, rather than Italian humanism. We must therefore consider what form this northern European movement took.

It is becoming increasingly clear that northern European humanism was decisively influenced by Italian humanism at every stage of its development. Three main channels for the diffusion of the methods and ideals of the Italian Renaissance into northern Europe have been identified:

1 Through northern European scholars moving south to Italy, perhaps to study at an Italian university or as part of a diplomatic mission. On returning to their homeland, they brought the spirit of the Renaissance back with them.
2 Through the foreign correspondence of the Italian humanists. Humanism was concerned with the promotion of written eloquence, and the writing of letters was seen as a means of embodying and spreading the ideals of the Renaissance. The foreign correspondence of Italian humanists was considerable, extending to most parts of northern Europe.
3 Through printed books, originating from sources such as the Aldine Press in Venice. These works were often reprinted by northern European presses, particularly those at Basel in Switzerland. Italian humanists often dedicated their works to northern European patrons, thus ensuring that they were taken notice of in potentially influential quarters.

Although there are major variations within northern European humanism, two ideals seem to have achieved widespread acceptance throughout the movement. First, we find the same concern for written and spoken eloquence, after the fashion of the classical period, as in the Italian Reformation. Second, we find a religious program directed toward the corporate revival of the Christian church. The Latin slogan *Christianismus renascens*, "Christianity being born again," summarizes the aims of this program, and indicates its relation to the "rebirth" of letters associated with the Renaissance.

In view of the importance of humanism to the Reformation in Europe, we shall consider some of its local variants, with particular reference to Switzerland, France, and England.

Swiss humanism

Perhaps on account of its geographical position, Switzerland proved especially receptive to the ideas of the Italian Renaissance. The University of Vienna attracted large numbers of students from this region. A palace revolution within the faculty of arts, engineered largely through the influence of Konrad Celtis, ensured that Vienna became a center of humanist learning in the final years of the fifteenth century, attracting individuals such as the great humanist writer Joachim von Watt, alias Vadian. Vadian, having gained every academic honor possible at Vienna, returned to his native town of St Gallen, becoming its leading citizen (Burgomeister) in 1529. The University of Basel also achieved a similar reputation in the 1510s, and became the center of a humanist group (usually known as a "sodality"), focusing on such individuals as Thomas Wyttenbach.

Swiss humanism has been the subject of intensive study, and its basic ethos is fairly well understood. For its leading representatives, Christianity was primarily a way of life, rather than a set of doctrines. Reform was indeed needed – but that reform related primarily to the morality of the church, and the need for personal moral renewal of individual believers. There was no pressure for a reform of church doctrine.

The ethos of Swiss humanism was strongly moralistic, with Scripture being regarded as prescribing correct moral behavior for Christians, rather than narrating the promises of God. This ethos has a number of significant implications, especially in relation to the doctrine of justification. In the first place, the questions which stimulated Luther's concern for the doctrine were quite absent from Swiss circles. Justification was something of a non-issue. Second, as it became an issue in Germany, a certain degree of anxiety became evident within Swiss humanist circles in the 1520s about Luther's doctrine of justification. To the Swiss humanists, Luther seemed to be developing ideas which were a radical threat to morality, and thus to the distinctive ethos of their movement.

The importance of these observations relates to Huldrych Zwingli, educated at the universities of Vienna (1498–1502) and Basel (1502–6). Zwingli's program of reform at Zurich, initiated in 1519, bears the hallmark of Swiss humanist moralism. Augustine, the "doctor of grace," does not appear to figure prominently in Zwingli's thought until the 1520s (and even then, his influence relates primarily to Zwingli's sacramental thinking). Zwingli finally broke with the moralism of Swiss humanism (probably around 1523, certainly by 1525), but until this point his program of reform was based upon the moralist educational outlook so characteristic of Swiss humanist sodalities of this period.

French humanism

In early sixteenth-century France, the study of law was in the process of radical revision. The absolutist French monarchy under Francis I, with its increasing trend toward administrative centralization, regarded legal reform as essential to the modernization of France. In order to speed up the process of reform, with its goal of formulating a legal system universally valid throughout France, it patronized a group of scholars, centered on the Universities of Bourges and Orléans, who were engaged on the theoretical aspects of general codes of law founded on universal principles. A pioneer amongst these latter was Guillaume Budé, who argued for a direct return to Roman law as a means of meeting the new legal needs of France which was both eloquent and economic. In contrast with the Italian custom (*mos italicus*) of reading classical legal texts in the light of the glosses and commentaries of medieval jurists, the French developed the procedure (*mos gallicus*) of appealing directly to the original classical legal sources in their original languages.

One direct result of the French humanist program of proceeding directly *ad fontes* was a marked impatience with glosses (annotations to the text) and commentaries. Far from being viewed as useful study tools, these became increasingly regarded as obstacles to engagement with the original text. The interpretations of classical Roman legal texts by writers such as Bartholus and Accursius came to be regarded as irrelevant. They were like distorting filters placed between the reader and the text. As humanist scholarship became more confident in its assertions, the reliability of Accursius and others was increasingly called into question. The great Spanish scholar Antonio Nebrija published a detailed account of errors he had detected in Accursius' glosses, while Rabelais wrote scornfully of "the inept opinions of Accursius."

The importance of this development to the Reformation must be noted. One student at Bourges and Orléans during the heyday of this French legal humanism was the future church reformer John Calvin, who probably arrived at Orléans in 1528. In studying civil law at Orléans and Bourges, Calvin came into first-hand contact with a major constituent element of the humanist movement. This encounter at least turned Calvin into a competent lawyer: when he was subsequently called upon to assist with the codification of the "laws and edicts" of Geneva, he was able to draw on his knowledge of the *corpus iuris civilis* for models of contract, property law, and judicial procedure. But Calvin learned more than this from French humanism.

The origins of Calvin's methods as perhaps the greatest biblical commentator and preacher of his age may be argued to lie in his study of law in the advanced atmosphere of Orléans and Bourges. There is every indication that Calvin learned from Budé the need to be a competent philologist, to approach a foundational text directly, to interpret it within the linguistic and historical parameters of its context, and apply it to the needs of his own day. It is precisely this attitude which undergirds Calvin's exposition of Scripture, especially in his sermons, in which he aims to fuse the horizons of Scripture and the context of his audience. French humanism gave Calvin both the incentive and the tools to enable the documents of yesteryear to interact with the situation of the city of Geneva in the 1550s.

English humanism

Perhaps the most important center of humanism in early sixteenth-century England was located at the University of Cambridge, although the importance of Oxford and London must not be understated. Cambridge was the home of the early English Reformation, centering on the "White Horse Circle" (named after a now-demolished tavern close to Queens' College), where individuals such as Robert Barnes met to devour and discuss the latest writings of Martin Luther during the early 1520s. It was only to be expected that the tavern should soon be nicknamed "little Germany," just as later the King Street area – once home of Cambridge's Communist Party – would be known as "little Moscow" during the 1930s.

KEY THEOLOGIANS

Of the many theologians of importance to have emerged during this period of enormous creativity, the following are of especial interest and importance.

Anselm of Canterbury (*c*.1033–1109)

Anselm was born in northern Italy, but soon moved to France, then establishing a reputation as a center for learning. He quickly mastered the arts of logic and grammar, and acquired a formidable reputation as a teacher at the Norman abbey of Bec. Standing at the dawn of the theological renaissance of the twelfth century, Anselm made decisive contributions in two areas of discussion: proofs for the existence of God, and the rational interpretation of Christ's death upon the cross.

The *Proslogion* (the word is virtually untranslatable) was written around 1079. It is a remarkable work, in which Anselm sets himself the task of formulating an argument which will lead to belief in the existence and character of God as highest good. The resulting analysis, often known as the "ontological argument," leads to the derivation of the existence of God from an affirmation of his being "that than which nothing greater can be conceived." Although the argument has been contested since its inception, it has remained one of the most intriguing components of philosophical theology to this day. The *Proslogion* is also of importance on account of its clear appeal to reason in matters of theology, and its appreciation of the role of logic. In many ways, the work anticipates the best aspects of scholastic theology. Anselm's phrase *fides quaerens intellectum* ("faith seeking understanding") has passed into widespread use.

Following the Norman invasion of England (1066), Anselm was invited to become Archbishop of Canterbury in 1093, thus ensuring the consolidation of Norman influence over the English church. It was not an entirely happy period of his life, due to a series of violent disputes between the church and the monarchy over land rights. During one period spent working away from England in Italy, Anselm penned perhaps his most important work, *Cur Deus homo* ("Why God became man"). In this work, Anselm seeks to set out a rational demonstration of the necessity of God becoming man, and an analysis of the benefits which accrue to humanity as a result of the incarnation and obedience of the Son of God. This argument, to be considered at length later in this work, remains of foundational importance to any discussion of "theories of the atonement" – in

113

other words, understandings of the meaning of the death and resurrection of Christ, and its significance for humanity. Once more, the work exhibits the characteristics which are typical of scholasticism at its best: The appeal to reason, the logical marshaling of arguments, the relentless exploration of the implications of ideas, and the fundamental conviction that, at its heart, the Christian gospel *is* rational, and can be *shown* to be rational.

Thomas Aquinas (*c.*1225–74)

Aquinas was born at the castle of Roccasecca in Italy, the youngest son of Count Landulf of Aquino. To judge by his nickname – "the dumb ox" – he was rather portly. In 1244, while in his late teens, Aquinas decided to join the Dominican order, also known as the "Order of Preachers." His parents were hostile to this idea: they rather hoped he would become a Benedictine, and perhaps end up as abbot of Monte Cassino, one of the most prestigious positions in the medieval church. His brothers forcibly imprisoned him in one of the family's castles for a year to encourage him to change his mind. Despite this intense opposition from his family, Aquinas eventually got his way, and ended up becoming one of the most important religious thinkers of the Middle Ages. One of his teachers is reported to have said that "the bellowing of that ox will be heard throughout the world."

Aquinas began his studies at Paris, before moving to Cologne in 1248. In 1252 he returned to Paris to study theology. Four years later, he was granted permission to teach theology at the university. For the next three years he lectured on Matthew's gospel and began to write the *Summa contra Gentiles*, "Summary against the Gentiles." In this major work, Aquinas provided important arguments in favor of the Christian faith for the benefit of missionaries working amongst Moslems and Jews. In 1266, he began the most famous of his many writings, usually known by its Latin title, *Summa Theologiae*. In this work, Thomas developed a detailed study of key aspects of Christian theology (such as the role of reason and faith), as well as a detailed analysis of key doctrinal questions (such as the divinity of Christ). The work is divided into three parts, with each of the first two parts subdivided into two. Part I deals chiefly with God the creator; Part II with the restoration of humanity to God; and Part III with the manner in which the person and work of Christ bring about the salvation of humanity.

On December 6, 1273, Aquinas declared that he could write no longer. "All that I have written seems like straw to me," he said. It is possible that he may have had some sort of breakdown, perhaps brought on by overwork. He died on March 7, 1274.

Amongst Aquinas' key contributions to theology, the following are of especial importance, and are discussed elsewhere in this volume:

- the "Five Ways" (arguments for the existence of God) (see pp. 127–33);
- the principle of analogy, which provides a theological foundation for knowing God through the creation;
- the relation between faith and reason (see pp. 118–20).

Duns Scotus (*c.*1265–1308)

Scotus was unquestionably one of the finest minds of the Middle Ages. In his short life, he taught at Cambridge, Oxford, and Paris, and produced three versions of a *Commentary on the Sentences.* Known as the "subtle doctor" on account of the very fine distinctions which he frequently drew between the possible meanings of terms, he was responsible for a number of developments of considerable significance to Christian theology. Only three can be noted here.

1   Scotus was a champion of the theory of knowledge associated with Aristotle. The earlier Middle Ages were dominated by a different theory of knowledge, going back to Augustine of Hippo, known as "illuminationism," in which knowledge was understood to arise from the illumination of the human intellect by God. This view, which was championed by writers such as Henry of Ghent, was subjected to devastating criticism by Scotus.

2   Scotus regarded the divine will as taking precedence over the divine intellect, a doctrine often referred to as *voluntarism*. Thomas Aquinas had argued for the primacy of the divine intellect; Scotus opened the way to new approaches to theology, based on the assumption of the priority of the divine will. An example illustrates the point. Consider the idea of merit – that is to say, a human moral action which is deemed worthy of reward by God. What is the basis of this decision? Aquinas argued that the divine intellect recognized the inherent worth of the human moral act. It then informed the will to reward it appropriately. Scotus argued along very different lines. The divine will to reward the moral action came before any evaluation of its inherent worth. This approach is of considerable importance in relation to the doctrines of justification and predestination, and will be considered in more detail later.

3   Scotus was a champion of the doctrine of the immaculate conception of Mary, the mother of Jesus. Thomas Aquinas had taught that Mary shared the common sinful condition of humanity. She was tainted by sin (Latin: *macula*), like everyone else, apart from Christ. Scotus, however, argued that Christ, by virtue of his perfect work of redemption, was able to keep Mary free from the taint of original sin. Such was the influence of Scotus that the "immaculate position" (from the Latin *immacula*, "free of sin") became dominant by the end of the Middle Ages.

William of Ockham (*c*.1285–1347)

In many ways, Ockham may be regarded as developing some of the lines of argument associated with Scotus. Of particular importance is his consistent defense of a voluntarist position, giving priority to the divine will over the divine intellect. It is, however, probably his philosophical position which has ensured his permanent place of note in the history of Christian theology. Two major elements of his teaching may be noted.

1   Ockham's Razor, often referred to as "the principle of parsimony." Ockham insisted that simplicity was both a theological and a philosophical virtue. His "razor" eliminated all hypotheses which were not absolutely essential. This had major implications for his theology of justification. Earlier medieval theologians (including Thomas Aquinas) had argued that God was obliged to justify sinful humanity by means of a "created habit of grace" – in other words, an intermediate supernatural entity, infused by God into the human soul, which permitted the sinner to be pronounced justified. Ockham dismissed this notion as an unnecessary irrelevance, and declared that justification was the direct acceptance of a sinner by God. The way was thus opened to the more personalist approach to justification associated with the early Reformation.

2   Ockham was a vigorous defender of nominalism. In part, this resulted from his use of the razor: Universals were declared to be a totally unnecessary hypothesis, and were thus eliminated. The growing impact of the "modern way" in western Europe owes a considerable debt to him. One aspect of his thought which proved to be of especial importance is the "dialectic between the two powers of God." This device allowed Ockham to contrast the way things are with the way things could have been. A full discussion of this follows later; for the moment, it is enough to note that Ockham made a decisive contribution to discussions of divine omnipotence, which are of continuing importance today.

Erasmus of Rotterdam (*c*.1469–1536)

Desiderius Erasmus is generally regarded as the most important humanist writer of the Renaissance, and had a profound impact upon Christian theology during the first half of the sixteenth century. Although not a Protestant in any sense of the term, Erasmus did much to lay the intellectual foundations of the Reformation, not least through his extensive editorial undertakings, including the production of the first printed text of the Greek New Testament. His *Enchiridion militis Christiani* ("Handbook of the Christian Soldier") was a landmark in religious publishing. Although the work was first published in 1503, and then reprinted in 1509, its real impact dates from its third printing in 1515. From that moment onward it became a cult work, apparently going through twenty-three editions in the next six years. Its appeal was to educated lay men and women, whom Erasmus regarded as the most important resource that the church possessed. Its amazing popularity in the years after 1515 makes it possible to suggest that it brought about a radical alteration in lay self-perception – and it can hardly be overlooked that the reforming rumbles at Zurich and Wittenberg date from soon after the *Enchiridion* became a best-seller.

The *Enchiridion* developed the revolutionary thesis that the church of the day could be reformed by a collective return to the writings of the fathers and Scripture. The regular reading of Scripture is put forward as the key to a new lay piety, on the basis of which the church may be renewed and reformed. Erasmus conceived of his work as a lay person's guide to Scripture, providing a simple yet learned exposition of the "philosophy of Christ." This "philosophy" is really a form of practical morality, rather than an academic philosophy: The New Testament concerns the knowledge of good and evil, in order that its readers may eschew the latter and love the former. The New Testament is the *lex Christi*, "the law of Christ," which Christians are called to obey. Christ is the example whom Christians are called to imitate. Yet Erasmus does not understand Christian faith to be a mere external observance of a moral code. His characteristically humanist emphasis upon inner religion leads him to suggest that reading of Scripture *transforms* its readers, giving them a new motivation to love God and their neighbors.

A number of features of this book are of particular importance. First, Erasmus understands the future vitality of Christianity to lie with the laity, not the clergy. The clergy are seen as educators, whose function is to allow the laity to achieve the same level of understanding as themselves. There is no room for any superstitions which give the clergy a permanent status superior to their lay charges. Second, Erasmus' strong emphasis upon the "inner religion" results in an understanding of Christianity which makes no reference to the church – its rites, priests, or institutions. Why bother confessing sins to another human, asks Erasmus, just because he's a priest, when you can confess them directly to God?

In addition to these radical suggestions, Erasmus undertook extensive scholarly projects. Two of these are of especial importance to the development of Christian theology:

1   The production of the first Greek New Testament. As noted earlier, this allowed theologians direct access to the original text of the New Testament, with explosive results.
2   The production of reliable editions of patristic works, including the writings of Augustine. Theologians thus had access to the full text of such major works, instead of having to rely upon second-hand quotations, often taken out of context. A new understanding of Augustine's theology began to

develop as a result, with significant implications for the theological development of the period.

KEY THEOLOGICAL DEVELOPMENTS

The major renaissance in theology which took place during the period under consideration focused on a number of issues, of which the following are of especial importance. They are simply noted at this point; detailed discussion of most of them will take place later in this work. The first six such developments are associated with scholasticism (see pp. 104–8), the last two with humanism (see pp. 108–13).

The Consolidation of the Patristic Heritage

When the Dark Ages lifted, Christian theologians tended to pick up where the great patristic writers had left off. In that the western church was Latin-speaking, it was natural that its theologians should turn to the substantial collection of works by Augustine of Hippo, and take this as a starting point for their own theological speculations. Peter Lombard's *Sentences* may be regarded as a critical compilation of quotations ("Sentences") drawn largely from the writings of Augustine, upon which medieval theologians were required to comment.

The Exploration of the Role of Reason in Theology

The new concern to establish Christian theology upon a totally reliable foundation led to a considered exploration of the role of reason in theology, a central and defining characteristic of scholasticism (see p. 104). As the theological renaissance of the early Middle Ages proceeded, two themes began to dominate theological debate: the need to *systematize* and *expand* Christian theology; and the need to *demonstrate the inherent rationality* of that theology. Although most early medieval theology was little more than a replay of the views of Augustine, there was growing pressure to systematize Augustine's ideas, and take them further. But how could this be done? A "theory of method" was urgently needed. And on the basis of what philosophical system could the rationality of Christian theology be demonstrated?

The eleventh-century writer Anselm of Canterbury gave expression to this basic belief of the rationality of the Christian faith in two phrases which have come to be linked with his name: *fides quaerens intellectum* ("faith seeking understanding"), and *credo ut intellegam* ("I believe, in order that I may understand"). His basic insight was that, while faith came before understanding, the content of that faith was nevertheless rational. These definitive formulae established the priority

118

of faith over reason, just as they asserted the entire reasonableness of faith. In the preface to his *Monologium*, Anselm stated explicitly that he would establish nothing in Scripture on the basis of Scripture itself; instead, he would establish everything that he could on the basis of "rational evidence and the natural light of truth." Nevertheless, Anselm is no rationalist; reason has its limits!

The eleventh and early twelfth centuries saw a growing conviction that philosophy could be an invaluable asset to Christian theology at two different levels. In the first place, it could demonstrate the reasonableness of faith, and thus defend it against non-Christian critics. In the second, it offered ways of systematically exploring and arranging the articles of faith, so that they could be better understood. But which philosophy? The answer to this question came through the rediscovery of the writings of Aristotle, in the late twelfth and early thirteenth centuries. By about 1270, Aristotle had become established as "the Philosopher." His ideas came to dominate theological thinking, despite fierce opposition from more conservative quarters.

Through the influence of writers such as Thomas Aquinas and Duns Scotus, Aristotle's ideas became established as the best means of consolidating and developing Christian theology. The ideas of Christian theology were thus arranged and correlated systematically, on the basis of Aristotelian presuppositions. Equally, the rationality of Christian faith was demonstrated on the basis of Aristotelian ideas. Thus some of Thomas Aquinas' famous "proofs" for the existence of God actually rely on principles of Aristotelian physics, rather than on any distinctively Christian insights.

Initially, this development was welcomed by many, who saw it as providing important ways of defending the rationality of the Christian faith – a discipline which has since come to be known as "apologetics," from the Greek word *apologia* (defense). Thomas Aquinas' *Summa contra Gentiles* is an excellent example of a work of theology which draws on Aristotelianism. At points, the argument seems to work like this: If you can agree with the Aristotelian ideas presented in this writing, then you ought to become a Christian. As Aristotle was highly regarded by many Moslem academics of the period, Thomas can be seen as exploiting the apologetic potential of this philosopher.

This development came to be viewed with concern by some later medieval writers, such as Hugolino of Orvieto. A number of central Christian insights seemed to have been lost, as a result of a growing reliance upon the ideas and methods of a pagan philosopher. Particular concern centered on the doctrine of justification. The idea of the "righteousness of God" came to be discussed in terms of the Aristotelian idea of "distributive justice." Here, "righteousness" (*iustitia*) was defined in terms of "giving someone what they were entitled to." This seemed to lead to a doctrine of justification by merit. In other words, justification takes place on the basis of entitlement, rather than grace. It can be shown without difficulty that this concern lies behind Martin Luther's growing dislike of Aristotle, and his eventual break with scholastic doctrines of justification.

The Development of Theological Systems

We have already noted the pressure to consolidate the patristic, and especially the Augustinian, heritage (p. 118). This pressure to systematize, which is integral to scholasticism, led to the development of sophisticated theological systems, which Etienne Gilson, a noted historian of the period, described as "cathedrals of the mind." This development is perhaps best seen in Thomas Aquinas' *Summa Theologiae*, which represents one of the most forceful statements of the comprehensive and all-embracing character of this approach to Christian theology.

The Development of Sacramental Theology

The early church had been somewhat imprecise in its discussion of the sacraments. There was little general agreement concerning either how a sacrament was to be defined, or what items were to be included in a list of the sacraments (see pp. 139–43). Baptism and eucharist were generally agreed to be sacramental; there was relatively little agreement on anything else. However, with the theological renaissance of the Middle Ages, the church was coming to play an increasingly important role in society. There was new pressure for the church to place its acts of public worship on a secure intellectual footing, and to consolidate the theoretical aspects of its worship. As a result, sacramental theology developed considerably during the period. Agreement was reached on the definition of a sacrament, the number, and the precise identity of these sacraments.

The Development of the Theology of Grace

A central element of the Augustinian heritage was a theology of grace. However, Augustine's theology of grace had been stated in a polemical context. In other words, Augustine had been obliged to state his theology of grace in the heat of a controversy, often in response to the challenges and provocations of his opponents. As a result, his writings on the subject were often unsystematic. Occasionally, Augustine developed distinctions in response to the needs of the moment, and failed to lay an adequate theological foundation for them. The theologians of the Middle Ages saw themselves as charged with the task of consolidating Augustine's doctrine of grace, placing it upon a more reliable foundation, and exploring its consequences. As a result, the doctrines of grace and justification were developed considerably during the period, laying the foundation for the Reformation debates over these central issues.

The Role of Mary in the Scheme of Salvation

This new interest in grace and justification led to a new concern to understand the role of Mary, the mother of Jesus Christ, in salvation. Growing interest in devotion to Mary, linked with intense theological speculation concerning the nature of original sin and redemption, led to a series of developments relating to Mary. Many of these are linked with Duns Scotus, who placed Mariology (that is, the area of theology dealing with Mary) on a considerably more developed foundation than hitherto. Intense debate broke out between "maculists" (who held that Mary was subject to original sin, like everyone else) and "immaculists" (who held that she was preserved from the taint of original sin). There was also considerable discussion over whether Mary could be said to be "coredemptrix" (that is to say, whether she was to be regarded as a figure of redemption, in a manner similar to Jesus Christ).

Returning Directly to the Sources of Christian Theology

A central element of the humanist agenda was the return to the original sources of western European culture in classical Rome and Athens. The theological counterpart to this element was the direct return to the foundational resources of Christian theology, above all in the New Testament. This agenda proved to be of major significance, as will be seen later (see p. 146). One of its most important consequences was a new appreciation of the foundational importance of Scripture as a theological resource. As interest in Scripture developed, it became increasingly clear that existing Latin translations of this source were inadequate. Supreme among these was the "Vulgate," a Latin translation of the Bible which achieved widespread influence during the Middle Ages. As revision of translations, especially the Vulgate, proceeded, it became clear that theological revision was inevitable.

The rise of humanist textual and philological techniques was to expose distressing discrepancies between the Vulgate and the texts it purported to translate – and thus open the way to doctrinal reform as a consequence. It is for this reason that humanism is of decisive importance to the development of medieval theology: It demonstrated the total unreliability of this translation of the Bible – and hence, it seemed, of theologies based upon it. The biblical basis of scholasticism seemed to collapse, as humanism uncovered error after error in its translation. We shall explore this point further in what follows; it is unquestionably one of the most significant developments in the history of Christian theology at this time.

The Critique of the Vulgate Translation of Scripture

The literary and cultural program of humanism can be summarized in the slogan *ad fontes* – "back to the original sources." The "filter" of medieval commentaries – whether on legal texts or on the Bible – is abandoned, in order to engage directly with the original texts. Applied to the Christian church, the slogan *ad fontes* meant a direct return to the title-deeds of Christianity – to the patristic writers, and supremely to the Bible, studied in its original languages. This necessitated direct access to the Greek text of the New Testament.

The first printed Greek New Testament was produced by Erasmus in 1516. Erasmus' text was not as reliable as it ought to have been: he had access to a mere four manuscripts for most of the New Testament, and only one for its final part, the Book of Revelation. As it happened, that manuscript left out five verses, which Erasmus himself had to translate into Greek from the Latin of the Vulgate. Nevertheless, it proved to be a literary milestone. For the first time, theologians had the opportunity of comparing the original Greek text of the New Testament with the later Vulgate translation into Latin.

Drawing on work carried out earlier by the Italian humanist Lorenzo Valla, Erasmus showed that the Vulgate translation of several major New Testament texts could not be justified. As a number of medieval church practices and beliefs were based upon these texts, Erasmus' allegations were viewed with consternation by many conservative Catholics (who wanted to retain these practices and beliefs) and with equally great delight by the reformers (who wanted to eliminate them). Three classic examples of translation errors will indicate the relevance of Erasmus' biblical scholarship.

1   Much medieval theology justified the inclusion of matrimony in the list of sacraments on the basis of a New Testament text which – at least, in the Vulgate translation – spoke of marriage being a *sacramentum* (Ephesians 5: 31–2). Erasmus pointed out that the Greek word (*musterion*) here translated as "sacrament" simply meant "mystery." There was no reference whatsoever to marriage being a "sacrament." One of the classic proof texts used by medieval theologians to justify the inclusion of matrimony in the list of sacraments was thus rendered virtually useless.

2   The Vulgate translated the opening words of Jesus' ministry (Matthew 4: 17) as "*do penance*, for the kingdom of heaven is at hand." This translation suggested that the coming of the kingdom of heaven had a direct connection with the sacrament of penance. Erasmus, again following Valla, pointed out that the Greek should be translated as "*repent*, for the Kingdom of heaven is at hand." In other words, where the Vulgate seemed to refer to an outward practice (the sacrament of penance), Erasmus insisted that the reference was to an inward

psychological attitude – that of "being repentant." Once more, an important justification of the sacramental system of the medieval church was challenged.

3 According to the Vulgate, Gabriel greeted Mary as "the one who is full of grace (*gratia plena*)" (Luke 1: 28), thus suggesting the image of a reservoir full of grace, which could be drawn upon at time of need. But, as Erasmus pointed out, the Greek simply meant "favored one," or "one who has found favor." Once more, an important feature of medieval theology seemed to be contradicted by humanist New Testament scholarship.

These developments undermined the credibility of the Vulgate translation, and opened the way to theological revision on the basis of a better understanding of the biblical text. It also demonstrated the importance of biblical scholarship in relation to theology. Theology could not be permitted to base itself upon translation mistakes! The recognition of the vitally important role of biblical scholarship to Christian theology thus dates from the second decade of the sixteenth century. It also led to the theological concerns of the Reformation, to which we shall turn in the next chapter.

Our attention now turns to Byzantine theology, which flourished in eastern Europe during the Middle Ages. Although pressure on space prevents a detailed discussion of its leading themes and theologians, we shall consider some of its more important features.

Byzantine Theology

"Byzantine theology" takes its name from the Greek city of Byzantium, which Constantine chose as the site of his new capital city in 330. At this point, it was renamed "Constantinople" ("city of Constantine"). However, the name of the older town remained, and gave its name to the distinctive style of theology which flourished in this region until the fall of Constantinople to invading Islamic armies in 1453. Constantinople was not the only center of Christian thought in the eastern Mediterranean. Egypt and Syria had been centers of theological reflection for some time. However, as political power increasingly came to be concentrated on the imperial city, so its status as a theological center advanced correspondingly. During the time of Justinian (527–65), Byzantine theology began to emerge as an intellectual force of some importance. As the eastern and western churches became increasingly alienated from each other (a process which had begun long before the final schism of 1054), so Byzantine thinkers often emphasized their divergence from western theology (for example, in relation to the *filioque* clause: see p. 61), thus reinforcing the distinctiveness of their approach through polemical writings. For example, Byzantine writers tended to understand salvation in terms of *deification*, rather than western legal or relational categories. In addition, they found themselves puzzled by the doctrines of purgatory which were gaining the ascendancy in western Catholic circles. Any attempt to achieve a degree of reunion between east and west during the Middle Ages was thus complicated by a complex network of political, historical and theological factors. By the time of the fall of Constantinople, the differences between east and west remained as wide as ever. With the fall of Byzantium, intellectual and political leadership within Orthodoxy tended to pass to Russia. The Russians had been converted through Byzantine missions in the tenth century, and took the side of the Greeks in the schism of 1054. By the end of the fifteenth century, Moscow and Kiev were firmly established as patriarchates, each with its own distinctive style of Orthodox theology.

In order to understand the distinctive nature of Byzantine theology, it is necessary to appreciate the ethos which lies behind it. Byzantine theologians were not particularly concerned with systematic formulations of the Christian faith. For them, Christian theology was something "given," and which therefore required to be defended against its opponents and explained to its adherents. The idea of "systematic theology" is somewhat foreign to the general Byzantine ethos. Even John of Damascus (*c.*675–*c.*749), whose work *de fide orthodoxa* ("On the Orthodox Faith") is of considerable importance in the consolidation of a distinctively eastern Christian theology, is to be seen as an expositor of the faith, rather than as a speculative or original thinker. Indeed, Byzantine theology can be regarded as remaining faithful to a principle originally set out by Athanasius, in his writing *de incarnatione* ("on the incarnation"), which affirmed that theology was the expression of the mind of the saints. Byzantine theology (including its modern descendants in both Greek and Russian Orthodoxy) is thus strongly orientated toward the idea of *paradosis* ("tradition"), particularly the writings of the Greek fathers. Writers such as Gregory of Nyssa, Maximus the Confessor, and the writer who adopted the pseudonym "Dionysius the Areopagite," are of particular importance in this respect.

Two controversies are of particular importance. The first, which broke out during the period 725–842, is usually referred to as the iconoclastic ("breaking of images") controversy. It erupted over the decision of Emperor Leo III (717–42) to destroy icons, on the grounds that they were barriers to the conversion of Jews and Moslems. The controversy was mainly political, although there were some serious theological issues at stake, most notably the extent to which the doctrine of the incarnation justified the depiction of God in the form of images. The second, which broke out in the fourteenth century, focused on the issue of hesychasm (Greek: *hesychia* = silence), a style of meditation through physical exercises which enabled believers to see the "divine light" with their own eyes. Hesychasm placed considerable emphasis upon the idea of "inner quietness" as a means of achieving a direct inner vision of God. It was particularly associated with writers such as Symeon the New Theologian and Gregory Palamas (*c.*1296–1359), who was elected as archbishop of Thessalonika in 1347. Its opponents argued that its methods tended to minimize the difference between God and creatures, and were particularly alarmed by the suggestion that God could be "seen."

In responding to this criticism, Palamas developed the doctrine now generally known as "Palamism," which draws a distinction between the divine energies and the divine essence. The distinction allowed Palamas to defend the Hesychastic approach by affirming that it enabled believers to encounter the divine energies, but not the unseen and ineffable divine essence. Believers cannot participate directly in the divine essence; however, they are able to participate directly in the uncreated energies, which are God's mode of union with believers. Palamas' theology was espoused and developed particularly by the lay theologian Nicolas Cabasilis (*c.*1320–*c.*1390), whose *Life in Christ* remains a classic work of Byzantine spirituality. His work has been reappropriated in more recent years by neo-Palamite writers such as Vladimir Lossky and John Meyendorff.

Constantinople soon became a center of missionary activity. At some point around the year 860, the Moravian ruler Rastislav asked the Byzantine emperor to send missionaries to his people in central Europe. Two Greek brothers, Cyril and Methodius, were sent in response to this request. This development was of particular importance to the formation of eastern European culture. Not only did it eventually lead to the dominance of Orthodoxy in the region of eastern Europe; it also had a major impact on the alphabets used in the region. Cyril devised an alphabet, suitable for writing down the Slavic languages. This became the basis for the modern Cyrillic alphabet, named after the younger of the two "apostles of the Slavs." The conversion of Moravia was followed by that of Bulgaria and Serbia later that century. This was followed by the conversion of the Russians, at some point around the year 988.

As the eastern and western churches became increasingly alienated from each other (a process which had begun long before the final schism of 1054), so Byzantine thinkers often emphasized their divergence from western theology (for example, in relation to the *filioque* clause: see p. 61), thus reinforcing the distinctiveness of their approach through polemical writings. For example, Byzantine writers tended to understand salvation in terms of *deification*, rather than western legal or relational categories. Any attempt to achieve a degree of reunion between east and west during the Middle Ages was thus complicated by a complex network of political, historical, and theological factors. It is worth repeating that by the time of the fall of Constantinople, the differences between east and west remained as wide as ever. With the fall of Byzantium, intellectual and political leadership within Orthodoxy tended to pass to Russia. The Russians, who had been converted through Byzantine missions in the tenth century, took the side of the Greeks in the schism of 1054. By the end of the fifteenth century,

Moscow and Kiev were firmly established as patriarchates, each with its own distinctive style of Orthodox Christianity, which remains of major importance today. Other regions which converted to Orthodoxy during this period include Serbia and Bulgaria.

It is clear that the flourishing of the eastern Orthodox church in Russia during the Middle Ages was of major importance to the shaping of Moscovite Russia. It is estimated that during the fourteenth, fifteenth, and sixteenth centuries, more than 250 monasteries and convents were established in the region. The monastic revival, under the guidance of leaders such as St Sergius of Radonezh (died 1392), gave further impetus to the missionary efforts of the Russian church. During the thirteenth century, for example, the Finnish-speaking peoples of the Karelia region were converted to Orthodoxy.

The fall of Constantinople in 1453 caused a major development within Russian Orthodoxy. Traditionally, each new metropolitan of the Russian church was installed by the patriarch of Constantinople, and looked to the Byzantine emperor (based in Constantinople) for its political leadership. The Russian church was very much a daughter of the Byzantine church. But with the fall of Constantinople, this traditional approach became a thing of the past. What could replace it? In the event, the eastern Orthodox church in Moscow became autocephalous – that is, self-governing. As a result, the political and cultural links between the Russian church and state became deeper. By 1523, the relation between church and state was so close that some writers began to refer to Moscow as the "Third Rome," to be treated with respect equal to Rome and Constantinople. Philotheus of Pskov proclaimed that, now that Rome and Byzantium had become corrupt, the leadership of the Christian world had passed to Moscow: "two Romes have fallen; the third stands; there will be no fourth."

It will be clear from the material presented in this chapter that both western and eastern Christian theology underwent significant development during the Middle Ages and Renaissance. Subsequent generations of theologians have regarded the period as being of landmark importance in relation to a number of areas of theological reflection, with a number of its writers being regarded as possessing permanent importance. The rise and fall of Byzantium is of particular importance to a full understanding of the subsequent development of eastern Orthodoxy in Russia and Greece (see pp. 241–2), just as the rise of scholasticism and humanism were of considerable importance to the shaping of western theology. In the following chapter, our attention focuses particularly on the western church, as we explore the emergence of the movement widely known as "the Reformation," which is generally regarded as establishing the distinctive features of modern western Christianity, whether Roman Catholic or Protestant.

KEY NAMES, WORDS, AND PHRASES

By the end of this chapter, you will have encountered the following terms, some of which will recur during the work. Ensure that you are familiar with them! They have been capitalized as you are likely to encounter them in normal use.

ad fontes	Middle Ages
apologetics	ontological argument
Byzantine	Renaissance
Five Ways	scholasticism
humanism	theories of the atonement
immaculate conception	voluntarism
medieval	Vulgate

QUESTIONS

1 What was the language spoken by most western theologians during this period?
2 "Humanists were people who were interested in studying classical Rome." How helpful is this definition of the term?
3 What were the major themes of scholastic theology?
4 Why was there such interest in the theology of the sacraments during the Middle Ages?
5 What is meant by the slogan *ad fontes*?

Case Study 2.1   Arguments for the Existence of God

CASE
STUDIES

The "ontological argument" is first set out in Anselm's *Proslogion*, a work which dates from 1079. (The term "ontological" refers to the branch of philosophy which deals with the notion of "being.") Anselm himself does not refer to his discussion as an "ontological" argument. When his contemporaries wished to refer to his approach, they dubbed it "Anselm's argument." In fact, there is really no "ontological" character to the argument, as Anselm presents it; and Anselm never presents his reflections as an "argument" for the existence of God. The *Proslogion* is really a work of meditation, not of logical argument. In the course of this work, Anselm reflects on how self-evident the idea of God has become to him, and what the implications of this might be.

In his *Proslogion*, Anselm offers a definition of God as "that than which no greater thing can be thought (*aliquid quo maius cogitari non potest*)." He argues that, if this definition of God is correct, it necessarily implies the existence of God.

> **Anselm of Canterbury (*c.*1033–1109).** Born in Italy, Anselm migrated to Normandy in 1059, entering the famous monastery of Bec, becoming its prior in 1063, and abbot in 1078. In 1093 he was appointed Archbishop of Canterbury. He is chiefly noted for his strong defense of the intellectual foundations of Christianity, and is especially associated with the "ontological argument" for the existence of God.

The reason for this is as follows. If God does not exist, the idea of God remains, yet the reality of God is absent. Yet the reality of God is greater than the idea of God. Therefore, if God is "that than which no greater thing can be thought," the idea of God must lead to accepting the reality of God, in that otherwise the mere idea of God is the greatest thing which can be thought. And this contradicts the definition of God on which the argument is based. Therefore, given the existence of the idea of God, and the acceptance of the definition of God as "that than which no greater thing can be thought," the reality of God necessarily follows. Note that the Latin verb *cogitare* is sometimes translated as "conceive," leading to the definition of God as "that than which no greater thing can be conceived." Both translations are acceptable.

It may be helpful to go over this again. God is defined as "that than which nothing greater can be conceived." Now the idea of such a being is one thing; the reality is another. Thinking of a 100-dollar bill is quite different from having a 100-dollar bill in your hands – and much less satisfying, as well. Anselm's point is this: the idea of something is inferior to the reality. So the idea of God as "that than which nothing greater can be conceived" contains a contradiction – because the reality of God would be superior to this idea. In other words, if this definition of God is correct, and exists in the human mind, then the corresponding reality must also exist.

2.1.1 Anselm of Canterbury on God's Existence

This [definition of God] is indeed so true that it cannot be thought of as not being true. For it is quite possible to think of something whose non-existence cannot be thought of. This must be greater than something whose non-existence can be thought of. So if this thing (than which no greater thing can be thought) can be
5   thought of as not existing, then, that very thing than which a greater thing cannot be thought is not that than which a greater cannot be thought. This is a contradiction. So it is true that there exists something than which nothing greater can be thought, that it cannot be thought of as not existing. And you are this thing, O Lord our God! So truly therefore do you exist, O Lord my God, that you cannot
10 be thought of as not existing, and with good reason; for if a human mind could

think of anything greater than you, the creature would rise above the Creator and judge you; which is obviously absurd. And in truth whatever else there be beside you may be thought of as not existing. So you alone, most truly of all, and therefore most of all, have existence: because whatever else exists, does not exist as truly as you, and therefore exists to a lesser degree.

15

This is an important argument, and it is worth focusing on its central elements.

1   Note the definition of God which Anselm offers (lines 4–6). No justification is offered for the notion of God as "that than which no greater thing can be thought." It is taken to be self-evidently true.
2   Anselm then argues that a real entity is greater than a mere idea (lines 4–9). This point, which is assumed to be obvious to the reader, is the second critical stage in the argument, the first being the definition of God which was offered earlier in the passage.
3   The conclusion of the argument is that, since the *idea* of God is clearly inferior to the *reality* of God, it must follow that God exists (lines 9–15). Otherwise, the definition of God which was set out is shown to be inconsistent.

This is an important argument, but it did not persuade one of his earliest critics, a Benedictine monk named Gaunilo who made a response known as "A Reply on Behalf of the Fool" (the reference being to Psalm 14: 1, cited by Anselm, "The fool says in his heart that there is no God"). There is, according to Gaunilo, an obvious logical weakness in Anselm's "argument" (although it must be stressed that Anselm does not really regard it as an argument in the first place). Imagine, Gaunilo suggests, an island, so lovely that a more perfect island cannot be conceived. By the same argument, Gaunilo suggests, that island must exist, in that the reality of the island is necessarily more perfect that the mere idea. In much the same way, we might argue that the idea of a 100-dollar bill seems, according to Anselm, to imply that we have such a bill in our hands. The mere idea of something – whether a perfect island or God – thus does not guarantee its existence.

2.1.2   Gaunilo's Reply to Anselm's Argument

People say that somewhere in the ocean there is an island which, because of the difficulty (or rather the impossibility) of finding that which does not exist, some have called the "Lost Island." And we are told that it is blessed with all manner of priceless riches and delights in abundance, far more than the Happy Isles, and,

5   having no owner or inhabitant, it is superior in every respect in the abundance of
     its riches to all those other lands that are inhabited by people. Now, if someone
     were to tell me about this, I shall easily understand what is said, since there is
     nothing difficult about it. But if I am then told, as though it were a direct
     consequence of this: "You cannot any more doubt that this island that is more
10   excellent than all other lands truly exists somewhere in reality than you can doubt
     that it is in your mind; and since it is more excellent to exist not just in your mind
     but in reality as well, therefore it must exist. For if it did not exist, any other land
     existing in reality would be more excellent than it, and so this island, already
     conceived by you to be more excellent than others, will not be more excellent."
15   I say that if anyone wanted to persuade me in this way that this island really exists
     beyond all doubt, I should either think that they were joking, or I should find it
     hard to decide which of us I ought to think of as the bigger fool: I myself, if I agreed
     with them, or they, if they thought that they had proved the existence of this island
     with any certainty, unless they had first persuaded me that its very excellence exists
20   in my mind precisely as a thing existing truly and indubitably and not just as
     something unreal or doubtfully real.

The response offered by Gaunilo is widely regarded as exposing a serious
weakness in Anselm's argument. The text itself is so clear that no comment is
needed. It may, however, be pointed out that Anselm is not so easily dismissed.
Part of his argument is that it is an essential part of the definition of God that he
is "that than which nothing greater can be conceived." God therefore belongs
to a totally different category than islands or dollar bills. It is part of the nature
of God to transcend everything else. Once the believer has come to understand
what the word "God" means, then God really does exist for him or her. This is
the intention of Anselm's meditation: to reflect on how the Christian understanding of the nature of God reinforces belief in his reality. The "argument"
does not really have force outside this context of faith, and Anselm never intended
it to be used in this general philosophical manner.

Furthermore, Anselm argued that Gaunilo had not entirely understood him.
The argument which he set out in the *Proslogion* did not involve the idea that
there is a being that is, as a matter of fact, greater than any other being; rather,
Anselm had argued for a being so great that a greater one could not even be
conceived. The argument continues, and it remains a disputed question to this
day as to whether Anselm's argument has a genuine basis.

A very different approach (or, perhaps we should say, range of approaches) is
offered by the great scholastic writer Thomas Aquinas. Aquinas believed that it
was entirely proper to identify pointers toward the existence of God, drawn from
general human experience of the world. So what kind of pointers does Aquinas
identify? The basic line of thought guiding Aquinas is that the world mirrors God,

Thomas Aquinas (*c*.1225–74). Probably the most famous and influential theologian of the Middle Ages. Born in Italy, he achieved his fame through his teaching and writing at the University of Paris and other northern universities. His fame rests chiefly on his *Summa Theologiae*, composed toward the end of his life and not totally finished at the time of his death. However, he also wrote many other significant works, particularly the *Summa contra Gentiles*, which represents a major statement of the rationality of the Christian faith.

as its creator – an idea which is given more formal expression in his doctrine of the "analogy of being." Just as an artist might sign a painting to identify it as his handiwork, so God has stamped a divine "signature" upon the creation. What we observe in the world – for example, its signs of ordering – can be explained on the basis of the existence of God as its creator. God is both its first cause and its designer. God both brought the world into existence, and impressed the divine image and likeness upon it.

So where might we look in creation to find evidence for the existence of God? Aquinas argues that the ordering of the world is the most convincing evidence of God's existence and wisdom. This basic assumption underlies each of the "Five Ways," although it is of particular importance in the case of the argument often referred to as the "argument from design" or the "teleological argument." We shall consider each of these "ways" individually.

The first way begins from the observation that things in the world are in motion or change. The world is not static, but is dynamic. Examples of this are easy to list. Rain falls from the sky. Stones roll down valleys. The earth revolves around the sun (a fact, incidentally, unknown to Aquinas). This, the first of Aquinas' arguments, is normally referred to as the "argument from motion"; however, it is clear that the "movement" in question is actually understood in more general terms, so that the term "change" is more appropriate as a translation at points.

So how did nature come to be in motion? Why is it changing? Why isn't it static? Aquinas argues that everything which moves is moved by something else. For every motion, there is a cause. Things don't just move – they are moved. Now each cause of motion must itself have a cause. And that cause must have a cause as well. And so Aquinas argues that there is a whole series of causes of motion lying behind the world as we know it. Now unless there is an infinite number of these causes, Aquinas argues, there must be a single cause right at the origin of the series. From this original cause of motion, all other motion is ultimately derived. This is the origin of the great chain of causality which we see reflected in the way the world behaves. From the fact that things are in motion, Aquinas thus argues for the existence of a single original cause of all this motion – and this, he concludes, is none other than God.

The second way begins from the idea of causation. In other words, Aquinas notes the existence of causes and effects in the world. One event (the effect) is explained by the influence of another (the cause). The idea of motion, which we looked at briefly above, is a good example of this cause-and-effect sequence. Using a line of reasoning similar to that used above, Aquinas thus argues that all effects may be traced back to a single original cause – which is God.

The third way concerns the existence of contingent beings. In other words, the world contains beings (such as human beings) which are not there as a matter of necessity. Aquinas contrasts this type of being with a necessary being (one who is there as a matter of necessity). Whilst God is a necessary being, Aquinas argues that humans are contingent beings. The fact that we *are* here needs explanation. Why are we here? What happened to bring us into existence? Aquinas argues that a being comes into existence because something which already exists brought it into being. In other words, our existence is caused by another being. We are the effects of a series of causation. Tracing this series back to its origin, Aquinas declares that this original cause of being can only be someone whose existence is necessary – in other words, God.

The fourth way begins from human values, such as truth, goodness, and nobility. Where do these values come from? What causes them? Aquinas argues that there must be something which is in itself true, good, and noble, and that this brings into being our ideas of truth, goodness, and nobility. The origin of these ideas, Aquinas suggests, is God, who is their original cause.

The fifth and final way is the teleological argument itself. Aquinas notes that the world shows obvious traces of intelligent design. Natural processes and objects seem to be adapted with certain definite objectives in mind. They seem to have a purpose. They seem to have been designed. But things don't design themselves: they are caused and designed by someone or something else. Arguing from this observation, Aquinas concludes that the source of this natural ordering must be conceded to be God.

It will be obvious that most of Aquinas' arguments are rather similar. Each depends on tracing a causal sequence back to its single origin, and identifying this with God. A number of criticisms of the "Five Ways" were made by Aquinas' critics during the Middle Ages, such as Duns Scotus and William of Ockham. The following are especially important:

1   Why is the idea of an infinite regression of causes impossible? For example, the argument from motion only really works if it can be shown that the sequence of cause and effect stops somewhere. There has to be, according to Aquinas, a Prime Unmoved Mover. But he fails to demonstrate this point.
2   Why do these arguments lead to belief in only *one* God? The argument from motion, for example, could lead to belief in a number of Prime Unmoved Movers. There seems to be no especially pressing reason for insisting that

there can only be one such cause, except for the fundamental Christian insistence that, as a matter of fact, there is only one such God.

3   These arguments do not demonstrate that God continues to exist. Having caused things to happen, God might cease to exist. The continuing existence of events does not necessarily imply the continuing existence of their originator. Aquinas' arguments, Ockham suggests, might lead to a belief that God existed once upon a time – but not necessarily now. Ockham developed a somewhat complex argument, based on the idea of God continuing to sustain the universe, which attempts to get round this difficulty.

In the end, Aquinas' arguments only go some way toward suggesting that it is reasonable to believe in a creator of the world, or an intelligent being who is able to cause effects in the world. Nevertheless, a leap of faith is still required. It still remains to be shown that this creator or intelligent being *is* the God which Christians know, worship, and adore. Aquinas' arguments could lead to faith in the existence of a god rather like that favored by the Greek philosopher Aristotle – an Unmoved Mover, who is distant from and uninvolved in the affairs of the world.

Case Study 2.2   Understandings of the Atonement

The medieval period saw considerable interest in the doctrine of the work of Christ (often also referred to as "the atonement"), both in academic theology and in popular religion.

One theme which became especially significant in popular religion was the idea of the "harrowing of Hell." The background to this idea is found in the New Testament itself. The New Testament and early church laid considerable emphasis upon the victory gained by Christ over sin, death, and Satan through Christ's Crucifixion and resurrection. This theme of victory, often linked liturgically with the Easter celebrations, was of major importance within the western Christian theological tradition until the Enlightenment. The theme of "Christ the victor (*Christus Victor*)" brought together a series of themes, centering on the idea of a decisive victory over forces of evil and oppression.

The image of Christ's death as a ransom came to be of central importance to Greek patristic writers, such as Irenaeus. But what were the implications of this idea? If Christ's death was a ransom, Origen argued, it must have been paid to someone. But to whom? It could not have been paid to God, in that God was not holding sinners to ransom. Therefore it had to be paid to the devil. Gregory the Great developed this idea still further. The devil had acquired rights over fallen humanity, which God was obliged to respect. The only means by which humanity could be released from this satanic domination and oppression was through the devil exceeding the limits of his authority, and thus being obliged to forfeit his rights. So how could this be achieved? Gregory suggests that it could come about if a sinless person were to enter the world, yet in the form of a normal sinful person. The devil would not notice until it was too late: in claiming authority over this sinless person, the devil would have overstepped the limits of his authority, and thus be obliged to abandon his rights.

Gregory suggested the image of a baited hook: Christ's humanity is the bait, and his divinity the hook. The devil, like a great sea-monster, snaps at the bait – and then discovers, too late, the hook. "The bait tempts in order that the hook may wound. Our Lord therefore, when coming for the redemption of humanity, made a kind of hook of himself for the death of the devil." Other writers explored other images for the same idea – that of trapping the devil. Christ's death was like a net for catching birds, or a trap for catching mice. It was this aspect of this approach to the meaning of the cross that caused the most disquiet subsequently. It seemed that God was guilty of deception. It was against any such idea of deception on the part of God that Anselm of Canterbury reacted – an idea to which we shall return presently.

The imagery of victory over the devil proved to have enormous popular appeal. The medieval idea of "the harrowing of hell" bears witness to its power. According to this, after dying upon the cross, Christ descended to hell, and broke down its gates in order that the imprisoned souls might go free. The idea rested (rather tenuously, it has to be said) upon 1 Peter 3: 18–22, which makes reference to Christ "preaching to the spirits in prison." The great medieval hymn "You choirs of New Jerusalem," written by Fulbert of Chartres, expresses this theme in two of its verses, picking up the theme of Christ, as the lion of Judah (Revelation 5: 5) defeating Satan, the serpent (Genesis 3: 15):

> For Judah's lion bursts his chains
> Crushing the serpent's head;
> And cries aloud through death's domain
> To wake the imprisoned dead.
>
> Devouring depths of hell their prey
> At his command restore;
> His ransomed hosts pursue their way
> Where Jesus goes before.

A similar idea can be found in a fourteenth-century English mystery play, which describes the "harrowing of hell" in the following manner:

> And when Christ was dead, his spirit went in haste to hell. And soon he broke down the strong gates that were wrongfully barred against him. . . . He bound Satan fast with eternal bonds, and so shall Satan ever remain bound until the day of doom. He took with him Adam and Eve and others that were dear to him . . . all these he led out of hell and set in paradise.

Anselm of Canterbury (*c.*1033–1109). Born in Italy, Anselm migrated to Normandy in 1059, entering the famous monastery of Bec, becoming its prior in 1063, and abbot in 1078. In 1093 he was appointed Archbishop of Canterbury. He is chiefly noted for his strong defense of the intellectual foundations of Christianity, and is especially associated with the "ontological argument" for the existence of God.

A very different approach was developed by Anselm of Canterbury, who reacted against any idea of God deceiving the devil, or any idea that the devil could be said to have "rights" of any kind over fallen humanity, or that God should be under any obligation to respect such "rights." At best, the devil might be allowed to have a *de facto* power over humanity – a power which exists as a matter of fact, even if it is an illegitimate and unjustified power. Yet this cannot be thought of as a *de jure* authority – that is, an authority firmly grounded in some legal or moral principle. "I do not see what force this has," he comments, in dismissing the notion. Equally, Anselm is dismissive of any notion that God deceives the devil in the process of redemption. The entire trajectory of redemption is grounded in and reflects the righteousness of God.

Anselm's emphasis falls totally upon the righteousness of God. God redeems humanity in a manner that is totally consistent with the divine quality of righteousness. His treatise *Cur Deus homo* ("Why God became human") is a sustained engagement with the question of the possibility of human redemption, cast in the form of a dialogue. In the course of his analysis, he demonstrates – although how successfully is a matter of dispute – both the necessity of the incarnation, and the saving potential of the death and resurrection of Jesus Christ. The argument is complex, and can be summarized as follows:

1   God created humanity in a state of original righteousness, with the objective of bringing humanity to a state of eternal blessedness.
2   That state of eternal blessedness is contingent upon human obedience to God. However, through sin, humanity is unable to achieve this necessary obedience, which appears to frustrate God's purpose in creating humanity in the first place.
3   In that it is impossible for God's purposes to be frustrated, there must be some means by which the situation can be remedied. However, the situation can only be remedied if a satisfaction is made for sin. In other words, something has to be done, by which the offense caused by human sin can be purged.
4   However, there is no way in which humanity can provide this necessary satisfaction. It lacks the resources which are needed. On the other hand, God possesses the resources needed to provide the required satisfaction.

5   Therefore a "God-man" would possess both the *ability* (as God) and the *obligation* (as a human being) to pay the required satisfaction. Therefore the incarnation takes place, in order that the required satisfaction may be made, and humanity redeemed.

A number of points require comment. First, sin is conceived as an offense against God. The weight of that offense appears to be proportional to the status of the offended party. For many scholars, this suggests that Anselm has been deeply influenced by the feudal assumptions of his time, perhaps regarding God as the equivalent of the "lord of the manor."

Second, there has been considerable debate over the origins of the idea of a "satisfaction." It is possible that the idea may derive from the Germanic laws of the period, which stipulated that an offense had to be purged through an appropriate payment. However, most scholars believe that Anselm is appealing directly to the existing penitential system of the church. A sinner, seeking penance, was required to confess every sin. In pronouncing forgiveness, the priest would require that the penitent should do something (such as go on a pilgrimage or undertake some charitable work) as a "satisfaction" – that is, a means of publicly demonstrating gratitude for forgiveness. It is possible that Anselm derived the idea from this source.

However, despite the obvious difficulties which attend Anselm's approach, an important advance had been made. Anselm's insistence that God is totally and utterly obliged to act according to the principles of justice throughout the redemption of humanity marks a decisive break with the dubious morality of the *Christus Victor* approach. In taking up Anselm's approach, later writers were able to place it on a more secure foundation by grounding it in the general principles of law.

> **Thomas Aquinas (*c*.1225–74).** Probably the most famous and influential theologian of the Middle Ages. Born in Italy, he achieved his fame through his teaching and writing at the University of Paris and other northern universities. His fame rests chiefly on his *Summa Theologiae*, composed toward the end of his life and not totally finished at the time of his death. However, he also wrote many other significant works, particularly the *Summa contra Gentiles*, which represents a major statement of the rationality of the Christian faith.

An early example of this can be found in Thomas Aquinas' The *Summa Theologiae* ("The Totality of Theology"), which he began to write in 1265 and left unfinished at the time of his death. This is widely regarded as the greatest work of medieval theology. In this important and influential analysis, Aquinas develops the idea of "satisfaction," as stated by Anselm, dealing with a number of objections which had been raised against it. His response to the criticism that the dignity of Christ was not sufficient to obtain God's forgiveness of human sin is of especial interest.

2.2.1 Thomas Aquinas on the Satisfaction of Christ

1   It seems that the passion of Christ did not effect our salvation by way of satisfaction. For it seems that to make satisfaction is the responsibility of the one who sins, as is clear from other aspects of penance, in that the one who sins is the one who must repent and confess. But Christ did not sin. As St Peter says,
5   "he committed no sin" (1 Peter 2: 22). He therefore did not make satisfaction through his passion.

2   Furthermore, satisfaction can never be made by means of a greater offense. But the greatest offense was perpetrated in the passion of Christ, since those who put him to death committed the most grievous of sins. For this reason,
10   satisfaction could not be made to God through the passion of Christ.

3   Furthermore, satisfaction implies a certain equality with the fault, since it is an act of justice. But the passion of Christ does not seem to be equal to all the sins of the human race, since Christ suffered according to the flesh, not according to his divinity. As St Peter says, "Christ has suffered in the flesh" (1 Peter 4: 1)
15   . . . Christ therefore did not make satisfaction for our sins by his passion. . . .

I reply that a proper satisfaction comes about when someone offers to the person offended something which gives him a delight greater than his hatred of the offense. Now Christ by suffering as a result of love and obedience offered to God something greater than what might be exacted in compensation for the whole
20   offense of humanity; firstly, because of the greatness of the love, as a result of which he suffered; secondly, because of the worth of the life which he laid down for a satisfaction, which was the life of God and of a human being; thirdly, because of the comprehensiveness of his passion and the greatness of the sorrow which he took upon himself. . . . And therefore the passion of Christ was not only sufficient
25   but a superabundant satisfaction for the sins of the human race. As John says, "he is a propitiation for our sins, not only for ours, but also for those of the whole world" (1 John 2: 2).

Hence, in reply to the first point, the head and the members are as it were one mystical person; and thus the satisfaction of Christ belongs to all the faithful as to
30   his members. . . .

In reply to the second, the love of Christ in his suffering outweighed the malice of them that crucified him. . . . In reply to the third, the worth of Christ's flesh is to be reckoned, not just according to the nature of flesh, but according to the person who assumed it, in that it was the flesh of God, from whom it gained an
35   infinite worth.

In this passage, Aquinas addresses a number of points of importance. The following should be noted in particular.

1 Aquinas demonstrates how the satisfaction which Christ offered on the cross can be considered to be greater than the offense committed by humanity in the first place (lines 16–24). The value of the satisfaction offered is determined by three factors: the greatness of the love of Christ; the intrinsic value of his life, in which humanity and divinity are combined; and the greatness of the burden which he bore. Anselm tended to focus only on the second of these three; Aquinas extends the analysis of Christ's satisfaction to include additional elements, reinforcing the theological foundations of the atonement in doing so.

2 Developing this point further, Aquinas stresses that the high value to be attributed to Christ's human nature is not to be understood purely in terms of the human nature which is assumed, but in the divinity of the person who assumed that nature (lines 32–35).

3 Note Aquinas' distinctive method of arguing in the *Summa Theologiae*. Various objections or difficulties are set out; a general response is made (usually beginning with the words "I reply that . . ."); and the individual points are then dealt with separately.

> **Peter Abelard (1079–1142).** French theologian, who achieved a considerable reputation as a teacher at the University of Paris. Among his many contributions to the development of medieval theology, his most noted is his emphasis upon the subjective aspects of the atonement.

Aquinas' analysis shows the theological potential of the "satisfaction" model of atonement. Other medieval writers were, however, uneasy about Anselm's approach, for different reasons. Some felt that it failed to deal adequately with the subjective aspects of salvation, including the personal appropriation of faith. Others wondered whether the theme of the "love of God" had really been adequately explored, and wished to see a greater emphasis placed upon the manner in which the death of Christ showed the love of God. Perhaps the most important medieval statement of this emphasis can be found in the writings of Peter Abelard. It must be stressed that Abelard does not, as some of his interpreters suggest, *reduce* the meaning of the cross to a demonstration of the love of God. This is one among many components of Abelard's soteriology, which includes traditional ideas concerning Christ's death as a sacrifice for human sin. It is Abelard's emphasis upon the subjective impact of the cross that is distinctive.

For Abelard, "the purpose and cause of the incarnation was that Christ might illuminate the world by his wisdom, and excite it to love of himself." In this, Abelard restates the Augustinian idea of Christ's incarnation as a public demonstration of the extent of the love of God, with the intent of evoking a response of love from humanity. "The Son of God took our nature, and in it took upon himself to teach us by both word and example, even to the point of death, thus binding us to himself through love." This insight is pressed home with considerable force, as the subjective impact of the love of God in Christ is explored further:

> Everyone is made more righteous, that is more loving towards God, after the passion of Christ than before, because people are incited to love. . . . And so our redemption is that great love for us shown in the passion of Christ, which not only sets us free from the bondage of sin, but also gains for us the true liberty of the children of God, so that we should fulfill all things not so much through fear as through love.

Abelard fails to provide an adequate theological foundation to allow us to understand precisely why Christ's death is to be understood as a demonstration of the love of God. Nevertheless, his approach to the meaning of the death of Christ brought home the powerful subjective impact of that death, which had been somewhat ignored or downplayed by contemporary writers, such as Anselm of Canterbury.

It will therefore be clear that the medieval period witnessed considerable interest in the doctrine of the work of Christ, and made significant contributions to its development. Much the same may be said of its approach to the question of the nature and function of the sacraments, to which we now turn.

Case Study 2.3   Discussion of the Sacraments

The first centuries of the Christian tradition were characterized by a relative lack of interest in the theology of the sacraments. During the second century, some discussions of a general sacramental nature can be found in such writings as the Didache, and the works of Irenaeus. It is only in the writings of Augustine that the issues, including that of the definition of a sacrament, begin to be fully addressed. Augustine is generally regarded as having laid down the general principles relating to the definition of sacraments. These principles are as follows:

1   A sacrament is a sign. "Signs, when applied to divine things, are called sacraments."
2   The sign must bear some relation to the thing which is signified. "If sacraments did not bear some resemblance to the things of which they are the sacraments, they would not be sacraments at all."

These definitions are, however, still imprecise and inadequate. For example, does it follow that every "sign of a sacred thing" is to be regarded as a sacrament? In practice, Augustine understands by "sacraments" a number of things that are no longer regarded as sacramental in character – for example, the creed and the Lord's Prayer. As time developed, it became increasingly clear that the definition of a sacrament simply as "a sign of a sacred thing" was inadequate.

> **Hugh of St Victor (died 1142).** A theologian, of Flemish or German origin, who entered the Augustinian monastery of St Victor in Paris around 1115. His most important work is *de sacramentis Christianae fidei* ("On the Sacraments of the Christian Faith"), which shows awareness of the new theological debates which were beginning to develop at this time.

It was during the earlier Middle Ages – the period of sacramental development *par excellence* – that further clarification took place. In this case study, we shall explore the general area of the definition of a sacrament. In the first half of the twelfth century, the Paris-based theologian Hugh of St Victor revised the very imprecise definition offered by Augustine. In his comprehensive account of the theology of the sacraments, written in the first half of the twelfth century, Hugh of St Victor set out a definition of a sacrament which included the need for a physical element which bore some resemblance to the grace it signified. This had the important consequence of excluding penance from the list of sacraments; it was only when Peter Lombard modified this definition (see 2.3.2) that the medieval formulation of the list of seven sacraments was standardized.

2.3.1 Hugh of St Victor on the Nature of a Sacrament

Not every sign of a sacred thing can properly be called a sacrament (for the letters in sacred writings, or statues and pictures, are all "signs of sacred things," but cannot be called sacraments for that reason). . . . Anyone wanting a fuller and better definition of a sacrament can define it as follows: "a sacrament is a physical
5   or material element set before the external senses, representing by likeness, signifying by its institution, and containing by sanctification, some invisible and spiritual grace." This definition is recognized as being so appropriate and perfect that it turns out to be appropriate in the case of every sacrament, yet only the sacraments. For everything that has these three elements is a sacrament; and
10   everything that lacks these three cannot be considered as a sacrament. For every sacrament ought to have a kind of likeness to the thing of which it is the sacrament, according to which it is capable of representing the same thing. It ought also to have been instituted in such a way that it is ordained to signify this thing. And

> finally, it ought to have been sanctified in such a way that it contains that thing,
> 15 and is efficacious in conferring the same on those who are to be sanctified.

Note that there are four essential elements in the understanding of the nature of a sacrament as "a physical or material element set before the external senses, representing by likeness, signifying by its institution, and containing by sanctification, some invisible and spiritual grace" (lines 4–7).

1 There must be a "physical or material" element involved (lines 4–5) – such as the water of baptism, the bread and wine of the eucharist, or the oil of extreme unction. ("Extreme unction" is the practice of anointing those who are terminally ill with consecrated olive oil.)
2 A "kind of likeness" to the thing which is signified, so that it can represent the thing signified (lines 10–12). Thus the eucharistic wine can be argued to have a "kind of likeness" to the blood of Christ, allowing it to represent that blood in a sacramental context.
3 Some form of "institution" through which it is "ordained to signify this thing" (lines 12–13). In other words, there must be a good reason for believing that the sign in question is authorized to represent the spiritual reality to which it points. An example – indeed, the primary example – of the "authorization" in question is institution at the hands of Jesus Christ himself.
4 An efficacy, by which the sacrament is capable of conferring the benefits which it signifies to those who partake in it (lines 14–15).

This third point is of especial importance. In medieval theology, a careful distinction was drawn between the "sacraments of the Old Covenant" (such as circumcision) and the "sacraments of the New Covenant." The essential distinction between them is that the sacraments of the Old Covenant merely signified spiritual realities, whereas the sacraments of the New Covenant actualized what they signified. The thirteenth-century Franciscan writer Bonaventure made this point as follows, using a medicinal analogy:

> In the Old Law, there were ointments of a kind, but they were figurative and did not heal. The disease was lethal, but the anointings were superficial. . . . Genuinely healing ointments must bring both spiritual anointing and a life-giving power; it was only Christ our Lord who did this, since . . . through his death, the sacraments have the power to bring to life.

However, Hugh of St Victor's definition of a sacrament remained unsatisfactory. According to Hugh, the following items were "sacraments": the incarnation, the church, and death. Something was still missing. By this time, there was general agreement that there were seven sacraments – baptism, confirmation, the eucharist, penance, marriage, ordination, and extreme unction. But by Hugh's definition, penance could not be a sacrament. It contained no material element. Theory and practice were thus seriously out of line.

The situation was resolved through the contribution of Peter Lombard. In his *Four Books of the Sentences*, compiled at Paris during the years 1155–8, Peter Lombard set out a definition of a sacrament which differed from that offered by Hugh of St Victor by avoiding any reference to any physical element (such as bread, wine, or water). Using this definition, Peter was able to set out a list of seven sacraments, which became definitive for medieval Catholic theology.

2.3.2   Peter Lombard on the Nature of Sacraments

A sacrament bears a likeness to the thing of which it is a sign. "For if sacraments did not have a likeness of the things whose sacraments they are, they would not properly be called sacraments" (Augustine). . . . Something can properly be called a sacrament if it is a sign of the grace of God and a form of invisible grace, so that
5   it bears its image and exists as its cause. Sacraments were therefore instituted for the sake of sanctifying, as well as of signifying. . . . Those things which were instituted for the purpose of signifying alone are nothing more than signs, and are not sacraments, as in the case of the physical sacrifices and ceremonial observances of the Old Law, which were never able to make those who offered them righteous.
10   . . . Now let us consider the sacraments of the New Law, which are baptism, confirmation, the bread of blessing (that is, the eucharist), penance, extreme unction, ordination, and marriage. Some of these, such as baptism, provide a remedy against sin and confer the assistance of grace; others, such as marriage, are only a remedy; and others, such as the eucharist and ordination, strengthen us with
15   grace and power. . . . So why were these sacraments not instituted soon after the fall of humanity, since they convey righteousness and salvation? We reply that the sacraments of grace were not given before the coming of Christ, who is the giver of grace, in that they receive their virtue from his death and suffering.

Note the following points:

1   A sacrament is defined as "a sign of the grace of God and a form of invisible grace, so that it bears its image and exists as its cause." Compare this with Hugh's definition of a sacrament as "a physical or material element set before the external senses, representing by likeness, signifying by its institution, and containing by sanctification, some invisible and spiritual grace." Hugh begins

by insisting on the need for a "a physical or material element", Peter makes no reference of any kind to such an element.

2 Note the list of seven sacraments provided by Peter: "baptism, confirmation, the bread of blessing (that is, the eucharist), penance, extreme unction, ordination, and marriage" (lines 10–12). This list would become normative in subsequent medieval Christian thought and practice.

Case Study 2.4   The Interpretation of the Bible

The question of how the Bible is to be interpreted has always been of theological importance, and was discussed at some length during the medieval period. It was during this era of Christian thought that the interpretive scheme usually known as the "Fourfold Sense of Scripture" received its final form. In view of the importance of this method, and its impact on the theology of the period, we shall consider it in a little detail.

It will be helpful if we begin by exploring the background to the development of this scheme in the patristic period. A major influence, especially within the Alexandrian school, at this time was the lengthening shadow of the Jewish writer Philo of Alexandria (*c.*30 BC – *c.* AD 45). Philo argued that it was necessary to look beneath the surface meaning of scripture, to discern a deeper meaning which lay beneath the surface of the text. In addition to the "literal" meaning of the text, there was a deeper "spiritual" meaning, which could be uncovered by treating the passages in question as allegories, pointing to these deeper truths.

These ideas were taken up by a group of theologians based in Alexandria, including Origen. The scope of the allegorical method can be seen from Origen's interpretation of key Old Testament images. Joshua's conquest of the promised land, interpreted allegorically, referred to Christ's conquest of sin upon the cross, just as the sacrificial legislation in Leviticus pointed ahead to the spiritual sacrifices of Christians. It might at first sight seem that this represents a degeneration into *eisegesis*, in which the interpreter simply reads any meaning he or she likes into the text of Scripture. However, as the writings of Didymus the Blind make clear, this need not be the case. It seems that a consensus developed about the images and texts of the Old Testament which were to be interpreted allegorically. For example, Jerusalem regularly came to be seen as an allegory of the church.

In contrast, the Antiochene school placed an emphasis upon the interpretation of Scripture in the light of its historical context. This school, especially associated with writers such as Diodore of Tarsus, John Chrysostom and Theodore of Mopsuestia, gave an emphasis to the historical location of Old Testament prophecies, which is quite absent from the writings of Origen and other representatives of the Alexandrian tradition. Thus Theodore, in dealing with Old Testament prophecy, stresses that the prophetic message was relevant to those to whom it was directly addressed, as well as having a developed meaning for a

Christian readership. Every prophetic oracle is to be interpreted as having a single consistent historical or literal meaning. In consequence, Theodore tended to interpret relatively few Old Testament passages as referring directly to Christ, whereas the Alexandrian school regarded Christ as the hidden content of many Old Testament passages, both prophetic and historical.

In the western church a slightly distinct approach can be seen to develop, which would eventually find full expression in the *Quadriga*. In many of his writings, Ambrose of Milan developed a threefold understanding of the senses of Scripture: in addition to the *natural* sense, the interpreter may discern a *moral* and *rational* or *theological* sense. Augustine chose to follow this approach, and instead argued for a twofold sense – a *literal–fleshly–historical* approach and an *Allegorical–mystical–spiritual* sense, although Augustine allows that some passages can possess both senses. "The sayings of the prophets are found to have a threefold meaning, in that some have in mind the earthly Jerusalem, others the heavenly city, and others refer to both." To understand the Old Testament at a purely historical level is unacceptable; the key to its understanding lies in its correct interpretation. Among the major lines of "spiritual" interpretation, the following should be noted: Adam represents Christ; Eve represents the church; Noah's ark represents the cross; the door of Noah's ark represents Christ's pierced side; the city of Jerusalem represents the heavenly Jerusalem:

> These hidden meanings of inspired Scripture we can track down to the best of our ability, with varying degrees of success. Yet we all hold firmly to the principle that all these historical events and their narrative always have some foreshadowing of things to come, and that they are always to be interpreted with reference to Christ and his church.

By the use of such lines of analysis, Augustine is able to stress the unity of both Old and New Testaments. They bear witness to the same faith, even if its modes of expression may be different. Augustine expresses this idea in a text which has become of major importance to biblical interpretation, especially as it bears on the relation between Old and New Testaments: "The New Testament is hidden in the Old; the Old is made accessible by the New (*In Vetere Novum latet et in Novo Vetus patet*)."

This distinction between the *literal* or *historical* sense of Scripture on the one hand, and a deeper *spiritual* or *allegorical* meaning on the other, came to be generally accepted within the church during the early Middle Ages. The standard method of biblical interpretation used during the Middle Ages is usually known as the *Quadriga*, or the "fourfold sense of Scripture." The origins of this method lie specifically in the distinction between the literal and spiritual senses. Scripture possesses four different senses. In addition to the literal sense, three non-literal senses can be distinguished: the allegorical, defining what Christians are to believe; the tropological or moral, defining what Christians are to do; and the anagogical, defining what Christians are to hope for. The four senses of Scripture were thus the following:

1   The *literal* sense of Scripture, in which the text could be taken at face value, referring to some historical event.
2   The *allegorical* sense, which interpreted certain passages of Scripture to produce statements of doctrine. Those passages tended either to be obscure, or to have a literal meaning which was unacceptable, for theological reasons, to their readers.
3   The *tropological or moral* sense, which interpreted such passages to produce ethical guidance for Christian conduct.
4   The *anagogical* sense, which interprets passages to indicate the grounds of Christian hope, pointing towards the future fulfillment of the divine promises in the New Jerusalem.

This scheme was often summed up by a Latin mnemonic, found in the writings of Augustine of Denmark and many other writers of the early Middle Ages:

Littera gesta docet, quid credas allegoria
Moralis quid agas, quid speres anagogia.

A rough translation would run like this: "The literal [sense] teaches about deeds; the allegorical [sense] what to believe; the moral [sense] what to do; the anagogical [sense] what to hope for."

A potential weakness was avoided by insisting that nothing should be believed on the basis of a non-literal sense of Scripture, unless it could first be established on the basis of the literal sense. This insistence on the priority of the literal sense of Scripture may be seen as an implied criticism of the allegorical approach adopted by Origen, which virtually allowed interpreters of Scripture to read whatever "spiritual" interpretations they liked into any passage.

So how was this method applied? An example will help understand the scope of the Quadriga, as well as indicate its potential limitations. In the course of his exposition of Song of Songs 1: 16, written in Latin in the first half of the twelfth century, Bernard of Clairvaux provides an allegorical interpretation of the phrase "the beams of our houses are of cedar, and our panels are of cypress." This extract is an excellent illustration of the way in which doctrinal or spiritual meaning was "read into" otherwise unpromising passages at this time. Note especially the way in which developed meanings, often with virtually no connection with the text itself, were drawn out of the passage in question. The advantages and disadvantages of the method will be immediately obvious. On the positive side, significant meanings can be attached to otherwise apparently unimportant passages of the

145

Bible; on the negative side, the meanings in question often rest on somewhat flimsy or even arbitrary foundations.

2.4.1   Bernard of Clairvaux and the Allegorical Sense of Scripture

By "houses" we are to understand the great mass of the Christian people, who are bound together with those who possess power and dignity, rulers of the church and the state, as "beams." These hold them together by wise and firm laws; otherwise, if each of them were to operate in any way that they pleased, the walls
5   would bend and collapse, and the whole house would fall in ruins. By the "panels," which are firmly attached to the beams and which adorn the house in a royal manner, we are to understand the kindly and ordered lives of a properly instructed clergy, and the proper administration of the rites of the church. Yet how can the clergy carry out their work, or the church discharge her duties, unless the princes,
10   like strong and solid beams, sustain them through their goodwill and munificence, and protect them through their power?

A further development of major importance to biblical interpretation in the later Middle Ages was the rise of Renaissance humanism, with its distinctive emphasis on returning to the original sources in the original languages. We shall explore this further in the following case study.

Case Study 2.5   Renaissance Humanism and the Bible

In our overview of the Middle Ages and Renaissance, we drew attention to the importance of humanism in relation to biblical scholarship in the fifteenth and sixteenth centuries, and touched on the importance of translation alterations to theological revisionism. So important is this theme for historical theology that a much more detailed examination of the matter is required. The present case study aims to set out the implications of the methods and goals associated with the Renaissance for Christian theology at the time. We begin by exploring what a typical medieval theologian would have understood by the phrase "the Bible."

When a medieval theologian refers to "Scripture," he almost invariably means the Latin translation of the Bible widely referred to as the *textus vulgatus* (literally, the "common text") drawn up by the great patristic biblical scholar Jerome in the late fourth and early fifth centuries. Although the term "Vulgate" did not come into general use in the sixteenth century, it is perfectly acceptable to use this term to refer to the specific Latin translation of the Bible prepared by Jerome in the late fourth and early fifth centuries. This text was passed down to the Middle Ages in a number of forms, with considerable variations between them. For example,

Theodulf and Alcuin, noted scholars of the Dark Ages, used quite different versions of the Vulgate text. A new period of intellectual activity opened up in the eleventh century, as the Dark Ages lifted. It was clear that a standard version of this text was required to service the new interest in theology which developed as part of this intellectual renaissance. If theologians were to base their theology upon different versions of the Vulgate, an equally great, if not greater, variation in their conclusions would be the inevitable result.

This need for standardization was met by what appears to have been a joint speculative venture by some Paris theologians and stationers in 1226, resulting in the "Paris version" of the Vulgate text. By then, Paris was recognized as the leading center of theology in Europe, with the inevitable result that – despite its many obvious imperfections – the "Paris version" of the Vulgate became established as normative. This version, it must be emphasized, was not commissioned or sponsored by any ecclesiastical figure: it appears to have been a purely commercial venture. History, however, concerns the fate of accidents, and it is necessary to note that medieval theologians, attempting to base their theology upon Scripture, were obliged to equate Scripture with a rather bad commercial edition of an already faulty Latin translation of the Bible. The rise of humanist textual and philological techniques would expose the distressing discrepancies between the Vulgate and the texts it purported to translate – and thus open the way to doctrinal reformation as a consequence.

So what was the significance of humanism in relation to the many theological questions concerning the authority, interpretation, and application of the Bible? The main elements of the humanist contribution to this important question are summarized below.

1   The great humanist emphasis upon the need to return *ad fontes* established the priority of Scripture over its commentators, particularly those of the Middle Ages. The text of Scripture was to be approached directly, rather than through a complicated system of glosses and commentaries.

2   Scripture was to be read directly in its original languages, rather than in Latin translation. Thus the Old Testament was to be studied in Hebrew (except for those few sections written in Aramaic), and the New Testament was to be read in Greek. The growing humanist interest in the Greek language (which many humanists held to be supreme in its capacity to mediate philosophical concepts) further consolidated the importance attached to the New Testament documents. The late Renaissance scholarly ideal was to be *trium linguarum gnarus*, "expert in three languages (Hebrew, Greek, and Latin)." Trilingual colleges were established at Alcalá in Spain, at Paris, and at Wittenberg. The new interest in, and availability of, Scripture in its original language soon brought to light a number of serious translation mistakes in the Vulgate, some of considerable importance.

3 The humanist movement made available two essential tools required for the new method of study of the Bible. First, it made available the printed text of Scripture in its original languages. For example, Erasmus' *Novum Instrumentum omne* of 1516, which allowed scholars direct access to the printed text of the Greek New Testament; and Jacques Lefèvre d'Etaples provided the Hebrew text of a group of important Psalms in 1509. Second, it made available manuals of classical languages, allowing scholars to learn languages which they otherwise could not have acquired. Reuchlin's Hebrew primer, *de rudimentis hebraicis* ("On the Basics of Hebrew," 1506), is an excellent example of this type of material. Greek primers were more common: the Aldine press produced an edition of Lascaris' Greek grammar in 1495, Erasmus' translation of the famous Greek grammar of Theodore of Gaza appeared in 1516, and Melanchthon produced a masterly Greek primer in 1518.

4 The humanist movement developed textual techniques capable of establishing accurately the best text of Scripture. These techniques had been used, for example, by Lorenzo Valla to demonstrate the inauthenticity of the famous *Donation of Constantine*. It was now possible to eliminate many of the textual errors which had crept into the Parisian edition of the Vulgate. Erasmus shocked his contemporaries by excluding a significant part of one verse of the Bible (1 John 5: 7), which he could not find in any Greek manuscript, as a later addition. The Vulgate version reads as follows: "For there are three that testify [in heaven: the Father, the Words and the Holy Spirit, and these three are one. And there are three that testify on earth]: the Spirit, the water and the blood." The bracketed section of the verse, omitted by Erasmus, was certainly there in the Vulgate – but not in the Greek texts which it purported to translate. As this text had become an important proof-text for the doctrine of the Trinity, many were outraged at his action. Theological conservatism here often triumphed over scholarly progress: even the famous King James Version (also known as the Authorized Version) of 1611, for example, included the spurious verse, despite its absence in the key Greek manuscripts.

5 The humanists tended to regard ancient texts as mediating an experience, which could be recaptured through appropriate literary methods. Included in the theme *ad fontes* is the notion of recapturing the experience mediated by the text. In the case of the New Testament, the experience in question was that of the presence and power of the risen Christ. Scripture was thus read with a sense of anticipation – it was believed that the vitality and excitement of the apostolic era could be regained in the sixteenth century, by reading and studying Scripture in the right manner.

6 In his *Enchiridion*, which became enormously influential in 1515, Erasmus argued that a biblically literate laity held the key to the renewal of the church.

Both clergy and church were marginalized: the lay reader of Scripture had therein a more than adequate guide to the essentials of Christian belief and especially practice. These views, which achieved wide circulation among the lay intelligentsia of Europe, unquestionably prepared the way for the scriptural reforming program of Luther and Zwingli in the period 1519–25.

In what follows, we shall look at two key passages in which humanist scholars detected translation errors, and consider the theological implications of the translation changes which were introduced through humanist scholarship.

1 Matthew 4: 17

This verse describes the beginning of the ministry of Jesus, and the basic content of his preaching at this stage. The gospel of Matthew was widely used in the Middle Ages as a source for Christian teaching in parish sermons, with the result that this verse appears to have had considerable impact on the popular understanding of what Christianity was all about. The Latin of the Vulgate text reads as follows:

> Exinde coepit Iesus praedicare et dicere paenitentiam agite
> adpropinquavit enim regnum caelorum.

A literal English translation of this would be: "Then Jesus began to preach and say: 'do penance (*paenitentiam agite*), for the kingdom of heaven has drawn near.' " The natural way of reading this would be to assume that Jesus was directing those who wished to respond to his preaching of the coming of the kingdom by "doing penance" – that is, by making use of the penitential system of the church. There is a clearly implied link between the preaching of Jesus and the institution of the church. The Greek original, however, does not bear this meaning. The most natural translation of the Greek text of Matthew's gospel at this point would be "repent," not "do penance." In other words, the Greek implies a personal transformation of the individual, with no implied connection with the institution or sacraments of the church. The translation change thus had considerable theological implications.

2 Luke 1: 28

This text describes what is generally known as "the annunciation" – that is, the declaration by Gabriel to Mary that she is to bear a child. The Latin of the Vulgate texts reads as follows:

> et ingressus angelus at eam dixit: ave gratia plena Dominus tecum benedicta tu in
> mulieribus.

A rough translation of this would be: "And the angel went in, and said to her: 'Hail, one that is full of grace (*ave gratia plena*) the Lord is with you, blessed are you among women.' " The implications of this greeting were considerable, in that the clear implication is that Mary is to be regarded as a person who is "full of grace." In medieval theology, grace was characteristically thought of as a divine or quasi-divine substance, rather than a gracious attitude on the part of God. This passage would therefore have been understood to imply that Mary was a vessel containing grace, and thus further to imply that access could be had to this grace by those who needed it in times of distress. These themes certainly became an important aspect of late medieval Marian spirituality. However, humanist scholars (such as Erasmus) argued that the Greek original of the gospel text could not be translated in this way. The natural interpretation of the text would be to refer to Mary as "one who has found favor" [with God], an idea which could be expressed in the Latin term *gratificata* rather than *gratia plena*. The implications of this translation alteration for both theology and spirituality were thus potentially considerable.

Case Study 2.6   Some Themes in Late Medieval Scholastic Theology

The late medieval period saw some fascinating theological developments taking place. These are often interpreted (especially in older textbooks) in terms of a confrontation between "Nominalism" and "Augustinianism" within the scholastic theology of the later Middle Ages. In recent years, however, considerable progress has been made in understanding the nature of late medieval scholasticism, leading to a rewriting of the intellectual history of the early Reformation. In what follows, we shall attempt to present an up-to-date account of trends in late medieval scholasticism, and assess their significance.

An earlier generation of scholars, writing in the period 1920–65, regarded "nominalism" as a religious school of thought which captured most northern European university faculties of theology in the later Middle Ages. It proved remarkably difficult, however, to identify the exact features of this theology. Some "nominalist" theologians (such as William of Ockham and Gabriel Biel) seemed to be very optimistic about human abilities, suggesting that it was possible for a human being to do everything that was necessary to enter into a relationship with God. Other "nominalist" theologians (such as Gregory of Rimini and Hugolino of Orvieto) appeared to be profoundly pessimistic about those same abilities, suggesting that without the grace of God, humanity was totally unable to enter into such a relationship. In desperation, scholars began to speak of "nominalistic diversity." Eventually, however, the real solution to the problem emerged: there were actually *two* different schools of thought, the sole common feature of which was antirealism. Both schools adopted a nominalist position in matters of logic and the theory of knowledge – but their theological positions differed radically.

The term *via moderna* is now becoming generally accepted as the best way of referring to the movement once known as "nominalism," including among its representatives such leading fourteenth- and fifteenth-century thinkers as William of Ockham, Pierre d'Ailly, Robert Holcot, and Gabriel Biel. During the fifteenth century, the *via moderna* began to make significant inroads into many northern European universities – for example, at Paris, Heidelberg, and Erfurt. In addition to its philosophical nominalism, the movement adopted a doctrine of justification which many of its critics branded "Pelagian." In view of the importance of this form of scholasticism to Luther's theological breakthrough, we shall explain its understanding of justification in some detail.

The central feature of the soteriology, or doctrine of salvation, of the *via moderna* is a covenant between God and humanity. The later Middle Ages saw the development of political and economic theories based upon the concept of a covenant (for example, between a king and his people), and the theologians of the *via moderna* were quick to realize the theological potential of this idea. Just as a political covenant between a king and his people defined the obligations of king to people, and people to king, so a religious covenant between God and his people defined God's obligations to his people, and their obligation to God. This covenant was not negotiated, of course, but was unilaterally imposed by God. The theologians of the *via moderna* were able to develop this theme – already familiar to readers of the Old Testament – using ideas borrowed from their own political and economic world.

According to these theologians, the covenant between God and human beings established the conditions necessary for justification. God has ordained to accept an individual, on condition that this individual first fulfills certain demands. These demands were summarized using the Latin tag *facere quod in se est*, literally "doing what lies within you," or "doing your best." When individuals met this precondition, God was obliged, by the terms of the covenant, to accept them. A Latin maxim was often used to express this point: *facienti quod in se est Deus non denegat gratiam*, "God will not deny grace to those who do what lies within them." The noted late medieval theologian Gabriel Biel, who is known to have influenced Luther through his writings, explained that "doing your best" meant rejecting evil and trying to do good.

At this point, the parallels between the *via moderna* and Pelagius become obvious. Both assert that men and women are accepted on the basis of their own efforts and achievements. Both assert that human works place God under an obligation to reward them. It would seem that the writers of the *via moderna* are simply reproducing the ideas of Pelagius, using a more sophisticated covenantal framework. At this point, however, the theologians of the *via moderna* drew upon contemporary economic theory to argue that they were doing nothing of the sort. Their use of late medieval economic theory is fascinating, in that it illustrates the extent to which medieval theologians were prepared to exploit ideas drawn from their social context. We shall consider their argument in some detail.

The classic example invariably cited by these theologians to illustrate the relation between good works and justification is the king and the small lead coin. Most medieval coinage systems used gold and silver coins. This had the advantage of guaranteeing the value of the coins, even if it also encouraged the practice of "clipping" precious metal from the coin's sides. The introduction of milled edges to coins represented an attempt to prevent removal of gold or silver in this way. Occasionally, however, kings found themselves in a financial crisis, through war for example. A standard way of meeting this was to recall gold and silver coins, and melt them down. The gold and silver thus retrieved could be used to finance a war.

In the meantime, however, currency of some sort was still required. To meet this need, small leaden coins were issued, which bore the same face value as the gold and silver coins. Although their inherent value was negligible, their ascribed or imposed value was considerable. The king would promise to replace the lead coins with their gold or silver equivalents once the financial crisis was past. The value of the lead coins thus resided in the king's promise to redeem them at their full ascribed value at a later date. The value of a gold coin derives from the gold – but the value of a lead coin derives from the royal covenant to treat that coin as if it were gold. A similar situation, of course, exists in most modern economies. For example, paper money is of negligible inherent value. Its value derives from the promise of the issuing bank to honor its notes to their full face value.

The theologians of the *via moderna* used this economic analogy to counter the charge of Pelagianism. To the suggestion that they were exaggerating the value of human works (in that they seemed to be making them capable of meriting salvation), they replied that they were doing nothing of the sort. Human works were like lead coins, they argued – of little inherent value. But God had ordained, through the covenant, to treat them as if they were of much greater value, in just the same way as a king could treat a lead coin as if it were gold. Pelagius, they conceded, certainly treated human works as if they were gold, capable of purchasing salvation. But they were arguing that human works were like lead: the only reason they were of any value was that God had graciously undertaken to treat them as if they were much more valuable. The theological exploitation of the difference between the inherent and imposed value of coins thus served to get the theologians of the *via moderna* out of a potentially awkward situation, even it if would not satisfy their more severe critics, such as Martin Luther.

It is this "covenantal" understanding of justification which underlies Martin Luther's theological breakthrough, to which we shall return in a later case study. Our attention now turns to a trend within late medieval scholastic theology which re-embraced the ideas of Augustine, in deliberate opposition to the *via moderna* – the movement which is now generally known as the *Schola Augustiniana Moderna*, the "modern Augustinian school."

It is known that the University of Oxford was one of the strongholds of the *via moderna* in the early fourteenth century. A group of thinkers, largely based in Merton College, developed the ideas on justification noted above, characteristic of the *via moderna*. And it was at Oxford that the first backlash against this movement occurred. The individual responsible for this backlash was Thomas Bradwardine, later to become Archbishop of Canterbury, who wrote a furious attack on the ideas of the Oxford representatives of the *via moderna*, entitled *De causa Dei contra Pelagium*, "The case of God against Pelagius." In this book, he charged his Merton colleagues with being "modern Pelagians," and developed a theory of justification which represents a return to the views of Augustine, as they are found in the anti-Pelagian writings. Important though Oxford was as a theological center, the Hundred Years War led to it becoming increasingly isolated from the continent of Europe.

Although Bradwardine's ideas would be developed in England by John Wycliffe, they were taken up on the mainland of Europe by Gregory of Rimini at the University of Paris. Gregory had one particularly significant advantage over Bradwardine: he was a member of a religious order (the Order of the Hermits of St Augustine, generally referred to as the "Augustinian Order"). And just as the Dominicans propagated the views of Thomas Aquinas, and the Franciscans those of Duns Scotus, so the Augustinians would promote the ideas of Gregory of Rimini. It is this transmission of an Augustinian tradition, deriving from Gregory of Rimini, within the Augustinian Order which is increasingly referred to as the *schola Augustiniana moderna*. Its general features can be described as follows.

First, Gregory adopted a nominalist view on the question of universals. Like many thinkers of his time, he had little time for the realism of Thomas Aquinas or Duns Scotus. In this respect, he has much in common with thinkers of the *via moderna*, such as Robert Holcot or Gabriel Biel. Second, Gregory developed a soteriology, or doctrine of salvation, which reflects the influence of Augustine. We find an emphasis upon the need for grace, upon the fallenness and sinfulness of humanity, upon the divine initiative in justification, and upon divine predestination. Salvation is understood to be totally a work of God, from its beginning to its end. Where the theologians of the *via moderna* held that humans could initiate their justification by "doing their best," Gregory insisted that only God could initiate justification. The *via moderna* held that most (but not all) necessary soteriological resources were located within human nature. The merits of Christ are an example of a resource lying outside humanity; the ability to desist from sin and turn to righteousness is, for a writer such as Biel, an example of a vital soteriological resource located within humanity. In marked contrast, Gregory of Rimini argued that these resources were located exclusively outside human nature. Even the ability to desist from sin and turn to righteousness arose through the action of God, not a human action. It is obvious that these represent two totally different ways of understanding the human and divine roles in justification.

Although this academic Augustinianism was particularly associated with the Augustinian Order, not every Augustinian monastery or university school seems to have adopted its ideas. Nevertheless, it seems that a school of thought which was strongly Augustinian in cast was in existence in the late Middle Ages on the eve of the Reformation. In many ways, the Wittenberg reformers, with their particular emphasis upon the anti-Pelagian writings of Augustine, may be regarded as having rediscovered and revitalized this tradition. As the views of some leading reformers, such as Luther or Calvin, seem to parallel those of this academic Augustinianism, the question has often been asked: were the reformers influenced, directly or indirectly, by this Augustinian tradition? While this question is too complex to be discussed in detail here, it may be noted that there are excellent reasons for suggesting that both may have been influenced by currents of thought in late medieval scholasticism (although the extent and nature of that influence is a matter for some debate).

We may illustrate this point by considering the case of Calvin. Calvin began his academic career at the University of Paris in the 1520s. As study after study has made clear, the University of Paris – and especially Calvin's college, the Collège de Montaigu – was a stronghold of the *via moderna*. During his four or five years studying at the faculty of arts at Paris, Calvin could not have avoided encountering the leading ideas of this movement. One especially obvious point of affinity between Calvin and late medieval theology concerns voluntarism – the doctrine that the ultimate grounds of merit lie in the will of God, not in the intrinsic goodness of an action. To explore this doctrine, let us consider a human moral action – for example, giving money to a charity. What is the meritorious value of this action? What is it worth in the sight of God? The relation between the moral (i.e., the human) and the meritorious (i.e., the divine) value of actions was of major concern to late medieval theologians. Two distinct approaches developed: the intellectualist and the voluntarist.

The intellectualist approach argued that the divine intellect recognized the inherent moral value of an act, and rewarded it accordingly. There was a direct connection between the moral and the meritorious. The voluntarist approach rejected this, arguing that it made God dependent upon his creatures. The meritorious value of a human action could not be allowed to be predetermined; God had to be free to choose whatever value he liked. There was thus no necessary connection between the moral and the meritorious. So the meritorious value of a human action does not rest upon its inherent value, but is grounded solely in the worth which God chooses to impose upon it. This principle is summarized in the maxim of Duns Scotus (usually, though not entirely correctly, regarded as the originator of the trend towards voluntarism in later medieval thought), to the

154

effect that the value of an offering is determined solely by the divine will, rather than by its inherent goodness. The divine will chose to impose whatever value it cared upon human actions, preserving the freedom of God. In the later Middle Ages, the voluntarist position gained increasing sympathy, especially within radical Augustinian circles. Most theologians of the *via moderna* and *schola Augustiniana moderna* adopted it.

In the *Institutes*, Calvin adopts exactly this voluntarist position in relation to the merit of Christ. Although this is implicit in earlier editions of the work, it is only explicitly stated in the 1559 edition, in the aftermath of Calvin's correspondence with Laelius Socinus on the subject. In 1555, Calvin responded to questions raised by Socinus concerning the merit of Christ and the assurance of faith, and appears to have incorporated these replies directly into the text of the 1559 edition of the *Institutes*.

The death of Christ on the cross is a central focus of Christian thought and worship. But why should the death of Christ have such enormous importance? What justification can be given for its centrality? Why is the death of Christ – rather than of any other individual – declared to be of unique significance? In the course of this correspondence, Calvin considers this question, known technically as the *ratio meriti Christi* (the basis of the merit of Christ). Why is Christ's death on the cross sufficient to purchase the redemption of humanity? Is it something intrinsic to the person of Christ, as Luther had argued? For Luther, the divinity of Christ was adequate grounds for declaring that his death was uniquely important. Or was it that God chose to accept his death as sufficient to merit the redemption of humanity? Was this value inherent within Christ's death, or was it imposed upon it by God? Calvin makes clear his view that the basis of Christ's merit is not located in Christ's offering of himself (which would correspond to an intellectualist approach to the *ratio meriti Christi*), but in the divine decision to accept such an offering as of sufficient merit for the redemption of mankind (which corresponds to the voluntarist approach). For Calvin, "apart from God's good pleasure, Christ could not merit anything." The continuity between Calvin and the late medieval voluntarist tradition will be evident.

In the past, this similarity between Calvin and Scotus has been taken to imply the direct influence of Scotus on Calvin. In fact, however, Calvin's continuity appears to be with the late medieval voluntarist tradition, deriving from William of Ockham and Gregory of Rimini, in relation to which Scotus marks a point of transition. No reason may be given for the meritorious nature of Christ's sacrifice, save that God benevolently ordained to accept it as such. The continuity of Calvin with this later tradition is evident.

This observation provides a convenient transition to the next part of this work, which deals with the period of the Reformation itself.

Chapter 3

THE REFORMATION AND POST-REFORMATION PERIODS, 1500–1750

A major new period in western Christian theology opened in the sixteenth century. The styles of Christian theology associated with the medieval period gave way to new paradigms. The most significant development was the Reformation, a movement which sought to return the western church to more biblical foundations in relation to its belief system, morality and structures. The Reformation initially led to the formation of a cluster of Protestant churches in Europe.

A major development to occur during this period is the expansion of western Christianity from its European context. The arrival of English Puritan communities in Massachusetts Bay and Spanish and Portuguese missionaries in South America opened the way to a further period of expansion of Christianity, which would become of increasing theological significance during the modern period.

We open our discussion of this pivotal period in the history of Christian theology by considering the theological developments associated with the Reformation.

The term "Reformation" is used by historians and theologians to refer to the western European movement, centering upon individuals such as Martin Luther, Huldrych Zwingli, and John Calvin, concerned with the moral, theological, and institutional reform of the Christian church in that region. Initially, up to about 1525, the Reformation may be regarded as revolving around Martin Luther and the University of Wittenberg, in modern-day north-eastern Germany. However, the movement also gained strength, independently at first, in the Swiss city of Zurich in the early 1520s. Through a complex series of developments, the Zurich Reformation gradually underwent a series of political and theological modifications, eventually coming to be associated primarily with the city of Geneva (now part of modern-day Switzerland, although then an independent city-state) and John Calvin.

The Reformation movement was complex and heterogeneous, and its agenda

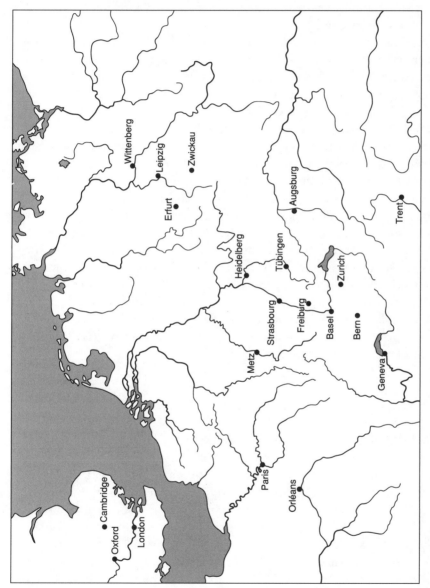

Map 3   Centers of theological and ecclesiastical activity at the time of the European Reformation

157

went far beyond the reform of the doctrine of the church. It addressed fundamental social, political, and economic issues, too complex to be discussed in any detail in this volume. The agenda of the Reformation varied from one country to another, with the theological issues which played major roles in one country (for example, Germany) often having relatively little impact elsewhere (for example, in England).

In response to the Reformation, the Catholic church moved to put its own house in order. Prevented from calling a council at an early date due to political instability in Europe resulting from tensions between France and Germany, the Pope of the day (Paul III) was eventually able to convene the Council of Trent (1545). This set itself the task of clarifying Catholic thought and practice and defending them against its evangelical opponents.

The Reformation itself was a western European phenomenon, concentrated especially in the central and northern parts of this region, although Calvinism penetrated as far east as Hungary. However, the emigration of large numbers of individuals to North America, which becomes increasingly significant from 1600 onward, led to post-Reformation Protestant and Catholic theologies being exported to that region. Harvard College is an example of an early center of theological education in New England. The Society of Jesus also undertook extensive missionary operations in the Far East, including India, China, and Japan. Christian theology gradually began to expand beyond its western European base and become a global phenomenon – a development which received final consolidation in the modern period, to which we shall turn shortly. Our attention now turns to a consideration of the terminology linked with the Reformation and post-Reformation periods.

A Clarification of Terms

The term "Reformation" is used in a number of senses, and it is helpful to distinguish them. Four elements may be involved in its definition, and each will be discussed briefly below: Lutheranism; the Reformed church, often referred to as "Calvinism"; the "radical Reformation," often still referred to as "Anabaptism"; and the "Counter-Reformation" or "Catholic Reformation." In its broadest sense, the term "Reformation" is used to refer to all four movements. The term is also used in a somewhat more restricted sense, meaning "the Protestant Reformation," excluding the Catholic Reformation. In this sense, it refers to the three Protestant movements noted above. In many scholarly works, however, the term "Reformation" is used to refer to what is sometimes known as the "magisterial Reformation," or the "mainstream Reformation" – in other words, that linked with the Lutheran and Reformed churches (including Anglicanism), and excluding the Anabaptists.

The unusual phrase "magisterial Reformation" needs a little explaining. The phrase draws attention to the manner in which the mainstream reformers related to secular authorities, such as princes, magistrates, or city councils. Whereas the radical reformers regarded such authorities as having no rights within the church, the mainstream reformers argued that the church was, at least to some extent, subject to the secular agencies of government. The magistrate had a right to authority within the church, just as the church could rely on the authority of the magistrate to enforce discipline, suppress heresy, or maintain order. The phrase "magisterial Reformation" is intended to draw attention to this close relationship between the magistracy and the church, which lay at the heart of the reforming program of writers such as Martin Luther or Martin Bucer. All three senses of the word "Reformation" will be encountered in the course of reading works dealing with Christian theology. The term "magisterial Reformation" is increasingly used to refer to the first two senses of the term (i.e. covering Lutheranism and the Reformed church), taken together, and the term "radical Reformation" to refer to the third (Anabaptism).

The term "Protestant" requires comment. It derives from the aftermath of the Diet of Speyer (February 1529), which voted to end the toleration of Lutheranism in Germany. In April of the same year, six German princes and fourteen cities protested against this oppressive measure, defending freedom of conscience and the rights of religious minorities. The term "Protestant" derives from this protest. It is therefore not strictly correct to apply the term "Protestant" to individuals prior to April 1529, or to speak of events prior to that date as constituting "the Protestant Reformation." The term "evangelical" is often used in the literature to refer to the reforming factions at Wittenberg and elsewhere (e.g. in France and Switzerland) prior to this date. Although the word "Protestant" is often used to refer to this earlier period, this use is, strictly speaking, an anachronism.

The Lutheran Reformation

The Lutheran Reformation is particularly associated with the German territories and the pervasive personal influence of one charismatic individual – Martin Luther. Luther was particularly concerned with the doctrine of justification, which formed the central point of his religious thought. The Lutheran Reformation was initially an academic movement, concerned primarily with reforming the teaching of theology at the University of Wittenberg. Wittenberg was an unimportant university, and the reforms introduced by Luther and his colleagues within the theology faculty attracted little attention. It was Luther's personal activities – such as his posting of the famous Ninety-Five Theses (October 31, 1517) – which attracted considerable interest, and brought the ideas in circulation at Wittenberg to the attention of a wider audience.

The Ninety-Five Theses were a protest against the practice of selling indulgences in order to raise money for the rebuilding of St Peter's basilica in Rome. The theory underlying the sale of indulgences is confused, but seems to have rested upon the idea of the gratitude of the sinner for forgiveness of sins. Once sinners were assured that their sins had been forgiven by the church, acting on behalf of Christ, they would naturally wish to express that gratitude in some positive manner. Gradually, the giving of money to charity, including directly to church funds, came to be seen as the normal way of expressing appreciation for such forgiveness. It must be noted that this was not understood to mean that a sinner *purchased* forgiveness. The gift of money was a result of, not a condition for, forgiveness. But by Luther's time, misrepresentation and misunderstanding had set in. People seem to have believed that indulgences were a quick and convenient way of buying forgiveness of sins. Luther protested. Forgiveness was a matter of a changed relationship between a sinner and God, not a matter of financial speculation. The idea of forgiveness by grace had become corrupted into that of the purchase of God's favor.

Strictly speaking, the Lutheran Reformation only began in 1522, when Luther returned to Wittenberg from his enforced isolation in the Wartburg. Luther was condemned for "false doctrine" by the Diet of Worms in 1521. Fearing for his life, certain well-placed supporters removed him in secrecy to the castle known as the Wartburg, until the threat to his safety ceased. In his absence, Andreas Bodenstein von Karlstadt, one of Luther's academic colleagues at Wittenberg, began a program of reform at Wittenberg, which seemed to degenerate into chaos. Convinced that he was needed if the Reformation was to survive Karlstadt's ineptitude, Luther emerged from his place of safety, and returned to Wittenberg.

At this point. Luther's program of academic reform changed into a program of reform of church and society. No longer was Luther's forum of activity the university world of ideas; he now found himself regarded as the leader of a religious, social, and political reforming movement which seemed to some contemporary observers to open the way to a new social and religious order in Europe. In fact, Luther's program of reform was much more conservative than that associated with his Reformed colleagues, such as Huldrych Zwingli. Furthermore, it met with considerably less success than some anticipated. The movement remained obstinately tied to the German territories, and – Scandinavia apart – never gained the foreign power bases which seemed to be like so many ripe apples, ready to fall into its lap. Luther's understanding of the role of the "godly prince" (which effectively ensured that the monarch had control of the church) does not seem to have had the attraction which might have been expected, particularly in the light of the generally republican sentiments of Reformed thinkers such as Calvin. The case of England is particularly illuminating: here, as in the Low Countries, the Protestant theology which gained the ascendancy was Reformed rather than Lutheran.

The Calvinist Reformation

The origins of the Calvinist Reformation, which brought the Reformed churches (such as the Presbyterians) into being, lie in developments within the Swiss Confederation. Whereas the Lutheran Reformation had its origins in an academic context, the Reformed church owed its origins to a series of attempts to reform the morals and worship of the church (but not necessarily its *doctrine*) according to a more biblical pattern. It must be emphasized that although Calvin gave this style of Reformation its definitive form, its origins are to be traced back to earlier reformers, such as Huldrych Zwingli and Heinrich Bullinger, based in the leading Swiss city of Zurich.

Although most of the early Reformed theologians, such as Zwingli, had an academic background, their reforming programs were not academic in nature. They were directed toward the church as they found it in Swiss cities such as Zurich, Berne, and Basel. Whereas Luther was convinced that the doctrine of justification was of central significance to his program of social and religious reform, the early Reformed thinkers had relatively little interest in doctrine, let alone one specific doctrine. Their reforming program was institutional, social, and ethical, in many ways similar to the demands for reform emanating from the humanist movement.

The consolidation of the Reformed church is generally thought to begin after Zwingli's death in battle (1531) with the stabilization of the Zurich Reformation under his successor, Heinrich Bullinger, and to end with the emergence of Geneva as its power base, and John Calvin as its leading spokesman, in the 1550s. The gradual shift in power within the Reformed church (initially from Zurich to Berne, and subsequently from Berne to Geneva) took place over the period 1520–60, eventually establishing the city of Geneva, its political system (republicanism), and its religious thinkers (initially Calvin, and after his death Theodore Beza) as predominant within the Reformed church. This development was consolidated through the establishment of the Genevan Academy (founded in 1559), at which Reformed pastors were trained.

The term "Calvinism" is often used to refer to the religious ideas of the Reformed church. Although still widespread in the literature relating to the Reformation, this practice is now generally discouraged. It is becoming increasingly clear that later sixteenth-century Reformed theology draws on sources other than the ideas of Calvin himself. To refer to later sixteenth- and seventeenth-century Reformed thought as "Calvinist" implies that it is essentially the thought of Calvin – and it is now generally agreed that Calvin's ideas were modified subtly by his successors. The term "Reformed" is now preferred, whether to refer to those churches (mainly in Switzerland, the Low Countries, and Germany) or religious thinkers (such as Theodore Beza, William Perkins, and John Owen) that based themselves upon Calvin's celebrated religious textbook, *The Institutes of the Christian Religion*, or church documents (such as the famous *Heidelberg Catechism*) based upon it.

Of the three constituents of the Protestant Reformation – Lutheran, Reformed or Calvinist, and Anabaptist – it is the Reformed wing which is of particular importance to the English-speaking world. Puritanism, which figures so prominently in seventeenth-century English history and is of such fundamental importance to the religious and political views of New England in the seventeenth century and beyond, is a specific form of Reformed Christianity. To understand the religious and political history of New England or the ideas of writers such as Jonathan Edwards, for example, it is necessary to come to grips with at least some of the theological insights and part of the religious outlook of Puritanism, which underlie their social and political attitudes.

The Radical Reformation (Anabaptism)

The term "Anabaptist" literally means "rebaptizer," and refers to what was perhaps the most distinctive aspect of Anabaptist practice: the insistence that only those who had made a personal, public profession of faith should be baptized. Anabaptism seems to have first arisen around Zurich, in the aftermath of Zwingli's reforms within the city in the early 1520s. It centered on a group of individuals (amongst whom we may note Conrad Grebel) who argued that Zwingli was not being faithful to his own reforming principles. He preached one thing, and practiced another. Although Zwingli professed faithfulness to the *sola scriptura*, "by scripture alone," principle, Grebel argued that he retained a number of practices – including infant baptism, the close link between church and magistracy, and the participation of Christians in warfare – which were not sanctioned or ordained by Scripture. In the hands of such thinkers as Grebel, the *sola scriptura* principle would be radicalized; reformed Christians would believe and practice only those things explicitly taught in Scripture. Zwingli was alarmed by this, seeing it as a destabilizing development which threatened to cut the Reformed church at Zurich off from its historical roots and its continuity with the Christian tradition of the past.

A number of common elements can be discerned within the various strands of the Anabaptist movement: a general distrust of external authority; the rejection of infant baptism in favor of the baptism of adult believers; the common ownership of property; and an emphasis upon pacifism and non-resistance. To take up the third of these points: in 1527, the governments of Zurich, Berne, and St Gallen accused the Anabaptists of believing "that no true Christian can either give or receive interest or income on a sum of capital; that all temporal goods are free and common, and that all can have full property rights to them." It is for this reason that "Anabaptism" is often referred to as the "left wing of the Reformation" (Roland H. Bainton) or the "radical Reformation" (George Hunston

Williams). For Williams, the "radical Reformation" was to be contrasted with the "magisterial Reformation," which he broadly identified with the Lutheran and Reformed movements. These terms are increasingly being accepted within Reformation scholarship, and you are likely to encounter them in your reading of more recent studies of the movement.

The Catholic Reformation

This term is often used to refer to the revival within Roman Catholicism in the period following the opening of the Council of Trent (1545). In older scholarly works, the movement is often designated the "Counter-Reformation": as the term suggests, the Roman Catholic church developed means of combating the Protestant Reformation, in order to limit its influence. It is, however, becoming increasingly clear that the Roman Catholic church countered the Reformation partly by reforming itself from within, in order to remove the grounds of Protestant criticism. In this sense, the movement was a reformation of the Roman Catholic church, as much as it was a reaction against the Protestant Reformation.

The same concerns underlying the Protestant Reformation in northern Europe were channeled into the renewal of the Catholic church, particularly in Spain and Italy. The Council of Trent, the foremost component of the Catholic Reformation, clarified Catholic teaching on a number of confusing matters, and introduced much-needed reforms in relation to the conduct of the clergy, ecclesiastical discipline, religious education, and missionary activity. The movement for reform within the church was greatly stimulated by the reformation of many of the older religious orders, and the establishment of new orders (such as the Jesuits). The more specifically theological aspects of the Catholic Reformation will be considered in relation to its teachings on Scripture and tradition, justification by faith, and the sacraments. As a result of the Catholic Reformation, many of the abuses which originally lay behind the demands for reform – whether these came from humanists or Protestants – were removed.

KEY THEOLOGIANS

The Reformation era is widely regarded as one of the most creative in the history of Christian theology. Three theologians are usually singled out as being of particular significance: Martin Luther, John Calvin, and Huldrych Zwingli. Of these, the first two are of especial importance. Although Zwingli is a major figure in his own right, he has been overshadowed by the creative talent and theological impact of Luther and Calvin.

Martin Luther (1483–1546)

Martin Luther was educated at the University of Erfurt, initially studying within the faculty of arts, before beginning the study of theology at the local Augustinian monastery. He gained an appointment as professor of biblical studies at the University of Wittenberg in 1512, and lectured on the Psalms (1513–15), Romans (1515–16), Galatians (1516–17), and Hebrews (1517–18). During this period, Luther's theology can be seen to have gone through a series of developments, especially in relation to the doctrine of justification. His close engagement with biblical texts during this period appears to have led him to become increasingly dissatisfied with the views of the *via moderna* on the subject.

Luther first came to public attention in 1517, through the publication of his Ninety-Five Theses on Indulgences. This was followed by the Leipzig Disputation (June–July 1519), in which Luther established a reputation as a radical critic of scholasticism. In 1520 he published three treatises which consolidated his growing reputation as a theological reformer. In the *Appeal to the Christian Nobility of the German Nation*, Luther argued passionately for the need for reform of the church. In both its doctrine and its practices, the church of the early sixteenth century had cast itself adrift from the New Testament. His pithy and witty German gave added popular appeal to some intensely serious theological ideas. Encouraged by the remarkable success of this work, Luther followed it up with *The Babylonian Captivity of the Christian Church*. In this powerful piece of writing, Luther argued that the gospel had become captive to the institutional church. The medieval church, he argued, had imprisoned the gospel in a complex system of priests and sacraments. The church had become the master of the gospel, where it should be its servant. This point was further developed in *The Liberty of a Christian*, in which Luther explored the implications of the doctrine of justification by faith for the Christian life.

Luther was perhaps the most creative of the reformers. Yet his theological impact does not rest upon any major work of theology. Most of Luther's writings were produced in response to some controversy. Only his two Catechisms can really be thought of as systematic presentations of the basic ideas of the Christian faith. Their largely pastoral role probably disqualifies them from being taken seriously as works of academic theology. Nevertheless, aspects of Luther's theology have had a deep impact upon western Christian thought. For example, his "theology of the cross," set out briefly in a document of 1518 (the *Heidelberg Disputation*), has had a considerable impact upon twentieth-century theology, as works such as Jürgen Moltmann's *Crucified God* indicate.

John Calvin (1509–64)

Calvin was born in Noyon, north-east of Paris, in 1509. Educated at the scholasticism-dominated University of Paris, he subsequently moved to the more humanist University of Orléans, at which he studied civil law. Although initially inclined to a career of scholarship, he underwent a conversion experience in his mid-twenties, which led to his becoming increasingly associated with reforming movements in Paris, and eventually being forced into exile in Basel.

The second generation of reformers were far more aware of the need for works of systematic theology than the first. Calvin, the major figure of the second period of the Reformation, saw the need for a work which would set out clearly the basic ideas of evangelical theology, justifying them on the basis of Scripture and defending them in the face of Catholic criticism. In 1536, he published a small work entitled *Institutes of the Christian Religion*, a mere six chapters in length. For the next quarter of a century, Calvin worked away at this, adding extra chapters and rearranging the material. By the time of its final edition (1559), the work had eighty chapters, and was divided into four books.

The first book deals with God the creator, and God's sovereignty over his creation. Book two concerns the human need for redemption, and the manner in which this redemption is achieved by Christ the mediator. The third book deals with the manner in which this redemption is appropriated by human beings, while the final book deals with the church and its relation to society. Although it is often suggested that predestination stands at the center of Calvin's system, this is not the case; the only principle which seems to govern Calvin's organization of his theological system is a concern to be faithful to Scripture on the one hand, and to achieve maximum clarity of presentation on the other.

After winding up his affairs in Noyon early in 1536, Calvin decided to settle down to a life of private study in the great city of Strasbourg. Unfortunately, the direct route from Noyon to Strasbourg was impassable, due to the outbreak of war between Francis I of France and the Emperor Charles V. Calvin had to make an extended detour, passing through the city of Geneva, which had recently gained its independence from the neighboring territory of Savoy. Geneva was then in a state of confusion, having just evicted its local bishop and begun a controversial program of reform under the Frenchmen Guillaume Farel and Pierre Viret. On hearing that Calvin was in the city, they demanded that he stay, and help the cause of the Reformation. They needed a good teacher. Calvin reluctantly agreed.

His attempts to provide the Genevan church with a solid basis of doctrine and discipline met with intense resistance. After a series of quarrels, matters reached a head on Easter Day 1538: Calvin was expelled from the city, and sought refuge in Strasbourg. Having arrived in Strasbourg two years later than he had anticipated, Calvin began to make up for lost time. In quick succession he produced a series of major theological works. Perhaps most importantly, he revised and expanded his *Institutes* (1539) and produced the first French translation of this work (1541). As pastor to the French-speaking congregation in the city, Calvin was able to gain experience of the practical problems facing Reformed pastors. Through his friendship with Martin Bucer, the Strasbourg reformer, Calvin was able to develop his thinking on the relation between the city and the church.

In Calvin's absence from Geneva, the religious and political situation had deteriorated. In September 1541 the city appealed to him to come back, and restore order and confidence there. The Calvin who returned to Geneva was a wiser and more experienced young man, far better equipped for the tasks awaiting him than he had been three years earlier. His experience at Strasbourg lent new realism to his theorizing about the nature of the church, which is reflected in his subsequent writings in the field. By the time of his death in 1564, Calvin had made Geneva the center of an international movement, which came to bear his name. Calvinism is still one of the most potent and significant intellectual movements in human history.

Huldrych Zwingli (1484–1531)

The Swiss reformer Huldrych Zwingli was educated at the universities of Vienna and Basel, before taking up parish duties in eastern Switzerland. It is clear that he took a keen interest in the agenda of Christian humanism, especially the writings of Erasmus, and became committed to belief in the need to reform the church of his day. In 1519, he took up a pastoral position in the city of Zurich, where he used the pulpit of the Great Minister, the chief church within the city, to propagate a program of reform. Initially, this program was primarily concerned with the reformation of the morals of the church. However, it soon extended to include criticism of the existing theology of the church, especially its sacramental theology. The term "Zwinglian" is used especially to refer to the belief, associated with Zwingli, that Christ is not present at the eucharist, which is best seen as a memorial of Christ's death.

Zwingli was of major importance in relation to the early propagation of the Reformation, especially in eastern Switzerland. However, he never achieved the same impact as Luther or Calvin, lacking the creativity of the former and the systematic approach of the latter. The reader will encounter considerable variation in the spelling of Zwingli's forename, with "Ulrich" and "Huldreich" often being used in preference to "Huldrych."

KEY THEOLOGICAL DEVELOPMENTS

The Reformation was a complex movement, with a very broad agenda. The debate centered in part upon the sources of Christian theology; in part upon the doctrines which resulted from the application of those sources. We shall consider these matters individually.

The Sources of Theology

The mainstream Reformation was concerned not with establishing a new Christian tradition, but with the renewal and correction of an existing tradition. Arguing that Christian theology was ultimately grounded in Scripture, reformers such as Luther and Calvin argued for the need to return to Scripture as the primary and critical source of Christian theology. The slogan "by Scripture alone" (*sola scriptura*) became characteristic of the reformers, expressing their basic belief that Scripture was the sole necessary and sufficient source of Christian theology. However, as we shall see later (pp. 177–84), this did not mean that they denied the importance of tradition.

This new emphasis upon Scripture had a number of direct consequences, of which the following are of especial importance:

1　Beliefs which could not be demonstrated to be grounded in Scripture were either to be rejected, or to be declared as binding on no one. For example, the reformers had little time for the doctrine of the immaculate conception of Mary (that is, the belief that Mary, as the mother of Jesus, was conceived without any taint from sin). They regarded this as lacking in Scriptural basis, and thus discarded it.
2　A new emphasis came to be placed upon the public status of Scripture within the church. The expository sermon, the biblical commentary, and works of biblical theology (such as Calvin's *Institutes*) came to be characteristic of the Reformation.

The Doctrine of Grace

The first period of the Reformation is dominated by the personal agenda of Martin Luther. Convinced that the church had lapsed into an unwitting Pelagianism, Luther proclaimed the doctrine of justification by faith to whomever would listen to him. The question "How can I find a gracious God?" and the slogan "by faith alone" (*sola fide*) resonated throughout much of western Europe, and attracted him a hearing amongst a substantial section of the church. The issues involved in this doctrine are complex, and will be discussed in detail at the appropriate point later in this volume (see pp. 184–90).

167

The doctrine of justification by faith is especially associated with the Lutheran Reformation. Calvin, while continuing to honor this doctrine, initiated a trend which became of increasing importance in later Reformed theology: the discussion of grace in relation to the doctrine of predestination, rather than justification. For Reformed theologians, the ultimate statement of the "grace of God" was not to be seen in the fact that God justified sinners; rather, it was to be seen in God's election of humanity without reference to their foreseen merits or achievements. The doctrine of "unconditional election" came to be seen as a concise summary of the unmerited nature of grace.

The Doctrine of the Sacraments

By the 1520s, the view had become well established within reforming circles that the sacraments were outward signs of the invisible grace of God. This forging of a link between the sacraments and the doctrine of justification (a development especially associated with Luther and his colleague at Wittenberg, Philip Melanchthon) led to a new interest in the theology of the sacraments. It was not long before this area of theology became the subject of considerable controversy, with the reformers disagreeing with their Catholic opponents over the number and nature of the sacraments, and Luther and Zwingli arguing furiously over whether Christ was really present at communion services (see pp. 195–200).

The Doctrine of the Church

If the first generation of reformers were preoccupied with the question of grace, the second generation turned to address the question of the church. Having broken away from the mainstream of the Catholic church over the doctrine of grace, the reformers came under increasing pressure to develop a coherent theory of the church which would justify this break, and give a basis for the new evangelical churches springing up in the cities of western Europe. Where Luther is especially linked with the doctrine of grace, it is Martin Bucer and John Calvin who made the decisive contributions to the development of Protestant understandings of the church. Those understandings have since become increasingly significant in global Christianity, and will be considered in greater detail later in the present work (see pp. 200–7).

POST-REFORMATION MOVEMENTS

The Reformations, both Protestant and Catholic, were followed by a period of theological consolidation within both movements. Within Protestantism, both Lutheran and Reformed (or "Calvinist"), the period known as "Orthodoxy" opened up, characterized by its emphasis on doctrinal norms and definitions. Although sympathetic to this doctrinal trend, Puritanism placed considerably greater emphasis on spiritual and pastoral application. Pietism, in contrast, was hostile to this emphasis on doctrine, feeling that the stress on doctrinal orthodoxy obscured the need for a "living faith" on the part of believers. Within post-Tridentine Roman Catholicism, increasing emphasis came to be placed on the continuity of the Catholic tradition, with Protestantism being viewed as innovative, and hence heterodox. We begin our analysis by considering the emergence of Protestant orthodoxy.

Protestant Orthodoxy

It seems to be a general rule of history that periods of enormous creativity are followed by eras of stagnation. The Reformation is no exception. Perhaps through a desire to preserve the insights of the Reformation, the post-Reformation period witnessed the development of a strongly scholastic approach to theology. The insights of the reformers were codified and perpetuated through the development of a series of systematic presentations of Christian theology.

In the period after Calvin's death a new concern for method – that is, the systematic organization and coherent deduction of ideas – gained momentum. Reformed theologians found themselves having to defend their ideas against both Lutheran and Roman Catholic opponents. Aristotelianism, regarded with a certain degree of suspicion by Calvin, was now seized upon as an ally. It became increasingly important to demonstrate the internal consistency and coherence of Calvinism. As a result, many Calvinist writers turned to Aristotle, in the hope that his writings on method would offer hints as to how their theology might be placed upon a firmer rational foundation.

Four characteristics of the new approach to theology which resulted may be noted.

1   Human reason was assigned a major role in the exploration and defense of Christian theology.
2   Christian theology was presented as a logically coherent and rationally defensible system, derived from syllogistic deductions based upon known axioms. In other words, theology began from first principles, and proceeded to deduce its doctrines on their basis.
3   Theology was understood to be grounded upon Aristotelian philosophy, and particularly Aristotelian insights into the nature of method; later Reformed writers are better described as philosophical, rather than biblical, theologians.
4   Theology became oriented toward metaphysical and speculative questions, especially relating to the nature of God, God's will for humanity and creation, and above all the doctrine of predestination.

169

The starting point of theology thus came to be general principles, not a specific historical event. The contrast with Calvin will be clear. For Calvin, theology centered on and derived from the event of Jesus Christ, as witnessed to by Scripture. But for later Calvinism, general principles came to take the central place hitherto assigned to Christ.

A point of major importance here concerns the political situation in Europe, especially Germany, in the later sixteenth century. In the 1550s, Lutheranism and Roman Catholicism were well established in different regions of Germany. A religious stalemate had developed, in which further expansion into Roman Catholic regions by Lutheranism was no longer possible. Lutheran writers therefore concentrated upon defending Lutheranism at the academic level, by demonstrating its internal consistency and faithfulness to Scripture. They believed that by showing Lutheranism to be intellectually respectable, they might make it attractive to Roman Catholics, disillusioned with their own system of beliefs. But this was not to be the case. Roman Catholic writers responded with increasingly sophisticated works of systematic theology, drawing on the writings of Thomas Aquinas. The Society of Jesus (founded in 1534) rapidly established itself as a leading intellectual force within the Roman Catholic church. Its leading writers, such as Roberto Bellarmine and Francisco de Suarez, made major contributions to the intellectual defense of Roman Catholicism.

The situation in Germany became even more complicated during the 1560s and 1570s, as Calvinism began to make major inroads into previously Lutheran territory. Three major Christian denominations were now firmly established in the same area: Lutheranism, Calvinism, and Roman Catholicism. All three were under considerable pressure to identify themselves. Lutherans were obliged to explain how they differed from Calvinists on the one hand, and Roman Catholics on the other. Doctrine proved the most reliable way of identifying and explaining these differences: "We believe this, but they believe that." The period 1559–1622, characterized by its new emphasis upon doctrine, is generally referred to as the "period of orthodoxy." A new form of scholasticism began to develop within both Protestant and Roman Catholic theological circles, as both sought to demonstrate the rationality and sophistication of their systems.

Lutheranism and Calvinism were, in many respects, very similar. Thus both claimed to be evangelical, and rejected more or less the same central aspects of medieval Catholicism. But they needed to be distinguished. On most points of doctrine, Lutherans and Calvinists were in broad agreement. Yet there was one matter upon which they were radically divided: the doctrine of predestination. The emphasis placed upon the doctrine of predestination by Calvinists in the period 1559–1662 partly reflects the fact that this doctrine most sharply distinguished them from their Lutheran colleagues.

The importance of this point can easily be appreciated by comparing the German situation with that of England. The sixteenth-century English Reformation under Henry VIII (1509–47) bore little relation to its German equivalent. In Germany, there was a protracted struggle between Lutheran and Roman Catholic, as each attempted to gain influence in a disputed region. In England, Henry VIII simply declared that there would only be one national church within his realm. By royal command, there would only be one Christian body within England. The Reformed English church was under no pressure to define itself in relation to any other Christian body in the region. The manner in which the English Reformation initially proceeded demanded no doctrinal self-definition, in that the church in England was defined socially in precisely the same way before the Reformation as after, whatever political alterations may have been introduced. This is not to say that no theological debates took place in England at the time of the Reformation; it is to note that they were not seen as of decisive importance. They were not regarded as identity-giving.

The Lutheran church in Germany was obliged to define and defend its existence and boundaries by doctrine because it had broken away from the medieval Catholic church. That church continued to exist around Lutheran regions, forcing Lutheranism to carry on justifying its existence. The Henrician church in England, however, regarded itself as continuous with the medieval church. The English church was sufficiently well defined as a social unit to require no further definition at the doctrinal level.

The situation in England remained much the same under Elizabeth I. The "Elizabethan Settlement" (1559) laid down that there would only be one Christian church in England: the Church of England, which retained the monopoly of the pre-Reformation church, while replacing it with a church which recognized royal) rather than papal, authority. Roman Catholicism, Lutheranism, and Calvinism – the three Christian churches fighting it out for dominance of the continent of Europe – would not be tolerated within England. There was thus no particular reason for the Church of England to bother much about doctrinal questions. Elizabeth ensured that it had no rivals within England. One of the purposes of doctrine is to divide – and there was nothing for the Church of England to divide itself from. England was insulated from the factors which made doctrine so significant a matter on the mainland of Europe in the Reformation and immediate post-Reformation periods.

The following two developments are of especial importance during this period.

1   *A new concern for method*   Reformers such as Luther and Calvin had relatively little interest in questions of method. For them, theology was primarily concerned with the exposition of Scripture. Indeed, Calvin's *Institutes* may be regarded as a work of "biblical theology," bringing together the basic ideas of Scripture into an orderly presentation. However, in the writings of Theodore Beza, Calvin's successor as director of the Genevan Academy (a training institute for Calvinist pastors throughout Europe), there is a new concern for questions

of method, as noted above. The logical arrangement of material, and its grounding in first principles, comes to assume paramount importance. The impact of this development is perhaps most obvious in the way in which Beza handled the doctrine of predestination, to be noted later.

2 *The development of works of systematic theology* The rise of scholasticism within Lutheran, Calvinist, and Roman Catholic theological circles led to the appearance of vast works of systematic theology, comparable in many ways to Thomas Aquinas' *Summa Theologiae*. These works aimed to present sophisticated and comprehensive accounts of Christian theology, demonstrating the strengths of their positions and the weaknesses of their opponents'.

The following writers should be noted as being of especial importance during this period.

1 *Theodore Beza (1519–1605)*, a noted Calvinist writer, served as professor of theology at the Genevan Academy from 1559 to 1599. The three volumes of his *Tractationes theologicae* ("Theological Treatises," 1570–82) present a rationally coherent account of the main elements of Reformed theology, using Aristotelian logic. The result is a tightly argued and rationally defensible account of Calvin's theology, in which some of the unresolved tensions of that theology (chiefly relating to the doctrines of predestination and atonement) are clarified. Some writers have suggested that Beza's concern for logical clarity leads him to misrepresent Calvin at a number of critical points; others have argued that Beza merely streamlined Calvin's theology, tidying up some loose ends.

2 *Johann Gerhard (1582–1637)*, a Lutheran writer, was appointed professor of theology at Jena in 1616, where he remained for the rest of his teaching career. Gerhard recognized the need for a systematic presentation of Lutheran theology in the face of intense Calvinist opposition. The basic form of Lutheran works of systematic theology had been laid down in 1521, when Philip Melanchthon published the first edition of his *Loci communes* ("Commonplaces"), in which subjects were treated topically, rather than systematically. Gerhard continued this tradition, but felt able to draw increasingly upon Aristotelian works of logic. His *Loci communes theologici* ("Theological Commonplaces," 1610–22) remained a classic of Lutheran theology for many years.

Roman Catholicism

The Council of Trent (1545–63) represented the definitive response of the Catholic church to the Reformation. The achievements of the Council may be thought of in two manners. First, the Council remedied the problems within the church which had contributed in no small way to the emergence of the Reformation in the first place. Measures were taken to end corruption and abuse within the church. Second, the Council set out the main lines of Catholic teaching on central areas of the Christian faith, including a series of issues which had become controversial as a result of the Reformation – such as the relation between Scripture and tradition, the doctrine of justification, and the nature and role of the sacraments. As a result, Roman Catholicism was well prepared to meet the challenges of its Protestant opponents. The final decades of the sixteenth century saw the emergence of a confident, sustained and significant critique of Protestantism from within the Catholic church.

One of the clearest signs of this new confidence can be seen in Catholic patristic scholarship. The Protestant appeal to the patristic period was initially so effective that some Catholic writers of the middle of the sixteenth century seem to have thought that patristic writers such as Augustine were actually proto-Protestants. However, the final third of the century saw increasing confidence among Roman Catholic writers concerning the continuity between the patristic writers and themselves. The most important work to establish this continuity was Marguérin de la Bigne's *Bibliotheca Patrum* ("Library of the Fathers"), whose eight folio volumes appeared in 1575. This was followed up by major contributions from writers such as Antoine Arnauld and Pierre Nicole.

This new confidence in the continuity of the Catholic tradition led to increasing emphasis being placed upon the constancy of Catholic teaching. The most noted writer to develop this emphasis was Jacques-Bénigne Bossuet (1627–1704), whose *Histoire des variations des églises protestantes* ("History of the Variations of the Protestant Churches") became a major weapon in the debates between Roman Catholics and Protestants. For Bossuet, the teaching of the church remained the same down the ages. As Protestants had departed from this teaching, either by introducing innovations or by denying some of its central elements, they had forfeited their right to be considered orthodox. The apostles had handed down to their successors a fixed deposit of truth, which had to be maintained from one generation to another.

> The teaching of the church is always the same. . . . The gospel is never different from what it was earlier. Therefore if anyone at any time should say that the faith includes something which was not said to be "of the faith" yesterday, it is *heterodoxy*, which is any teaching different from *orthodoxy*. There is no difficulty in recognizing false teaching, or argument about it: it is recognized at once, whenever it appears, simply because it is new.

The slogan *semper eadem* ("always the same") became a significant element in Catholic polemics against Protestantism. For Bossuet, Protestantism was easily shown to be an innovation – and hence heterodox for that very reason.

Of the theologians to achieve eminence during this golden period of Catholic theology, the most important is probably Roberto Bellarmine (1542–1621), who entered the Society of Jesus in 1560, and subsequently became professor of controversial theology at Rome in 1576. He remained in this position until 1599, when he became a cardinal. His most significant work is generally regarded to be the *Disputationes de Controversiis Christianae Fidei* ("Disputations concerning the controversies of the Christian faith," 1586–93), in which he argued forcibly for the rationality of Catholic theology against its Protestant (both Lutheran and Calvinist) critics.

Puritanism

One of the most important styles of theology associated with the English-speaking world emerged in late sixteenth-century England. Puritanism is probably best understood as a version of Reformed orthodoxy which laid particular emphasis on the experiential and pastoral aspects of faith. The writings of the leading Puritan theologians William Perkins (1558–1602), William Ames (1576–1633), and John Owen (1618–83) are clearly heavily influenced by Beza, particularly in relation to their teaching on the extent of the death of Christ, and the divine sovereignty in providence and election.

In recent years, particular scholarly attention has focused on the pastoral theology of Puritanism. Early seventeenth-century figures such as Laurence Chaderton, John Dod, and Arthur Hildersam were concerned to bring theology to focus on pastoral issues. The Puritan pastoral tradition is widely regarded as having reached its zenith in the ministry and writings of Richard Baxter (1615–91). Baxter's reputation rests in part on his massive *Christian Directory* (1673), whose four parts set out a vision of theology actualized in everyday Christian life. However, his most celebrated work of pastoral theology remains the *Reformed Pastor* (1656), which addresses ministerial issues from a Puritan perspective.

Although Puritanism was a major theological and political force in early seventeenth-century England, its most significant development took place in the New World. The repressive religious policies of King Charles I forced many Puritans to leave England, and settle in North America. As a result, Puritanism became a major shaping force in North American Christianity during the seventeenth century. The most significant American Puritan theologian was Jonathan Edwards (1703–58), who combined a Puritan emphasis upon divine sovereignty with a willingness to engage with the new questions being raised through the rise of a rational worldview. Although Edwards was much in demand as a spiritual director, especially in the aftermath of the eighteenth-century "Great Awakening" (in which he played a prominent, and probably decisive, role), his theology found its practical expression particularly in his ethics. His sermon series on 1 Corinthians 13 was published in 1746 as *Charity and Its Fruits*.

In some respects, particularly in relation to the issue of Christian experience, Puritanism shows affinities with Pietism, to which we may now turn.

Pietism

As orthodoxy became increasingly influential within mainstream Protestantism, so its defects became clear. At its best, orthodoxy was concerned with the rational defense of Christian truth claims, and a concern for doctrinal correctness. Yet, too often, this came across as an academic preoccupation with logical niceties, rather than a concern for relating theology to the issues of everyday life. The term "Pietism" derives from the Latin word *pietas* (best translated as "piety" or "godliness"), and was initially a derogatory term used by the movement's opponents to describe its emphasis upon the importance of Christian doctrine for the everyday Christian life.

The Pietist movement is usually regarded as having been inaugurated with the publication of Philip Jakob Spener's *Pia desideria* ("Pious Wishes," 1675). In this work, Spener lamented the state of the German Lutheran church in the aftermath of the Thirty Years War (1618–48), and set out proposals for the revitalization of the church of his day. Chief among these was a new emphasis upon personal Bible study. These proposals were treated with derision by academic theologians; nevertheless, they were to prove influential in German church circles, reflecting a growing disillusionment and impatience with the sterility of orthodoxy in the face of the shocking social conditions endured during the war. For Pietism, a reformation of doctrine must always be accompanied by a reformation of life.

Pietism developed in a number of different directions, especially in England and Germany. Among the representatives of the movement, two in particular should be noted.

1   *Nikolaus Ludwig Graf von Zinzendorf (1700–60)* founded the Pietist community generally known as the "Herrnhuter," named after the German village of Herrnhut. Alienated from what he regarded as the arid rationalism and barren orthodoxy of his time, he stressed the importance of a "religion of the heart," based on an intimate and personal relationship between Christ and the believer. A new emphasis was placed upon the role of "feeling" (as opposed to reason or doctrinal orthodoxy) within the Christian life, which may be regarded as laying the foundations of Romanticism in later German religious thought. Zinzendorf's emphasis upon a personally appropriated faith finds expression in the slogan "a living faith," which he opposed to the dead credal assent of Protestant orthodoxy. These ideas would be developed

in one direction by F. D. E. Schleiermacher, and in another by John Wesley, who may be regarded as introducing Pietism to England.

2   *John Wesley (1703–91)* founded the Methodist movement within the Church of England, which subsequently gave birth to Methodism as a denomination in its own right. Convinced that he "lacked the faith whereby alone we are saved," Wesley discovered the need for a "living faith" and the role of experience in the Christian life through his conversion experience at a meeting in Aldersgate Street in May 1738, in which he felt his heart to be "strangely warmed." Wesley's emphasis upon the experiential side of Christian faith, which contrasted sharply with the dullness of contemporary English Deism, led to a major religious revival in England.

Despite their differences, the various branches of Pietism succeeded in making Christian faith relevant to the experiential world of ordinary believers. The movement may be regarded as a reaction against a onesided emphasis upon doctrinal orthodoxy, in favor of a faith which relates to the deepest aspects of human nature.

KEY NAMES, WORDS, AND PHRASES

Anabaptism	Methodism
Calvinist	orthodoxy
Catholic Reformation	Pietism
confessionalism	Protestant
Deism	Puritan
evangelical	Reformed
Lutheran	

QUESTIONS

1   What does the term "Reformation" mean?
2   Which reformer is especially associated with the doctrine of justification by faith alone?
3   How important was humanism to the origins and development of the Reformation?
4   Why did the reformers come to place such emphasis upon revising existing doctrines of the church?
5   What factors led to the development of (a) confessionalism and (b) Pietism?
6   Why did post-Tridentine (Council of Trent) Roman Catholic writers place such an emphasis on continuity with the early church?

Case Study 3.1   Bible and Tradition in the Reformation

The sixteenth century witnessed a major debate over the authority and interpretation of the Bible, which continues to be both interesting and significant. The Reformation called into question established understandings of the matter, and forced a debate over an issue which had hitherto not been considered to be especially significant. The present case study explores this debate, and the positions associated with three participants: the magisterial, radical, and catholic Reformations respectively.

"The Bible," wrote William Chillingworth, "I say, the Bible only, is the religion of Protestants." These famous words of this seventeenth-century English Protestant summarize the Reformation attitude to Scripture. Calvin stated the same principle less memorably, if more fully: "Let this then be a sure axiom: that nothing ought to be admitted in the church as the Word of God, save that which is contained, first in the Law and the Prophets, and secondly in the writings of the Apostles; and that there is no other method of teaching in the church than according to the prescription and rule of his Word." For Calvin, as we shall see, the institutions and regulations of both church and society were required to be grounded in Scripture: "I approve only of those human institutions which are founded upon the authority of God and derived from Scripture." Zwingli entitled his 1522 tract on Scripture *On the Clarity and Certainty of the Word of God*, stating that "the foundation of our religion is the written word, the Scriptures of God." Such views indicate the consistently high view of Scripture adopted by the reformers. This view is not, it must be stressed, a novelty; it represents a major point of continuity with medieval theology, which – certain later Franciscan writers excepted – regarded Scripture as the most important source of Christian doctrine. The difference between the reformers and medieval theology at this point concerns how Scripture is *defined* and *interpreted* rather than the status which it is given. We shall explore these points further in what follows.

The canon of Scripture

Central to any program which treats Scripture as normative is the delimitation of Scripture. In other words, what is Scripture? The term "canon" (a Greek word meaning "rule" or "norm") came to be used to refer to those Scriptures recognized as authentic by the church. For medieval theologians, "Scripture" meant "those works included in the Vulgate." The reformers, however, called this judgment into question. While all the New Testament works were accepted as canonical – Luther's misgivings concerning four of them gaining little support – doubts were raised concerning the canonicity of a group of Old Testament works. A comparison of the contents of the Old Testament in the Hebrew Bible on the one hand, and the Greek and Latin versions (such as the Vulgate) on the other, shows that the latter contain a number of works not found in the former. Following the lead of Jerome, the reformers argued that the only Old Testament writings which could be regarded as belonging to the canon of Scripture were those originally included in the Hebrew Bible. A distinction was thus drawn between the "Old Testament" and "Apocrypha": the former consisted of works found in the Hebrew Bible, while the latter consisted of works found in the Greek and Latin Bibles (such as the Vulgate), but not in the Hebrew Bible. While some reformers allowed that the apocryphal works were edifying reading, there was general agreement that these works could not be used as the basis of doctrine. Medieval theologians, however, to be followed by the Council of Trent in 1546, defined the "Old Testament" as "those Old Testament works contained in the Greek and Latin bibles," thus eliminating any distinction between "Old Testament" and "Apocrypha."

A fundamental distinction thus developed between Roman Catholic and Protestant understandings of what the term "Scripture" actually meant. This distinction persists to the present day. A comparison of Protestant versions of the Bible – the two most important being the *New Revised Standard Version* (NRSV) and *New International Version* (NIV) – with a Roman Catholic Bible, such as the *Jerusalem Bible*, will reveal these differences. For the reformers, the slogan *scriptura sola* ("by Scripture alone") thus implied not merely one, but two, differences from their Catholic opponents: not only did they attach a different status to Scripture, but they disagreed over what Scripture actually was. But what is the relevance of this dispute?

In practice, it has to be said, the distinction was of little practical importance. It certainly had a bearing on one Catholic practice to which the reformers took particular exception – praying for the dead. To the reformers, this practice rested upon a non-biblical foundation (the doctrine of purgatory), and encouraged popular superstition and ecclesiastical exploitation. Their Catholic opponents, however, were able to meet this objection by pointing out that the practice of praying for the dead was explicitly mentioned in Scripture, at 2 Maccabees 12: 40–6. The reformers, having declared that this book was apocryphal (and hence not part of the Bible), were able to respond that, in their view at least, the practice was not scriptural. This merited the obvious riposte from the Catholic side – that the reformers based their theology on Scripture, only after having excluded from the canon of Scripture any works which happened to contradict this theology.

One outcome of this debate was the production and circulation of authorized lists of books which were to be regarded as "scriptural." The fourth session of the Council of Trent (1546) produced a detailed list, which included the works of the Apocrypha as authentically scriptural, while the Protestant congregations in Switzerland, France, and elsewhere produced lists which deliberately omitted reference to these works, or else indicated that they were of no importance in matters of doctrine.

The authority of Scripture

The reformers grounded the authority of Scripture in its relation to the Word of God. For some, that relation was an absolute identity: Scripture is the Word of God. For others, the relation was slightly more nuanced: Scripture contains the Word of God. Nevertheless, there was a consensus that Scripture was to be received as if it were God himself speaking. For Calvin, the authority of Scripture was grounded in the fact that the biblical writers were "secretaries of the Holy Spirit." As Heinrich Bullinger stated it, the authority of Scripture was absolute and autonomous: "Because it is the Word of God, the holy biblical Scripture has adequate standing and credibility in itself and of itself." Here was the gospel itself, able to speak for itself and challenge and correct its inadequate and inaccurate representations in the sixteenth century. Scripture was able both to pass judgment upon the late medieval church (and find it wanting) and also to provide the model for the new Reformed church which would arise in its wake.

The Catholic opponents of the Reformation, however, argued that, in that the church had defined the canon of Scripture and chosen to treat canonical biblical works as possessing authority, it followed that the church took precedence over the Bible.

A number of points will bring out the importance of the *sola scriptura* principle. First, the reformers insisted that the authority of popes, councils, and theologians is subordinate to that of Scripture. This is not necessarily to say that they have no authority: as a matter of fact, the mainline reformers allowed certain councils and theologians of the patristic era a genuine authority in matters of doctrine. Nevertheless, the mainstream reformers argued that such authority is derived from Scripture, and is thus subordinate to Scripture. The Bible, as the Word of God, must be regarded as superior to fathers and councils. As Calvin stated this point:

> For although we hold that the Word of God alone lies beyond the sphere of our judgment, and that fathers and councils are of authority only in so far as they agree with the rule of the Word, we still give to councils and fathers such rank and honour as it is appropriate for them to hold under Christ.

Second, the reformers argued that authority within the church does not derive from the status of the office-bearers, but from the Word of God which they serve. Traditional Catholic theology tended to ground the authority of the office-bearer in the office itself – for example, the authority of a bishop resides in the fact that he is a bishop – and emphasized the historical continuity of the office of bishop with the apostolic era. The reformers grounded the authority of bishops (or their Protestant equivalent) in their faithfulness to the Word of God. As Calvin stated this point:

> The difference between us and the papists is that they believe that the church cannot be the pillar of the truth unless she presides over the Word of God. We, on the other hand, assert that it is *because* she reverently subjects herself to the Word of God that the truth is preserved by her, and passed on to others by her hands.

Historical continuity is of little importance in relation to the faithful proclamation of the Word of God. The breakaway churches of the Reformation were obviously denied historical continuity with the institutions of the Catholic church: no Catholic bishop would ordain their clergy, for example. Yet the reformers argued that the authority and functions of a bishop ultimately derived from faithfulness to the Word of God. Similarly, the decisions of bishops (and also of councils and popes) are authoritative and binding to the extent that they are faithful to Scripture. Where the Catholics stressed the importance of institutional or historical continuity, the reformers emphasized equally the importance of doctrinal continuity. While the Protestant churches could not generally provide historical continuity with the episcopacy (except, as in the case of the English or the Swedish reformations, through defections of Catholic bishops), they could supply the necessary fidelity to Scripture – thus, in their view, legitimizing the Protestant ecclesiastical offices. There might not be an unbroken historical link between the leaders of the Reformation and the bishops of the early church – but, the reformers argued, as they believed and taught the same faith as those early church bishops (rather than the distorted gospel of the medieval church), the necessary continuity was there nonetheless.

The *sola scriptura* principle thus involved the claim that the authority of the church was grounded in its fidelity to Scripture. The opponents of the Reformation, however, were able to draw upon a dictum of Augustine: "I should not have believed the gospel, unless I was moved by the authority of the Catholic church." Did not the very existence of the canon of Scripture point to the church having authority over Scripture? After all, as we have seen, it was the church which defined what "Scripture" was – and this would seem to suggest that the church had an authority over, and independent of, Scripture. Thus John Eck, Luther's opponent at the famous Leipzig Disputation of 1519, argued that "Scripture is not authentic without the authority of the church." This clearly raises the question of the relation between Scripture and tradition, to which we may now conveniently turn.

The role of tradition

The *scriptura sola* principle of the reformers would seem to eliminate any reference to tradition in the formation of Christian doctrine. In fact, however, the magisterial reformers had a very positive understanding of tradition, as we shall see, although the radical reformers did indeed adopt the more negative attitude toward tradition which the slogan might seem to imply. It will be helpful if we begin our discussion of this matter by exploring some understandings of the role of tradition found in the Middle Ages; readers might also like to look at case study 1.1, which examines the issues as they were set out during the patristic period.

For most medieval theologians, Scripture was the materially sufficient source of Christian doctrine. In other words, everything that was of essential importance to the Christian faith was contained in Scripture. There was no need to look anywhere else for material relevant to Christian theology. There were certainly matters on which Scripture had nothing to say – for example, who wrote the Apostles' Creed, at what precise moment during the celebration of the eucharist the bread and wine became the body and blood of Christ, or whether the practice of baptism was intended solely for adult believers. On these matters, the church felt at liberty to attempt to work out what Scripture implied, although their judgments were regarded as subordinate to Scripture itself.

By the end of the Middle Ages, however, the concept of "tradition" had come to be of major importance in relation to the interpretation and authority of Scripture. Scholars such as Heiko A. Oberman have shown that two quite different concepts of tradition were in circulation in the late Middle Ages, which may be designated as "Tradition 1" and "Tradition 2." As we noted earlier (see case study 1.1), in response to various controversies within the early church, especially the threat from Gnosticism, a "traditional" method of understanding certain passages of Scripture began to develop. Second-century patristic theologians such as Irenaeus of Lyons began to develop the idea of an authorized way of interpreting certain texts of Scripture, which he argued went back to the time of the apostles themselves. Scripture couldn't be interpreted in any random way: it had to be interpreted within the context of the historical continuity of the Christian church. The parameters of its interpretation were historically fixed and "given." Oberman designates this understanding of tradition as "Tradition 1." "Tradition" here means simply "a traditional way of interpreting Scripture within the community of faith."

In the fourteenth and fifteenth centuries, however, a somewhat different understanding of tradition developed. "Tradition" is now understood to be a separate and distinct source of revelation *in addition to Scripture*. Scripture, it was argued, was silent on a number of points – but God had providentially arranged for a second source of revelation to supplement this deficiency: a stream of unwritten tradition, going back to the apostles themselves. This tradition was passed down from one generation to another within the church. Oberman designates this understanding of tradition as "Tradition 2."

To summarize this important distinction: "Tradition 1" is a *single-source* theory of doctrine: doctrine is based upon Scripture, and "tradition" refers to a "traditional way of interpreting Scripture." "Tradition 2" is a *dual-source* theory of doctrine: doctrine is based upon two quite distinct sources, Scripture and unwritten tradition. A belief which is not to be found in Scripture may thus, on the basis of this dual-source theory, be justified by an appeal to an unwritten tradition. It was primarily against this dual-source theory of doctrine that the reformers directed their criticisms.

During the sixteenth century, the option of totally rejecting tradition was vigorously defended by representatives of the radical Reformation. For radicals such as Thomas Müntzer and Caspar Schwenkfeld, every individual had the right to interpret Scripture as he pleased, subject to the guidance of the Holy Spirit. For Sebastian Franck, the Bible "is a book sealed with seven seals which none can open unless he has the key of David, which is the illumination of the Spirit." The way was thus opened for individualism, with the private judgment of the individual raised above the corporate judgment of the church. Thus the radicals rejected the practice of infant baptism (to which the magisterial Reformation remained committed) as non-scriptural. (There is no explicit reference to the practice in the New Testament.) Similarly, doctrines such as the Trinity and the divinity of Christ were rejected as resting upon inadequate scriptural foundations. What we might therefore term "Tradition 0" rejects tradition, and in effect places the private judgment of the individual or congregation in the present above the corporate traditional judgment of the Christian church concerning the interpretation of Scripture.

The three main understandings of the relation between Scripture and tradition current in the sixteenth century can thus be summarized as follows:

Tradition 0: The radical Reformation
Tradition 1: The magisterial Reformation
Tradition 2: The Council of Trent

At first, this analysis might seem surprising. Did not the reformers *reject* tradition, in favour of the scriptural witness alone? In fact, however, the reformers were concerned with the elimination of human additions to or distortions of the scriptural witness. The idea of a "traditional interpretation of Scripture" – embodied in the concept of "Tradition 1" – was perfectly acceptable to the magisterial reformers, provided that this traditional interpretation could be justified.

As has been noted, the magisterial Reformation was theologically conservative. It retained most traditional doctrines of the church – such as the divinity of Jesus Christ and the doctrine of the Trinity – on account of the reformers' conviction that these traditional interpretations of Scripture were correct. Equally, many traditional practices (such as infant baptism) were retained, on account of the reformers' belief that they were consistent with Scripture. The magisterial Reformation was painfully aware of the threat of individualism, and attempted to avoid this threat by placing emphasis upon the church's traditional interpretation of Scripture, where this traditional interpretation was regarded as correct. Doctrinal criticism was directed against those areas in which Catholic theology or practice appeared to have gone far beyond, or to have contradicted, Scripture. As most of these developments took place in the Middle Ages, it is not surprising that the reformers spoke of the period 1200–1500 as an "era of decay" or a "period of corruption" which they had a mission to reform. Equally, it is hardly surprising that we find the reformers appealing to the early church fathers as generally reliable interpreters of Scripture.

This point is of particular importance, and has not received the attention it merits. One of the reasons why the reformers valued the writings of the fathers, especially Augustine, was that they regarded them as exponents of a biblical theology. In other words, the reformers believed that the fathers were attempting to develop a theology based upon Scripture alone – which was, of course, precisely what they were also trying to do in the sixteenth century. Of course, the new textual and philological methods available to the reformers meant that they could correct the fathers on points of detail – but the reformers were prepared to accept the "patristic testimony" as generally reliable. As that testimony included such doctrines as the Trinity and the divinity of Christ, and such practices as infant baptism, the reformers were predisposed to accept these as authentically scriptural. It will thus be obvious that this high regard for a traditional interpretation of Scripture (i.e., "Tradition 1") gave the magisterial Reformation a strong bias towards doctrinal conservatism.

The Catholic position

The Council of Trent, meeting in 1546, responded to the threat of the Reformation by affirming a two-source theory. This affirmation by the Catholic Reformation of "Tradition 2" declares that the Christian faith reaches every generation through two sources: Scripture and an unwritten tradition. This extra-scriptural tradition is to be treated as having equal authority with Scripture. In making this declaration, the Council of Trent appears to have picked up the later, and less influential, of the two main medieval understandings of "tradition" – leaving the more influential to the reformers. It is interesting to note that in recent years there has been a certain degree of "revisionism" within Roman Catholic circles on this point, with several contemporary theologians arguing that Trent excluded the view that "the Gospel is only partly in Scripture and partly in the traditions."

The Fourth Session of the Council, which concluded its deliberations on April 8, 1546, laid down the following challenges to the Protestant position.

1 Scripture could not be regarded as the only source of revelation; tradition was a vital supplement, which Protestants irresponsibly denied. "All saving truths and rules of conduct . . . are contained in the written books and in the unwritten traditions, received from the mouth of Christ himself or from the apostles themselves."

2 Trent ruled that Protestant lists of canonical books were deficient, and published a full list of works which it accepted as authoritative. This included all the apocryphal books, which Protestant writers had rejected.

3 The Vulgate edition of Scripture was affirmed to be reliable and authoritative. It declared that "the old Latin Vulgate edition, which has been used for many centuries, has been approved by the church, and should be defended as authentic in public lectures, disputations, sermons or expositions, and that no one should dare or presume, under any circumstances, to reject it."

4 The authority of the church to interpret Scripture was defended, against what the Council of Trent clearly regarded as the rampant individualism of Protestant interpreters:

To check reckless spirits, this council decrees that no one, relying on his or her own judgement, in matters of faith and morals relating to Christian doctrine (distorting the Holy Scriptures in accordance with their own ideas), shall presume to interpret Scripture contrary to that sense which holy mother . . .

Case Study 3.2   Justification by Faith: Martin Luther and the Council of Trent

It is widely agreed that the doctrine of justification by faith was of critical importance to the Reformation. The present case study will focus on two understandings of this doctrine to be set out at the time of the Reformation – that adopted by the great German reformer Martin Luther, and that set out by the Council of Trent.

At the heart of the Christian faith lies the idea that human beings, finite and frail though they are, can enter into a relationship with the living God. The New Testament articulates this fundamental idea through a number of metaphors or images, such as "salvation" and "redemption," initially in the writings of the New Testament (especially the Pauline letters) and subsequently in Christian theological reflection, based upon these texts. By the late Middle Ages, one image had come to be seen as especially significant: justification.

The term "justification" and the verb "to justify" came to signify "entering into a right relationship with God," or perhaps "being made righteous in the sight of God." The doctrine of justification came to be seen as dealing with the question of what an individual had to do in order to be saved. As contemporary sources indicate, this question came to be asked with increasing frequency as the sixteenth century dawned. The rise of humanism brought with it a new emphasis upon individual consciousness, and a new awareness of human individuality. In the wake of this dawn of the individual consciousness came a new interest in the doctrine of justification – the question of how human beings, as individuals, could enter into a relationship with God. How could a sinner hope to do this? This question lay at the heart of the theological concerns of Martin Luther, and came to dominate the early phase of the Reformation. In view of the importance of the doctrine to this period, we shall consider Luther's discussion of the doctrine, and the response of the Council of Trent.

Martin Luther

In 1545, the year before he died, Luther contributed a preface to the first volume of the complete edition of his Latin writings, in which he described how he came to break with the church of his day. The preface is clearly written with the aim of introducing Luther to a readership which may not know how Luther came to hold the radical reforming views linked with his name. In this "autobiographical fragment" (as it is usually known), Luther aims to provide those readers with background information about the development of his vocation as a reformer. After dealing with some historical preliminaries, taking his narrative up to the year 1519, he turns to describe his personal difficulties with the problem of the "righteousness of God":

> I had certainly wanted to understand Paul in his letter to the Romans. But what prevented me from doing so was not so much cold feet as that one phrase in the first chapter: "the righteousness of God is revealed in it" (Romans 1: 17). For I hated that phrase, "the righteousness of God," which I had been taught to understand as the righteousness by which God is righteous, and punishes unrighteous sinners.
>
> Although I lived a blameless life as a monk, I felt that I was a sinner with an uneasy conscience before God. I also could not believe that I had pleased him with my works. Far from loving that righteous God who punished sinners, I actually hated him. . . . I was in desperation to know what Paul meant in this passage. At last, as I meditated day and night on the relation of the words "the righteousness of God is revealed in it, as it is written, the righteous person shall live by faith," I began to understand that "righteousness of God" as that by which the righteous person lives by the gift of God (faith); and this sentence, "the righteousness of God is revealed," to refer to a passive righteousness, by which the merciful God justifies us by faith, as it is written, "the righteous person lives by faith." This immediately made me feel as though I had been born again, and as though I had entered through open gates

into paradise itself. From that moment, I saw the whole face of Scripture in a new light. . . . And now, where I had once hated the phrase, "the righteousness of God," I began to love and extol it as the sweetest of phrases, so that this passage in Paul became the very gate of paradise to me.

What is Luther talking about in this famous passage, which vibrates with the excitement of discovery? It is obvious that his understanding of the phrase "the righteousness of God" has changed radically. But what is the nature of this change?

> **Martin Luther (1483–1546).** Perhaps the greatest figure in the European Reformation, noted particularly for his doctrine of justification by faith alone, and his strongly Christocentric understanding of revelation. His "theology of the cross" has aroused much interest in the late twentieth century. Luther's posting of the Ninety-Five Theses in Ocober 1517 is generally regarded as marking the beginning of the Reformation.

The basic change is fundamental. Originally Luther regarded the precondition for justification as a human work, something which the sinner had to perform, before he or she could be justified. Increasingly convinced, through his reading of Augustine, that this was an impossibility, Luther could only interpret the "righteousness of God" as a punishing righteousness. But in this passage, he narrates how he discovered a "new" meaning of the phrase – a righteousness which God gives to the sinner. In other words, God meets this precondition, graciously giving sinners what they require if they are to be justified. An analogy (not used by Luther) may help bring out the difference between these two approaches.

Let us suppose that you are in prison, and are offered your freedom on condition that you pay a heavy fine. The promise is real – so long as you can meet the precondition, the promise will be fulfilled. As we noted earlier, Pelagius works on the presupposition, initially shared by Luther, that you have the necessary money stacked away somewhere. As your freedom is worth far more, you are being offered a bargain. So you pay the fine. This presents no difficulties, so long as you have the necessary resources. Luther increasingly came to share the view of Augustine – that sinful humanity just doesn't have the resources needed to meet this precondition. To go back to our analogy, Augustine and Luther work on the assumption that, as you don't have the money, the promise of freedom has little relevance to your situation. For both Augustine and Luther, therefore, the good news of the gospel is that you have been *given* the necessary money with which to buy your freedom. In other words, the precondition has been met for you by someone else.

Luther's insight, which he describes in this autobiographical passage, is that the God of the Christian gospel is not a harsh judge who rewards individuals according to their merits, but a merciful and gracious God who bestows righteousness upon sinners as a gift. The general consensus among Luther scholars is that his theology of justification underwent a decisive alteration at some point in 1515.

Central to Luther's insights was the doctrine of "justification by faith alone." The idea of "justification" is already familiar. But what about the phrase "by faith alone"? What is the nature of justifying faith? "The reason why some people do not understand why faith alone justifies is that they do not know what faith is." In writing these words, Luther draws our attention to the need to inquire more closely concerning that deceptively simple word "faith." Three points relating to Luther's idea of faith may be singled out as having special importance to his doctrine of justification. Each of these points is taken up and developed by later writers, such as Calvin, indicating that Luther has made a fundamental contribution to the development of Reformation thought at this point. These three points are:

1 Faith has a personal, rather than a purely historical, reference.
2 Faith concerns trust in the promises of God.
3 Faith unites the believer to Christ.

We shall consider each of these points individually.

1 First, faith is not simply historical knowledge. Luther argues that a faith which is content to believe in the historical reliability of the gospels is not a faith which justifies. Sinners are perfectly capable of trusting in the historical details of the gospels; but these facts of themselves are not adequate for true Christian faith. Saving faith concerns believing and trusting that Christ was born *pro nobis*, born for us personally, and has accomplished for us the work of salvation.

2 Second, faith is to be understood as "trust (*fiducia*)." The notion of trust is prominent in the Reformation conception of faith, as a nautical analogy used by Luther indicates: "Everything depends upon faith. The person who does not have faith is like someone who has to cross the sea, but is so frightened that he does not trust the ship. And so he stays where he is, and is never saved, because he will not get on board and cross over." Faith is not merely believing that something is true; it is being prepared to act upon that belief, and relying upon it. To use Luther's analogy: faith is not simply about believing that a ship exists – it is about stepping into it, and entrusting ourselves to it.

3 In the third place, faith unites the believer with Christ. Luther states this principle clearly in his writing of 1520, *The Liberty of a Christian*. Faith is not assent to an abstract set of doctrines, but is a union between Christ and the

believer. It is the response of the whole person of the believer to God, which leads in turn to the real and personal presence of Christ in the believer. "To know Christ is to know his benefits," wrote Philip Melanchthon, Luther's colleague at Wittenberg. Faith makes both Christ and his benefits – such as forgiveness, justification, and hope – available to the believer.

The doctrine of "justification by faith" thus does not mean that the sinner is justified because he or she believes, on account of that faith. This would be to treat faith as a human action or work. Luther insists that God provides everything necessary for justification, so that all that the sinner needs to do is to receive it. God is active, and humans are passive, in justification. The phrase "justification by grace through faith" brings out the meaning of the doctrine more clearly: the justification of the sinner is based upon the grace of God, and is received through faith. The doctrine of justification by faith alone is an affirmation that God does everything necessary for salvation. Even faith itself is a gift of God, rather than a human action. God meets the precondition for justification. Thus, as we saw, the "righteousness of God" is not a righteousness which judges whether or not we have met the precondition for justification, but the righteousness which is given to us so that we may meet that precondition.

One of the central insights of Luther's doctrine of justification by faith alone is that the individual sinner is incapable of self-justification. It is God who takes the initiative in justification, providing all the resources necessary to justify that sinner. One of those resources is the "righteousness of God." In other words, the righteousness on the basis of which the sinner is justified is not his own righteousness, but a righteousness which is given to him by God. Augustine had made this point earlier: Luther, however, gives it a subtle new twist, which leads to the development of the concept of "forensic justification."

The point at issue is difficult to explain, and centers on the question of the location of justifying righteousness. Both Augustine and Luther are agreed that God graciously gives sinful humans a righteousness which justifies them. But where is that righteousness located. Augustine argued that it was to be found within believers; Luther insisted that it remained outside believers. For Augustine, the righteousness in question is internal; for Luther, it is external.

For Augustine, God bestows justifying righteousness upon the sinner, in such a way that it becomes part of his or her person. As a result, this righteousness, although originating from outside the sinner, becomes part of his or her person. For Luther, the righteousness in question remains outside the sinner: it is an "alien righteousness" (*iustitia aliena*). God treats, or "reckons," this righteousness *as if* it is part of the sinner's person. In his Romans lectures of 1515–16, Luther develops the idea of the "alien righteousness of Christ," imputed – not imparted – to us by faith, as the grounds of justification. His comments on Romans 4: 7 are especially important:

> The saints are always sinners in their own sight, and therefore always justified outwardly. But the hypocrites are always righteous in their own sight, and thus always sinners outwardly. I use the term "inwardly" to show how we are in ourselves, in our own sight, in our own estimation; and the term "outwardly" to indicate how we are before God and in his reckoning. Therefore we are righteous outwardly when we are righteous solely by the imputation of God and not of ourselves or of our own works.

Believers are righteous on account of the alien righteousness of Christ, which is imputed to them – that is, treated as if it were theirs through faith. Earlier, we noted that an essential element of Luther's concept of faith is that it unites the believer to Christ. Justifying faith thus allows the believer to link up with the righteousness of Christ, and be justified on its basis. Christians are thus "righteous by the imputation of a merciful God."

Through faith, the believer is clothed with the righteousness of Christ, in much the same way, Luther suggests, as Ezekiel 16: 8 speaks of God covering our nakedness with his garment. For Luther, faith is the right (or righteous) relationship to God. Sin and righteousness thus coexist; we remain sinners inwardly, but are righteous extrinsically, in the sight of God. By confessing our sins in faith, we stand in a right and righteous relationship with God. From our own perspective we are sinners; but in the perspective of God, we are righteous.

Luther does not necessarily imply that this coexistence of sin and righteousness is a permanent condition. The Christian life is not static, as if – to use a very loose way of speaking – the relative amounts of sin and righteousness remain constant throughout. Luther is perfectly aware that the Christian life is dynamic, in that the believer grows in righteousness. Rather, his point is that the existence of sin does not negate our status as Christians.

God shields our sin through his righteousness. This righteousness is like a protective covering, under which we may battle with our sin. This approach accounts for the persistence of sin in believers, while at the same time accounting for the gradual transformation of the believer and the future elimination of that sin. But it is not necessary to be perfectly righteous to be a Christian. Sin does not point to unbelief, or a failure on the part of God; rather, it points to the continued need to entrust one's person to the gentle care of God. Luther thus declares, in a famous phrase, that a believer is "at one and the same time righteous and a sinner (*simul iustus et peccator*)"; righteous in hope, but a sinner in fact; righteous in the sight and through the promise of God, yet a sinner in reality.

These ideas were subsequently developed by Luther's follower Philip Melanchthon to give the doctrine now generally known as "forensic justification." Where Augustine taught that the sinner is made righteous in justification, Melanchthon taught that he is counted as righteous or pronounced to be righteous. For Augustine, "justifying righteousness" is imparted; for Melanchthon,

189

it is imputed. Melanchthon drew a sharp distinction between the event of being declared righteous and the process of being made righteous, designating the former "justification" and the latter "sanctification" or "regeneration." For Augustine, both were simply different aspects of the same thing. According to Melanchthon, God pronounces the divine judgment – that the sinner is righteous – in the heavenly court. This legal approach to justification gives rise to the term "forensic justification," from the Latin word *forum* ("market place" or "courtyard") – the place traditionally associated with the dispensing of justice in classical Rome.

> **Philip Melanchthon (1497–1560).** A noted early Lutheran theologian, and close personal associate of Martin Luther. He was responsible for the systematization of early Lutheran theology, particularly through his *Loci Communes* (first edition published in 1521) and his "Apology for the Augsburg Confession."

The importance of this development lies in the fact that it marks a complete break with the teaching of the church up to that point. From the time of Augustine onward, justification had always been understood to refer to both the event of being declared righteous and the process of being made righteous. Melanchthon's concept of forensic justification diverged radically from this. As it was taken up by virtually all the major reformers subsequently, it came to represent a standard difference between Protestant and Roman Catholic from that point onward. In addition to their differences on how the sinner was justified, there was now an additional disagreement on what the word "justification" designated in the first place. As we shall see, the Council of Trent, the Roman Catholic church's definitive response to the Protestant challenge, reaffirmed the views of Augustine on the nature of justification, and censured the views of Melanchthon.

The Council of Trent

It was obvious that the church needed to make an official and definitive response to Luther. By 1540, Luther had become something of a household name throughout Europe. His writings were being read and digested with various degrees of enthusiasm, even in the highest ecclesiastical circles in Italy. Something had to be done. The Council of Trent, summoned in 1545, began the long process of formulating a comprehensive response to Luther. High on its agenda was the doctrine of justification.

The sixth session of the Council of Trent was brought to its close on January 13, 1547. The Tridentine Decree on Justification, as the substantial product of this session has generally come to be known, probably represents the most significant achievement of this council. Its sixteen chapters set out the Roman Catholic teaching on justification with a considerable degree of clarity. A series of 33 canons condemn specific opinions attributed to opponents of the Roman Catholic church, including Luther. Interestingly, the council seems unaware of the threat posed by Calvin, and directs the vast bulk of its criticisms against views which were known to be held by Luther himself.

Trent's critique of Luther's doctrine of justification can be broken down into four main sections:

1 The nature of justification.
2 The nature of justifying righteousness.
3 The nature of justifying faith.
4 The assurance of salvation.

We shall consider each of these four matters individually.

1 The nature of justification

In his earlier phase, around the years 1515–19, Luther tended to understand justification as a process of becoming, in which the sinner was gradually conformed to the likeness of Jesus Christ through a process of internal renewal. Luther's analogy of a sick person under competent medical care points to this understanding of justification, as does his famous declaration in the 1515–16 Romans lectures, "justification is about becoming." In his later writings, however, dating from the mid-1530s and beyond, perhaps under the influence of Melanchthon's more forensic approach to justification (see pp. 189–90), Luther tended to treat justification as a matter of being declared to be righteous, rather than a process of becoming righteous. Increasingly, he came to see justification as an event, which was complemented by the distinct process of regeneration and interior renewal through the action of the Holy Spirit. Justification alters the outer status of the sinner in the sight of God, while regeneration alters the sinner's inner nature.

The Council of Trent. A major gathering of Catholic bishops and theologians, which aimed to reform the church in the face of Protestant criticisms, and clarify and defend Catholic doctrine. The Sixth Session, focusing on the doctrine of justification, concluded in 1547; the Thirteenth Session, dealing with the real presence, ended in 1551.

Trent strongly opposes this view, and vigorously defends the idea, originally associated with Augustine of Hippo, that justification is the process of regeneration and renewal within human nature, which brings about a change in both the outer status and inner nature of the sinner. Its fourth chapter provides the following precise definition of justification:

> The justification of the sinner may be briefly defined as a translation from that state in which a human being is born a child of the first Adam, to the state of grace and of the adoption of the sons of God through the second Adam, Jesus Christ our Saviour. According to the gospel, this translation cannot come about except through the cleansing of regeneration, or a desire for this, as it is written, "Unless someone is born again of water and the Holy Spirit, he or she cannot enter into the Kingdom of God" (John 3: 5).

Justification thus includes the idea of regeneration. This brief statement is amplified in the seventh chapter, which stresses that justification "is not only a remission of sins but also the sanctification and renewal of the inner person through the voluntary reception of the grace and gifts by which an unrighteous person becomes a righteous person." This point was given further emphasis through canon 11, which condemned anyone who taught that justification takes place "either by the sole imputation of the righteousness of Christ or by the sole remission of sins, to the exclusion of grace and charity . . . or that the grace by which we are justified is only the goodwill of God."

For Trent, justification is closely linked with the sacraments of baptism and penance. The sinner is initially justified through baptism; however, on account of sin, that justification may be forfeited. It can, however, be renewed by penance, as the fourteenth chapter makes clear:

> Those who through sin have forfeited the received grace of justification can be justified again when, moved by God, they exert themselves to obtain through the sacrament of penance the recovery, by the merits of Christ, of the grace which was lost. Now this manner of justification is restoration for those who have lapsed into sin. The holy fathers have properly called this a "second plank after the shipwreck of lost grace." For Christ Jesus instituted the sacrament of penance, on behalf of those who lapse into sin after baptism. . . . The repentance of a Christian after a lapse into sin is thus very different from that at baptism.

Briefly, then, Trent maintains the medieval tradition, stretching back to Augustine, which saw justification as comprising both an event and a process – the event of being declared to be righteous through the work of Christ, and the process of being made righteous through the internal work of the Holy Spirit. Reformers such as Melanchthon and Calvin distinguished these two matters, treating the word "justification" as referring only to the process of being declared to be righteous; the accompanying process of internal renewal, which they termed "sanctification" or "regeneration," they regarded as theologically distinct.

Serious confusion thus resulted: Roman Catholics and Protestants both used the same word "justification" to mean very different things. Trent used the term "justification" to mean what, to Protestants, was *both* justification *and* sanctification.

2 The nature of justifying righteousness

Luther placed emphasis upon the fact that sinners possessed no righteousness in themselves. They had nothing within them which could ever be regarded as the basis of God's gracious decision to justify them. Luther's doctrine of the "alien righteousness of Christ (*iustitia Christi aliena*)" made it clear that the righteousness which justified sinners was outside them. It was imputed, not imparted; external, not internal.

Early critics of the Reformation argued, following Augustine of Hippo, that sinners were justified on the basis of an internal righteousness, graciously infused or implanted within their persons by God. This righteousness was itself given as an act of grace; it was not something merited. But, they argued, there had to be something within individuals which could allow God to justify them. Luther dismissed this idea. If God had decided to justify someone, he might as well do it directly, rather than through an intermediate gift of righteousness.

Trent strongly defended the Augustinian idea of justification on the basis of an internal righteousness. The seventh chapter makes this point crystal clear:

> The single formal cause (of justification) is the righteousness of God – not the righteousness by which he himself is righteous, but the righteousness by which he makes us righteous, so that, when we are endowed with it, we are "renewed in the spirit of our mind" (Ephesians 4: 23), and are not only counted as righteous, but are called, and are in reality, righteous. . . . Nobody can be righteous except God communicates the merits of the passion of our Lord Jesus Christ to him or her, and this takes place in the justification of the sinner.

The phrase "single formal cause" needs explanation. A "formal" cause is the *direct*, or most immediate, cause of something. Trent is thus stating that the direct cause of justification is the righteousness which God graciously imparts to us – as opposed to more distant causes of justification, such as the "efficient cause" (God), or the "meritorious cause" (Jesus Christ). But the use of the word "single" should also be noted. One proposal for reaching agreement between Roman Catholic and Protestant, which gained especial prominence at the Colloquy of Ratisbon in 1541, was that *two* causes of justification should be recognized – an external righteousness (the Protestant position) and an internal righteousness (the Roman Catholic position). This compromise seemed to hold some potential. Trent, however, had no time for it. The use of the word "single" was deliberate, intended to eliminate the idea that there could be more than one such cause. The only direct cause of justification was the interior gift of righteousness.

3 The nature of justifying faith

Luther's doctrine of justification by faith alone came in for severe criticism. Canon 12 condemns a central aspect of Luther's notion of justifying faith, when it rejects the idea that "justifying faith is nothing other than confidence in the mercy of God, which remits sin for the sake of Christ." In part, this rejection of Luther's doctrine of justification reflects the ambiguity, noted above, concerning the meaning of the term "justification." Trent was alarmed that anyone should believe that they could be justified – in the Tridentine sense of the term – by faith, without any need for obedience or spiritual renewal. Trent, interpreting "justification" to mean both the beginning of the Christian life and its continuation and growth, believed that Luther was suggesting that simply trusting in God (without any requirement that the sinner be changed and renewed by God) was the basis of the entire Christian life.

In fact, Luther meant nothing of the sort. He was affirming that the Christian life was begun through faith, and faith alone; good works followed justification, and did not cause that justification in the first place. Trent itself was perfectly prepared to concede that the Christian life was begun through faith, thus coming very close indeed to Luther's position. As chapter 8 of the Decree on Justification declares, "we are said to be justified by faith, because faith is the beginning of human salvation, the foundation and root of all justification, without which is it impossible to please God." This is perhaps a classic case of a theological misunderstanding, resting upon the disputed meaning of a major theological term.

4 The assurance of salvation

For Luther, as for the reformers in general, one could rest assured of one's salvation. Salvation was grounded upon the faithfulness of God to his promises of mercy; to fail to have confidence in salvation was, in effect, to doubt the reliability and trustworthiness of God. Yet this must not be seen as a supreme confidence in God, untroubled by doubt. Faith is not the same as certainty; although the theological foundation of Christian faith may be secure, the human perception of and commitment to this foundation may waver.

This point is brought out clearly by Calvin, often thought to be the most confident of all the reformers in relation to matters of faith. His definition of faith certainly seems to point in this direction:

> Now we shall have a right definition of faith if we say that it is a steady and certain knowledge of the divine benevolence towards us, which is founded upon the truth of the gracious promise of God in Christ, and is both revealed to our minds and sealed in our hearts by the Holy Spirit.

Yet the theological certainty of this statement does not, according to Calvin, necessarily lead to psychological security. It is perfectly consistent with a sustained wrestling with doubt and anxiety on the part of the believer:

> When we stress that faith ought to be certain and secure, we do not have in mind a certainty without doubt, or a security without any anxiety. Rather, we affirm that believers have a perpetual struggle with their own lack of faith, and are far from possessing a peaceful conscience, never interrupted by any disturbance. On the other hand, we want to deny that they may fall out of, or depart from, their confidence in the divine mercy, no matter how much they may be troubled.

The Council of Trent regarded the reformers' doctrine of assurance with considerable scepticism. Chapter 9 of the Decree on Justification, entitled "Against the vain confidence of heretics," criticized the "ungodly confidence" of the reformers. While no one should doubt God's goodness and generosity, the reformers erred seriously when they taught that "nobody is absolved from sins and justified, unless they believe with certainty that they are absolved and justified, and that absolution and justification are effected by this faith alone." Trent insisted that "nobody can know with a certainty of faith which is not subject to error, whether they have obtained the grace of God."

Trent's point is that the reformers seemed to be making human confidence or boldness the grounds of justification, so that justification rested upon a fallible human conviction, rather than upon the grace of God. The reformers, however, saw themselves as stressing that justification rested upon the promises of God; a failure to believe boldly in such promises was tantamount to calling the reliability of God into question.

The debate between Trent and the Reformation remains significant, as recent ecumenical dialogues between various Protestant denominations and the Roman Catholic church make clear. The same could be said of the Reformation debates over the sacraments, to one of which we now turn.

Case Study 3.3   The Nature of the Real Presence: Luther, Zwingli, and the Council of Trent

What happens at the eucharist? In what way do the eucharistic bread and wine change, if any, as a result of being used in this service? A number of approaches to the question were explored during the sixteenth century, of which three are of especial importance. We shall explore them individually, beginning with the traditional Catholic concept of transubstantiation, which affirms that the inward reality of the eucharistic bread and wine are transformed into the body and blood of Christ.

Transubstantiation: the Council of Trent

The doctrine of transubstantiation, formally defined by the Fourth Lateran Council (1215), rests upon Aristotelian foundations – specifically, on Aristotle's distinction between "substance" and "accident." The *substance* of something is its essential nature, whereas its *accidents* are its outward appearances (for example, its colour, shape, smell, and so forth). The theory of transubstantiation affirms that the accidents of the bread and wine remain unchanged at the moment of consecration, while their substance changes from that of bread and wine to that of the body and blood of Christ.

As we shall see, this understanding of the nature of the real presence was contested during the early sixteenth century. Martin Luther put forward an approach, often referred to as "consubstantiation," which differed from this view at points (although there are significant similarities, as we shall see). More radically, Huldrych Zwingli adopted a purely symbolic or "memorialist" approach to the issue. The traditional viewpoint was, however, vigorously defended by the Council of Trent.

> **The Council of Trent.** A major gathering of Catholic bishops and theologians, which aimed to reform the church in the face of Protestant criticisms, and clarify and defend Catholic doctrine. The Sixth Session, focusing on the doctrine of justification, concluded in 1547; the Thirteenth Session, dealing with the real presence, ended in 1551.

During the course of its thirteenth session, which ended on October 11, 1551, the Council of Trent set out a definitive statement on its understanding of the nature of the real presence of Christ in the eucharist, affirming that the term "transubstantiation" was appropriate to refer to the change in the substance of the bread and wine resulting from their consecration. The Decree opens with a vigorous affirmation of the real substantial presence of Christ: "After the consecration of the bread and wine, our Lord Jesus Christ is truly, really and substantially contained in the venerable sacrament of the holy eucharist under the appearance of those physical things." The Council thus vigorously defended both the doctrine and the terminology of transubstantiation:

> Because Christ our Redeemer declared that it was truly his body that he was offering under the species of bread, it has always been the belief of the Church of God, which

this sacred council reaffirms, that by the consecration of the bread and wine a change takes place in which the entire substance of the bread becomes the substance of the body of Christ our Lord, and the whole substance of the wine becomes the substance of his blood. This change the holy Catholic Church has fittingly and correctly called "transubstantiation."

Note especially the vigorous defense of the change of the substance of the bread and wine into that of the body and blood of Christ, which can be regarded as the real theological meat of this doctrine.

Luther: consubstantiation

This view, especially associated with Martin Luther, insists upon the simultaneous presence of both bread and the body of Christ at one and the same time. There is no change in substance; the substance of both bread and the body of Christ are present together. The doctrine of transubstantiation seemed to Luther to be an absurdity, an attempt to rationalize a mystery. For Luther, the crucial point was that Christ was really present at the eucharist – not some particular theory as to how he was present. He deploys an image borrowed from Origen to make his point: if iron is placed in a fire and heated, it glows – and in that glowing iron, both the iron and heat are present. Why not use some simple everyday analogy such as this to illustrate the mystery of the presence of Christ at the eucharist, instead of rationalizing it using some scholastic subtlety?

> For my part, if I cannot fathom how the bread is the body of Christ, yet I will take my reason captive to the obedience of Christ, and clinging simply to his words, firmly believe not only that the body of Christ is in the bread, but that the bread is the body of Christ. My warrant for this is the words which say: "He took bread, and when he had given thanks, he broke it and said, Take, eat, this [that is, this bread, which he had taken and broken] is my body." (1 Corinthians 11: 23–4)

It is not the doctrine of transubstantiation which is to be believed, but simply that Christ really is present at the eucharist. This fact is more important than any theory or explanation.

These points can be seen clearly from his 1520 treatise *The Babylonian Captivity of the Church*, in which Luther set out a fundamental criticism of the teachings of the medieval church concerning the sacraments, Luther argues that the concept of "transubstantiation" is untenable. While Luther maintains a doctrine of the real presence of Christ in the eucharist, he refuses to accept the specifically Aristotelian interpretation of it associated with transubstantiation.

3.3.1 Martin Luther on Transubstantiation

For more than twelve hundred years the church believed rightly, during which time the holy fathers never, at any time or place, mentioned this "transubstantiation" (a pretentious word and idea) until the pseudo-philosophy of Aristotle began to make its inroads into the church in these last three hundred years, in which many
5   things have been incorrectly defined, as for example, that the divine essence is neither begotten nor begets; or that the soul is the substantial form of the human body. . . . But why could not Christ include his body in the substance of the bread just as well as in the accidents? In red-hot iron, for example, the two substances, fire and iron, are so mingled that every part is both iron and fire. Why should it not
10   be even more possible that the glorious body of Christ be contained in every part of the substance of the bread? ... What is true concerning Christ is also true concerning the sacrament. In order for the divinity to dwell in a human body, it is not necessary for the human nature to be transubstantiated and the divinity contained under the accidents of the human nature. Both natures are simply there
15   in their entirety, and it is true to say: "This man is God; this God is man." Even though philosophy is not capable of grasping this, faith is. And the authority of God's Word is greater than the capacity of our intellect to grasp it. In the same way, it is not necessary in the sacrament that the bread and wine be transubstantiated and that Christ be contained under their accidents in order that the real body and
20   real blood may be present. But both remain there at the same time, and it is truly said: "This bread is my body; this wine is my blood," and vice versa. (I will understand it in this way for the time being on account of the honor of the holy words of God, to which I will allow no violence to be done by petty human arguments, nor will I allow them to be twisted into meanings which are foreign
25   to them.)

Zwingli: memorialism

For Zwingli, the eucharist is "a memorial of the suffering of Christ, and not a sacrifice." For reasons which we shall explore below, Zwingli insists that the words "this is my body" cannot be taken literally, thus eliminating any idea of the "real presence of Christ" at the eucharist. Just as a man, on setting off on a long journey from home, might give his wife his ring to remember him by until his return, so Christ leaves his church a token to remember him by until the day on which he should return in glory.

But what of the words "this is my body" (Matthew 26: 26), which had been the cornerstone of traditional Catholic views of the real presence, and which Luther had seized upon in his defense of the real presence? Zwingli argued that "there are innumerable passages in Scripture where the word 'is' means 'signifies.' " The question that must therefore be addressed is

> whether Christ's words in Matthew 26, "This is my body" can also be taken metaphorically or *in tropice*. It has already become clear enough that in this context the word "is" cannot be taken literally. Hence it follows that it must be taken metaphorically or figuratively. In the words "This is my body," the word "this" means the bread, and the word "body" means the body which was put to death for us. Therefore the word "is" cannot be taken literally, for the bread is not the body.

John Calvin

As we have seen, the central debate between Luther and Zwingli concerned the relation between the sacramental sign and the spiritual gift which it signified. Calvin may be regarded as occupying a position roughly midway between these two extremes. In the sacraments, he argues, there is such a close connection between the symbol and the gift which it symbolizes that we can "easily pass from one to the other." The sign is visible and physical, whereas the thing signified is invisible and spiritual – yet the connection between the sign and the thing signified is so intimate that it is permissible to apply the one to the other. The thing that is signified is effected by its sign.

> Believers ought always to live by this rule: whenever they see symbols appointed by the Lord, to think and be convinced that the truth of the thing signified is surely present there. For why should the Lord put in your hand the symbol of his body, unless it was to assure you that you really participate in it? And if it is true that a visible sign is given to us to seal the gift of an invisible thing, when we have received the symbol of the body, let us rest assured that the body itself is also given to us.

Calvin can thus maintain the difference between sign and thing signified, while insisting that the sign really points to the gift it signifies.

> I therefore say . . . that the sacred mystery of the Lord's Supper consists in two things: physical signs, which, when placed in front of our eyes, represent to us (according to our feeble capacity) invisible things; and spiritual truth, which is at the same time represented and displayed through the symbols themselves.

It might be possible to regard Calvin's position as an attempt to reconcile the views of Zwingli and Luther, an exercise in ecclesiastical diplomacy at an opportune moment in the history of the Reformation. In fact, there is little evidence to support this suggestion; Calvin's theology of the sacraments cannot be regarded as a compromise reached on political grounds, but rather reflects his understanding of the way in which the knowledge of God is given to us, particularly in relation to the idea of "accommodation."

It will be clear that there were substantial disagreements within Christianity during the sixteenth century over this important issue, which remain to this day.

Case Study 3.4   The Doctrine of the Church: Trends within Protestantism

The Reformation arose within an intellectual context which placed new emphasis upon the importance of this great Christian writer of the late fourth and early fifth centuries, reflected in the publication of the Amerbach edition of Augustine's works in 1506. In many ways, however, the reformers' views on the church represent their Achilles' heel. The reformers were confronted with two consistent rival views of the church the logic of which they could not match – those of their opponents within the Catholic and Radical Reformations. For the former, the church was a visible, historic institution, possessing historical continuity with the apostolic church; for the latter, the true church was in heaven, and no institution of any kind on earth merited the name "church of God." The magisterial reformers attempted to claim the middle ground somewhere between these two rival views, and found themselves involved in serious inconsistencies as a result. In the present case study, we will explore the various views on the doctrine of the church found within the Protestant Reformation, noting the remarkable parallels which exist with the Donatist controversy (on which see case study 1.6).

Luther was convinced that the church of their day and age had lost sight of the doctrine of grace, which Luther regarded as the center of the Christian gospel. Convinced that the Catholic church had lost sight of this doctrine, he concluded (with some reluctance, it would seem) that it had lost its claim to be considered as the authentic Christian church. The Catholics responded to this suggestion with derision: Luther was simply creating a breakaway faction which had no connection with the church. In other words, he was a schismatic – and had not Augustine himself condemned schism? Had not he placed enormous emphasis upon the unity of the church, which Luther now threatened to disrupt? Here we can see an important historical reference point, which would play a major role in sixteenth-century debates over the church: the Reformation can, at least in some respects, be seen as a replay of the Donatist controversy of the fourth century. Luther, it seemed, could only uphold Augustine's doctrine of grace by rejecting Augustine's doctrine of the church. "The Reformation, inwardly considered, was just the ultimate triumph of Augustine's doctrine of grace over Augustine's doctrine of the church" (Benjamin B. Warfield). It is in the context of this tension between two aspects of Augustine's thought, which proved to be incompatible in the sixteenth century, that the Reformation understandings of the nature of the church are to be seen.

Luther was a reluctant schismatic. In his period as an academic reformer,

Luther shared a profound distaste for schism. Even the row over the Ninety-Five Theses on indulgences of October 31, 1517 did not persuade Luther to break away from the church. In the twentieth century, we have become used to the phenomenon of "denominationalism" – but the very idea of the western church breaking up into smaller parts was completely alien to the medieval period. Schism, to put it bluntly, was unthinkable. As Luther himself wrote in early 1519: "If, unfortunately, there are things in Rome which cannot be improved, there is not – and cannot be – any reason for tearing oneself away from the church in schism. Rather, the worse things become, the more one should help her and stand by her, for by schism and contempt nothing can be mended." Luther's views here parallel those of other reforming groups throughout Europe: the church must be reformed from within.

The assumption that the growing alienation of the Wittenberg Reformation from the Catholic church was purely temporary seems to underlie much of the thinking of Lutheran writers in the period 1520–41. It seems that the evangelical faction at Wittenberg believed that the Catholic church would indeed reform itself, perhaps through convening a reforming council, within a matter of years, thus allowing the Lutherans to rejoin a renewed and reformed church. Thus the Augsburg Confession (1530), setting out the main lines of Lutheran belief, is actually remarkably conciliatory toward Catholicism. Such hopes of reunion were, however, dashed in the 1540s. In 1541, the Colloquy of Regensburg (sometimes also known as Ratisbon) seemed to offer the hope of reconciliation, as a group of Protestant and Catholic theologians met to discuss their differences. Those discussions ended in failure.

In 1545, the Council of Trent finally met to hammer out the response of the Catholic church to the Reformation, and institute a major program of reform within that church. Some present at that Council, such as Cardinal Reginald Pole, had hoped that it would prove to be conciliatory toward the Protestants: in the event, however, the Council identified and condemned the leading ideas of Protestantism. Any hopes of reconciliation had been dashed. The Protestant churches now had to recognize that their existence as separate entities was permanent, rather than temporary. They had to justify their existence as Christian "churches" alongside a body which seemed to have a much stronger claim to that title – the Roman Catholic church itself.

On the basis of this brief historical introduction, it will be obvious that the reformers' concern with the theory of the church dates mainly from the 1540s. It is a question which preoccupied the second, rather than the first, generation of reformers. If Luther was concerned with the question, "How may I find a gracious God?," his successors were obliged to deal with the question which arose out of this – "Where can I find the true church?" Theoretical justification had to be given for the separate existence of the evangelical churches. Most influential among second-generation reformers, of course, is John Calvin, and it is in his writings that we find perhaps the most important contributions to this debate. In what follows, we shall explore some seminal sixteenth-century discussions of the nature of the church.

Martin Luther

As we have seen, the early reformers were convinced that the medieval church had become corrupted and its doctrine distorted by a departure from Scripture on the one hand and by human additions to Scripture on the other. Luther's early views on the nature of the church reflect his emphasis on the Word of God: the Word of God goes forth conquering, and wherever it conquers and gains true obedience to God is the church.

3.4.1 Martin Luther on the Nature of the Church

This holy Christian people is to be recognized as having possession of the holy word of God, even if all do not possess it in equal measure, as St Paul says (1 Corinthians 3: 12–14). Some possess it completely purely, others not so purely. . . . This holy thing is the true holy thing, the true anointing that anoints with
5   eternal life, even though you may not have a papal crown or a bishop's hat, but will die bare and naked, just like children (as we all are), who are baptized naked and without any such adornment. But we are speaking of the external word, preached orally by people like you and me, for this is what Christ left behind as an external sign, by which his church, or his Christian people in the world,
10   should be recognized. . . . Now, anywhere you hear or see such a word preached, believed, confessed, and acted upon, do not doubt that the true *ecclesia sancta catholica*, a "holy Christian people" must be there, even though there are very few of them.

Note that Luther's views here stress the central role of the word of God in constituting a true church. An episcopally ordained ministry is therefore not necessary to safeguard the existence of the church, whereas the preaching of the gospel is essential to the identity of that church. "Where the word is, there is faith; and where faith is, there is the true church." The visible church is constituted by the preaching of the Word of God: no human assembly may claim to be the "church of God" unless it is founded on this gospel. Historical continuity with the early church is not sufficient to establish its credentials in this matter. Luther's understanding of the church is thus *functional*, rather than *historical*: what legitimates a church or its office-bearers is not historical continuity with the apostolic church, but theological continuity. It is more important to preach the same gospel as the apostles than to be a member of an institution which is historically derived from them.

The radical Reformation

For the radicals, such as Sebastian Franck, the apostolic church had been totally compromised through its close links with the state, dating back to the conversion of the Emperor Constantine. Franck here sets out the characteristic radical view that the true church ceased to exist after the apostles. His frequent reference to "external things (*externa*)" is a reference to external ceremonies, including the sacraments, which he regards as being "fallen (*lapsus*)." The true church will only come into being at the end of time, when Christ returns in glory to gather the scattered people of his church into his kingdom. Until then, the true church will remain concealed.

> I maintain, against all the doctors, that all external things which were in use in the church of the apostles have been abolished, and none of them are to be restored or reinstituted, even though they have gone beyond their authorization or calling and attempted to restore these fallen sacraments. For the church will remain scattered among the heathen until the end of the world. Indeed, the Antichrist and his church will only be defeated and swept away at the coming of Christ, who will gather together in his kingdom Israel, which has been scattered to the four corners of the world. . . . The works [of those who understood this] have been suppressed as godless heresies and rantings, and pride of place has instead been given to foolish Ambrose, Augustine, Jerome, Gregory – of whom not even one knew Christ, nor was sent by God to teach. But rather all were and shall remain the apostles of Antichrist.

Just as most of the radicals were utterly consistent in their application of the *scriptura sola* principle, so they were equally consistent in their views on the institutional church. The true church was in heaven, and its institutional parodies were on earth.

In responding to this radical approach Luther was forced to deal with two difficulties. If the church was not institutional, but was defined by the preaching of the gospel, how could he distinguish his views from those of the radicals? He himself had conceded that "the church is holy even where the fanatics (Luther's term for the radicals) are dominant, so long as they do not deny the word and the sacraments." Alert to the political realities of his situation, he countered by asserting the need for an institutional church. Just as Luther tempered the radical implications of the *scriptura sola* principle by an appeal to tradition (see case study 3.1), so he tempered his potentially radical views on the nature of the true church by insisting that it had to be viewed as an historical institution. The institution of the church is the divinely ordained means of grace. But in countering the radicals by asserting that the church was indeed visible and institutional, Luther found himself having difficulty in distinguishing his views from those of his Catholic opponents. He himself fully appreciated this problem:

> We on our part confess that there is much that is Christian and good under the papacy; indeed, everything that is Christian and is good is to be found there and has come to us from this source. For instance, we confess that in the papal church there are the true Holy Scriptures, true baptism, the true sacrament of the altar, the true keys to the forgiveness of sins, the true office of the ministry, the true catechism in the form of the Lord's Prayer, the Ten Commandments and the articles of the Creed.

Luther is thus obliged to assert that "the false church has only the appearance, although it also possesses the Christian offices." In other words, the medieval church may have looked like the real thing, but it was really something rather different.

It will be helpful to bring out the parallel with the Donatist controversy (see case study 1.6). The Donatists were a breakaway movement in the North African church, who insisted that the Catholic church of their day had become compromised through its attitude to the Roman authorities during a period of persecution. Only those who had not compromised their personal religious integrity could be recognized as members of the true church. Augustine argued the Catholic case: the church must be recognized as having a mixed membership, both saints and sinners. The righteous and the wicked coexisted within the same church, and no human had the authority to weed out the wicked from the church.

Augustine drew upon the parable of the "wheat and the weeds" (Matthew 13: 24–31) to support this point. In this parable, the owner of a field arrives one morning to find both wheat and weeds ("tares," in older English) growing side by side. Selective herbicides being unknown, he is reluctant to try to remove the weeds: by doing so, he would inevitably damage some of the wheat as well. His solution to the problem is to wait until the wheat is ready to harvest, and then separate them. According to Augustine, this parable applies to the church. Like the field in the parable, the church contains both wheat and weeds, the just and the wicked, which coexist until the day of judgment. On that day, God will judge between them – and no human is permitted to pre-empt God's judgment. The church will thus contain both good and evil until the end of time. Augustine argues that the term "catholic" (which literally means "whole"), as applied to the church, describes its mixed membership of saints and sinners.

The "Donatist" and "Augustinian" views of the church are thus very different. Luther accepted Augustine's view of the church as a "mixed" body, whereas the radicals developed a Donatist view of the church as a body of the just, and the just alone. Like the Donatists, the radicals demanded moral perfection of their members. The church and the world were opposed to one another as light and darkness, and they had no time for what they regarded as the political compromises of Luther and Zwingli. For Luther, however, corrupt churchmen are found in the church "just as mouse droppings are found among peppercorns, or tares among the grain." It is one of the ecclesiastical facts of life, recognized by Augustine, which Luther endorses. The magisterial Reformation thus leads to the establishment of a church, whereas the radical Reformation leads to the formation of sects. The sociological distinction between the two movements reflects their different understandings of the nature of the church. Theology and sociology are closely linked at this point. (Earlier, we noted the famous maxim which represents the Reformation as the triumph of Augustine's doctrine of grace over his doctrine of the church: it is necessary at this point to note that Luther and the other magisterial reformers retained at least this aspect of Augustine's theory of the church.) But what basis does Luther then have for breaking away from the Catholic church? Does not this aspect of his theory of the church necessarily imply that there will always be corruption in the true church? On the basis of Augustine's theory, corruption in the Catholic church does not necessarily mean that it is a "false church."

John Calvin

If any reformer wrestled with the problem posed by the doctrine of the church, it was Calvin. The first major discussion of the theory of the church is to be found in the second edition of his *Institutes of the Christian Religion*, published in 1539. Although Calvin deals with the subject in the first edition of the *Institutes* (1536), he was then quite innocent of any experience of ecclesiastical management or responsibility, which accounts for the curiously unfocused nature of his discussion. By the time of the second edition of this work, Calvin had gained more experience of the problems presented to the new evangelical churches.

For Calvin, the marks of the true church were that the Word of God should be preached, and that the sacraments be rightly administered. Since the Roman Catholic church did not conform even to this minimalist definition of the church, the evangelicals were perfectly justified in leaving it. And as the evangelical churches conform to this definition of a church, there was no justification for further division within them. This point is of particular importance, reflecting Calvin's political judgment that further fragmentation of the evangelical congregations would be disastrous to the cause of the Reformation.

By 1543, Calvin had gained considerably more experience of ecclesiastical responsibility, particularly during his period at Strasbourg. Martin Bucer, the intellectual force behind the Reformation at Strasbourg, had a considerable reputation as an ecclesiastical administrator, and it is probable that Calvin's later theory of the church reflects his personal influence. The fourfold office of pastor, doctor (or teacher), elder, and deacon owes its origins to Bucer, as does the distinction between the visible and the invisible church (explored below). Nevertheless, Bucer's suggestion that ecclesiastical discipline was an essential feature (technically, a "note" or "mark") of the church is not echoed by Calvin. Although Calvin includes "example of life" among the "certain sure marks" of the church in the 1536 edition of the *Institutes*, later editions lay stress upon the proper preaching of the word of God and the administration of the sacraments. Discipline strengthens the nerve of the church – but the saving doctrine of Christ establishes its heart and soul.

Calvin draws an important distinction between the visible and invisible church. At one level, the church is the community of Christian believers, a visible group. It is also, however, the fellowship of saints and the company of the elect – an invisible entity. In its invisible aspect, the church is the assembly of the elect, known only to God; in its visible aspect, it is the community of believers on earth. The former consists only of the elect; the latter includes both good and evil, elect and reprobate. The former is an object of faith and hope, the latter of present experience. Calvin stresses that all believers are obliged to honor and to remain committed to the visible church, despite its weaknesses, on account of the invisible church, the true body of Christ. Despite this, there is only one church, a single entity with Jesus Christ as its head.

The distinction between the visible and invisible churches has two important consequences. In the first place, it is to be expected that the visible church will include both the elect and the reprobate. Augustine of Hippo had made this point against the Donatists, using the parable of the tares (Matthew 13: 24–31) as his basis. It lies beyond human competence to discern their difference, correlating human qualities with divine favor (in any case, Calvin's doctrine of predestination precludes such grounds of election). In the second, however, it is necessary to ask which of the various visible churches corresponds to the invisible church. Calvin thus recognizes the need to articulate objective criteria by which the authenticity of a given church may be judged. Two such criteria are stipulated: "Wherever we see the Word of God preached purely and listened to, and the sacraments administered according to the institution of Christ, we cannot doubt that a church exists." It is thus not the quality of its members, but the presence of the authorized means of grace, which constitutes a true church. This can be seen clearly in Calvin's discussion of the identifying features of a church, to which we now turn.

3.4.2   John Calvin on the Distinguishing Features of the Church

Wherever we see the Word of God purely preached and listened to, and the sacraments administered according to Christ's institution, it is in no way to be

doubted that a church of God exists. . . . If the ministry has the Word and honors it, if it has the administration of the sacraments, it deserves without doubt to be
5   held and considered a church. . . . When we say that the pure ministry of the Word and pure mode of celebrating the sacraments are a sufficient pledge and guarantee by which we may recognize as a church any society, we mean where both these marks exist, it is not to be rejected, even if it is riddled with faults in other respects. What is more, some shortcoming may find its way into the administration of either
10   doctrine or sacraments, but this ought not to estrange us from communion with this church. For not all articles of true doctrine are of equal weight. Some are so necessary to know that they should be certain and unquestioned by everyone as proper to religion, such as: God is one; Christ is God and the Son of God; our salvation rests in God's mercy; and the like. There are other [articles of doctrine]
15   disputed among the churches which still do not break the unity of faith. . . . I am not condoning error, no matter how insignificant it may be, nor do I wish to encourage it. But I am saying that we should not desert a church on account of some minor disagreement, if it upholds sound doctrine over the essentials of piety, and maintains the use of the sacraments established by the Lord.

Note especially Calvin's constant emphasis on the central role played by the preaching of the word of God and the right administration of the sacraments. In that Calvin regards there as being a close link between the word of God and its embodiment or representation in the sacraments, it is understandable why he chose to link these two matters together. It may also be noted that Calvin makes no reference to bishops, or *historical* continuity with the early church, in his definition of a church. For Calvin, such matters may be useful, but they are not definitive. What really matters is that the church should believe and preach the teachings of the apostles, which are contained in the New Testament.

Case Study 3.5   Theology and Astronomy: The Copernican and Galileian Debates

One of the most important developments during the period under study is the growing importance of the natural sciences, and the recognition of the potential implications of the new insights and methods for Christian theology. In the present case study, we shall examine the controversy which centered on the views of Nicholas Copernicus and Galileo Galilei concerning the solar system.

In May 1543, Nicholas Copernicus' *De revolutionibus orbium coelestium* ("On the revolutions of the heavenly bodies") was finally published. According to a long-standing tradition, the book appeared just in time to allow Copernicus to see a copy before he died on May 24 of that year. The book set out a heliocentric

207

view of the solar system. According to Copernicus, the Earth and other planets rotated around the sun, which stood at the center of the solar system. (The moon, of course, was agreed to revolve around the earth.) This marked a significant departure from the older view, which held that all heavenly bodies – including both the sun and the planets – rotated around the earth.

The older model (often referred to as a "geocentric" theory) was widely accepted by theologians of the Middle Ages, who had become so familiar with reading the text of the Bible through geocentric spectacles that they had some difficulty coping with the new approach. Early published defenses of the Copernican theory (such as G. J. Rheticus' *Treatise on Holy Scripture and the Motion of the Earth*, which is widely regarded as the earliest known work to deal explicitly with the relation of the Bible and the Copernican theory) thus had to deal with two issues. First, they had to set out the observational evidence which led to the conclusion that the earth and other planets rotated around the sun. Second, they had to demonstrate that this viewpoint was consistent with the Bible, which had long been read as endorsing a geocentric view of the Universe.

The rise of the heliocentric theory of the solar system thus caused theologians to re-examine the manner in which certain biblical passages were interpreted. Three broad approaches can be identified in the Christian tradition of biblical interpretation.

1 A *literal* approach, which argues that the passage in question is to be taken at its face value. For example, a literal interpretation of the first chapter of Genesis would argue that creation took place in six periods of twenty-four hours.

2 An *allegorical* approach, which stresses that certain sections of the Bible are written in a style which it is not appropriate to take absolutely literally. During the Middle Ages, three non-literal senses of Scripture were recognized; this was regarded by many sixteenth-century writers as somewhat elaborate. This view regards the opening chapters of Genesis as poetic or allegorical accounts, from which theological and ethical principles can be derived; it does *not* treat them as literal historical accounts of the origins of the earth.

3 An approach based on the idea of *accommodation*. This has been by far the most important approach in relation to the interaction of biblical interpretation and the natural sciences. The approach argues that revelation takes place in culturally and anthropologically conditioned manners and forms, with the result that it needs to be appropriately interpreted. This approach has a long tradition of use within Judaism and subsequently within Christian theology, and can easily be shown to have been influential within the patristic period. Nevertheless, its mature development can be found within the sixteenth century. This approach argues that the opening chapters of Genesis use language and imagery appropri-

ate to the cultural conditions of its original audience; it is not to be taken "literally," but is to be interpreted for a contemporary readership by extracting the key ideas, which have been expressed in forms and terms which are specifically adapted or "accommodated" to the original audience.

The third approach proved to be of especial importance during the debates over the relation between theology and astronomy during the sixteenth and seventeenth centuries. The noted reformer John Calvin (1509–64) may be regarded as making two major and positive contributions to the appreciation and development of the natural sciences. First, he positively encouraged the scientific study of nature; second, he eliminated a major obstacle to the development of that study, through his understanding of the way in which the Bible was to be interpreted in terms of "accommodation" (as explained above). His first contribution is specifically linked with his stress upon the orderliness of creation; both the physical world and the human body testify to the wisdom and character of God:

> In order that no one might be excluded from the means of obtaining happiness, God has been pleased, not only to place in our minds the seeds of religion of which we have already spoken, but to make known his perfection in the whole structure of the universe, and daily place himself in our view, in such a manner that we cannot open our eyes without being compelled to observe him. ... To prove his remarkable wisdom, both the heavens and the earth present us with countless proofs – not just those more advanced proofs which astronomy, medicine and all the other natural sciences are designed to illustrate, but proofs which force themselves on the attention of the most illiterate peasant, who cannot open his eyes without seeing them.

Calvin thus commends the study of both astronomy and medicine. They are able to probe more deeply than theology into the natural world, and thus uncover further evidence of the orderliness of the creation and the wisdom of its creator. It may thus be argued that Calvin gave a new religious motivation to the scientific investigation of nature. This was now seen as a means of discerning the wise hand of God in creation. The *Confessio Belgica* (1561), a Calvinist statement of faith which exercised particular influence in the Lowlands (an area which would become particularly noted for its botanists and physicists), declared that nature is "before our eyes as a most beautiful book in which all created things, whether great or small, are as letters showing the invisible things of God to us." God can thus be discerned in the detailed study of the creation through the natural sciences.

Calvin's second major contribution was to eliminate a significant obstacle to the development of the natural sciences – biblical literalism. Calvin points out that the Bible is primarily concerned with the knowledge of Jesus Christ. It is not an astronomical, geographical or biological textbook. And when the Bible is intepreted, it must be borne in mind that God "adjusts" to the capacities of the human mind and heart. God has to come down to our level if revelation is to take place. Revelation thus presents a scaled-down or "accommodated" version of God to us, in order to meet our limited abilities. Just as a human mother stoops down to reach her child, so God stoops down to come to our level. Revelation is an act of divine condescension.

In the case of the biblical accounts of the creation (Genesis 1), Calvin argues that they are accommodated to the abilities and horizons of a relatively simple and unsophisticated people; they are not intended to be taken as literal representations of reality. The author of Genesis, he declares, "was ordained to be a teacher of the unlearned and primitive, as well as the learned; and so could not achieve his goal without descending to such crude means of instruction." The phrase "six days of creation" does not designate six periods of twenty-four hours, but is simply an accommodation to human ways of thinking to designate an extended period of time. The "water above the firmament" is simply an accommodated way of speaking about clouds.

The impact of both these ideas upon scientific theorizing, especially during the seventeenth century, was considerable. For example, the English writer Edward Wright defended Copernicus' heliocentric theory of the solar system against biblical literalists by arguing, in the first place, that Scripture was not concerned with physics, and in the second, that its manner of speaking was "accommodated to the understanding and way of speech of the common people, like nurses to little children." Both these arguments derive directly from Calvin, who may be argued to have made a fundamental contribution to the emergence of the natural sciences in this respect.

Similar arguments emerged in Italy during the early decades of the seventeenth century, as fresh controversy broke out over the heliocentric model of the solar system. This eventually led to the Roman Catholic church condemning Galileo Galilei, in what is widely regarded as a clear error of judgment on the part of some ecclesiastical bureaucrats. Galileo mounted a major defense of the Copernican theory of the solar system. Galileo's views were initially received sympathetically within senior church circles, partly on account of the fact that he was held in high regard by a papal favorite, Giovanni Ciampoli. Ciampoli's fall from power led to Galileo losing support within papal circles, and is widely regarded as opening the way to Galileo's condemnation by his enemies.

Although the controversy centering on Galileo is often portrayed as science versus religion, or libertarianism versus authoritarianism, the real issue concerned the correct interpretation of the Bible. Appreciation of this point is thought to have been hindered in the past on account of the failure of historians to engage with the theological (and, more precisely, the hermeneutical) issues attending the debate. In part, this can be seen as reflecting the fact that many of the scholars interested in this particular controversy were scientists or historians of science, who were not familiar with the intricacies of the debates on biblical interpretation of this remarkably complex period. Nevertheless, it is clear that the issue which dominated the discussion between Galileo and his critics was that of how to interpret certain biblical passages. The issue of accommodation was of major importance to that debate, as we shall see.

To explore this point, we may turn to a significant work published in January 1615. In his *Lettera sopra l'opinione de' Pittagorici e del Copernico* ("Letter on the opinion of the Pythagoreans and Copernicus"), the Carmelite friar Paolo Antonio Foscarini argued that the heliocentric model of the solar system was not incompatible with the Bible. Foscarini did not introduce any new principles of biblical interpretation in his analysis; rather, he sets out and applies traditional rules of interpretation:

> When Holy Scripture attributes something to God or to any other creature which would otherwise be improper and incommensurate, then it should be interpreted and explained in one or more of the following ways. First, it is said to pertain metaphorically and proportionally, or by similitude. Second, it is said . . . according to our mode of consideration, apprehension, understanding, knowing, etc. Thirdly, it is said according to vulgar opinion and the common way of speaking.

The second and third ways which Foscarini identifies are generally regarded as types of "accommodation," the third model of biblical interpretation noted above. As we have seen, this approach to biblical interpretation can be traced back to the first Christian centuries, and was not regarded as controversial.

Foscarini's innovation did not lie in the interpretive method he adopted, but in the biblical passages to which he applied it. In other words, Foscarini suggested that certain passages, which many had interpreted literally up to this point, were to be interpreted in an accommodated manner. The passages to which he applied this approach were those which seemed to suggest that the earth remained stationary, and the sun moved. Foscarini argued as follows:

> Scripture speaks according to our mode of understanding, and according to appearances, and in respect to us. For thus it is that these bodies appear to be related to us and are described by the common and vulgar mode of human thinking, namely, the earth seems to stand still and to be immobile, and the sun seems to rotate around it. And hence Scripture serves us by speaking in the vulgar and common manner; for from our point of view it does seem that the earth stands firmly in the center and that the sun revolves around it, rather than the contrary.

Galileo's growing commitment to the Copernican position led him to adopt an approach to biblical interpretation similar to Foscarini's.

The real issue was how to interpret the Bible. Galileo's critics argued that some biblical passages contradicted him. For example, they argued, Joshua 10: 12 spoke of the sun standing still at Joshua's command. Did not that prove beyond reasonable doubt that it was the sun which moved around the earth? In his *Letter to the Grand Countess Christina*, Galileo countered with an argument that this was simply a common way of speaking. Joshua could not be expected to know the intricacies of celestial mechanics, and therefore used an "accommodated" way of speaking.

The official condemnation of this viewpoint was based on two considerations:

1 Scripture is to be interpreted according "to the proper meaning of the words." The accommodated approach adopted by Foscarini is thus rejected in favour of a more literal approach. As we have stressed, both methods of interpretation were accepted as legitimate, and had a long history of use within Christian theology. The debate centered on the question of which was appropriate to the passages in question.

2 The Bible is to be interpreted "according to the common interpretation and understanding of the Holy Fathers and of learned theologians." In other words, it was being argued that nobody of any significance had adopted Foscarini's interpretation in the past; it was therefore to be dismissed as an innovation.

It therefore followed that the views of both Foscarini and Galileo were to be rejected as innovations, without any precedent in Christian thought.

This second point is of major importance, and needs to be examined more carefully, in that it is to be set against the long-standing and bitter debate, fueled during the seventeenth century by the Thirty Years War (1618–48), between Protestantism and Roman Catholicism over whether the former was an innovation or a recovery of authentic Christianity. The idea of the unchangeability of the Catholic tradition became an integral element of Roman Catholic polemic against Protestantism. As Jacques-Bénigne Bossuet (1627–1704), one of the most formidable apologists for Roman Catholicism, put this point in 1688:

> The teaching of the church is always the same. . . . The gospel is never different from what it was before. Hence, if at any time someone says that the faith includes something which yesterday was not said to be of the faith, it is always heterodoxy, which is any doctrine different from orthodoxy. There is no difficulty about recognizing false doctrine; there is no argument about it. It is recognized at once, whenever it appears, simply because it is new.

These same arguments were widely used at the opening of the century, and are clearly reflected and embodied in the official critique of Foscarini. The interpretation which he offered had never been offered before – and it was, for that reason alone, wrong.

It will therefore be clear that this critical debate over the interpretation of the Bible must be set against a complex background. The highly charged and politicized atmosphere at the time seriously prejudiced theological debate, for fear that the concession of any new approach might be seen as an indirect concession of the Protestant claim to legitimacy. To allow that Roman Catholic teaching on any matter of significance had "changed" was potentially to open the floodgates which would inevitably lead to demands for recognition of the orthodoxy of central Protestant teachings – teachings that the Roman Catholic church had been able to reject as "innovations" up to this point.

It was thus inevitable that Galileo's views would meet with resistance. They key factor was that of theological innovation: to concede Galileo's interpretation of certain biblical passages would seriously undermine the Catholic criticisms of Protestantism, which involved the assertion that Protestantism introduced new (and therefore erroneous) interpretations of certain biblical passages. It was only a matter of time before his views would be rejected. It is generally agreed that Galileo's positive reputation in ecclesiastical circles until a surprisingly late date was linked to his close relationship with the papal favourite, Giovanni Ciampoli. When Ciampoli fell from grace in the spring of 1632, Galileo found his position seriously weakened, perhaps to the point of being fatally compromised. Without the protection of Ciampoli, Galileo was vulnerable to the charges of "heresy through innovation" which were leveled against him by his critics.

The controversy which focused on Galileo is often presented in a highly simplified form in textbooks, typically as an example of "science versus religion." As this case study will have made clear, the issues were much more complex than this. The controversy has to be set against a background of court politics, personality clashes, and a ferocious struggle on the part of the Catholic church to defend itself against Protestantism – as well as a genuine attempt to understand the Bible correctly!

Chapter 4

THE MODERN PERIOD,
1750–THE PRESENT DAY

During the second half of the fifteenth century, Christianity became increasingly a European religion. Islam had launched a *jihad* ("holy war") against Christianity several centuries earlier. By about 1450, as a direct result of its military conquests, Islam was firmly established in the southwestern and southeastern parts of Europe. Although Christian communities continued to exist outside Europe (most notably in Egypt, Ethiopia, India, and Syria), Christianity was becoming geographically restricted. Its future seemed insecure.

One of the most dramatic developments to take place during the last few centuries has been the recovery of Christianity from this crisis. By the twentieth century, Christianity was firmly established as the dominant religion in the Americas, Australasia, southern Africa, and throughout many of the island nations of the South Pacific. We shall explore how this took place during the present chapter. However, despite this dramatic expansion outside Europe, Christianity suffered a series of internal setbacks in its former heartland – western Europe. We may begin our discussion of the modern period by trying to understand how an indifference to religion began to arise in this region of the world.

THE RISE OF INDIFFERENCE TO RELIGION IN EUROPE

With the ending of the European Wars of Religion, a degree of stability settled upon the continent. Although religious controversy continued intermittently, it became generally accepted that certain parts of Europe were Lutheran, Catholic, Orthodox or Reformed. The sense of weariness which had been created by the Wars of Religion led to a new interest in religious toleration. The classic argument for toleration of diversity in matters of religion may be found in John Locke's *Letters Concerning Toleration* (1689–92). Locke argues for religious toleration on the basis of three general considerations, as follows.

First, it is impossible for the state to adjudicate between competing religious truth-claims. This does not mean that there is no truth in matters of religion, or that all religions are equal in terms of their insights into reality. The modern view, associated with writers such as John Hick, that all religions are equally valid can be seen as the extrapolation of a political judgment to a metaphysical plane. Instead, Locke points out that no earthly judge can be brought forward to settle the matter. For this reason, religious diversity is to be tolerated.

Second, Locke argues that, even if it could be established that one religion was superior to all others, the legal enforcement of this religion would not lead to the desired objective of that religion. Locke's argument here is based upon the notion that "true and saving religion consists in the inward persuasion of the mind, without which nothing is acceptable to God. And such is the nature of the understanding, that it cannot be compelled to the belief of any thing by outward force." It is interesting to note that Locke's argument here is shaped by the Christian conception of salvation; a religion which demanded external conformity to a set of regulations would not fit in to his analysis).

Third, Locke argues, on pragmatic grounds, that the results of trying to impose religious uniformity are far worse than those which result from the continuing existence of diversity. Religious coercion leads to internal discord, or even civil war. Locke thus argues that religious truth cannot be established with certainty. Even if it could be established with certainty, its imposition would not lead to inward faith. And if it were imposed, the negative results would far outweigh the advantages gained.

Yet Locke does not see this toleration of religious diversity as leading to moral diversity. Theological disputations may be tolerated, precisely because they do not, in Locke's view, have any impact upon the core moral agreement which his commonwealth presupposes. Indeed, at several points, Locke suggests that the religions – Jewish, Christian, and Muslim – are consistent with, and supportive of, public morality. Alexis de Tocqueville provided much support for this view in the nineteenth century, with his observation that, although there was "an innumerable multitude of sects in the United States," there was nevertheless agreement concerning duty and morality.

Locke's analysis can be seen as leading to the view that religion is a private matter of public indifference. What individuals believe should be regarded as private, with no relevance to the public field. This approach at one and the same time upheld religious toleration, while indicating that religion was a purely private matter. This perception was strengthened by the rise of the Enlightenment, which regarded the religions as different expressions of the same ultimate reality, which could be known through reason.

The notion of religious toleration was of especial importance in relation to the emergence of the United States of America during the eighteenth century. We shall turn to explore this issue now.

CHRISTIANITY IN NORTH AMERICA: THE GREAT AWAKENING AND THE AMERICAN REVOLUTION

The United States of America is today widely regarded as the most important Christian nation. Christianity plays a major role in the national and international politics of this superpower. It is therefore of importance to appreciate how Christianity came to be of such importance to the life of this nation. As we noted earlier, Christianity was brought to North America largely by refugees seeking to escape from religious persecution then endemic in Europe. In 1620 the Pilgrim Fathers sailed from Plymouth. Between 1627 and 1640 some 4,000 individuals made the hazardous crossing of the Atlantic Ocean, and settled on the coastline of Massachusetts Bay. The first settlers in North America were generally deeply committed to their Christian beliefs. Most early settlers were English-speaking Protestants; an important exception to this is found in the case of Maryland, which was a Catholic enclave for a period during the 1630s. (It was not until the nineteenth century that large numbers of Catholic immigrants from Ireland and Italy would swell the numbers of Catholics in the region.)

A renewed interest in the Christian faith resulted from the "Great Revival," which broke out in the Massachusetts town of Northampton during the 1730s, and initially centered on the ministry of Jonathan Edwards (1703–58). The first signs of revival began to be noticed in 1727 by Theodore Freylinghausen, a Dutch pastor ministering to a congregation in the Raritan Valley of New Jersey. It was not until the winter of 1734–5 that the revival can be said to have started at Northampton. The revival continued into the new year, reaching its peak during the months of March and April 1735. Edwards published accounts of the events at Northampton in the form of a book, *A Faithful Narrative of the Surprising Work of God*, which drew international attention to the awakening. Between 1737 and 1739 the book went through three editions and 20 printings. As the revival continued in New England, it was given a new sense of direction by George Whitefield (1714–70), recently arrived from England. In 1740, he undertook a preaching tour of the colonies, from Georgia in the south to Maine in the north. The tour of New England, undertaken in the fall of that year, caused a sensation. Crowds of up to 8,000 people are said to have come to hear him preach every day for the best part of a month. Benjamin Franklin heard Whitefield preach in Philadelphia, and was amazed both by the size of the crowd which had gathered to hear him, and by the quality of his voice.

This revival had a lasting impact on American Christianity. It established the role of wandering preachers, unattached to any particular church. It undermined the authority of the clergy of established churches, who felt their positions to be deeply theatened by the upsurge in popular religious interest. The foundations of a mass popular culture were laid, in which Christianity was not the preserve of a clerical élite committed to the preservation of the existing social order, but a popular movement with a direct appeal to the masses. The established clergy refused to allow Whitefield to preach in their churches; he responded by preaching in the fields around towns, and attracting vast audiences which could never have been contained within the churches from which he was barred. Perhaps the group to be most deeply threatened by this development was the colonial clergy of the Church of England – the guardians of the existing social order. It is no exaggeration to say that the roots of the American Revolution lay in the growing religious alienation between the new popular American religion and the established religion of England. Within a generation of the Great Awakening, the colonies were in revolt.

The causes of the American Revolution are complex, involving a number of interrelated issues. Perhaps the dominant theme is that of a desire to break free from the influence of England, which was increasingly seen as paternalist, oppressive, and exploitative. This desire for freedom expressed itself in the political, economic, and religious arenas. The Church of England was increasingly viewed as the religious dimension of British colonialism. During the 1760s, vigorous efforts were made by American Protestants to resist the expansion of the Church of England's authority in the region. The Church of England was established by law in all the southern colonies, and its influence seemed destined to increase still further. The Quebec Act of 1774, which established Catholicism in French-speaking regions of Canada, was seen as particularly provocative. If Britain could decide what was the established religion in Canada, what would it do in America? Suspicion and hostility grew unchecked.

The imposition of the Stamp Tax (1764) brought cries for "no taxation without representation." The 1773 decision of the British parliament to give the East India Company exclusive rights to sell tea in North America led to the "Boston Tea Party," and widespread unrest in Massachusetts. British troops were sent to restore order; this action was interpreted as an act of war by the colonists. A series of battles were fought in 1775, leading to the Declaration of Independence on July 4, 1776. A full-scale war of independence ensued, in which church pulpits often served as rallying points for revolutionary activity. In effect, the Revolution united Christian groups of more or less all persuasions in the service of a greater goal. The Church of England was isolated, and would lose any privileges it once possessed.

The First Amendment to the Constitution declared that "Congress shall make no law respecting an establishment of religion or restricting the free exercise thereof." The Constitution thus prevented the formal establishment of religion, meaning that no Christian church (such as the Church of England) was to be given a favored legal status by the state. Although some modern constitutional theorists argue that this was intended to remove religion from American public life, or that it justifies this practice today, it is clear that the intention of the

Constitution was simply to avoid giving legal or social precedence to any specific Christian grouping.

The American Revolution led to the consolidation of Christianity in the United States. However, on the continent of Europe, another revolution was about to break out. In this case, the consequences were more far-reaching and negative.

THE WATERSHED IN EUROPE: THE FRENCH REVOLUTION

The French Revolution is usually singled out as marking the high point of anti-religious feeling in Europe. In 1789, the established social structure in France was shaken to its foundations by a popular uprising, which eventually led to the ending of the monarchy and the establishment of a secular republic. The church and the monarchy were the two pillars of this established order (usually referred to as the *ancien régime*). What began as an attempt to reform both institutions ended up as a revolution, in which power was decisively transferred from the old feudal aristocracy to the rising middle classes.

There was little to indicate that such a radical shake-up was on the way. There was a parallel to be drawn with the American Revolution of the previous decade, which had led to the consolidation of the influence of various forms of Protestant Christianity in the region. While the established religion of the area (the religion of the colonial power – the Church of England) suffered a serious setback, other forms of Christianity strengthened their position. The disestablishment of Christianity in the region is widely regarded as contributing to its future success. Yet the situation in France proved to be very different.

It was clear that both the pillars of traditional French society – the monarchy and the church – needed reform. Even late in the summer of the momentous year 1789, the general feeling was that the French monarch had allowed a series of measures which would abolish feudalism and remove some of the grievances felt by ordinary people against the power and privileges of the church. On November 2, it was agreed that all church lands should be nationalized, with a basic minimum wage for priests being set in place, guaranteed by the state. The Civil Constitution of the Clergy (July 1790) rejected the authority of the Pope, reorganized and slimmed down the dioceses and the cathedral clergy. Although radical, the measures were not anti-Christian. The clergy split into a group which wished to remain loyal to Rome, and another wishing to comply with the new civil authority.

All changed soon afterward. A more radical revolutionary faction, headed by Robespierre, gained power, and launched its celebrated "Reign of Terror." Louis XVI was publicly guillotined on January 21, 1793. A program of dechristianization was put in place during the period 1793–4; the cult of the Goddess Reason was given official sanction. The old calendar was replaced by a republican calendar which eliminated Sundays and Christian festivals, replacing them with secular alternatives. Priests were placed under pressure to renounce their faith. A program of church closure was initiated. Although the impact of these measures seems to have been felt mostly in urban areas, they caused considerable disruption and hardship to the church throughout France.

The religious policies of the French Revolution were soon extended to neighboring regions. In November 1792, French revolutionary armies embarked on a campaign of conquest in the region. By 1799, six satellite republics had been established, embracing areas such as the Netherlands, Switzerland, parts of northern Italy, and areas of the Rhineland. In February 1798, the papal states were occupied, and the Pope was deported to France, where he died six months later. The French Revolution, it seemed to many, had destroyed not only the French church, but also the papacy.

On the eve of the nineteenth century, the future of Christianity in Europe thus seemed remarkably fragile. Many saw it as linked with the politics of a bygone era, an obstacle to progress and liberty. Its faith and its institutions seemed to be in irreversible decline. In fact, this would prove to be a false perception. The revolutionary experimentation with a secular state eventually fizzled out. Under Napoleon, relations with the Pope were re-established, although on very different terms from those in operation before the Revolution.

The Bourbon monarchy was restored: in 1814, Louis XVIII returned to claim the throne of France, and re-established Catholicism. The situation was never easy, and real tensions between church and state continued unabated throughout most of the nineteenth century. Nevertheless, the church was able to regain at least some of its lost influence, prestige, and clergy. The period 1815–48 witnessed a series of popular revivals (usually referred to as "le Réveil") in French-speaking Europe.

It is clear that the French Revolution drew at least some of its strength from the rationalist worldview which pervaded the writings of leading French writers of the period – such as Denis Diderot (1713–84), Jean-Jacques Rousseau (1712–78), and Voltaire (1694–1778). This leads us to consider some of the worldviews which dominated western thinking in the modern period, and their impact on Christianity. The most important of these is the movement which is generally known as "the Enlightenment," to which we now turn.

THE ENLIGHTENMENT

The English term "Enlightenment" passed into general circulation only in the closing decades of the nineteenth century. The German term *die Aufklärung* (which literally means "the clearing up") and the French term *les lumières* ("the lights") date from the eighteenth century, but do not convey much information about the nature of the movement in question. "Enlightenment" is a loose term, defying precise definition, embracing a cluster of ideas and attitudes characteristic of the period 1720–80, such as the free and constructive use of reason in an attempt to demolish old myths which were seen to have bound individuals and societies to the oppression of the past. If there is any common element underlying the movement, it perhaps lies more in *how* those who were sympathetic to its outlook thought than in *what* they thought.

The term "Age of Reason," often used as a synonym for the Enlightenment, is misleading. It implies that reason had been hitherto ignored or marginalized. Yet, as we saw earlier, the Middle Ages was just as much an "Age of Reason" as the Enlightenment; the crucial difference lay in the manner in which reason was used, and the limits which were understood to be imposed upon it. Nor was the eighteenth century consistently rational in every aspect. In fact, the Enlightenment included a remarkable variety of anti-rational movements, such as Mesmerism and Masonic rituals. Nevertheless, an emphasis upon the ability of human reason to penetrate the mysteries of the world is rightly regarded as a defining characteristic of the Enlightenment.

The term "rationalism" should also be used with caution when referring to the Enlightenment. In the first place, it should be noted that the term is often used in an uncritical and inaccurate way, designating the general atmosphere of optimism, grounded in a belief in scientific and social progress, which pervades much of the writing of the period. This use of the term is confusing, and should be avoided. Rationalism, in its proper sense, is perhaps best defined as the doctrine that the external world can be known by reason, and reason alone. This doctrine, which is characteristic of earlier writers such as Descartes, Leibniz, Spinoza, and Wolff, was subjected to intense criticism during the later eighteenth century, as the influence of John Locke's empiricist epistemology became widespread. Kant, often portrayed as an exponent of the sufficiency of pure reason, was in reality acutely aware of its limitations. The theory of knowledge developed in the *Critique of Pure Reason* (1781) may be regarded as an attempt to synthesize the insights of pure rationalism (which relies upon reason alone) and pure empiricism (which appeals to experience alone). This work may be regarded as bringing the early period of rationalism to a close. Despite according a particularly significant role to reason in his thought (as seen in *Religion within the Limits of Reason Alone*), Kant showed a keen appreciation of the implications of the empiricist emphasis upon sense experience. Nevertheless, rationalist attitudes persisted well into the nineteenth century, and constitute an important element of the general Enlightenment critique of Christianity.

The Enlightenment ushered in a period of considerable uncertainty for Christianity in western Europe and North America. The trauma of the Reformation and the resulting Wars of Religion had barely subsided on the continent of Europe before a new and more radical challenge to Christianity arose. If the sixteenth-century Reformation challenged the church to rethink its external forms and the manner in which it expressed its beliefs, the Enlightenment saw the intellectual credentials of Christianity itself (rather than any one of its specific forms) facing a major threat on a number of fronts. The origins of this challenge may be traced back to the seventeenth century, with the rise of Cartesianism on the continent of Europe, and the increasing influence of Deism in England. The growing emphasis upon the need to uncover the rational roots of religion had considerable negative implications for Christianity, as subsequent events were to prove.

At this point, it may be noted that it was Protestant theology, rather than its Roman Catholic or Eastern Orthodox counterparts, which was especially open to the new currents which arose from the Enlightenment and its aftermath. A number of factors appear to have influenced this development, of which the following are of particular importance.

1 Protestantism was at its strongest in those areas of Europe in which the influence of the Enlightenment was at its greatest.
2 Protestant ecclesiastical institutions were weaker than their Roman Catholic counterparts, with the result that Protestant university and seminary teachers enjoyed a greater degree of academic freedom than their Roman Catholic counterparts.
3 Protestantism enjoyed especially close links with many northern European universities, with the result that shifts in the academic culture were felt particularly strongly in Protestant faculties of theology.

As will become clear from the material to be presented in the following section, this means that any account of the influence of the Enlightenment on modern theology will focus on Protestant theology.

The Enlightenment Critique of Christian Theology: A General Overview

The Enlightenment criticism of traditional Christianity was based upon the principle of the omnicompetence of human reason. A number of stages in the development of this belief may be discerned. First, it was argued that the beliefs of Christianity were rational, and thus capable of standing up to critical examination. This type of approach may be found in John Locke's *Reasonableness of Christianity* (1695), and within the early Wolffian school in Germany. Christianity was a reasonable supplement to natural religion. The notion of divine revelation was thus maintained.

Second, it was argued that the basic ideas of Christianity, being rational, could be derived from reason itself. There was no need to invoke the idea of divine revelation. According to this idea, as it was developed by John Toland in

Christianity not Mysterious (1696) and by Matthew Tindal in *Christianity as Old as Creation* (1730), Christianity was essentially the re-publication of the religion of nature. It did not transcend natural religion, but was merely an example of it. All so-called "revealed religion" was actually nothing other than the reconfirmation of what can be known through rational reflection on nature. "Revelation" was simply a rational reaffirmation of moral truths already available to enlightened reason.

Third, the ability of reason to judge revelation was affirmed. As critical reason was omnicompetent, it was argued that it was supremely qualified to judge Christian beliefs and practices, with a view, to eliminating any irrational or superstitious elements. This view, associated with Hermann Samuel Reimarus in Germany and the *philosophes* in France, placed reason firmly above revelation, and may be seen as symbolized in the enthronement of the Goddess of Reason in Notre Dame de Paris in 1793.

The Enlightenment was primarily a European and American phenomenon, and thus took place in cultures in which the most numerically significant form of religion was Christianity. This historical observation is of importance: The Enlightenment critique of religion in general was often particularized as a criticism of Christianity in general. It was Christian doctrines which were subjected to a critical assessment of unprecedented vigor. It was Christian sacred writings – rather than those of Islam or Hinduism – which were subjected to an unprecedented critical scrutiny, both literary and historical, with the Bible being treated "as if it were any other book" (Benjamin Jowett). It was the life of Jesus of Nazareth which was subjected to critical reconstruction, rather than that of Mohammed or the Buddha.

The Enlightenment attitude to religion was subject to a considerable degree of regional variation, reflecting a number of local factors peculiar to different situations. One of the most important such factors is Pietism, perhaps best known in its English and American form of Methodism. As noted earlier, this movement placed considerable emphasis upon the experiential aspects of religion – see, for example, John Wesley's notion of "experimental religion" (note that Wesley uses the word "experimental" to mean "experiential"). This concern for religious experience served to make Christianity relevant and accessible to the experiential situation of the masses, contrasting sharply with the intellectualism of, for example, Lutheran orthodoxy, which was perceived to be an irrelevance. Pietism forged a strong link between Christian faith and experience, thus making Christianity a matter of the heart, as well as of the mind.

As noted earlier, Pietism was well established in Germany by the end of the seventeenth century, whereas the movement developed in England only during the eighteenth century, and in France not at all. The Enlightenment thus preceded the rise of Pietism in England, with the result that the great evangelical revivals of the eighteenth century significantly blunted the influence of rationalism upon religion. In Germany, however, the Enlightenment followed after the rise of Pietism, and thus developed in a situation which had been significantly shaped by religious faith, even if it would pose a serious challenge to the received forms and ideas of that faith. (Interestingly, English Deism began to become influential in Germany at roughly the same time as German Pietism began to exert influence in England.) The most significant intellectual forces in the German Enlightenment were thus directed toward the reshaping (rather than the rejection or demolition) of the Christian faith.

In France, however, Christianity was widely perceived as both oppressive and irrelevant, with the result that the writers of the French Enlightenment – often referred to simply as *les philosophes* – were able to advocate the total rejection of Christianity as an archaic and discredited belief system. In his *Treaty on Tolerance*, Denis Diderot argued that English Deism had compromised itself, permitting religion to survive where it ought to have been eradicated totally.

The Enlightenment Critique of Christian Theology: Specific Issues

Having outlined the general principles of the Enlightenment challenge to traditional Christian thought, it is now appropriate to explore how these impacted on specific matters of doctrine. The rational religion of the Enlightenment found itself in conflict with six major areas of traditional Christian theology.

The possibility of miracles

Much traditional Christian apologetics concerning the identity and significance of Jesus Christ was based upon the "miraculous evidences" of the New Testament, culminating in the resurrection. The new emphasis upon the mechanical regularity and orderliness of the universe, perhaps the most significant intellectual legacy of Newtonianism, raised doubts about the New Testament accounts of miraculous happenings. Hume's *Essay on Miracles* (1748) was widely regarded as demonstrating the evidential impossibility of miracles. Hume emphasized that there were no contemporary analogues of New Testament miracles, such as the resurrection, thus forcing the New Testament reader to rely totally upon human testimony to such miracles. For Hume, it was axiomatic that no human testimony was adequate to establish the occurrence of a miracle, in the absence of a present-day analogue. Reimarus and G. E. Lessing denied that human testimony to a past event (such as the resurrection) was sufficient to make it credible if it appeared to be contradicted by present-day direct experience, no matter how well documented the original event may have been.

Similarly, Diderot declared that if the entire population of Paris were to assure him that a dead man had just been raised from the dead, he would not believe

223

a word of it. This growing skepticism concerning the "miraculous evidences" of the New Testament forced traditional Christianity to defend the doctrine of the divinity of Christ on grounds other than miracles – which, at the time, it proved singularly incapable of doing. Of course, it must be noted that other religions claiming miraculous evidences were subjected to equally great skeptical criticism by the Enlightenment: Christianity happened to be singled out for particular comment on account of its religious domination of the cultural milieu in which the Enlightenment developed.

The notion of revelation

The concept of revelation was of central importance to traditional Christian theology. While many Christian theologians (such as Thomas Aquinas and John Calvin) recognized the possibility of a natural knowledge of God, they insisted that this required supplementation by supernatural divine revelation, such as that witnessed to in Scripture. The Enlightenment witnessed the development of an increasingly critical attitude to the very idea of supernatural revelation. In part, this new critical attitude was also due to the Enlightenment depreciation of history.

For Lessing, there was an "ugly great ditch" between history and reason. Revelation took place in history – but of what value were the contingent truths of history in comparison with the necessary truths of reason? The *philosophes* in particular asserted that history could at best confirm the truths of reason, but was incapable of establishing those truths in the first place. Truths about God were timeless, open to investigation by human reason but not capable of being disclosed in "events" such as the history of Jesus of Nazareth.

The doctrine of original sin

The idea that human nature is in some sense flawed or corrupted, expressed in the orthodox doctrine of original sin, was vigorously opposed by the Enlightenment. Voltaire and Jean-Jacques Rousseau criticized the doctrine as encouraging pessimism with regard to human abilities, thus impeding human social and political development and encouraging *laissez-faire* attitudes. German Enlightenment thinkers tended to criticize the doctrine on account of its historical origins in the thought of Augustine of Hippo, dating from the fourth and fifth centuries, which they regarded as debarring it from permanent validity and relevance.

The rejection of original sin was of considerable importance, as the Christian doctrine of redemption rested upon the assumption that humanity required to be liberated from bondage to original sin. For the Enlightenment, it was the idea of original sin itself which was oppressive, and from which humanity required liberation. This intellectual liberation was provided by the Enlightenment critique of the doctrine.

The problem of evil

The Enlightenment witnessed a fundamental change in attitude toward the existence of evil in the world. For the medieval period, the existence of evil was not regarded as posing a threat to the coherence of Christianity. The contradiction implicit in the existence both of a benevolent divine omnipotence and of evil was not regarded as an obstacle to belief, but simply as an academic theological problem. The Enlightenment saw this situation change radically: The existence of evil metamorphosed into a challenge to the credibility and coherence of Christian faith itself. Voltaire's novel *Candide* was one of many works to highlight the difficulties caused for the Christian worldview by the existence of natural evil (such as the famous Lisbon earthquake). The term "theodicy," coined by Leibniz, derives from this period, reflecting a growing recognition that the existence of evil was assuming a new significance within the Enlightenment critique of religion.

The status and interpretation of Scripture

Within orthodox Christianity, whether Protestant or Roman Catholic, the Bible was still widely regarded as a divinely inspired source of doctrine and morals, to be differentiated from other types of literature. The Enlightenment saw this assumption called into question, with the rise of the critical approach to Scripture. Developing ideas already current within Deism, the theologians of the German Enlightenment developed the thesis that the Bible was the work of many hands, at times demonstrating internal contradiction, and that it was open to precisely the same method of textual analysis and interpretation as any other piece of literature. These ideas may be seen in developed forms in works by J. A. Ernesti (1761) and J. J. Semler (1771). The effect of these developments was to weaken still further the concept of "supernatural revelation," and call into question the permanent significance of these foundational documents of the Christian faith.

The identity and significance of Jesus Christ

A final area in which the Enlightenment made a significant challenge to orthodox Christian belief concerns the person of Jesus of Nazareth. Two particularly important developments may be noted: the origins of the "quest of the historical Jesus" (see pp. 270–5), and the rise of the "moral theory of the atonement" (pp. 282–97).

Both Deism and the German Enlightenment developed the thesis that there was a serious discrepancy between the real Jesus of history and the New Testament interpretation of his significance. Underlying the New Testament portrait of the supernatural redeemer of humanity lurked a simple human figure, a glorified teacher of common sense. While a supernatural redeemer was unacceptable to Enlightenment rationalism, the idea of an enlightened moral teacher was not.

This idea, developed with particular rigor by Reimarus, suggested that it was possible to go behind the New Testament accounts of Jesus and uncover a simpler, more human Jesus, who would be acceptable to the new spirit of the age. And so the quest for the real and more credible "Jesus of history" began. Although this pursuit would ultimately end in failure, the later Enlightenment regarded the quest as holding the key to the credibility of Jesus within the context of a rational natural religion. Jesus' moral authority resided in the quality of his teaching and religious personality, rather than in the unacceptable orthodox suggestion that he was God incarnate.

The second area in which the ideas of orthodoxy concerning Jesus were challenged concerned the significance of his death. For orthodoxy, Jesus' death on the cross was interpreted from the standpoint of the resurrection (which the Enlightenment was not prepared to accept as an historical event) as a way in which God was able to forgive the sins of humanity. During the Enlightenment this "theory of the atonement" was subjected to increasing criticism, as involving arbitrary and unacceptable hypotheses such as that of original sin.

Jesus' death on the cross was reinterpreted in terms of a supreme moral example of self-giving and dedication, intended to inspire similar dedication and self-giving on the part of his followers. Where orthodox Christianity tended to treat Jesus' death (and resurrection) as possessing greater inherent importance than his religious teaching, the Enlightenment marginalized his death and denied his resurrection, in order to emphasize the quality of his moral teaching.

WESTERN THEOLOGICAL MOVEMENTS
SINCE THE ENLIGHTENMENT

It will be clear from the above that the Enlightenment had a major impact upon Christian theology, raising a series of critical questions concerning its sources, methods, and doctrines. However, despite its continuing influence over the modern period, the Enlightenment is generally regarded as having reached the zenith of its impact around the time of the French Revolution. A series of developments since then have moved Christian theology away from the agenda of the movement, even if its influence can still be discerned at points. In what follows, we shall consider major developments within western Christian theology since the time of the Enlightenment.

In the course of discussing these movements, the contributions of several major theologians will be considered. In particular, the following should be noted: F. D. E. Schleiermacher (Romanticism); Karl Barth (neo-orthodoxy);

Paul Tillich (liberal Protestantism). However, the modern period includes a galaxy of stars, and we do not propose to single out any individual writers for special discussion.

Romanticism

In the closing decade of the eighteenth century, increasing misgivings came to be expressed concerning the arid quality of rationalism. Reason, once seen as a liberator, was increasingly regarded as spiritually enslaving. These anxieties were not expressed so much within university faculties of philosophy, as within literary and artistic circles, particularly in the Prussian capital, Berlin, where the brothers Friedrich and August William Schlegel became particularly influential.

"Romanticism" is notoriously difficult to define. The movement is perhaps best seen as a reaction against certain of the central themes of the Enlightenment, most notably the claim that reality can be known to the human reason. This reduction of reality to a series of rationalized simplicities seemed, to the Romantics, to be a culpable and crude misrepresentation. Where the Enlightenment appealed to the human reason, Romanticism made an appeal to the human imagination, which was capable of recognizing the profound sense of mystery which arises from realizing that the human mind cannot comprehend even the finite world, let alone the infinity beyond this. This ethos is expressed well by the English poet William Wordsworth, who spoke of the human imagination in terms of transcending the limitations of human reason, and reaching beyond its bounds to sample the infinite through the finite. Imagination, he wrote,

> Is but another name for absolute power
> And clearest insight, amplitude of mind,
> And Reason in her most exalted mood.

Romanticism thus found itself equally unhappy with both traditional Christian doctrines and the rationalist moral platitudes of the Enlightenment: both failed to do justice to the complexity of the world, in an attempt to reduce the "mystery of the universe" – to use a phrase found in the writings of August William Schlegel – to neat formulae.

A marked limitation of the competence of reason may be discerned in such sentiments. Reason threatens to limit the human mind to what may be deduced; the imagination is able to liberate the human spirit from this self-imposed bondage, and allow it to discover new depths of reality – a vague and tantalizing "something," which can be discerned in the world of everyday actualities. The infinite is somehow present in the finite, and may be known through feeling and the imagination. As John Keats put it, "I am certain of nothing except the holiness of the heart's affections, and the truth of the imagination."

227

The reaction against the aridity of reason was thus complemented by an emphasis upon the epistemological significance of human feelings and emotions. Under the influence of Novalis (Friedrich von Hardenberg), German Romanticism came to develop two axioms concerning *das Gefühl*. (This German term is perhaps best translated as "feeling" or "sentiment," though neither conveys the full range of meanings associated with the original. For this reason, it is often left untranslated; readers disliking the use of foreign-language terms can, however, replace it with "feeling.") First, "feeling" has to do with the individual subjective thinker, who becomes aware of his or her subjectivity and inward individuality. Rationalism may have made its appeal to individual reason; Romanticism retained the emphasis upon the individual, but supplanted a concern with reason by a new interest in the imagination and persona; feeling. The Enlightenment looked inward to human reason; Romanticism looked inward to human feelings, seeing in these "the way to all mysteries" (Novalis).

Second, "feeling" is oriented toward the infinite and eternal, and provides the key to these higher realms. It is for this reason, Novalis declares, that the Enlightenment proscribed the imagination and feeling as "heretical," in that they offered access to the "magical idealism" of the infinite; by its wooden appeal to reason alone, the Enlightenment attempted to suppress knowledge of these higher worlds through an appeal to the aridities of philosophy. Human subjectivity and inwardness were now seen as a mirror of the infinite. A new emphasis came to be placed upon music as a "revelation of a higher order than any morality or philosophy" (Bettina von Arnim).

The development of Romanticism had considerable implications for Christianity in Europe. Those aspects of Christianity (especially Roman Catholicism) which rationalism found distasteful came to captivate the imaginations of the Romantics. Rationalism was seen to be experientially and emotionally deficient, incapable of meeting real human needs that were traditionally addressed and satisfied by Christian faith. As F. R. de Chateaubriand remarked of the situation in France in the first decade of the nineteenth century, "there was a need for faith, a desire for religious consolation, which came from the very lack of that consolation for so long." Similar sentiments can be instanced from the German context in the closing years of the eighteenth century.

That rationalism had failed to undermine religion is clear from developments in England, Germany, and North America. The new strength evident in German Pietism and English evangelicalism in the eighteenth century is evidence of the failure of rationalism to provide a cogent alternative to the prevailing human sense of personal need and meaning. Philosophy came to be seen as sterile, academic in the worst sense of the word, in that it was detached from both the outer realities of life and the inner life of the human consciousness.

It is against this background of growing disillusionment with rationalism, and a new appreciation of human "feeling," that the contribution of Friedrich Daniel

Ernst Schleiermacher (1768–1834) is to be seen. Schleiermacher capitalized on this interest in feeling. He argued that religion in general, and Christianity in particular, was a matter of feeling or "self-consciousness." His major work of systematic theology, *The Christian Faith* (1821; revised 1830), is an attempt to show how Christian theology is related to a feeling of "absolute dependence." The structure of *The Christian Faith* is complex, centering on the dialectic between sin and grace. The work is organized in three parts. The first deals with the consciousness of God, concentrating upon such matters as creation. The second part handles the consciousness of sin, and its implications, such as an awareness of the possibility of redemption. The final part considers the consciousness of grace, and deals with such matters as the person and work of Christ. In this way, Schleiermacher is able to argue that "everything is related to the redemption accomplished by Jesus of Nazareth."

Schleiermacher's contribution to the development of Christian theology is considerable, and will be examined in depth at the appropriate points in this volume. However, our attention now turns to a movement which, although not strictly theological – indeed, it could be termed atheological – has had a major impact upon modern western theology. The movement in question is Marxism.

Marxism

Marxism, probably one of the most significant worldviews to emerge during the modern period, has had a major impact upon Christian theology during the last century, and is likely to continue to be an important dialogue partner in the years to come. Marxism may be regarded as the body of ideas associated with the German writer Karl Marx (1818–83). Until recently, however, the term also referred to a state ideology, characteristic of a number of states in eastern Europe and elsewhere, which regarded Christianity and other religions as reactionary, and adopted repressive measures to eliminate them.

The notion of materialism is fundamental to Marxism. This is not some metaphysical or philosophical doctrine which affirms that the world consists only of matter. Rather, it is an assertion that a correct understanding of human beings must begin with material production. The way in which human beings respond to their material needs determines everything else. Ideas, including religious ideas, are responses to material reality. They are the superstructure which is erected upon a socio-economic substructure. In other words, ideas and belief systems are a response to a quite definite set of social and economic conditions. If these are radically altered (for example, by a revolution), the belief systems which they generated and sustained will pass away with them.

This first idea flows naturally into the second: the alienation of humanity. A number of factors bring about alienation within the material process, of which the two most significant are the division of labor and the existence of private property. The former causes the alienation of the worker from his product, whereas the second brings about a situation in which the interest of the individual no longer coincides with that of society as a whole. As productive forces are owned by a small minority of the population, it follows that societies are divided along class lines, with political and economic power being concentrated in the hands of the ruling class.

If this analysis is correct, Marx believed, then, that the third conclusion naturally followed: Capitalism – the economic order just described – was inherently unstable, due to the tensions arising from productive forces. As a result of these internal contradictions, it would break down. Some versions of Marxism present this breakdown as happening without any need for assistance. Others present it as the result of a social revolution, led by the working class. The closing words of the *Communist Manifesto* (1848) seem to suggest the latter: "Workers have nothing to lose but their chains. They have a world to gain. Workers of the world, unite!"

So how do these ideas relate to Christian theology? In his 1844 political and economic manuscripts, Marx develops the idea that religion in general (he does not distinguish the individual religions) is a direct response to social and economic conditions. "The religious world is but the reflex of the real world." There is an obvious and important allusion here to Feuerbach's critique of religion, which we shall consider in a later section. Thus Marx argues that "religion is just the imaginary sun which seems to man to revolve around him, until he realizes that he himself is the center of his own revolution." In other words, God is simply a projection of human concerns. Human beings "look for a superhuman being in the fantasy reality of heaven, and find nothing there, but their own reflection."

But why should religion exist at all? If Marx is right, why should people continue to believe in such a crude illusion? Marx's answer centers on the notion of alienation. "Humans make religion; religion does not make humans. Religion is the self-consciousness and self-esteem of people who either have not found themselves or who have already lost themselves again." Religion is the product of social and economic alienation. It arises from that alienation, and at the same time encourages that alienation by a form of spiritual intoxication which renders the masses incapable of recognizing their situation, and doing something about it. Religion is a comfort, which enables people to tolerate their economic alienation. If there were no such alienation, there would be no need for religion.

Materialism affirms that events in the material world bring about corresponding changes in the intellectual world. Religion is thus the result of a certain set of social and economic conditions. Change those conditions, so that economic alienation is eliminated, and religion will cease to exist. It will no longer serve any useful function. Unjust social conditions produce religion, and are in turn supported by religion. "The struggle against religion is therefore indirectly a struggle against *the world* of which religion is the spiritual fragrance."

Marx thus argues that religion will continue to exist, as long as it meets a need in the life of alienated people. "The religious reflex of the real world can . . . only then vanish when the practical relations of everyday life offer to man none but perfectly intelligible and reasonable relations with regard to his fellow men and to nature." In other words, a shake-up in the real world is needed to get rid of religion. Marx thus argues that when a non-alienating economic and social environment is brought about through communism, the needs which gave rise to religion will vanish. And with the elimination of those material needs, spiritual hunger will also vanish.

In practice, Marxism had virtually no influence until the period of World War I. This can be put down partly to some disagreements within the movement, and is partly due to the lack of any real opportunities for political expansion. The internal problems are especially interesting. The suggestion that the working class could liberate itself from its oppression, and bring about a political revolution, soon proved to be illusory. It rapidly became clear that Marxists, far from being drawn from the ranks of the politically conscious working class, were actually depressingly middle-class (like Marx himself). Aware of this problem, Lenin developed the idea of a "vanguard party." The workers were so politically naïve that they needed to be led by professional revolutionaries, who alone could provide the overall vision and practical guidance that would be needed in bringing about and sustaining a world revolution.

The Russian Revolution gave Marxism the break it needed. However, although Marxism established itself in a modified form (Marxism–Leninism) within the Soviet Union, it proved unsuccessful elsewhere. Its successes in eastern Europe after World War II can be put down mainly to military strength and political destabilization. Its successes in Africa were largely due to the seductive appeal of Lenin's carefully devised concept of "imperialism," which allowed alienated elements in certain African and Asian countries to put their backwardness down to ruthless and systematic exploitation by the external agency of western capitalism, rather than to any inherent deficiencies.

The economic failure and political stagnation which resulted when such countries experimented with Marxism in the 1970s and 1980s soon led to disillusionment with this new philosophy. In Europe, Marxism found itself locked into a spiral of decline. Its chief advocates increasingly became abstract theoreticians, detached from working-class roots, with virtually no political experience. The idea of a socialist revolution gradually lost its appeal and its credibility. In the United States and Canada, Marxism had little, if any, social appeal in the first place, although its influence upon the academic world was more noticeable. The Soviet invasion of Czechoslovakia in 1968 resulted in a noticeable cooling in enthusiasm for Marxism within western intellectual circles.

231

However, Marx's ideas have found their way, suitably modified, into modern Christian theology. Latin American liberation theology can be shown to have drawn appreciatively on Marxist insights, even if the movement cannot really be described as "Marxist." We shall consider liberation theology in a later section (see pp. 254–6).

Liberal Protestantism

Liberal Protestantism is unquestionably one of the most important movements to have arisen within modern Christian thought. Its origins are complex. However, it is helpful to think of it as having arisen in response to the theological program set out by F.D.E. Schleiermacher, especially in relation to his emphasis upon human "feeling" (see pp. 333–5) and the need to relate Christian faith to the human situation. Classic liberal Protestantism had its origins in the Germany of the mid-nineteenth century, amidst a growing realization that Christian faith and theology alike required reconstruction in the light of modern knowledge. In England, the increasingly positive reception given to Charles Darwin's theory of natural selection (popularly known as the "Darwinian theory of evolution") created a climate in which some elements of traditional Christian theology (such as the doctrine of the seven days of creation) seemed to be increasingly untenable. From its outset, liberalism was committed to bridging the gap between Christian faith and modern knowledge.

Liberalism's program required a significant degree of flexibility in relation to traditional Christian theology. Its leading writers argued that reconstruction of belief was essential if Christianity were to remain a serious intellectual option in the modern world. For this reason, they demanded a degree of freedom in relation to the doctrinal inheritance of Christianity on the one hand, and traditional methods of biblical interpretation on the other. Where traditional ways of interpreting Scripture, or traditional beliefs, seemed to be compromised by developments in human knowledge, it was imperative that they should be discarded or reinterpreted to bring them into line with what was now known about the world.

The theological implications of this shift in direction were considerable. A number of Christian beliefs came to be regarded as seriously out of line with modern cultural norms; these suffered one of two fates:

1 They were *abandoned*, as resting upon outdated or mistaken presuppositions. The doctrine of original sin is a case in point; this was put down to a misreading of the New Testament in the light of the writings of St Augustine, whose judgment on these matters had become clouded by his overinvolvement with a fatalist sect (the Manichees).

2 They were *reinterpreted*, in a manner more conducive to the spirit of the age.

A number of central doctrines relating to the person of Jesus Christ may be included in this category, including his divinity (which was reinterpreted as an affirmation of Jesus exemplifying qualities which humanity as a whole could hope to emulate).

Alongside this process of doctrinal reinterpretation (which continued in the "history of dogma" movement) may be seen a new concern to ground Christian faith in the world of humanity – above all, in human experience and modern culture. Sensing potential difficulties in grounding Christian faith in an exclusive appeal to Scripture or the person of Jesus Christ, liberalism sought to anchor that faith in common human experience, and interpret it in ways that made sense within the modern worldview.

Liberalism was inspired by the vision of a humanity which was ascending upward into new realms of progress and prosperity. The doctrine of evolution gave new vitality to this belief, which was nurtured by strong evidence of cultural stability in western Europe in the late nineteenth century. Religion came increasingly to be seen as relating to the spiritual needs of modern humanity, and giving ethical guidance to society. The strongly ethical dimension of liberal Protestantism is especially evident in the writings of Albrecht Benjamin Ritschl.

For Ritschl, the idea of the "kingdom of God" was of central importance. Ritschl tended to think of this as a static realm of ethical values, which would undergird the development of German society at this point in its history. History, it was argued, was in the process of being divinely guided toward perfection. Civilization is seen as part of this process of evolution. In the course of human history, a number of individuals appear who are recognized as being the bearers of special divine insights. One such individual was Jesus. By following his example and sharing in his inner life, other human beings are able to develop. The movement showed enormous and unbounded optimism in human ability and potential. Religion and culture were, it was argued, virtually identical. Later critics of the movement dubbed it "culture Protestantism" (*Kultur-protestantismus*), on account of their belief that it was too heavily dependent upon accepted cultural norms.

Many critics – such as Karl Barth in Europe and Reinhold Niebuhr in North America – regarded liberal Protestantism as based upon a hopelessly optimistic view of human nature. They believed that this optimism had been destroyed by the events of World War I, and that liberalism would henceforth lack cultural credibility. This has proved to be a considerable misjudgment. At its best, liberalism may be regarded as a movement committed to the restatement of Christian faith in forms which are acceptable within contemporary culture. Liberalism has continued to see itself as a mediator between two unacceptable alternatives: the mere restatement of traditional Christian faith (usually described as "traditionalism" or "fundamentalism" by its liberal critics), and the total

233

rejection of Christianity. Liberal writers have been passionately committed to the search for a middle road between these two stark alternatives.

Perhaps the most developed and influential presentation of liberal Protestantism is to be found in the writings of Paul Tillich (1886–1965), who rose to fame in the United States in the late 1950s and early 1960s, toward the end of his career, and who is widely regarded as the most influential American theologian since Jonathan Edwards. Tillich's program can be summarized in the term "correlation." By the "method of correlation," Tillich understands the task of modern theology to be to establish a conversation between human culture and Christian faith. Tillich reacted with alarm to the theological program set out by Karl Barth, seeing this as a misguided attempt to drive a wedge between theology and culture. For Tillich, existential questions – or "ultimate questions," as he often terms them – are thrown up and revealed by human culture. Modern philosophy, writing, and the creative arts point to questions which concern humans. Theology then formulates answers to these questions, and by doing so it correlates the gospel to modern culture. The gospel must speak to culture, and it can do so only if the actual questions raised by that culture are heard. For David Tracy of the University of Chicago, the image of a dialogue between the gospel and culture is controlling: that dialogue involves the mutual correction and enrichment of both gospel and culture. There is thus a close relation between theology and apologetics, in that the task of theology is understood to be that of interpreting the Christian response to the human needs disclosed by cultural analysis.

The term "liberal" is thus probably best interpreted as applying to "a theologian in the tradition of Schleiermacher and Tillich, concerned with the reconstruction of belief in response to contemporary culture," in which form it describes many noted modern writers. However, it must be noted that the term "liberal" is widely regarded as imprecise and confusing. The British theologian John Macquarrie notes this point with characteristic clarity:

> What is meant by "liberal" theology? If it means only that the theologian to whom the adjective is applied has an openness to other points of view, then liberal theologians are found in all schools of thought. But if "liberal" becomes itself a party label, then it usually turns out to be extremely illiberal.

In fact, one of the more curious paradoxes of recent Christian theology is that some of the most dogmatic of its representatives actually lay claim to be liberals! Liberalism, in the traditional and honorable sense of the word, carries with it an inalienable respect for and openness to the views of others; as such, it ought to be a fundamental element of every branch of Christian theology (including neo-orthodoxy and evangelicalism, to be discussed shortly). However, the term has now come to have a developed meaning, often carrying with it overtones of suspicion, hostility, or impatience toward traditional Christian formulations and doctrines. This can be seen clearly in the popular use of the term, which often includes ideas such as the denial of the resurrection or of the uniqueness of Christ.

Liberalism has been criticized on a number of points, of which the following are typical.

1   It tends to place considerable weight upon the notion of a universal human religious experience. Yet this is a vague and ill-defined notion, incapable of being examined and assessed publicly. There are also excellent reasons for suggesting that "experience" is shaped by interpretation to a far greater extent than liberalism allows.
2   Liberalism is seen by its critics as placing too great an emphasis upon transient cultural developments, with the result that it often appears to be uncritically driven by a secular agenda.
3   It has been suggested that liberalism is too ready to surrender distinctive Christian doctrines in an effort to become acceptable to contemporary culture.

Liberalism probably reached its zenith in North America during the late 1970s and early 1980s. Although continuing to maintain a distinguished presence in seminaries and schools of religion, it is now widely regarded as a waning force both in modern theology and in church life in general. The weaknesses of liberalism have been seized upon by critics within the postliberal school, to be considered shortly. Much the same criticism can also be directed against a movement known loosely as "modernism," to which we may now turn.

Modernism

The term "modernist" was first used to refer to a school of Roman Catholic theologians operating toward the end of the nineteenth century, which adopted a critical and skeptical attitude to traditional Christian doctrines, especially those relating to Christology and soteriology. The movement fostered a positive attitude toward radical biblical criticism, and stressed the ethical, rather than the more theological, dimensions of faith. In many ways, modernism may be seen as an attempt by writers within the Roman Catholic church to come to terms with the outlook of the Enlightenment, which it had, until that point, largely ignored.

"Modernism" is, however, a loose term, and should not be understood to imply the existence of a distinctive school of thought, committed to certain common methods or indebted to common teachers. It is certainly true that most modernist writers were concerned to integrate Christian thought with the spirit of the Enlightenment, especially the new understandings of history and the natural sciences which were then gaining the ascendancy. Equally, some drew

235

inspiration from writers such as Maurice Blondel (1861–1949), who argued that the supernatural was intrinsic to human existence, or Henri Bergson (1859–1941), who stressed the importance of intuition over intellect. Yet there is not sufficient commonality amongst the French, English, and American modernists, nor between Roman Catholic and Protestant modernism, to allow the term to be understood as designating a rigorous and well-defined school.

Amongst Roman Catholic modernist writers, particular attention should be paid to Alfred Loisy (1857–1940) and George Tyrrell (1861–1909). During the 1890s, Loisy established himself as a critic of traditional views of the biblical accounts of creation, and argued that a real development of doctrine could be discerned within Scripture. His most significant publication, *L'évangile et l'église* ("The gospel and the church"), appeared in 1902. This important work was a direct response to the views of Adolf von Harnack, published two years earlier as *What is Christianity?*, on the origins and nature of Christianity. Loisy rejected Harnack's suggestion that there was a radical discontinuity between Jesus and the church; however, he made significant concessions to Harnack's liberal Protestant account of Christian origins, including an acceptance of the role and validity of biblical criticism in interpreting the gospels. As a result, the work was placed upon the list of prohibited books by the Roman Catholic authorities in 1903.

The British Jesuit writer George Tyrrell followed Loisy in his radical criticism of traditional Catholic dogma. In common with Loisy, he criticized Harnack's account of Christian origins in *Christianity at the Crossroads* (1909), dismissing Harnack's historical reconstruction of Jesus as "the reflection of a Liberal Protestant face, seen at the bottom of a deep well." The book also included a defense of Loisy's work, arguing that the official Roman Catholic "hostility to the book and its author has created a general impression that it is a defence of Liberal Protestant against Roman Catholic positions, and that 'Modernism' is simply a protestantizing and rationalizing movement."

In part, this perception may be due to the growing influence of modernist attitudes within the mainstream Protestant denominations. In England, the Churchmen's Union was founded in 1898 for the advancement of liberal religious thought; in 1928, it altered its name to the Modern Churchmen's Union. Amongst those especially associated with this group may be noted Hastings Rashdall (1858–1924), whose *Idea of Atonement in Christian Theology* (1919) illustrates the general tenor of English modernism. Drawing somewhat uncritically upon the earlier writings of liberal Protestant thinkers such as Ritschl, Rashdall argued that the theory of the atonement associated with the medieval writer Peter Abelard was more acceptable to modern thought forms than traditional theories which made an appeal to the notion of a substitutionary sacrifice. This strongly moral or exemplarist theory of the atonement, which interpreted Christ's death virtually exclusively as a demonstration of the love of God, made a considerable impact upon English, and especially Anglican, thought in the 1920s and 1930s. Nevertheless, the events of World War I, and the subsequent rise of fascism in Europe in the 1930s, undermined the credibility of the movement. It was not until the 1960s that a renewed modernism or radicalism became a significant feature of English Christianity.

The rise of modernism in the United States follows a similar pattern. The growth of liberal Protestantism in the late nineteenth and early twentieth centuries was widely perceived as a direct challenge to more conservative evangelical standpoints. Newman Smyth's *Passing Protestantism and Coming Catholicism* (1908) argued that Roman Catholic modernism could serve as a mentor to American Protestantism in several ways, not least in its critique of dogma and its historical understanding of the development of doctrine. The situation became increasingly polarized through the rise of fundamentalism in response to modernist attitudes.

World War I ushered in a period of self-questioning within American modernism which was intensified through the radical social realism of writers such as H. R. Niebuhr. By the mid-1930s, modernism appeared to have lost its way. In an influential article in *The Christian Century* of December 4, 1935, Harry Emerson Fosdick declared the need to go beyond modernism. In his *Realistic Theology* (1934), Walter Marshall Horton spoke of the rout of liberal forces in American theology. However, the movement gained new confidence in the post-war period, and arguably reached its zenith during the period of the Vietnam War.

However, we must now turn back to the opening of the twentieth century, to consider an earlier reaction against liberalism, which is especially associated with the name of Karl Barth: neo-orthodoxy.

Neo-Orthodoxy

World War I witnessed a disillusionment with, although not a final rejection of, the liberal theology which had come to be associated with Schleiermacher and his followers. A number of writers argued that Schleiermacher had, in effect, reduced Christianity to little more than religious experience, thus making it a human-centered rather than a God-centered affair. The war, it was argued, destroyed the credibility of such an approach. Liberal theology seemed to be about human values – and how could these be taken seriously, if they led to global conflicts on such a massive scale? By stressing the "otherness" of God, writers such as Karl Barth (1886–1968) believed that they could escape from the doomed human-centered theology of liberalism.

These ideas were given systematic exposition by Barth in the *Church Dogmatics* (1936–69), probably the most significant theological achievement of the twentieth century. Barth did not live to finish this enterprise, so that his exposition of the doctrine of redemption is incomplete. The primary theme which resonates

237

throughout the *Dogmatics* is the need to take seriously the self-revelation of God in Christ through Scripture. Although this might seem to be little more than a reiteration of themes already firmly associated with Calvin or Luther, Barth brought a degree of creativity to his task which firmly established him as a major thinker in his own right.

The work is divided into five volumes, each of which is further subdivided. Volume I deals with the Word of God – for Barth, the source and starting point of Christian faith and Christian theology alike. Volume II deals with the doctrine of God, and Volume III with the doctrine of the creation. Volume IV deals with the doctrine of reconciliation (or, perhaps one might say, atonement; the German term *Versöhnung* can mean both), and the incomplete Volume V with the doctrine of redemption.

Apart from the predictable (and relatively non-informative) "Barthianism," two terms have been used to describe the approach associated with Barth. The term "dialectical theology" has been used, taking up the idea, found especially in Barth's 1919 commentary on Romans, of a "dialectic between time and eternity," or a "dialectic between God and humanity." The term draws attention to Barth's characteristic insistence that there is a contradiction or dialectic, rather than a continuity, between God and humanity. The second term is "neo-orthodoxy," which draws attention to the affinity between Barth and the writings of the period of Reformed orthodoxy, especially during the seventeenth century. In many ways, Barth can be regarded as entering into dialogue with several leading Reformed writers of this period.

Perhaps the most distinctive feature of Barth's approach is his "theology of the Word of God." According to Barth, theology is a discipline which seeks to keep the proclamation of the Christian church faithful to its foundation in Jesus Christ, as he has been revealed to us in Scripture. Theology is not a response to the human situation or to human questions; it is a response to the Word of God, which demands a response on account of its intrinsic nature.

Neo-orthodoxy became a significant presence in North American theology during the 1930s, especially through the writings of Reinhold Niebuhr and others, which criticized the optimistic assumptions of much liberal Protestant social thinking of the time.

Neo-orthodoxy has been criticized at a number of points. The following are of especial importance:

1   Its emphasis upon the transcendence and "otherness" of God leads to God being viewed as distant and potentially irrelevant. It has often been suggested that this leads to extreme skepticism.
2   There is a certain circularity to the claim of neo-orthodoxy to be based only upon divine revelation, in that this cannot be checked out by anything other than an appeal to that same revelation. In other words, there are no

recognized external reference points by which neo-orthodoxy's truth claims can be verified. This has led many of its critics to suggest that it is a form of *fideism* – that is to say, a belief system which is impervious to any criticism from outside.

3 Neo-orthodoxy has no helpful response to those who are attracted to other religions, which it is obliged to dismiss as distortions and perversions. Other theological approaches are able to account for the existence of such religions, and place them in relation to the Christian faith.

Roman Catholicism

It is widely accepted that the most significant developments in modern Roman Catholic theology have their origins in the period immediately preceding the Second Vatican Council (1962–5). It would be unfair to inscribe the words "not much happened" against the history of Roman Catholic theology during the eighteenth and nineteenth centuries. Nevertheless, the conditions which the Roman Catholic church encountered in Europe during this period were not particularly suitable for theological reflection. In predominantly Protestant northern Europe, the church often found itself being placed on the defensive, so that polemical rather than constructive theology was of paramount importance. This was even the case during the nineteenth century, when Bismark launched his *Kulturkampf* ("Culture War") against the German Roman Catholic church. Yet secularizing forces were also of major importance. The French Revolution and its aftermath posed a powerful challenge to the church, once more placing it on the defensive.

However, there were also theological reasons for this lack of creativity. Roman Catholicism had been deeply influenced by the ideas of Bossuet, particularly his emphasis on the constancy of the Catholic tradition (see p. 212). Theology was frequently understood in terms of the faithful repetition of the legacy of the past, a trend encouraged by the First Vatican Council (1869–70). One development of particular importance in this respect was Pope Leo XIII's decision to confer a privileged status on the writings of Thomas Aquinas, in effect (if not in intention) establishing Aquinas as normative in matters of theology.

Nevertheless, definite anticipations of the trend toward theological renewal can be discerned in the nineteenth century. German Roman Catholicism was deeply touched by the rise of the idealism of the Romantic movement, which reawakened interest in many aspects of Catholic faith and practice, including its experiential aspects. This new interest in experience can be seen in the rise of the Catholic Tübingen school during the 1830s, when writers such as Johann Sebastian von Drey (1777–1853) and Johann Adam Möhler (1796–1838) began to place an emphasis on the idea of tradition as the living voice of the church. John Henry Newman (1801–90), who was initially an Anglican, also

239

provided a major injection of confidence and theological acumen into later nineteenth-century Catholic theology, even if his influence has arguably been greater in the twentieth century than in his own. Perhaps the most important of his contributions to the development of Catholic theology relate to the areas of the development of doctrine and the role of the laity in the church.

Signs of a major revival in Roman Catholic theology can be seen after the Second World War (1939–45). One of the most important themes is that of the retrieval of the patristic and medieval heritage of Catholicism, evident in the writings of Henri de Lubac and Yves Congar. The Second Vatican Council promoted interest in the discussion of the nature and role of the church and sacraments, and also established a more positive environment in which Catholic theologians could operate. The writings of Hans Küng, Piet Schoonenberg, and Edward Schillebeeckx illustrate the new vitality within Catholic theology since the Council.

The two most significant theologians to emerge within twentieth-century Roman Catholicism are universally agreed to be Hans Urs von Balthasar (1905–88) and Karl Rahner (1904–84). Von Balthasar's chief work, published over the period 1961–9, is entitled *Herrlichkeit* ("The Glory of the Lord"). It sets out the idea of Christianity as a response to God's self-revelation, laying special emphasis upon the notion of faith as a response to the vision of the beauty of the Lord.

One of Karl Rahner's most impressive achievements is the rehabilitation of the essay as a tool of theological construction. The most significant source for Rahner's thought is not a substantial work of dogmatic theology, but a relatively loose and unstructured collection of essays published over the period 1954–84, and known in English as *Theological Investigations*. These essays, which extend over sixteen volumes in the original German (*Schriften zur Theologie*), and twenty volumes in the still incomplete English edition, bring out the way in which a relatively unsystematic approach to theology can nevertheless give rise to a coherent theological program. Perhaps the most important aspect of Rahner's theological program is his "transcendental method," which he saw as a Christian response to the secular loss of the transcendence of God. Whereas earlier generations attempted to meet this challenge through liberal or modernist accommodationist strategies, Rahner argued that the recovery of a sense of the transcendent could only be achieved through a reappropriation of the classical sources of Christian theology, especially Augustine and Thomas Aquinas. Rahner's particular approach involves the fusion of Thomism with central aspects of German idealism and existentialism.

A document of major importance appeared in 1994. The *Catechism of the Catholic Church* represents a lucid summary of some of the major themes of modern Roman Catholic thought, updated in the light of the Second Vatican Council. This work represents a convenient summary of contemporary Roman Catholic thinking, and will be cited on occasion in the course of this book.

Eastern Orthodoxy

The Byzantine tradition continued to develop after the fall of Byzantium (see pp. 123–7), although in modified forms. With the fall of Constantinople to Islamic invaders, the main centers of eastern Christian thought shifted to Russia, and especially the cities of Kiev and Moscow. Writers such as A. S. Khomyakov (1804–60) and Vladimir Soloviev (1853–1900) did much to develop the intellectual foundations of Russian Orthodox theology during the nineteenth century. The repressive religious policies associated with the Russian Revolution, however, made it impossible for theological education to continue in the homeland of Orthodoxy. Various Russian émigré writers, such as Georges Florovsky (1893–1979) and Vladimir Lossky (1903–58), continued to develop the tradition in exile. Although the collapse of the Soviet Union has opened the way for the re-establishment of a vigorous tradition of Russian Orthodox theology and spirituality in its homeland, it is likely that the Russian diaspora (from the Greek word for "dispersion," often used to refer to groups of people exiled from their homeland) will continue to be of major importance in this respect, particularly in the United States.

Greece was finally liberated from Turkish rule in the 1820s, thus opening the way to a renewal of this theological tradition within Orthodoxy. However, this renewal did not really get off the ground until the 1960s. Indeed, much Greek theological writing in the nineteenth century shows a considerable degree of dependence on western ideas, largely alien to Greece itself. Since then, writers such as John Zizioulas and Christos Yannaras have provided a major stimulus to the recovery of the distinctive ideas of the eastern Christian tradition. Despite the growing importance of Greek diasporas in cities such as New York and Melbourne, it seems likely that Greece itself will continue to provide a major theological influence within Orthodoxy in the future.

Feminism

Feminism has come to be a significant component of modern western culture. At its heart, feminism is a global movement working toward the emancipation of women. The older term for the movement – "women's liberation" – expressed the fact that it is at heart a liberation movement directing its efforts toward achieving equality for women in modern society, especially through the removal of obstacles – including beliefs, values, and attitudes – which hinder that process. Of late, the movement has become increasingly heterogeneous, partly on account of a willingness to recognize a diversity of approaches on the part of women within different cultures and ethnic groupings. Thus the religious writings of black women in North America are increasingly coming to be referred to as "black womanist theology."

Feminism has come into conflict with Christianity (as it has with most religions) on account of the perception that religions treat women as second-rate human beings, in terms of both the roles which those religions allocate to women, and the manner in which they are understood to image God. The writings of Simone de Beauvoir – such as *The Second Sex* (1945) – developed such ideas at length. A number of post-Christian feminists, including Mary Daly in her *Beyond God the Father* (1973) and Daphne Hampson in *Theology and Feminism* (1990), argue that Christianity, with its male symbols for God, its male savior figure, and its long history of male leaders and thinkers, is biased against women, and incapable of redemption. Women, they urge, should leave its oppressive environment. Others, such as Carol Christ in *Laughter of Aphrodite* (1987) and Naomi Ruth Goldenberg in *Changing of the Gods* (1979), argue that women may find religious emancipation by recovering the ancient goddess religions (or inventing new ones), and abandoning traditional Christianity altogether.

Yet the feminist evaluation of Christianity is far from as monolithically hostile toward Christianity as these writers might suggest. Feminist writers have stressed how women have been active in the shaping and development of the Christian tradition, from the New Testament onward, and have exercised significant leadership roles throughout Christian history. Indeed, responsible feminist writers have shown the need to reappraise the Christian past, giving honor and recognition to an army of faithful women, whose practice, defense, and proclamation of their faith had hitherto passed unnoticed by much of the Christian church and its (mainly male) historians.

The most significant contribution of feminism to Christian thought may be argued to lie in its challenge to traditional theological formulations. These, it is argued, are often patriarchal (that is, they reflect a belief in domination by males) and sexist (that is, they are biased against women). The following areas of theology are especially significant in this respect.

1   *The maleness of God* (see pp. 323–7)   The persistent use of male pronouns for God within the Christian tradition is a target of criticism by many feminist writers. It is argued that the use of female pronouns is at least as logical as the use of their male counterparts, and might go some way toward correcting an excessive emphasis upon male role models for God. In her *Sexism and God-Talk* (1983), Rosemary Radford Ruether suggests that the term "God/ess" is a politically correct designation for God, although the verbal clumsiness of the term is unlikely to enhance its appeal.

Sallie McFague's *Metaphorical Theology* (1982) argues for the need to recover the idea of the metaphorical aspects of male models of God, such as "father": *analogies* tend to stress the similarities between God and human beings; *metaphors* affirm that, amidst these similarities, there are significant dissimilarities between God and humans (for example, in the realm of gender).

2 *The nature of sin* Many feminist writers have suggested that notions of sin as pride, ambition, or excessive self-esteem are fundamentally male in orientation. This, it is argued, does not correspond to the experience of women, who tend to experience sin as *lack* of pride, *lack* of ambition, and *lack* of self-esteem. Of particular importance in this context is the feminist appeal to the notion of non-competitive relationships, which avoids the patterns of low self-esteem and passivity which have been characteristic traditional female responses to male-dominated society. This point is made with particular force by Judith Plaskow in *Sex, Sin and Grace* (1980), a penetrating critique of Reinhold Niebuhr's theology from a feminist perspective.

3 *The person of Christ* A number of feminist writers, most notably Rosemary Radford Ruether in *Sexism and God-Talk*, have suggested that Christology is the ultimate ground of much sexism within Christianity. In her *Consider Jesus: Waves of Renewal in Christology* (1990), Elizabeth Johnson has explored the manner in which the maleness of Jesus has been the subject of theological abuse, and suggests appropriate correctives. Two areas of especial importance may be noted.

First, the maleness of Christ has sometimes been used as the theological foundation for the belief that only the male human may adequately image God, or that only males provide appropriate role models or analogies for God. Second, the maleness of Christ has sometimes been used as the foundation for a network of beliefs concerning norms within humanity. It has been argued, on the basis of the maleness of Christ, that the norm of humanity is the male, with the female being somehow a second-rate, or less than ideal, human being. Thomas Aquinas, who describes women as misbegotten males (apparently on the basis of an obsolete Aristotelian biology), illustrates this trend, which has important implications for issues of leadership within the church.

In responding to these points, feminist writers have argued that the maleness of Christ is a contingent aspect of his identity, on the same level as his being Jewish. It is a contingent element of his historical reality, not an essential aspect of his identity. Thus it cannot be allowed to become the basis of the domination of females by males, any more than it legitimates the domination of Gentiles by Jews, or plumbers by carpenters.

The relevance of the feminist critique of traditional theology will be noted at appropriate points during the course of this volume.

Postmodernism

Postmodernism is generally taken to be something of a cultural sensibility without absolutes, fixed certainties, or foundations, which takes delight in pluralism and divergence, and which aims to think through the radical "situatedness" of all human thought. Postmodernism is a vague and ill-defined notion, which perhaps could be described as the general intellectual outlook arising after the collapse of modernism. Although a number of writers still maintain that modernism is alive and active, this attitude is becoming increasingly rare.

Further, it should be noted that modernism itself is a vague idea. The very idea of postmodernism might be argued to "presuppose that our age is unified enough that we can speak of its ending" (David Kolb); nevertheless, much of western culture disagrees. The trauma of Auschwitz is a powerful and shocking indictment of the "pretense of new creation, the hatred of tradition, the idolatry of self" (Kolb) characteristic of modernism. It was modernism, especially with its compulsive desire to break totally with the past, which gave rise to the Nazi Holocaust and the Stalinist purges. There has been a general collapse of confidence in the Enlightenment trust in the power of reason to provide foundations for a universally valid knowledge of the world, including God. Reason fails to deliver a morality suited to the real world in which we live. And with this collapse in confidence in universal and necessary criteria of truth, relativism and pluralism have flourished.

To give a full definition of postmodernism is virtually impossible; nevertheless, it is possible to identify its leading general features, in so far as it is likely to be encountered by the student of Christian theology, especially on North American college and university campuses. This is the precommitment to relativism or pluralism in relation to questions of truth. To use the language which has become characteristic of the movement, one could say that postmodernism represents a situation in which the signifier (or signifying) has replaced the signified as the focus of orientation and value.

In terms of the structural linguistics developed initially by Ferdinand de Saussure, and subsequently by Roman Jakobson and others, the recognition of the *arbitrariness* of the linguistic sign and its interdependence with other signs marks the end of the possibility of fixed, absolute meanings. Thus writers such as Jacques Derrida, Michel Foucault, and Jean Baudrillard argued that language was whimsical and capricious, and did not reflect any overarching, absolute linguistic laws. It was arbitrary, incapable of disclosing meaning. Baudrillard argued that modern society was trapped in an endless network of artificial sign systems, which *meant* nothing, and merely perpetuated the belief systems of those who created them.

One aspect of postmodernism which illustrates this trend particularly well, while also indicating its obsession with texts and language, is *deconstruction* – the critical method which virtually declares that the identity and intentions of the author of a text are irrelevant to the interpretation of the text, prior to insisting that, in any case, no meaning can be found in it. All interpretations are equally valid, or equally meaningless (depending upon your point of view). As Paul de

Man, one of the leading American proponents of this approach, declared, the very idea of "meaning" smacked of fascism. It implied that someone had authority to define how a work of literature *ought* to be understood, and denied others the opportunity to exercise freedom of interpretation, thus stifling their creativity. This approach, which blossomed in the cultural situation of post-Vietnam America, was given intellectual respectability by academics such as de Man, Geoffrey Hartman, Harold Bloom, and J. Hillis Miller.

Theologically, the two following developments should be noted as being of especial importance. Although it is not clear what their long-term influence may be, they are likely to remain significant until the end of the twentieth century.

1 *Biblical interpretation* Traditional academic biblical interpretation had been dominated by the historico-critical method. This approach, which developed during the nineteenth century, stressed the importance of the application of critical historical methods, such as establishing the *Sitz im Leben*, or "situation in life," of gospel passages. It was challenged in the 1970s and 1980s through the rise of structuralism and poststructuralism.

A number of leading literary critics of the 1980s (such as Harold Bloom and Frank Kermode) ventured into the field of biblical interpretation, and challenged such ideas as "institutionally legitimized" or "scholarly respectable" interpretations of the Bible. The notion that there is *a* meaning to a biblical text – whether laid down by a church authority or by the academic community – is regarded with intense suspicion within postmodernism.

Amongst specific influences upon biblical interpretation, the following are of especial interest. Michel Foucault's analysis of the power relationship between the interpreter and the community raised a cluster of important questions concerning the potentially repressive function of "authorized" biblical interpreters. The works of Jacques Derrida raised the question of how a range of conflicting readings of Scripture could be created by the differential interpretation of biblical texts. Jean-François Lyotard suggested that what he styled *les grands récits*, the great biblical narratives, did little more than perpetuate secular ideologies based loosely on those narratives. This raised the question of how the Bible can be interpreted in such a way as to challenge, rather than endorse, the assumptions of western capitalism (although the writings of Latin American liberation theologians – see below – suggest that this problem is considerably less serious than Lyotard's rhetoric allows).

2 *Systematic theology* Postmodernism is, by its very nature, hostile to the notion of "systematization," or any claims to have discerned "meaning." Mark Taylor's study *Erring* is an excellent illustration of the impact of postmodernism on systematic theology. The image of "erring" – rather than more traditional approaches to theological system-building – leads Taylor to develop an anti-

systematic theology which offers polyvalent approaches to questions of truth or meaning. Taylor's study represents an exploration of the consequences of Nietzsche's declaration of the "death of God." On the basis of this, Taylor argues for the elimination of such concepts as self, truth, and meaning. Language does not refer to anything, and truth does not correspond to anything.

Black Theology

"Black theology" is the movement, especially significant in the United States during the 1960s and 1970s, which concerned itself with ensuring that the realities of Black experience were represented at the theological level. The first major evidence of the move toward theological emancipation within the American Black community dates from 1964, with the publication of Joseph Washington's *Black Religion*, a powerful affirmation of the distinctiveness of Black religion within the North American context. Washington emphasized the need for integration and assimilation of Black theological insights within mainstream Protestantism; however, this approach was largely swept to one side with the appearance of Albert Cleage's *Black Messiah*. Cleage, pastor of the Shrine of the Black Madonna in Detroit, urged Black people to liberate themselves from White theological oppression. Arguing that Scripture was written by Black Jews, Cleage claimed that the gospel of a Black Messiah had been perverted by Paul in his attempt to make it acceptable to Europeans. Despite the considerable overstatements within the work, *Black Messiah* came to be a rallying point for Black Christians, determined to discover and assert their distinctive identity.

The movement made several decisive affirmations of its theological distinctiveness during 1969. The "Black Manifesto" issued at the Inter-religious Foundation for Community Organization meeting in Detroit, Michigan, placed the issue of the Black experience firmly on the theological agenda. The statement by the National Committee of Black Churchmen emphasized the theme of liberation as a central motif of Black theology:

> Black Theology is a theology of black liberation. It seeks to plumb the black condition in the light of God's revelation in Jesus Christ, so that the black community can see that the gospel is commensurate with the achievement of black humanity. Black Theology is a theology of "blackness." It is the affirmation of black humanity that emancipates black people from white racism, thus providing authentic freedom for both white and black people.

Although there are evident affinities between this statement and the aims and emphases of Latin American liberation theology, it must be stressed that, at this stage, there was no formal interaction between the two movements. Liberation theology arose primarily within the Roman Catholic church in South America, whereas Black theology tended to arise within Black Protestant communities in North America.

The origins of the movement can be traced to the rise in Black consciousness which was so distinctive a feature of American history in the 1960s. Three main stages can be distinguished within the development of the movement.

1 *1966–70* During this developmental phase, Black theology emerged as a significant aspect of the civil rights struggle in general, and as a reaction against the dominance of Whites in both seminaries and churches. At this stage, Black theology was developed within the Black-led churches, and was not particularly academic in its outlook. The issues of primary importance centered on the use of violence to achieve justice, and the nature of Christian love.

2 *1970–77* In this period of consolidation, the movement appears to have moved away from the churches to the seminaries, as the movement became increasingly accepted within theological circles. The focus of the movement shifted from issues of practical concern to more explicitly theological issues, such as the nature of liberation and the significance of suffering.

3 *1977 onwards* A new awareness of the development of liberation movements in other parts of the world, especially in Latin America, became of importance within Black theology. Alongside this new sense of perspective came a new commitment to serving Black-led churches, and the fostering of fellowship and collaboration amongst those churches.

The most significant writer within the movement is generally agreed to be James H. Cone, whose *Black Theology of Liberation* (1970) appealed to the central notion of a God who is concerned for the Black struggle for liberation. Noting the strong preference of Jesus for the oppressed, Cone argued that "God was Black" – that is, identified with the oppressed. However, Cone's use of Barthian categories was criticized: Why, it was asked, should a Black theologian use the categories of a White theology in articulating the Black experience? Why had he not made fuller use of Black history and culture? In later works, Cone responded to such criticisms by making a more pervasive appeal to "the Black experience" as a central resource in Black theology. Nevertheless, Cone has continued to maintain a Barthian emphasis upon the centrality of Christ as the self-revelation of God (while identifying him as "the Black Messiah"), and the authority of Scripture in interpreting human experience in general.

Postliberalism

One of the most significant developments in theology since about 1980 has been a growing skepticism over the plausibility of a liberal worldview. A number of developments have accompanied this retreat from liberalism, perhaps the most important of which has been the repristination of more conservative viewpoints. One such development has been postliberalism, which has become especially associated with Yale Divinity School. Its central foundations are narrative approaches to theology, such as those developed by Hans Frei, and the schools of social interpretation which stress the importance of culture and language in the generation and interpretation of experience and thought.

Building upon the work of philosophers such as Alasdair MacIntyre, postliberalism rejects both the traditional Enlightenment appeal to a "universal rationality" and the liberal assumption of an immediate religious experience common to all humanity. Arguing that all thought and experience is historically and socially mediated, postliberalism bases its theological program upon a return to religious traditions, whose values are inwardly appropriated. Postliberalism is thus *anti-foundational* (in that it rejects the notion of a universal foundation of knowledge), *communitarian* (in that it appeals to the values, experiences, and language of a community, rather than prioritizing the individual), and *historicist* (in that it insists upon the importance of traditions and their associated historical communities in the shaping of experience and thought).

The most significant statement of the postliberal agenda remains George Lindbeck's *Nature of Doctrine* (1984). Rejecting "cognitive-propositional" approaches to doctrine as premodern, and liberal "experiential-expressive" theories as failing to take account of both human experiential diversity and the mediating role of culture in human thought and experience, Lindbeck develops a "cultural-linguistic" approach which embodies the leading features of postliberalism.

The "cultural-linguistic" approach denies that there is some universal unmediated human experience which exists apart from human language and culture. Rather, it stresses that the heart of religion lies in living within a specific historical religious tradition, and interiorizing its ideas and values. This tradition rests upon a historically mediated set of ideas, for which the narrative is an especially suitable means of transmission.

Postliberalism is of particular importance in relation to two areas of Christian theology.

1 *Systematic theology* Theology is understood to be primarily a descriptive discipline, concerned with the exploration of the normative foundations of the Christian tradition, which are mediated through the scriptural narrative of Jesus Christ. Truth can be, at least in part, equated with fidelity to the

distinctive doctrinal traditions of the Christian faith. This has caused critics of postliberalism to accuse it of retreating from the public arena into some kind of Christian ghetto. If Christian theology, as postliberalism suggests, is intrasystemic (that is, concerned with the exploration of the internal relationships of the Christian tradition), its validity is to be judged with reference to its own internal standards, rather than some publicly agreed or universal criteria. Once more, this has prompted criticism from those who suggest that theology ought to have external criteria, subject to public scrutiny, by which its validity can be tested.

2   *Christian ethics* Stanley Hauerwas is one of a number of writers to explore postliberal approaches to ethics. Rejecting the Enlightenment idea of a universal set of moral ideals or values, Hauerwas argues that Christian ethics is concerned with the identification of the moral vision of a historical community (the church), and with bringing that vision to actualization in the lives of its members. Thus ethics is intrasystemic, in that it concerns the study of the internal moral values of a community. To be moral is to identify the moral vision of a specific historical community, to appropriate its moral values, and to practice them within that community.

Evangelicalism

The term "evangelical" dates from the sixteenth century, and was then used to refer to Catholic writers wishing to revert to more biblical beliefs and practices than those associated with the late medieval church. It was used especially in the 1520s, when the terms *évangélique* (French) and *evangelisch* (German) came to feature prominently in polemical writings of the early Reformation. The term is now used widely to refer to a transdenominational trend in theology and spirituality, which lays particular emphasis upon the place of Scripture in the Christian life. Evangelicalism now centers upon a cluster of four assumptions:

1   The authority and sufficiency of Scripture.
2   The uniqueness of redemption through the death of Christ upon the cross.
3   The need for personal conversion.
4   The necessity, propriety, and urgency of evangelism.

All other matters have tended to be regarded as adiaphora, "matters of indifference," upon which a substantial degree of pluralism may be accepted.

Of particular importance is the question of ecclesiology, an issue which will be considered at a later stage in this work (pp. 312–20). Historically, evangelicalism has never been committed to any particular theory of the church, regarding the New Testament as being open to a number of interpretations in this respect, and treating

249

denominational distinctives as of secondary importance to the gospel itself. This most emphatically does not mean that evangelicals lack commitment to the church as the body of Christ; rather, it means that evangelicals are not committed to any one theory of the church. A corporate conception of the Christian life is not understood to be specifically linked with any one denominational understanding of the nature of the church. In one sense, this is a "minimalist" ecclesiology; in another, it represents an admission that the New Testament itself does not stipulate with precision any single form of church government, which can be made binding upon all Christians. This has had several major consequences, which are of central importance to an informed understanding of the movement.

1   Evangelicalism is transdenominational. It is not confined to any one denomination, nor is it a denomination in its own right. There is no inconsistency involved in speaking of "Anglican evangelicals," "Presbyterian evangelicals," "Methodist evangelicals," or even "Roman Catholic evangelicals."

2   Evangelicalism is not a denomination in itself, possessed of a distinctive ecclesiology, but is a trend within the mainstream denominations.

3   Evangelicalism itself represents an ecumenical movement. There is a natural affinity amongst evangelicals, irrespective of their denominational associations, which arises from a common commitment to a set of shared beliefs and outlooks. The characteristic evangelical refusal to allow any specific ecclesiology to be seen as normative, while honoring those which are clearly grounded in the New Testament and Christian tradition, means that the potentially divisive matters of church ordering and government are treated as of secondary importance.

An essential question which demands clarification at this point concerns the relation between fundamentalism and evangelicalism. Fundamentalism arose as a reaction within some of the American churches to the rise of a secular culture. It was from its outset, and has remained, a counter-cultural movement, using central doctrinal affirmations as a means of defining cultural boundaries. Certain central doctrines – most notably, the absolute literal authority of Scripture and the second coming of Christ before the end of time (a doctrine usually referred to as "the premillennial return of Christ") – were treated as barriers, intended as much to alienate secular culture as to give fundamentalists a sense of identity and purpose. A siege mentality became characteristic of the movement; fundamentalist counter-communities viewed themselves as walled cities, or (to evoke the pioneer spirit) circles of wagons, defending their distinctiveness against an unbelieving culture.

The emphasis upon the premillennial return of Christ is of especial significance. This view has a long history; it never attained any especial degree of significance prior to the nineteenth century. However, fundamentalism appears to have discerned in the idea an important weapon against the liberal Christian idea of a kingdom of God upon earth, to be achieved through social action. "Dispensationalism," especially of a premillenarian type, became an integral element of fundamentalism.

Yet disquiet became obvious within American fundamentalism during the late 1940s and early 1950s. Neo-evangelicalism (as it has subsequently come to be known) began to emerge, committed to redressing the unacceptable situation created by the rise of fundamentalism. Fundamentalism and evangelicalism can be distinguished at three general levels.

1   Biblically, fundamentalism is totally hostile to the notion of biblical criticism, in any form, and is committed to a literal interpretation of Scripture. Evangelicalism accepts the principle of biblical criticism (although insisting that it be applied responsibly), and recognizes the diversity of literary forms within Scripture.

2   Theologically, fundamentalism is narrowly committed to a set of doctrines, some of which evangelicalism regards as at best peripheral (such as those specifically linked with dispensationalism), and at worst utterly irrelevant. There is an overlap of beliefs (such as the authority of Scripture), which can too easily mask profound differences in outlook and temperament.

3   Sociologically, fundamentalism is a reactionary counter-cultural movement, with tight criteria of membership, and is especially associated with a "blue-collar" constituency. Evangelicalism is a cultural movement with increasingly loose criteria of self-definition, which is more associated with a professional or "white-collar" constituency. The element of irrationalism often associated with fundamentalism is lacking in evangelicalism, which has produced significant writings in areas of the philosophy of religion and apologetics.

The break between fundamentalism and neo-evangelicalism in the late 1940s and early 1950s changed both the nature and the public perception of the latter. Billy Graham, perhaps the most publicly visible representative of this new evangelical style, became a well-known figure in English society, and a role model for a younger generation of evangelical ordinands. The public recognition in America of the new importance and public visibility of evangelicalism dates from the early 1970s. The crisis of confidence within American liberal Christianity in the 1960s was widely interpreted to signal the need for the emergence of a new and more publicly credible form of Christian belief. In 1976, America woke up to find itself living in the "Year of the Evangelical," with a born-again Christian

(Jimmy Carter) as its President, and an unprecedented media interest in evangelicalism, linked with an increasing involvement on the part of evangelicalism in organized political action.

A number of evangelical theologians have emerged as significant within the movement since the Second World War. Carl F. H. Henry (b. 1913) is noted for his six-volume *God, Revelation and Authority* (1976–83), which represents a vigorous defense of traditional evangelical approaches to biblical authority. Donald G. Bloesch (b. 1928) maintains this emphasis, especially in his *Essentials of Evangelical Theology* (1978–9), setting out an evangelical theology which is distinguished from liberalism on the one hand, and fundamentalism on the other. James I. Packer (b. 1926) has also maintained an emphasis on the importance of biblical theology, while pioneering the exploration of the relation between systematic theology and spirituality in his best-selling *Knowing God* (1973). One of evangelicalism's most significant areas of theological activity is the field of apologetics, in which writers such as Edward John Carnell (b. 1919) and Clark H. Pinnock (b. 1939) have made considerable contributions. Yet despite the growing theological renaissance within the movement, evangelicalism has yet to make a significant impact on mainline theology. This situation is certain to change, especially if postliberalism continues to expand its influence within North America and beyond. Despite major differences between the two movements, it is becoming increasingly clear that there are also significant convergences, thus facilitating an evangelical contribution to the mainline discussion.

Pentecostal and Charismatic Movements

One of the most significant developments in Christianity in the twentieth century has been the rise of charismatic and Pentecostal groupings, which affirm that modern Christianity can rediscover and reappropriate the power of the Holy Spirit, described in the New Testament and particularly in the Acts of the Apostles. The term "charismatic" derives from the Greek word *charismata* ("gifts," and particularly "spiritual gifts"), which charismatic Christians believe to be accessible today. The related term "Pentecostal" refers to the events which are described as having taken place on the Day of Pentecost (Acts 2: 1–12), which charismatic Christians see as setting a pattern for the normal Christian life.

The modern rediscovery of spiritual gifts is linked with the movement known as Pentecostalism, generally regarded as the first modern movement to demonstrate clearly charismatic inclinations. In his study of the development of charismatic movements in the twentieth century, C. Peter Wagner distinguishes three "waves" within the movement. The first wave was classic Pentecostalism, which arose in the early 1900s, and was characterized by its emphasis upon speaking in tongues. The second wave took place in the 1960s and 1970s, and was associated with the mainline denominations, including Roman Catholicism, as they appropriated spiritual healing and other charismatic practices. The third wave, exemplified by individuals such as John Wimber, places emphasis upon "signs and wonders."

Although the charismatic movement can be argued to have long historical roots, its twentieth-century development is generally traced back to the ministry of Charles Fox Parham (1873–1929). In 1901, Parham set out the basic ideas which would become definitive for Pentecostalism, including the practice of "speaking in tongues" and the belief that the "baptism of the Holy Spirit" was a second blessing after the conversion of a believer. These ideas were developed and consolidated by Joseph William Seymour (1870–1922), a black pastor who presided over a major charismatic revival at the Azusa Street Mission in downtown Los Angeles during the years 1906–8. Most major North American Pentecostalist groupings, such as the Assemblies of God, trace their origins back to this period.

The full impact of the charismatic movement, however, dates from the 1960s. The incident which brought it to public attention took place in Van Nuys, California, in 1959, when a local episcopal rector told his congregation that he had been filled with the Holy Spirit and had spoken in tongues. This led to widespread attention being focused on charismatic renewal within mainline churches in Europe, North America and South Africa. The rapid rise of Pentecostalist groupings in Latin America can also be traced back to this period.

The more recent "signs and wonders" movement, which places considerable emphasis on the importance of spiritual healing, has caused controversy. Some critics have argued that it presents the gospel in terms which make no reference to repentance or forgiveness, charges which were pressed particularly forcefully after the 1990 Spiritual Warfare Conference at Sydney, Australia. Further controversy centers on the theology of healing itself. However, it is clear that a major movement is in the process of emerging, with the potential for articulating a distinctive theology of its own. The new awareness and experience of the presence of the Holy Spirit in the modern church has raised a series of debates over the nature of baptism of the Spirit, and which of the various "spiritual gifts" (*charismata*) are of greatest importance in relation both to personal faith and spirituality, and to the upbuilding of the church as a whole.

THE GROWTH OF CHRISTIANITY IN THE DEVELOPING WORLD

Although Christianity originated in Palestine, it rapidly spread throughout the Mediterranean world. Although many of its initial regions of influence were subsequently subjected to a process of Islamization as a result of the Arab invasions of the seventh century and beyond, Europe remained Christian. Even

Turkey, the most Islamic nation in Europe, retained a significant Christian presence (largely in the form of Armenian Christians) until a program of genocide by the Islamic government led to the virtual elimination of Christianity in the region by the end of the First World War. As the great European powers – such as England, France, Portugal, and Spain – began to expand their spheres of influence, so Christianity began its process of transformation from a primarily European to a global faith.

The establishment by the Catholic church of the commission *de propaganda fide* ("for the spreading of the faith") in the second half of the sixteenth century is to be regarded as a landmark in this process. It reflected the Catholic church's awareness of large populations in newly-discovered territories outside Europe, and the need to create missionary and pastoral agencies to deal with territories in which there was no formally established system of church administration.

Protestants were much slower to meet the challenge of the newly-discovered territories, such as the Americas. Although a Calvinist missionary is known to have been active in Brazil during the sixteenth century, the general picture is that of a missionary situation dominated by the Catholic church, with a particularly important role being played by the Society of Jesus. The evangelical revival in England during the eighteenth century led to a dramatic increase in the number of evangelical missionaries active in regions in which Britain had political or economic interests. A missionary enterprise of major proportions began in southern Africa, India, and the vast sprawling island territories of the southern Pacific.

The outcome of this transformation can be clearly seen from a simple statistic. In the early nineteenth century, the vast majority of Christians lived in the northern hemisphere, and were primarily concentrated in Europe. By the middle of the twentieth, the balance had shifted decisively. Most Christians now live in the southern hemisphere. It is no longer Europe or North America which constitutes the numerical center of gravity of the Christian faith. That center has shifted decisively to South America, southern Africa, and parts of Asia.

So how did Christianity come to be present in such societies? In what follows, we shall explore the origins and development of Christianity in several significant regions of the world, beginning with the case of South America.

Latin America: Liberation Theology

The colonial powers in South America were Spain and Portugal. During the sixteenth century, these two nations established their presence in the region. This was consolidated during the following centuries. Mission settlements were developed, particularly by the Jesuits. The missionaries moved north from their Latin American bases, establishing missions in what is now California, New Mexico, Texas, and Arizona. Although territorial disputes between Spain and

Portugal often hindered missionary work, South America had been extensively Christianized by the end of the eighteenth century.

More recent developments have been of particular interest, and we may turn to consider one of these – Latin American liberation theology – in what follows.

The term "liberation theology" could, in theory, be applied to any theology which is addressed to or deals with oppressive situations. However, in practice, the term is used to refer to a quite distinct form of theology, which has its origins in the Latin American situation in the 1960s and 1970s. In 1968, the Catholic bishops of Latin America gathered for a congress at Medellín, Colombia. This meeting – often known as CELAM II – sent shock waves throughout the region, by acknowledging that the church had often sided with oppressive governments in the region, and declaring that in future it would be on the side of the poor.

This pastoral and political stance was soon complemented by a solid theological foundation. In his *Theology of Liberation* (1971), the Peruvian theologian Gustavo Gutiérrez introduced the characteristic themes that would become definitive of the movement, and which we shall explore presently. Other writers of note include the Brazilian Leonardo Boff, the Uruguayan Juan Luis Segundo, and the Argentinian José Míguez Bonino. This last is unusual in one respect, in that he is a Protestant (more precisely, a Methodist) voice in a conversation dominated by Catholic writers.

The basic themes of Latin American liberation theology may be summarized as follows.

1   Liberation theology is oriented toward the poor and oppressed. "The poor are the authentic theological source for understanding Christian truth and practice" (Sobrino). In the Latin American situation, the church is on the side of the poor. "God is clearly and unequivocally on the side of the poor" (Bonino). The fact that God is on the side of the poor leads to a further insight: the poor occupy a position of especial importance in the interpretation of the Christian faith. All Christian theology and mission must begin with the "view from below," with the sufferings and distress of the poor.

2   Liberation theology involves critical reflection on practice. As Gutiérrez puts it, theology is a "critical reflection on Christian praxis in the light of the word of God." Theology is not, and should not be, detached from social involvement or political action. Whereas classical western theology regarded action as the result of reflection, liberation theology inverts the order: action comes first, followed by critical reflection. "Theology has to stop explaining the world, and start transforming it" (Bonino). True knowledge of God can never be disinterested or detached, but comes in and through commitment to the cause of the poor. There is a fundamental rejection of the Enlightenment view that commitment is a barrier to knowledge.

At this point, the indebtedness of liberation theology to Marxist theory becomes evident. Many western observers have criticized the movement for this reason, seeing it as an unholy alliance between Christianity and Marxism. Liberation theologians have vigorously defended their use of Marx, on two major grounds. First, Marxism is seen as a "tool of social analysis" (Gutiérrez), which allows insights to be gained concerning the present nature of Latin American society, and the means by which the appalling situation of the poor may be remedied. Second, it provides a political program by which the present unjust social system may be dismantled, and a more equitable society created. In practice, liberation theology is intensely critical of capitalism and affirmative of socialism. Liberation theologians have noted the way in which the medieval scholastic writer Thomas Aquinas used Aristotle in his writings, arguing that they were merely doing the same thing – using a secular philosopher to give substance to fundamentally Christian beliefs. For, it must be stressed, liberation theology declares that God's preference for and commitment to the poor is a fundamental aspect of the gospel, not some bolt-on option arising from the Latin American situation or based purely in Marxist political theory.

It will be clear that liberation theology is of major significance to recent theological debate. For example, Scripture is read as a narrative of liberation. Particular emphasis is laid upon the liberation of Israel from bondage in Egypt, the prophet's denunciation of oppression, and Jesus' proclamation of the gospel to the poor and outcast. Scripture is read, not from a standpoint of wishing to understand the gospel, but out of a concern to apply its liberating insights to the Latin American situation. Western academic theology has tended to regard this approach with some impatience, believing that it has no place for the considered insights of biblical scholarship concerning the interpretation of such passages.

Liberation theology also has important concerns relating to the nature of salvation. It often seems to equate salvation with liberation, and stresses the social, political, and economic aspects of salvation. The movement has laid particular emphasis upon the notion of "structural sin," noting that it is society, rather than individuals, who are corrupted and require redemption. To its critics, liberation theology has reduced salvation to a purely worldly affair, and neglected its transcendent and eternal dimensions. This aspect of the movement is probably reflected to some extent in the rapid growth of forms of Christianity (such as the charismatic movement) which stress the transcendent and spiritual aspects of life.

South-East Asia

In 1521, the great Spanish explorer Ferdinand Magellan discovered a group of some 3,141 islands. The islands, now known as "the Philippines," became a Spanish colony. Under Spanish rule, a program of evangelization was undertaken by various religious orders, especially the Franciscans and Dominicans. The islands came under American rule in 1898. The Philippines are unusual, in that they constitute the only predominantly Christian country in South-East Asia. Although Catholicism is the dominant form of Christianity in the region at present, many Protestant missionary societies established a presence following the end of Spanish rule. While various forms of Protestantism are now firmly rooted in the region, they constitute a minority.

Elsewhere in South-East Asia, Christianity is best described as a growing minority presence. In Japan, Christianity first gained a presence in 1549, when the Jesuit missionary Francis Xavier landed at Kagoshima. The small church in the country experienced a long period of isolation from the west during the Tokugawa shogunate. It was only in 1865 that Japan opened its doors to the west, revealing the continuing presence of about 60,000 Christian believers in the country. During the Meiji period (1868–1912), Christianity gained a growing following in the country. However, it has never achieved the substantial levels of growth seen in China or Korea in recent years. For many Japanese, Christianity, like butter, is seen as a western import. This is evident from the colloquial Japanese term for Christianity, which can be translated as "it tastes of butter."

Perhaps the most interesting developments in South-East Asia are to be found in China and Korea. It is known that Christianity established a presence in China in 1294, when Franciscan missionaries reached the country. There is, however, evidence that Christianity reached China much earlier. The Sigan-Fu Tablet, generally thought to date from 781, refers to a Nestorian missionary who had arrived in the region 146 years earlier, pointing to the strongly missionary activity of this eastern form of Christianity around this time. However, the church never achieved any great success in conversions. One of the many effects of the Opium Wars of the 1840s was to open the "Middle Kingdom" up to at least some western attitudes. China chose to remain isolated from the west until the nineteenth century, when growing interest in commerce opened up the region to western missionaries. Of these, James Hudson Taylor (1832–1905) may be singled out for special comment.

Hudson Taylor was initially a missionary with the Chinese Evangelization Society. Dissatisfaction with this organization led him to found the China Inland Mission in 1865. This Mission was unusual in several aspects, not least its willingness to accept single women as missionaries and its interdenominational character. Hudson Taylor showed an awareness of the cultural barriers facing Christian missionaries in China, and did what he could to remove them – for example, he required his missionaries to wear Chinese, rather than western, dress.

Nevertheless, western attempts to evangelize Christianity were of very limited value. Christianity was seen as something western, and hence un-Chinese. The defeat of China by Japan in an ill-fated war during the years 1894–5 was widely regarded as a direct result of the presence of foreigners in the country. This led to the I Ho Ch'uan crusade of 1899–1900, with its fanatical opposition to foreign investment and religious activity. With the establishment of the Republic of China in 1911, Christianity received a degree of official toleration. This ended abruptly in 1949, with the communist victory which led to the foundation of the Peoples' Republic of China, and the ejection of all western missionaries from the country. The "cultural revolution" of the 1960s involved the forcible suppression of Christianity. It was far from clear what was happening to Christianity; many came to the conclusion that it had been eradicated.

In 1979, the horrors of the cultural revolution came to an end. It became clear that Christianity had survived the revolution. In broad terms, three main strands can be discerned within modern Chinese Christianity.

1   The Three Self Patriotic Movement, founded in 1951, is the "official" church. The phrase "Three Self" refers to the three principles of self-supporting, self-administering, and self-propagating. The general idea was to ensure that the church was totally independent of any foreign influence. However, it is also clear that the state exercises considerable control over this church.

2   The Catholic church remains important within China. The government insistence that churches shall not be dependent on or obedient to foreign agencies clearly causes some difficulties for Catholics, on account of their loyalty to the Pope. In general terms, there seem to be two groups within modern Chinese Catholicism, one of which is independent of the Vatican (the "Catholic Patriotic Association"), the other of which is not. The former group seems to be in the ascendancy.

3   The house church movement is now the most important Christian movement within China. Strongly charismatic in orientation, the movement has witnessed spectacular numerical gains, particularly in the rural areas of China. While it is impossible to obtain reliable figures, there are indications that possibly as many as 50 million Chinese belong to such churches.

Outside mainland China, Christianity has made considerable inroads into Chinese expatriate communities in Singapore and Malaysia. A similar picture emerges in Chinese communities in large western cities, such as Los Angeles, Vancouver, Toronto, and Sydney.

The situation in Korea is of importance to the future of Christianity in the region. The Christian population in Korea prior to 1883 was miniscule. However, in 1883, the Korean government ended a long period of international isolation by signing the Korean–American treaty. This led to the establishment of American Presbyterian missions in the country in 1884. Initial evangelistic efforts centered on women and other marginalized groups, and stressed the importance of training native Korean evangelists. The evangelistic campaign of

1909–11 met with a considerable response. In 1910, however, Japan annexed Korea as a colony, and eventually forcibly imposed Shintoism on the population. With the liberation of Korea after the Second World War, Christianity enjoyed massive growth in the region. At present, some 30 percent of the Korean population is Christian, predominantly Presbyterian. One of the factors which may help explain the growth of Christianity is that western culture was not seen as oppressive (as in China), but as liberating (particularly in the war with Japan).

Africa

Christianity became established in North Africa during the first centuries of the Christian era. Churches were established along much of the North African coast, in the areas now known as Algeria, Tunisia, and Libya. A particularly strong Christian presence developed in Egypt, with the city of Alexandria emerging as a leading center of Christian thought and life. Much of this Christian presence was swept away by the Arab invasions of the seventh century. Christianity survived in Egypt, although as a minority faith. Only the small kingdom of Ethiopia (which designates a territory much smaller than the modern nation of the same name) can be said to have remained a Christian nation. At the opening of the sixteenth century, Africa was dominated by Islam in its north, and by native forms of religion in the south. Apart from the isolated case of Ethiopia, there was no significant Christian presence whatsoever.

The situation began to change gradually during the later sixteenth century. Portuguese settlers occupied previously uninhabited islands off the west African coast, such as the Cape Verdes Islands. However, such settlement had little impact in the mainland of Africa. The coming of Christianity to southern Africa is to be dated from the eighteenth century, and is closely linked with the great evangelical awakening in England at this time.

Major British missionary societies which were active in Africa during the late eighteenth or early nineteenth centuries include the Baptist Missionary Society (founded 1792, and initially known as "The Particular Baptist Society for the Propagation of the Gospel"); the London Missionary Society (founded 1795, and initially known as "The Missionary Society"); and the Church Missionary Society (founded 1799, and originally known as "The Church Missionary Society for Africa and the East"). Each of these societies developed a particular focus on specific regions: the BMS focused on the Congo basin, the LMS on southern Africa (including Madagascar), and the CMS on west and east Africa. All of these societies were Protestant, and generally strongly evangelical in their outlook. It was not until the middle of the nineteenth century that Catholic mission groups began to become seriously involved in the region. The trauma of the French Revolution (1789) and its aftermath had severely shaken the Catholic church. Only after the Congress of Vienna (1815) had settled the future shape of Europe could the church turn its attention to evangelism.

The dominant feature of sub-Saharan Africa in the nineteenth century is the growing importance of colonialism. Belgium, Britain, France, and Germany had all established colonies in this region during the period. The forms of Christianity dominant in these European nations varied substantially, with the result that a considerable diversity of churches became established in Africa. Anglicanism, Catholicism, and Lutheranism were all well established by the end of the century; in South Africa, the Dutch Reformed church had a particularly strong influence among European settlers. It must, however, be stressed that other missionaries from radically different backgrounds were also active in the region. For example, at least 115 Black American missionaries are known to have been present and active in Africa during the period 1875–99.

African Christians of this period can be broadly divided into two categories: expatriate Europeans, and indigenous Africans. The former tended to maintain as much of the Christian life of their homeland as possible, often for sentimental or cultural reasons. Thus the external trappings of the Church of England found themselves replicated to various extents in the many British colonies to spring up in southern Africa during this period. More significant, however, was the gradual adoption of Christianity by native African people. The early converts to Christianity were often those who were on the margins of traditional African societies – such as slaves, women, and the poor. In several areas in which missionaries were active, the number of Christian women became far greater than the number of Christian men, causing severe difficulties. How were they to find Christian husbands? It is clear that the most successful missionaries here were not Europeans, but Africans themselves. The dramatic growth in African Christianity is mainly subsequent to the establishment of African Christian communities, which provided catechists and pastors to the growing number of converts which they attracted.

Despite this, the names of several European missionaries stand out as being of particularly important, David Livingstone (1813–73) is a case in point. Livingstone was convinced of the importance of commerce in relation to the Christianization of Africa. He declared his intention to go to Africa "to make an open path for commerce and Christianity." Exploiting the British government's interest in replacing the banned slave trade with more legitimate forms of commerce, Livingstone obtained government backing for an expedition to explore the Zambezi river as a potential gateway to the interior. He believed that the interior would be capable of commercial exploitation (such as the growing of cotton, then greatly in demand by the cotton mills of Lancashire). Although the expedition was a commercial failure, it opened up the interior to missionary activity.

The case of South Africa is of particular interest, given the difficulties experienced by the country in the second half of the twentieth century. A

European presence was established in 1658 by the Dutch East India Company in the Cape of Good Hope region. The region became a British colony in 1795, with a polarization developing between Dutch- and English-speaking European populations which would eventually reach a climax in the Boer War at the end of the nineteenth century. Christianity (although in very different forms) was integral to the identity of both European communities. Missionary work in the 1790s led to the establishment of small Christian communities amongst native tribes, particularly the Khoi. Gradually, surrounding tribes began to convert to Christianity. Here, as in many other situations, the motivation for conversion varied considerably. Some conversions clearly reflect a deep spiritual experience; others reflect a conviction of the truth of the Christian gospel; other conversions may reflect a belief that Christianity would make the benefits of western civilization more widely available to African culture. This is particularly clear in the case of the Ganda tribe of east Africa, where the decision to convert to Christianity (rather than Islam) seems to have been partly influenced by the superiority of British technology.

Enormous difficulties were experienced at the level of communication of ideas. How could the distinctive ideas of Christianity be explained to peoples who had no understanding of any of its concepts? It was all very well for English evangelical missionaries to urge their African audiences to be "washed in the blood of the Lamb" (a reference to receiving forgiveness through the death of Christ); the evidence suggests that this bewildered many potential converts.

Christianity also caused tensions to arise within traditional African societies. Western Christianity was strongly monogamist; African culture had long recognized the merits of polygamy. Increasingly, the European Christian insistence upon a man having only one wife was seen as a western import, having no place in traditional African society. The United African Methodist Church, an indigenous church which recognized polygamy, traces its origins back to a meeting of the Methodist Church in Lagos, Nigeria, in 1917, when a large group of leading lay people were debarred from the church on account of polygamy. They responded by forming their own Methodist church, which adopted native African values frowned on by the European missionaries.

In several cases, these tensions led to bloodshed. A case in point is provided by the Baganda people, who lived in a region which is now incorporated into modern Uganda. The persecution of Christians by the Baganda king, Mwanga, in 1886 is an important example, as it points to the threat posed by the growing influence of Christianity to more traditional power structures in the region. The occasion for the massacre was the refusal of some court pages to take part in homosexual activities on the basis of their Christian faith. The issue was not so much whether homosexuality was right or wrong, as whether the pages would obey the king or their Christian beliefs. It was clear that Christianity was threatening traditional tribal loyalties. It is thought that about 100 were executed, including 31 who were burned alive. All were native Africans; no expatriate missionaries were affected. The persecution simply increased the determination of the Christians to persevere in their faith. By 1911, slightly less than half of the population of the region was Christian.

In the period following the First World War (1914–18), Christianity underwent significant transformation and developments. The most obvious of these is the growing numerical strength of Christianity in the region, which is having major effects on the politics of the region. Of particular importance is the Islam–Christianity interface, which is potentially the cause of considerable conflict in the region. For example, the southern part of Nigeria is predominantly Christian, and the north predominantly Muslim. This raises the question of whether Nigeria can survive as a single nation, or whether some form of partition – such as that introduced between predominantly Muslim Pakistan and predominantly Hindu India in 1947 – will be necessary in future.

Yet other issues are of importance. Two related developments may be singled out as being of particular interest. The period after the Second World War saw the end of colonialism. The colonial powers – such as Belgium, France, and Great Britain – gradually withdrew from the region, leaving behind independent nation states. Accompanying this transition to independence, the churches in the region gradually cast off their dependence on their mother churches in Europe. For example, the Anglican churches in regions such as South Africa, Uganda, and Zimbabwe originally depended on expatriate Britons to assume senior positions of leadership – such as bishops, deans of cathedrals, and heads of seminaries. These positions are now being filled by native Africans. Although many of these senior clergy have been educated in Britain, it is clear that the churches in the region now regard themselves as self-sufficient in terms of personnel and resources.

A related development concerns the rise of African Independent Churches, a term which refers to a very broad range of Christian churches which place an emphasis on retaining a traditional African heritage within the context of their Christian faith. These churches are often strongly charismatic, placing an emphasis on the importance of spiritual healing, exorcism, the interpretation of dreams, and prophetic guidance. Reacting against the word-based culture of the nineteenth-century west, these churches place an emphasis on experience and symbolism. A further factor of importance here is the racism of some White churches, particularly in South Africa under the apartheid regime. The Zionist churches of this region can be seen as a celebration and affirmation of Black African identity in the face of such official hostility. In the last few decades, these churches have often been influenced by the charismatic movement, which has proved to be an important catalyst for further growth in the region. In 1967, a reliable survey suggested that there were at least 5,000 independent churches of this kind, with 7,000,000 members drawn from 290 tribes across 34 countries. Substantial further growth has taken place subsequently.

The South Pacific

The term "Oceania" is now generally used to refer to the 1,500 or so islands in the Pacific Ocean. This is further subdivided into three general regions. *Polynesia* designates the group of islands stretching from Hawaii (known as the "Sandwich Islands" in earlier centuries) in the north to New Zealand in the south, including Tahiti and Pitcairn Island. *Micronesia* refers to the group of small islands between Hawaii and the Philippines, including the Caroline, Gilbert, and Marshall Islands. *Melanesia* refers to the group of islands south of Micronesia and north of Australia, including Fiji, the Solomon Islands, and the New Hebrides. The population of this vast and dispersed region is relatively small; however, it was considered to be of major importance by Christian missionaries in the nineteenth century.

Interest in the region was first awakened by reports of the voyages of Captain Cook during the eighteenth century. In 1795, the London Missionary Society was founded with the primary objective of sending missionaries to "the islands of the South Sea." The first major missionary expedition to the region set off in August 1796, when 30 missionaries set sail for Tahiti. Although this mission faced considerable difficulties – not least of which related to the very different sexual mores of England and Tahiti – it can be seen as marking the beginning of a sustained effort to establish Christianity in the region.

The geographical nature of the region made one of the most reliable means of evangelization – the establishment of mission stations – impossible. The populations of the islands were generally too small to justify the building and maintenance of such settlements. The most successful strategy to be adopted was the use of missionary vessels, which allowed European missionaries to direct and oversee the operations of native evangelists, pastors, and teachers in the region.

The most significant Christian missions in the region were located in Australia and New Zealand, which eventually came to serve as the base for most missionary work in the region. Christianity came to Australia in 1788. The circumstances of its arrival were not entirely happy. The fleet which arrived in New South Wales was transporting convicts to the penal settlements which were being established in the region. At the last moment, William Wilberforce persuaded the British naval authorities to allow a chaplain to sail with the fleet. With the dramatic increase in immigration to the region from Britain in the following century, the various forms of British Christianity became established in the region. The formation of the "Bush Brotherhoods" in 1897 laid the basis for the evangelization of the interior of the continent.

The first missionaries arrived in New Zealand in 1814. The consolidation of

Christianity in the region was largely due to Bishop George Augustus Selwyn (1809–78), who was appointed missionary bishop of New Zealand in 1841. During his time in the region, he had a marked impact on the development of Christianity, particularly in relation to education. He returned to England in 1867, becoming bishop of Lichfield the following year.

Throughout the South Pacific region, a major issue has concerned the relation of Christianity to the native peoples of the area, particularly the Australian Kuri (often still inappropriately referred to as "Aborigines") and New Zealand Maori peoples. For some, Christianity is a western colonial phenomenon, which is to be rejected as destructive of indigenous culture; for others, Christianity has no necessary connection with western culture or power, and can be put at the service of indigenous peoples and cultures. This debate can be seen arising as a result of the rise of Christianity in India, to which we now turn.

India

Christianity became established on the Indian subcontinent at a relatively early stage. Traditionally, it is believed that the apostle Thomas founded the Indian Mar Thoma church in the first century; even allowing for a degree of pious exaggeration here, there are excellent reasons for believing that Christianity was an indigenous element of the Indian religious scene by the fourth century. It seems likely that western merchants discovered the existence of the Palghat gap at an early stage, thus facilitating trade with southern India. European travellers reaching India by land, prior to the opening of the ocean trading tour by the Portuguese navigator Vasco da Gama in May 1498, regularly reported the presence of Christians in the region.

The arrival of the Portuguese may be taken to signal the opening of a significant new period in Indian Christianity, in which indigenous Christian traditions were supplemented by imported versions of the gospel, each reflecting aspects of its European context. The papal Bull *Aeternia regis clementia* (June 21, 1481) gave the Portuguese monarch the authority to trade with hitherto undiscovered lands, as well as investing him with "spiritual power and authority from Capes Bojador and Nam as far as the Indies." The Bishopric of Goa was established as the potential base for a campaign of Portuguese evangelization of the interior.

The importance of this settlement was considerably enhanced through the arrival of Francis Xavier on May 6, 1542. A mere two years after having been formally recognized by the Pope, the Society of Jesus was thus established in India. Xavier organized an extensive missionary enterprise, including the trans-lation of Christian works into Tamil. As time went on, Dutch, English, and French settlers moved into India, bringing their own versions of Christianity with them.

Initially, evangelization was seen as peripheral to the more serious business of trading. The first Anglican clergy in India, for example, were ship's chaplains, appointed by the English East India Company to provide pastoral care and spiritual support for the crews of their ships. However, a growing European presence in the region brought with it the tensions of the European religious situation of the seventeenth century, in which Protestantism and Catholicism were viewed as mutually incompatible and radically divergent versions of Christianity. The establishment of Christianity in Europe inevitably meant that the political interests of Protestant and Catholic nations, such as England and France, were seen as possessing strongly religious dimensions. Religion was one aspect of a broader struggle for political and economic supremacy. As a result, evangelization became increasingly imperative.

Humphrey Prideaux, an Anglican dean of Norwich (1648–1724), may be regarded as indicative of this spirit of evangelistic adventurism. In his *Account of the English Settlements in the East Indies, together with some proposals for the propagation of Christianity in those parts of the world*, Prideaux pointed to the need to train people for the specific work of evangelism. Prideaux's idea was prophetic: a "seminary" was to be established in England, with a view to prepare mission workers, until such time as the work could be handed over to agencies based in India itself. In this proposal may be seen the basis of the missionary movement, which was destined to make a significant impact upon Indian Christianity.

Among the major contributions to European missionary work in India, the following may be singled out for special mention. The first major Protestant mission to India was based at Tranquebar on the Coromandel Coast, about 200 kilometers south of Madras. Among the German Lutheran missionaries of note were Bartholomäus Ziegenbalg (who directed the mission from its founding in 1706 to 1719) and Christian Frederick Schwartz (director from 1750 to 1787). However, the growing political power of Britain in the region inevitably favored the activities of British missionaries, the first of which (the Baptist, William Carey) began work in Bengal in 1793. This was assisted to no small extent by the decision of Clement XIV to suppress the Society of Jesus. The bull *Dominus ac Redemptor* (July 21, 1773) formally terminated "all and every one of its functions and ministries." The missionary activity of the Jesuits in India and elsewhere was thus terminated. Nevertheless, at least 50 Jesuits are known to have continued missionary work in India after the suppression of their order, despite the efforts of the Portuguese to repatriate them.

British missionary societies and individuals were thus able to operate in India without any major opposition from other European agencies. Nevertheless, they received no support from the British authorities; the East India Company, for example, was opposed to their activities, on the grounds that they might create ill will amongst native Indians, and thus threaten the trade upon which it depended. However, the Charter Act (passed by the British parliament on July

13, 1813) revised the conditions under which the Company was permitted to operate: the new charter gave British missionaries protected status, and a limited degree of freedom to carry out evangelistic work on the Indian subcontinent. The result was inevitable: "since 1813, Christian missions have never been wholly free from the stigma of undue dependence on government" (Stephen Charles Neill). The new charter also made provision for the establishment of an Anglican bishopric at Calcutta. Under Reginald Heber (1783–1826; bishop of Calcutta, 1823–6), missionary work was expanded considerably, and restricted to Anglicans (Lutheran missionaries being obliged to be reordained to allow them to continue operating in the region). Further revisions to the East India Company's charter in 1833 removed some of the restrictions imposed earlier upon missionary work.

It was inevitable that religious tensions would develop. In 1830, the Dharma Sabha was formed, apparently as a reaction against intrusive forms of westernization in Bengal. The uprising of 1857 (generally referred to as "the Indian Mutiny" by contemporary English writers) is often regarded as the outcome of this growing resentment about westernization. It is therefore important to note the development of indigenous Indian approaches to Christianity, rather than theologies of essentially European provenance in the region. In its initial phases, such a theology tended to arise through Hindus assimilating Christianity to their own worldview. Rammohun Roy (1772–1833) was born of a Brahmin family in Bengal. His early contacts with Islam (and particularly the mystical tradition of the Sufis) led him to conclude that his Hindu religion was corrupt, and required to be reformed. In 1815 he founded the Atmiya Sabha, a movement dedicated to the reform of Hinduism, which advocated the abolition of *sati* (often spelled "*suttee*": the practice of burning Hindu widows alive on their husbands' funeral pyres). His growing alienation from orthodox Hinduism led to an increasing interest in Christianity, which he came to regard as embodying a moral code which would be acceptable to right-thinking Hindus. This idea, which he promoted in his *Precepts of Jesus* (1820), attracted considerable attention.

It also provoked considerable criticism from within European Christian circles, most notably from the more conservative Protestants, such as the Lutheran pastor Deocar Schmidt. Schmidt argued that the moral precepts of Christ could not be separated from the theological question of the identity of Christ, and the subsequent implications of this for a Trinitarian concept of God. Rammohun Roy replied that it was impossible for a Hindu to accept a Trinitarian concept of God; nevertheless, a Unitarian understanding of God, linked with an emphasis upon the gospel as a moral code, might well prove acceptable. It was possible for sins to be forgiven without the need for the atonement of Christ, an idea which he regarded as utterly alien to Hinduism (Brahmo theism, for example, rejects the ideas of both revelation and atonement). In 1829, he founded the Brahmo

Samaj, a theistic society which drew upon ideas derived from both Hinduism and Christianity; among the ideas derived from the latter was the practice of regular congregational worship, then unknown in Hinduism. Under his successor Devendranath Tagore, however, the Samaj moved in a more definitely Hindu direction. However, aspects of Rammohun Roy's understanding of the relation between Christianity and Hinduism were criticized by other Hindus who had converted to Christianity. Thus the Bengali writer Krishna Mohan Banerjee argued that there were close affinities between the Vedic idea of Purusha sacrifice and the Christian doctrine of atonement, thus challenging Rammohun Roy's view that there were radical differences at this point.

A highly influential approach to understanding the relation between Christianity and Hinduism was developed by Keshub Chunder Sen (1838–84), who argued that Christ brought to fulfillment all that was best in Indian religion. This approach bears a direct resemblance to the western European idea, associated with writers as diverse as Thomas Aquinas and John Calvin, that Christianity brings to fulfillment the aspirations of classic antiquity, as expressed in the culture of ancient Greece and Rome. Unlike Rammohun Roy, however, Keshub embraced the doctrine of the Trinity with enthusiasm. He argued that although *Brahman* was indivisible and indescribable, it could nevertheless be considered in terms of its inner relations of *Sat* ("being"), *Cit* ("reason"), and *Ananda* ("bliss"). These three relations paralleled the Christian understanding of God the Father as "Being," God the Son as "Word," and God the Holy Spirit as "comforter" or "bringer of joy and love."

> The New Testament commenced with the birth of the Son of God. The Logos was the beginning of creation and its perfection too was the Logos – the culmination of humanity in the divine son. We have arrived at the last link in the series of created organisms. The last expression of Divinity is Divine Humanity. Having exhibited itself in endless varieties of progressive existence, the primary creative force at last took the form of the Son in Jesus Christ.

This approach was developed by Nehemiah Goreh (1825–95), who stressed the facility with which it was possible to move from a Hindu notion of God to that now offered by Christianity:

> May we, the sons of India, say that the unity with God, whom our fathers delighted to call "Sat, Cit, Ananda Brahman," after which they ardently aspired, but in a wrong sense . . . God has granted us, their children, to realise in the right sense? Was that aspiration and longing, though misunderstood by them, a presentiment of the future gift? I have often delighted to think so.

A related idea was developed more recently by Raimundo Panikkar in his *Unknown Christ of Hinduism* (1981), in which he argued for the hidden presence of Christ in Hindu practice, especially in relation to matters of justice and compassion.

A similar approach to that of Goreh was developed, but with considerably greater acumen, by Brahmabandhab Upadhyaya (1861–1907), based on an analysis of the relation of the Christian faith and its articulation in terms of non-Christian philosophical systems (as in Thomas Aquinas' use of Aristotelianism as a vehicle for his theological exposition). Why should Indian Christians not be at liberty to draw upon indigenous Indian philosophical systems, in undertaking a similar task? Why should not Vedanta be used in the expression of Christian theology, and the Vedas be regarded as the Indian Old Testament? Increasingly, the issue of an authentically Indian Christian theology came to be seen as linked with that of independence from Britain: theological and political self-determination came to be seen as inextricably linked.

The growing emphasis in the second half of the twentieth century was on growing into nationhood (eventually achieved in 1947). Among contributions to a Christian approach to independence, the following may be noted as having particular significance: C. F. Andrews' *The Ideal of Indian Nationality (1907)*, S. K. Datta's *Desire of India* (1908), S. K. Rudra's *Christ and Modern India* (1910), and K. T. Paul's *British Connection with India* (1928).

The move towards independence resulted in Christianity finding itself in competition with rival ideologies: Gandhism and Marxism. A particularly important participant in this debate is Madathiparamil Mammen Thomas (1916–). From a Mar Thoma Christian background, M. M. Thomas has come to be regarded as a leading representative of an authentically Indian voice in modern theology. Thomas's critique of Gandhism is of especial interest. In the first place, Thomas was himself initially a Gandhian, only to become disillusioned with what he regarded as its inadequacies and fallacies. In the second, it represents an Indian Christian response to a distinctively Indian ideology. While appreciating its moral strengths, and particularly its protests against the dehumanizing tendencies of "the machine age," Thomas argues that Gandhism elevated pragmatic strategies – such as *satyagraha* and *swadeshi* – into absolute moral principles, thus initiating a shift towards a form of pharisaic self-righteousness. Thomas argues that this ultimately represents an inadequate understanding of the human predicament, minimizing the effects of sin and masking the human need for redemption:

> To attempt to "spiritualize our politics" on the political plane, if seriously meant, is an expression of human self-righteousness and the doctrine of justification by works. And there may be a lot of difference from the political and ethical point of view between the "holy war of the past" and "a war for holiness," but from a religious perspective both equally arise out of man seeking a righteousness of the law in rebellion against the grace of God, and reveal the denial of one's own sinfulness and need of divine redemption.

Thomas regards Gandhi as having reduced Christianity to little more than a moral code or set of principles, and quotes with approval the letter to Gandhi from E. Stanley Jones: "I think you have grasped certain principles of the Christian faith. You have grasped the principles but missed the person." A similar criticism is directed against Indian Marxist writers, most notably E. M. Sankaran Namboodiripad, whose ideas Thomas declares to rest upon an inadequate anthropology.

Other issues have come to be of major importance within the Indian context in recent years, most notably the relation of the Christian gospel to the poor. Ideas which apparently owe their origins largely to Latin American liberation theology (see p. 254) have made their appearance in such writings as John Desrochers' *Jesus the Liberator* (1976) and Sebastian Kappen's *Jesus and Freedom* (1978). It seems, however, that the continuing exploration of the relationship between Christianity and Hinduism is likely to remain a significant feature of Indian Christian theology for some time. For example, the relation between the Christian doctrine of incarnation and the Hindu notion of *avatar* has emerged as a significant debate within Indian theology (see V. Chakkarai's *Jesus the Avatar*).

Eight general approaches to this question may be discerned within contemporary Indian Christian thought:

1 The cosmic Christ includes all the various pluralities of religious experience.
2 Christianity takes shape within a pluralist environment, and so becomes a Christ-centered syncretism.
3 Christ is the unknown force for justice within Hinduism.
4 Christ is the goal of the religious quest of Hinduism.
5 The relation of Hinduism to Christianity is parallel to that of Judaism to Christianity, so that Hinduism can be seen as the Old Testament Scriptures appropriate to the Indian context.
6 Christianity is totally discontinuous with Hinduism.
7 The Hindu context gives rise to a specifically Indian form of Christianity.
8 Hinduism is to be addressed with the question of the poor and marginalized within society, a question which Jesus himself validated and addressed.

One final development should be noted in relation to Indian Christianity. On September 27, 1947, shortly after independence, several major Christian denominations in the region agreed to form a single body, known as the "Church of South India." The original pressure which led to this development was an awareness that Christian mission in the region was being hindered by denominational rivalry. Other denominations subsequently joined the body, which is regarded by some western Christians as a model for future cooperation between the churches in their region. The development has important implications for ecclesiology, not least in regard to the question of the role of the episcopacy in relation to ecclesial identity and the place of tradition in theology.

This brief survey of developments within Christian theology since about 1750 has documented the way in which Christianity has become a global religion, with its numerical center of gravity increasingly shifting to the developing world. It will be clear that theological education and reflection is increasingly likely to follow this global shift, with seminaries in the developing world emerging as centers of theological development in the next millennium.

KEY NAMES, WORDS, AND PHRASES

Black theology

charismatic movement

dialectical theology

Enlightenment

evangelicalism

feminism

Great Awakening

liberalism

liberation theology

Marxism

modernism

neo-orthodoxy

postliberalism

postmodernism

Quest of the Historical Jesus

Romanticism

Three Self Patriotic Movement

QUESTIONS

1 For what reasons did indifference to religion arise in western Europe during the seventeenth and eighteenth centuries?

2 What are the main features of the Enlightenment?

3 For what reasons did the "Quest of the Historical Jesus" get under way?

4 What were the main lines of the Marxist critique of Christianity?

5 Summarize the leading features of the following theological movements: liberal Protestantism; neo-orthodoxy; liberation theology; evangelicalism; Black theology.

6 With which theological movements would you associate the following individuals: Karl Barth; Leonardo Boff; James Cone; Stanley Hauerwas; Rosemary Radford Ruether; F. D. E. Schleiermacher; Paul Tillich?

7 What issues became significant for Christian theology as a result of the expansion of Christianity in Africa and Asia?

CASE STUDIES

Case Study 4.1   The Quests of the Historical Jesus

The modern period has seen a series of developments of fundamental importance to Christology, which have no real parallel in previous Christian history. The rise of a rationalist worldview saw a series of challenges to traditional understandings of the identity and significance of Jesus, without any real parallel with earlier times. In view of the importance of these developments, they are considered here in some detail. Earlier case studies explored the development of classical Christology, which continues to be a major aspect of theological reflection within the church. The present case study explores this issue further, focusing on three "Quests of the Historical Jesus" – the "original," "new," and "third" quests.

The term "quest" has strongly romantic overtones, suggesting an affinity with the great Arthurian "quest for the Holy Grail." In fact, the term was introduced into the English-language discussion of the (much more prosaically entitled) "Historical Jesus Question" by the translator of Albert Schweitzer's masterpiece of 1906 (published in English translation, 1911). A rough English translation of the German title is: "From Reimarus to Wrede: On the History of the Question of the Historical Jesus." The English translator, doubtless concerned lest such an uninspiring title featuring two unknown German scholars might damage its sales potential, transferred their names to a subtitle, and inserted a new title: "The Quest of the Historical Jesus: A Study of its Progress from Reimarus to Wrede." The term was neither used nor intended to be used by Schweitzer; nevertheless, it passed into general use, and continues to be used to this day.

The original quest for the historical Jesus

Both Deism and the German Enlightenment developed the thesis that there was a serious discrepancy between the real Jesus of history and the New Testament interpretation of his significance. Underlying the New Testament portrait of the supernatural redeemer of humanity lurked a simple human figure, a glorified teacher of common sense. While a supernatural redeemer was unacceptable to Enlightenment rationalism, the idea of an enlightened moral teacher was not. This idea, developed with particular rigor by Reimarus, suggested that it was possible to go behind the New Testament accounts of Jesus, and uncover a simpler, more human Jesus, who would be acceptable to the new spirit of the age. And so the quest for the real and more credible "Jesus of history" began. Although this quest would ultimately end in failure, the later Enlightenment regarded this "quest" as holding the key to the credibility of Jesus within the context of a rational natural religion. Jesus' moral authority resided in the quality of his teaching and religious personality, rather than in the unacceptable orthodox suggestion that he was God incarnate. And it is this suggestion which underlies the celebrated "Quest of the Historical Jesus," to which we may now turn.

The original "Quest of the Historical Jesus" was based upon the presupposition that there was a radical gulf between the historical figure of Jesus, and the interpretation which the Christian church had placed upon him. The "historical

Jesus," who lies behind the New Testament, was a simple religious teacher; the "Christ of faith" was a misrepresentation of this simple figure by early church writers. By going back to the historical Jesus, a more credible version of Christianity would result, stripped of all unnecessary and inappropriate dogmatic additions (such as the idea of the resurrection or the divinity of Christ). Such ideas, although frequently expressed by English Deists of the seventeenth century, received their classic statements in Germany in the late eighteenth century, especially through the posthumously published writings of Hermann Samuel Reimarus (1694–1768).

Reimarus became increasingly convinced that both Judaism and Christianity rested upon fraudulent foundations, and conceived the idea of writing a major work which would bring this fact to public attention. The resulting work – *An Apology for the Rational Worshipper of God* – subjected the entire biblical canon to the standards of rationalist criticism. However, reluctant to cause any controversy, he did not publish the work. It remained in manuscript form until his death. At some point, however, the manuscript fell into the hands of G. E. Lessing, who decided to have it published as a selection of extracts from the work. These were published as "fragments of an unknown writer" in 1774, and promptly caused a sensation. The work, which is now generally known as the "Wolfenbüttel Fragments," included a sustained attack on the historicity of the resurrection.

Gotthold Ephraim Lessing (1729–81). A significant representative of the German Enlightenment, noted for his strongly rationalist approach to Christian theology.

The final fragment, entitled "On the aims of Jesus and his disciples," concerned the nature of our knowledge of Jesus Christ, and raised the questions of whether the gospel accounts of Jesus had been tampered with by the early Christians. Reimarus argued that there was a radical difference between the beliefs and intentions of Jesus himself, and those of the apostolic church. Jesus' language and images of God were, according to Reimarus, those of a Jewish apocalyptic visionary, with a radically limited chronological and political reference and relevance. Jesus accepted the late Jewish expectation of a Messiah who would deliver his people from Roman occupation, and believed that God would assist him in this task. His cry of dereliction on the cross represented his final realization that he had been deluded and mistaken.

However, the disciples were not prepared to leave things like this. They invented the idea of a "spiritual redemption," in the place of Jesus' concrete political vision of an Israel liberated from foreign occupation. They invented the idea of the resurrection of Jesus, in order to cover up the embarrassment caused by the death of Jesus. As a result, the disciples invented doctrines quite unknown to Jesus, such as his death being an atonement for human sin, adding such ideas to the biblical text to make it harmonize with their beliefs. As a result, the New Testament as we now have it is riddled with fraudulent interpolations. The real Jesus of history is concealed from us by the apostolic church, which substitutes a fictitious Christ of faith, the redeemer of humanity from sin.

In his masterly survey *The Quest of the Historical Jesus*, Albert Schweitzer summarizes the importance of Reimarus' radical suggestions as follows:

> [if] we desire to gain an historical understanding of Jesus' teaching, we must leave behind what we learned in the catechism regarding the metaphysical divine sonship, the Trinity, and similar dogmatic conceptions, and go out into a wholly Jewish world of thought. Only those who carry the teachings of the catechism back into the preaching of the Jewish Messiah will arrive at the idea that he was the founder of a new religion. To all unprejudiced persons it is manifest that "Jesus has not the slightest intention of doing away with the Jewish religion and putting another in its place."

Jesus was, according to this view, simply a Jewish political figure, who confidently expected to cause a decisive and victorious popular rising against Rome, and was shattered by his failure.

Although Reimarus found few, if any, followers at the time, he raised questions which would become of fundamental importance in subsequent years. In particular, his explicit distinction between the legitimate historical Jesus and the fictitious Christ of faith proved to be of enormous significance. The resulting "quest of the historical Jesus" arose as a direct result of the growing rationalist suspicion that the New Testament portrayal of Christ was a dogmatic invention. It was geuinely believed to be possible to reconstruct the real historical figure of Jesus, and disentangle him from the dogmatic ideas in which the apostles had clothed him.

The critique of the quest, 1890–1910

The illusion could not last. The most sustained challenge to the "life of Jesus" movement developed on a number of fronts during the final decade of the

Albert Schweitzer (1875–1965). This leading German Protestant theologian was noted particularly for his work on the historical Jesus, which led to a series of influential publications calling the validity and presuppositions of the "quest of the historical Jesus" into question. In 1913, he gave up his theological career to undertake medical work in Africa.

nineteenth century. Three main criticisms of the "religious personality" Christology of liberal Protestantism emerged in the two decades before the First World War; we shall consider them individually.

1   The *apocalyptic critique*, primarily associated with Johannes Weiss (1863–1914) and Albert Schweitzer (1875–1965), maintained that the strongly eschatological bias of Jesus' proclamation of the Kingdom of God called the essentially Kantian liberal interpretation of the concept into question. In 1892, Johannes Weiss published *Jesus' Proclamation of the Kingdom of God*. In this book, he argued that the idea of the "Kingdom of God" was understood by liberal Protestantism to mean the exercise of the moral life in society, or a supreme ethical ideal. In other words, it was conceived primarily as something subjective, inward or spiritual, rather than in spatio-temporal terms. For Weiss himself, Ritschl's concept of the Kingdom of God was essentially continuous with that of the Enlightenment. It was a static moral concept without eschatological overtones. The rediscovery of the eschatology of the preaching of Jesus called not merely this understanding of the Kingdom of God, but also the liberal portrait of Christ in general, into question. The "Kingdom of God" was thus not to be seen as a settled and static realm of liberal moral values, but as a devastating apocalyptic moment which overturned human values.

For Schweitzer, however, the whole character of Jesus' ministry was conditioned and determined by his apocalyptic outlook. It is this idea which has become familiar to the English-speaking world as "thoroughgoing eschatology." Where Weiss regarded a substantial part (but not all) of the teaching of Jesus as being conditioned by his radical eschatological expectations, Schweitzer argued for the need to recognize that every aspect of the teaching and attitudes of Jesus was determined by his eschatological outlook. Where Weiss believed that only part of Jesus' preaching was affected by this outlook, Schweitzer argued that the entire content of Jesus' message was consistently and thoroughly conditioned by apocalyptic ideas – ideas which were quite alien to the settled outlook of late nineteenth-century western Europe.

The result of this consistent eschatological interpretation of the person and message of Jesus of Nazareth was a portrait of Christ as a remote and strange figure, an apocalyptic and wholly unworldly figure, whose hopes and expectations finally came to nothing. Far from being an incidental and dispensable "husk" which could be discarded in order to establish the true "kernel" of Jesus' teaching concerning the universal fatherhood of God, eschatology was an essential and dominant characteristic of his outlook. Jesus thus appears to us as a strange figure from an alien first-century Jewish apocalyptic milieu, so that, in Schweitzer's famous words, "he comes to us as one unknown."

2   The *skeptical critique*, associated particularly with William Wrede (1859–1906), called into question the historical status of our knowledge of Jesus in the first place. History and theology were closely intermingled in the synoptic narratives, and could not be disentangled. According to Wrede, Mark was painting a theological picture in the guise of history, imposing his theology upon the material which he had at his disposal. The Second Gospel was thus not objectively historical, but was actually a creative theological reinterpretation of history. It was thus impossible to go behind Mark's narrative and reconstruct the history of Jesus, since – if Wrede is right – this narrative is itself a theological construction, beyond which one cannot go. The "quest of the historical Jesus" thus comes to an end, in that it proves impossible to establish an historical foundation for the "real" Jesus of history. Wrede identified the following three radical and fatal errors underlying the Christologies of liberal Protestantism:

1   Although the liberal theologians appealed to later modifications of an earlier tradition when faced with unpalatable features of the synoptic accounts of Jesus (such as miracles, or obvious contradictions between sources), they failed to apply this principle consistently. In other words, they failed to realize that the later belief of the community had exercised a normative influence over the evangelist at every stage of his work.

2   The motives of the evangelists were not taken into account. The liberal theologians tended simply to exclude those portions of the narratives they found unacceptable, and contented themselves with what remained. By doing so, they failed to take seriously the fact that the evangelist himself had a positive statement to make, and substituted for this something quite distinct. The first priority should be to approach the gospel narratives on their own terms, and to establish what the evangelist wished to convey to his readers.

3   The psychological approach to the gospel narratives tends to confuse what is conceivable with what actually took place, being based upon an inadequate foundation. In effect, liberal theologians tended to find in the gospels precisely what they were seeking, on the basis of a "sort of psychological guesswork" which appeared to value emotive descriptions more than strict accuracy and certainty of knowledge.

Martin Kähler (1835–1912). A German Lutheran theologian with a particular concern for the theological aspects of New Testament criticism and interpretation. He was appointed to the chair of systematic theology at Halle in 1867. His most famous work is an essay of 1892, in which he subjected the theological assumptions of the "Life of Jesus Movement" to devastating criticism.

3 The *dogmatic critique*, due to Martin Kähler (1835–1912), challenged the theological significance of the reconstruction of the historical Jesus. The "historical Jesus" was an irrelevance to faith, which was based upon the "Christ of faith." Kähler rightly saw that the dispassionate and provisional Jesus of the academic historian cannot become the object of faith. Yet how can Jesus Christ be the authentic basis and content of Christian faith, when historical science can never establish certain knowledge concerning the historical Jesus? How can faith be based upon an historical event without being vulnerable to the charge of historical relativism? It was precisely these questions which Kähler addressed in his book *The So-Called Historical Jesus and the Historic Biblical Christ*.

Kähler states his two objectives in this work as follows: first, to criticize and reject the errors of the "life of Jesus" movement; and second, to establish the validity of an alternative approach. For Kähler:

> The historical Jesus of modern writers conceals the living Christ from us. The Jesus of the "life of Jesus" movement is merely a modern example of a brain-child of the human imagination, no better than the notorious dogmatic Christ of Byzantine Christology. They are both equally far removed from the real Christ. In this respect, historicism is just as arbitrary, just as humanly arrogant, just as speculative and "faithlessly gnostic," as that dogmatism which was itself considered modern in its own day.

Kähler concedes immediately that the "life of Jesus" movement was completely correct in so far as it contrasted the biblical witness to Christ with an abstract dogmatism. He nevertheless insists upon its futility, a view summarized in his well-known statement to the effect that the entire life of Jesus movement is a blind alley. His reasons for making this assertion are complex.

The most fundamental reason is that Christ must be regarded as what Kähler terms a "supra-historical" rather than an "historical" figure, so that the critical historical method cannot be applied in his case. The critical historical method could not deal with the supra-historical (and hence supra-human) characteristics of Jesus, and hence was obliged to ignore or deny them. In effect, the critical historical method could only lead to an Arian or Ebionite Christology, on account of its latent dogmatic presuppositions. This point, made frequently throughout the essay, is developed with particular force in relation to the psychological interpretation of the personality of Jesus, and the related question concerning the use of the principle of analogy in the critical historical method.

Kähler notes that the psychological interpretation of the personality of Jesus is dependent upon the (unrecognized) presupposition that the distinction between ourselves and Jesus is one of degree rather than kind, which Kähler suggests must be criticized on dogmatic grounds. More significantly, Kähler challenged the principle of analogy in the interpretation of the New

Testament portrayal of Christ in general which inevitably led to Jesus being treated as analogous to modern human beings, and hence to a reduced Christology). If it is assumed from the outset that Jesus is an ordinary human being, who differs from other humans only in degree and not in nature, then this assumption will be read back into the biblical texts, and dictate the resulting conclusion – that Jesus of Nazareth is a human being who differs from us only in degree.

Second, Kähler argued that "we do not possess any sources for a life of Jesus which an historian could accept as reliable and adequate." This is not to say that the sources are unreliable and inadequate for the purposes of faith. Rather, Kähler wants to emphasize that the gospels are not the accounts of disinterested, impartial observers, but rather accounts of the faith of believers, which cannot be isolated, in either form or content, from that faith: the gospel accounts "are not the reports of alert impartial observers, but are throughout the testimonies and confessions of believers in Christ." In that "it is only through these accounts that we are able to come into contact with him," it will be clear that the "biblical portrait of Christ" is of decisive importance for faith.

What is important for Kähler is not who Christ was, but what he presently does for believers. The "Jesus of history" lacks the soteriological significance of the "Christ of faith." The thorny problems of Christology may therefore be left behind in order to develop what he termed "soterology," and defined as "the knowledge of faith concerning the person of the savior." In effect, Kähler argues that the "life of Jesus" movement has done little more than create a fictitious and pseudo-scientific Christ, devoid of existential significance. For Kähler, "the real Christ is the preached Christ." Christian faith is not based upon this historical Jesus, but upon the existentially significant and faith-evoking figure of the Christ of faith. Considerations such as these gradually came to dominate the theological scene, and may be regarded as reaching their climax in the writings of Rudolf Bultmann, to which we may now turn.

The retreat from history: Rudolf Bultmann

Bultmann regarded the entire enterprise of the historical reconstruction of Jesus as a blind alley. History was not of fundamental importance to Christology; it was merely necessary that Jesus existed, and that the Christian proclamation (which

Rudolf Bultmann (1884–1976). A German Lutheran writer, who was appointed to a chair of theology at Marburg in 1921. He is chiefly noted for his program of "demythologization" of the New Testament, and his use of existential ideas in the exposition of the twentieth-century meaning of the gospel.

277

Bultmann terms the *kerygma* is somehow grounded in his person. Bultmann thus famously reduced the entire historical aspect of Christology to a single word – "that." It is necessary only to believe "that" Jesus Christ lies behind the gospel proclamation (or *kerygma*).

For Bultmann, the cross and the resurrection are indeed historical phenomena (in that they took place within human history) – but they must be discerned by faith as divine acts. The cross and the resurrection are linked in the *kerygma* as the divine act of judgment and the divine act of salvation. It is this divine act which is of continuing significance, and not the historical phenomenon which acted as its bearer. The *kerygma* is thus not concerned with matters of historical fact, but with conveying the necessity of a decision on the part of its hearers, and thus transferring the eschatological moment from the past to the here and now of the proclamation itself:

> This means that Jesus Christ encounters us in the *kerygma* and nowhere else, just as he confronted Paul himself and forced him to a decision. The *kerygma* does not proclaim universal truths or a timeless idea – whether it is an idea of God or of the redeemer – but an historical fact. . . . Therefore the *kerygma* is neither a vehicle for timeless ideas nor the mediator of historical information: what is of decisive importance is that the *kerygma* is Christ's "that," his "here and now," a "here and now" which becomes present in the address itself.

One cannot therefore go behind the *kerygma*, using it as a "source" in order to reconstruct an "historical Jesus" with his "messianic consciousness," his "inner life," or his "heroism." That would merely be "Christ according to the flesh," who no longer exists. It is not the historical Jesus, but Jesus Christ, the one who preached, who is the Lord.

This radical move away from history alarmed many. How could anyone rest assured that Christology was properly grounded in the person and work of Jesus Christ? How could anyone begin to check out Christology, if the history of Jesus was an irrelevance? It seemed to an increasing number of writers, within the fields of both New Testament and dogmatic studies, that Bultmann had merely cut a Gordian knot, without resolving the serious historical issues at stake. For Bultmann, all that could be, and could be required to be, known about the historical Jesus was the fact that he existed. For the New Testament scholar Gerhard Ebeling, the person of the historical Jesus is the fundamental basis of Christology, and if it could be shown that Christology was a misinterpretation of the significance of the historical Jesus, Christology would be brought to an end. In this, Ebeling may be seen as expressing the concerns which underlie the "new quest of the historical Jesus," to be discussed in the following section.

The new quest of the historical Jesus

Ebeling pointed to a fundamental deficiency in Bultmann's Christology: its total lack of openness to investigation (perhaps "verification" is too strong a term) in the light of historical scholarship. Might not Christology rest upon a mistake? How can we rest assured that there is a justifiable transition from the preaching *of* Jesus to the preaching *about* Jesus? Ebeling develops criticisms which parallel those of Ernst Käsemann, but with a theological, rather than a purely historical, focus.

The "new quest of the historical Jesus" is generally regarded as having been inaugurated with Ernst Käsemann's lecture of October 1953 on the problem of the historical Jesus. The full importance of this lecture only emerges if it is viewed in the light of the presuppositions and methods of the Bultmannian school up to this point. Käsemann concedes that the synoptic gospels are primarily theological documents, and that their theological statements are often expressed within the form of the historical. In this, he endorses and recapitulates key axioms of the Bultmann school, here based upon insights of Kähler and Wrede.

Nevertheless, Käsemann immediately went on to qualify these assertions in a significant manner. Despite their obviously theological concerns, the evangelists nevertheless believed that they had access to historical information concerning Jesus of Nazareth, and that this historical information is expressed and embodied in the text of the synoptic gospels. The gospels include both the *kerygma* and historical narrative.

Building on this insight, Käsemann points to the need to explore the continuity between the preaching of Jesus and the preaching about Jesus. There is an obvious discontinuity between the earthly Jesus and the exalted and proclaimed Christ; yet a thread of continuity links them, in that the proclaimed Christ is already present, in some sense, in the historical Jesus. It must be stressed that Käsemann is not suggesting that a new inquiry should be undertaken concerning the historical Jesus in order to provide historical legitimation for the *kerygma*; still less is he suggesting that the discontinuity between the historical Jesus and the proclaimed Christ necessitates the deconstruction of the latter in terms of the former. Rather, Käsemann is pointing to the theological assertion of the identity of the earthly Jesus and the exalted Christ being historically grounded in the actions and preaching of Jesus of Nazareth. The theological affirmation is, Käsemann argues, dependent upon the historical demonstration that the *kerygma* concerning Jesus is already contained in a nutshell or embryonic form in the ministry of Jesus. In that the *kerygma* contains historical elements, it is entirely proper and necessary to inquire concerning the relation of the Jesus of history and the Christ of faith.

It will be clear that the "new quest of the historical Jesus" is qualitatively different from the discredited quest of the nineteenth century. Käsemann's argument rests upon the recognition that the discontinuity between the Jesus of history and the Christ of faith does not imply that they are unrelated entities, with the latter having no grounding or foundation in the former. Rather, the *kerygma* may be discerned in the actions and preaching of Jesus of Nazareth, so that there is a continuity between the preaching of Jesus and the preaching about Jesus. Where the older quest had assumed that the discontinuity between the historical Jesus and the Christ of faith implied that the latter was potentially a fiction, who required to be reconstructed in the light of objective historical investigation, Käsemann stresses that such reconstruction is neither necessary nor possible.

The growing realization of the importance of this point led to intensive interest developing in the question of the historical foundations of the *kerygma*. Four positions of interest may be noted.

1   Joachim Jeremias, perhaps representing an extreme element in this debate, seemed to suggest that the basis of the Christian faith lies in what Jesus actually said and did, in so far as this can be established by theological scholarship. The first part of his *New Testament Theology* was thus devoted in its totality to the "proclamation of Jesus" as a central element of New Testament theology.
2   Käsemann himself identified the continuity between the historical Jesus and the kerygmatic Christ in their common declaration of the dawning of the eschatological kingdom of God. Both in the preaching of Jesus and in the early Christian *kerygma*, the theme of the coming of the kingdom is of major importance.
3   As we saw above, Gerhard Ebeling locates the continuity in the notion of the "faith of Jesus," which he understands to be analogous to the "faith of Abraham" (described in Romans 4) – a prototypical faith, historically exemplified and embodied in Jesus of Nazareth, and proclaimed to be a contemporary possibility for believers.
4   Günter Bornkamm laid particular emphasis upon the note of authority evident in the ministry of Jesus. In Jesus, the actuality of God confronts humanity, and calls it to a radical decision. Whereas Bultmann located the essence of Jesus' preaching in the future coming of the Kingdom of God, Bornkamm shifted the emphasis from the future to the present confrontation of individuals with God through the person of Jesus. This theme of "confrontation with God" is evident in both the ministry of Jesus and the proclamation about Jesus, providing a major theological and historical link between the earthly Jesus and the proclaimed Christ.

The "New Quest of the Historical Jesus" was thus concerned to stress the continuity between the historical Jesus and the Christ of faith. Whereas the "Old Quest" had the aim of discrediting the New Testament portrayal of Christ, the

New Quest ended up consolidating it, by stressing the continuities between the preaching of Jesus himself, and the church's preaching about Jesus. Since then, there have been other developments in the field. In the last two decades, particular attention has been directed toward exploring the relation between Jesus and his environment in first-century Judaism. This development, which is especially associated with English and American writers such as Geza Vermes and E. P. Sanders, has renewed interest in the Jewish background to Jesus, and further emphasized the importance of history in relation to Christology. The Bultmannian approach – which devalues the significance of history in Christology – is widely regarded as discredited, at least for the moment. We shall turn to consider this "Third Quest" in the concluding section of this case study.

The third quest

Since the general collapse of the "New Quest" during the 1960s, a series of works have appeared offering re-evaluations of the historical Jesus. The term "Third Quest" has often been applied to this group of works. The designation has been called into question by a number of writers, who point out that the works and scholars who are gathered together under this term do not have enough in common to categorize them in this way. For example, some writers within the group make an appeal to sources outside the New Testament, especially the Coptic Gospel of Thomas, in their analysis; others restrict their analysis to the New Testament materials, especially the synoptic gospels. Despite this reservation, the term seems to be gaining acceptance, and it is therefore appropriate to include it in this survey.

The "original quest" approached the stories of Jesus in the light of its strongly rationalist presuppositions, and filtered out the miraculous aspects of the gospel narratives. The "new quest" tended to focus on the words of Jesus. The "Third Quest" seems to involve a focus on the healings and exorcisms of Jesus as indicative of the distinctive character of his mission, and his understanding of his own goals. Among significant contributions to the "Third Quest," the following should be noted in particular:

1 John Dominic Crossan argues that Jesus was essentially a poor Jewish peasant with a particular concern to challenge the power structures of contemporary society. In his *The Historical Jesus* (1991) and *Jesus: A Revolutionary Biography* (1994), Crossan argues that Jesus broke down prevailing social conventions, especially through his table fellowship with sinners and social outcasts.
2 In books such as *Jesus: A New Vision* (1988) and *Meeting Jesus Again for the First Time* (1994), Marcus L. Borg suggests that Jesus was a subversive sage concerned to renew Judaism in a manner which posed a powerful challenge to the ruling temple elite.

3   In his *Myth of Innocence* (1988) and *The Lost Gospel* (1993), Burton L. Mack argues that Jesus was an individualistic sage along the lines of a Cynic. As a "Hellenistic Cynic Sage" Jesus had little interest in specifically Jewish issues (such as the place of the Temple, or the role of the Law); rather, he was concerned to identify and mock the conventions of contemporary society.

4   E. P. Sanders insists that Jesus is to be seen as a prophetic figure who was concerned with the restoration of the Jewish people. In works such as *Jesus and Judaism* (1985) and *The Historical Figure of Jesus* (1993), Sanders suggests that Jesus envisaged an eschatological restoration of Israel. God would bring the present age to an end, and usher in a new order focusing on a new temple, with Jesus himself acting as God's representative.

On the basis of this brief analysis of a few writers generally regarded as representative of the "Third Quest," it will be clear that it lacks a coherent theological or historical core. There is significant disagreement concerning whether Jesus is to be seen against a Jewish or Hellenistic background; about his attitude to the Jewish law and its religious institutions; his view of the future of Israel; and the personal significance of Jesus in relation to that future. Nevertheless, the term has found at least a degree of acceptance, despite its clear weaknesses, and it is likely to remain an integral part of scholarly discussion of this important issue.

Case Study 4.2   The Basis and Nature of Salvation

The question of how salvation is attained, and how that salvation is to be understood, has been the subject of discussion throughout Christian history. The patristic period witnessed the exploration of a variety of approaches, often with a particular concentration on the theme of Christ's victory over death or his transformation of corporate humanity through deification. The Middle Ages witnessed a new interest in the morality or legality of atonement (see case study 2.2). In the modern period, the discussion has continued. The present case study offers a survey of that discussion, beginning with a consideration of the relation between the doctrines of the person and work of Christ – or, to use more technical language, between Christology and soteriology.

The relation between Christology and soteriology

In the great works of systematic theology dating from the periods of high scholasticism and Protestant orthodoxy, a rigorous distinction was made between the "person of Christ" and the "work of Christ." In the modern period, this distinction has been generally abandoned, on account of an increasing recognition of the inextricable connection of these two areas of theology.

Christology and soteriology are increasingly being regarded as the two sides of one and the same coin. A number of considerations have led to this development.

The first is the influence of a Kantian epistemology. Kant argued that we can only know the *Ding-an-sich* in terms of its effect upon us. If this general approach is translated to the cluster of issues centring upon the identity and significance of Jesus Christ, it would seem to follow that the essence or identity of Christ (i.e. Christology) cannot be separated from his effect or impact upon us (i.e. soteriology). This is the approach adopted by Albrecht Ritschl in his *Christian Doctrine of Justification and Reconciliation* of 1874. Ritschl argued that it was improper to separate Christology and soteriology, in that we perceive "the nature and attributes, that is the determination of being, only in the effect of a thing upon us, and we think of the nature and extent of its effect upon us as its essence."

The second consideration is the general recognition that, even in the New Testament, there is a strong correlation between the Christological titles of Jesus and their soteriological substructure. "A separation between Christology and soteriology is not possible, because in general the soteriological interest, the interest in salvation, in the *beneficia Christi*, is what causes us to ask about the figure of Jesus" (Wolfhart Pannenberg).

Despite this consensus, there is continuing disagreement over the emphasis to be given to soteriological considerations in Christology. For example, the approach adopted by Rudolf Bultmann appears to reduce Christology to *das Dass* – the mere fact "that" a historical figure existed, to whom the *kerygma* can be traced and attached. The primary function of the *kerygma* is to transmit the soteriological content of the Christ-event. A related approach, found in A. E. Biedermann and Paul Tillich, draws a distinction between the "Christ principle" and the historical person of Jesus. This has led some writers, most notably Pannenberg, to express anxiety that a Christology might simply be constructed out of soteriological considerations (and thus be vulnerable to the criticisms of Ludwig Feuerbach), rather than grounded in the history of Jesus himself.

Interpretations of the work of Christ

Modern discussions of the meaning of the cross and resurrection of Christ are best grouped around four central controlling themes or images. It must be stressed that these are not mutually exclusive, and that it is normal to find writers adopting approaches which incorporate elements drawn from more than one such category. Indeed, it can be argued that the views of most writers on this subject cannot be reduced to or confined within a single category without doing serious violence to their ideas.

Sacrifice. The New Testament, drawing on Old Testament imagery and expectations, presents Christ's death upon the cross as a sacrifice. This approach, which is especially associated with the Letter to the Hebrews, presents Christ's sacrificial offering as an effective and perfect sacrifice, which was able to accomplish that which the sacrifices of the Old Testament were only able to intimate, rather than achieve. This idea is developed subsequently within the Christian tradition. For example, in taking over the imagery of sacrifice, Augustine states that Christ "was made a sacrifice for sin, offering himself as a whole burnt offering on the cross of his passion." In order for humanity to be restored to God, the mediator must sacrifice himself; without this sacrifice, such restoration is an impossibility. For Augustine, this sacrifice is commemorated in the Eucharist:

> Before the coming of Christ, the flesh and blood of his sacrifice were foreshadowed in the animals which were killed; in the passion of Christ, these types were fulfilled by the true sacrifice [of Christ on the cross]; after the ascension of Christ, this sacrifice is commemorated in the sacrament.

Similar ideas may be discerned in the theology of the Middle Ages, and into the early modern period.

The sacrificial offering of Christ on the cross came to be linked especially with one aspect of the threefold office of Christ (*munus triplex Christi*). According to this typology, which dates from the middle of the sixteenth century, the work of Christ could be summarized under three "offices": prophet (by which Christ declares the will of God), priest (by which he makes sacrifice for sin) and king (by which he rules with authority over his people). The general acceptance of this taxonomy within Protestantism in the late sixteenth and seventeenth centuries led to a sacrificial understanding of Christ's death becoming of central importance within Protestant soteriologies. Thus John Pearson's *Exposition of the Creed* of 1659 insists upon the necessity of the sacrifice of Christ in redemption, and specifically links this with the priestly office of Christ.

> The redemption or salvation which the Messiah was to bring consisteth in the freeing of a sinner from the state of sin and eternal death into a state of righteousness and eternal life. Now a freedom from sin could not be wrought without a sacrifice propitiatory, and therefore there was a necessity of a priest.

Since the Enlightenment, however, there has been a subtle shift in the meaning of the term. A metaphorical extension of meaning has come to be given priority over the original. Whereas the term originally referred to the ritual offering of slaughtered animals as a specifically *religious* action, the term increasingly came to mean heroic or costly action on the parts of individuals, especially the giving up of one's life, with no transcendent reference or expectation.

This trend may be seen developing in John Locke's *Reasonableness of Christianity* of 1695. Locke argues that the only article of faith required of Christians is that of belief in Christ's Messiahship; the idea of a sacrifice for sin is studiously set to one side. "The faith required was to believe Jesus to be the Messiah, the anointed, who had been promised by God to the world. . . . I do not remember that [Christ] anywhere assumes to himself the title of a priest, or mentions anything relating to his priesthood."

These arguments are developed further by Thomas Chubb (1679–1747), especially in his *True Gospel of Jesus Christ Vindicated* of 1739. Arguing that the true religion of reason was that of conformity to the eternal rule of right, Chubb argues that the idea of Christ's death as a sacrifice arises from the apologetic concerns of the early Christian writers, which led them to harmonize this religion of reason with the cult of the Jews: "As the Jews had their temple, their altar, their high priest, their sacrifices and the like, so the apostles, in order to make Christianity bear a resemblance to Judaism, found out something or other in Christianity, which they by a figure of speech called by those names." Chubb, in common with the emerging Enlightenment tradition, dismissed this as spurious. "God's disposition to show mercy . . . arises wholly from his own innate goodness or mercifulness, and not from anything external to him, whether it be the sufferings and death of Jesus Christ or otherwise."

Even Joseph Butler, in attempting to reinstate the notion of sacrifice in his *Analogy of Religion* of 1736, found himself in difficulty, given the strongly rationalist spirit of the age. In upholding the sacrificial nature of Christ's death, he found himself obliged to concede more than he cared to:

> How and in what particular way [the death of Christ] had this efficacy, there are not wanting persons who have endeavoured to explain; but I do not find that Scripture has explained it. We seem to be very much in the dark concerning the manner in which the ancients understood atonements to be made, i.e., pardon to be obtained by sacrifice.

Horace Bushnell's *Vicarious Sacrifice* of 1866 illustrates this same trend in the Anglo-American theology of the period, but in a more constructive manner. Through his suffering, Christ awakens our sense of guilt. His vicarious sacrifice demonstrates that God suffers on account of evil. In speaking of the "tender appeals of sacrifice," Bushnell might seem to align himself with purely exemplarist understandings of the death of Christ; however, Bushnell is adamant that there are objective elements to atonement. Christ's death affects God, and expresses God. There are strong anticipations of later theologies of the suffering of God, when Bushnell declares:

> Whatever we may say or hold or believe concerning the vicarious sacrifice of Christ, we are to affirm in the same manner of God. The whole Deity is in it, in it from eternity. . . . There is a cross in God before the wood is seen on the hill. . . . It is as if there were a cross unseen, standing on its undiscovered hill, far back in the ages.

The use of sacrificial imagery has become noticeably less widespread since 1945, especially in German-language theology. It is highly likely that this relates directly to the rhetorical debasement of the term in secular contexts, especially in situations of national emergency. The secular use of the imagery of sacrifice, often degenerating to little more than slogan-mongering, is widely regarded as having tainted and compromised both the word and the concept. The frequent use of such phrases as "he sacrificed his life for King and country" in British circles during the First World War, and Adolf Hitler's extensive use of sacrificial imagery in justifying economic hardship and the loss of civil liberties as the price of German national revival in the late 1930s, served to render the term virtually unusable for many in Christian teaching and preaching, on account of its negative associations. Nevertheless, the idea continues to be of importance in modern Roman Catholic sacramental theology, which continues to regard the eucharist as a sacrifice, and to find in this image a rich source of theological imagery.

Christus Victor. The New Testament and early church laid considerable emphasis upon the victory gained by Christ over sin, death and Satan through his cross and resurrection. This theme of victory, often linked liturgically with the Easter celebrations, was of major importance within the western Christian theological tradition until the Enlightenment. With the advent of the Enlightenment, however, it began to fall out of theological favor, increasingly being regarded as outmoded and unsophisticated. The following factors appear to have contributed to this development.

1   Rational criticism of belief in the resurrection of Christ raised doubts concerning whether one could even begin to speak of a "victory" over death.
2   The imagery traditionally linked with this approach to the cross – such as the existence of a personal devil in the form of Satan, and the domination of human existence by oppressive or satanic forces of sin and evil – was dismissed as premodern superstition.

The rehabilitation of this approach in the modern period is usually dated to 1931, with the appearance of Gustaf Aulén's *Christus Victor.* This short book, which originally appeared in German as an article in *Zeitschrift für systematische Theologie* (1930), has exercised a major influence over English-language approaches to the subject. Aulén argued that the classic Christian conception of the work of Christ was summed up in the belief that the risen Christ had brought new possibilities of life to humanity through his victory over the powers of evil. In a brief and very compressed account of the history of theories of the atonement, Aulén argued that this highly dramatic "classic" theory had dominated Christianity until the Middle Ages, when more abstract legal theories began to gain ground. The situation was radically reversed through Martin Luther, who reintroduced the theme. However, the scholastic concerns of Protestant orthodoxy led to its being relegated once more to the background. Aulén argued that this approach could no longer be allowed to be the victim of historical circumstances; it demanded a full and proper hearing.

Historically, Aulén's case was soon found to be wanting. Its claims to be treated as the "classic" theory of the atonement had been overstated. It was indeed an important component of the general patristic understanding of the nature and mode of procurance of salvation; nevertheless, if any theory could justly lay claim to the title of "the classic theory of the atonement," it would be the notion of redemption through unity with Christ.

Nevertheless, Aulén's views were sympathetically received. In part, this reflects growing disenchantment with the Enlightenment worldview in general; more fundamentally, perhaps, it represents a growing realization of the reality of evil in the world, fostered by the horrors of the First World War. The insights of Sigmund Freud, drawing attention to the manner in which adults could be spiritually imprisoned by their subconscious, raised serious doubts about the Enlightenment view of the total rationality of human nature, and lent new credibility to the idea that humans are held in bondage to unknown and hidden forces. Aulén's approach seemed to resonate with a growing realization of the darker side of human nature. It had become intellectually respectable to talk about "forces of evil."

His approach also offered a *tertium quid*, a third possibility, which mediated between the two alternatives then on offer within mainstream liberal Protestantism – both of which were regarded as flawed. The classic legal theory was regarded as raising difficult theological questions, not least concerning the morality of atonement; the subjective approach, which regarded Christ's death as doing little more than arousing human religious sentiment, seemed to be seriously religiously inadequate. Aulén offered an approach to the meaning of the death of Christ which bypassed the difficulties of legal approaches, yet vigorously defended the objective nature of the atonement. Nevertheless, Aulén's *Christus Victor* approach did raise some serious questions. If offered no rational justification for the manner in which the forces of evil are defeated through the cross of Christ. Why the cross? Why not in some other manner?

Since then, the image of victory has been developed in writings on the cross. Rudolf Bultmann extended his programme of demythologization to the New Testament theme of victory, interpreting it as a victory over inauthentic existence and unbelief. Paul Tillich offers a reworking of Aulén's theory, in which the victory of Christ on the cross is interpreted as a victory over existential forces which threaten to deprive us of authentic existence. Bultmann and Tillich, in adopting such existentialist approaches, thus convert a theory of the atonement which was originally radically objective into a subjective victory within the human consciousness.

In his *Past Event and Present Salvation* (1989), Oxford theologian Paul Fiddes emphasizes that the notion of "victory" retains a place of significance within Christian thinking about the cross. Christ's death does more than impart some new knowledge to us, or express old ideas in new manners. It makes possible a new mode of existence:

> The victory of Christ actually *creates* victory in us. . . . The act of Christ is one of those moments in human history that "opens up new possibilities of existence." Once a new possibility has been disclosed, other people can make it their own, repeating and reliving the experience.

Legal approaches. A third approach centres on the idea of the death of Christ providing the basis by which God is enabled to forgive sin. This notion is traditionally associated with the eleventh-century writer Anselm of Canterbury, who developed an argument for the necessity of the incarnation on its basis. This model became incorporated into classical Protestant dogmatics during the period of orthodoxy, and finds its expression in many hymns of the eighteenth and nineteenth centuries. Three main models were used to understand the manner in which the forgiveness of human sins is related to the death of Christ.

1   Representation. Christ is here understood to be the covenant represent-ative of humanity. Through faith, believers come to stand within the covenant between God and humanity. All that Christ has achieved through the cross is available on account of the covenant. Just as God entered into a covenant with his people Israel, so he has entered into a covenant with his church. Christ, by his obedience upon the cross, represents his covenant people, winning benefits for them as their representative. By coming to faith, individuals come to stand within the covenant, and thus share in all its benefits, won by Christ through his cross and resurrection – including the full and free forgiveness of our sins.

2   Participation. Through faith, believers participate in the risen Christ. They are "in Christ," to use Paul's famous phrase. They are caught up in him, and share in his risen life. As a result of this, they share in all the benefits won by Christ, through his obedience upon the cross. One of those benefits is the forgiveness of sins, in which they share through their faith. Participating in Christ thus entails the forgiveness of sins, and sharing in his righteousness.

3   Substitution. Christ is here understood to be a substitute, the one who goes to the cross in our place. Sinners ought to have been crucified, on account of their sins. Christ was crucified in their place. God allows Christ to stand in our place, taking our guilt upon himself, so that his righteousness – won by obedience upon the cross – might become ours.

With the onset of the Enlightenment, this approach to the atonement was subjected to a radical critique. The following major points of criticism were directed against it.

1 It appeared to rest upon a notion of original guilt, which Enlightenment writers found unacceptable. Each human being was responsible for his or her own moral guilt; the very notion of an *inherited* guilt, as it was expressed in the traditional doctrine of original sin, was to be rejected.
2 The Enlightenment insisted upon the rationality, and perhaps above all the *morality*, of every aspect of Christian doctrine. This theory of the atonement appeared to be morally suspect, especially in its notions of transferred guilt or merit. The central idea of "vicarious satisfaction" was also regarded with acute suspicion: in what sense was it *moral* for one human being to bear the penalties due for another?

These criticism were given added weight through the development of the discipline of the "history of dogma" (*Dogmengeschichte*). The representatives of this movement, from G. S. Steinbart through to Adolf von Harnack, argued that a series of assumptions, each of central importance to the Anselmian doctrine of penal substitution, had become incorporated into Christian theology by what were little more than historical accidents. For example, in his *System of Pure Philosophy* of 1778, Steinbart argued that historical investigation disclosed the intrusion of three "arbitrary assumptions" into Christian reflection on salvation:

1 the Augustinian doctrine of original sin;
2 the concept of satisfaction;
3 the doctrine of the imputation of the righteousness of Christ.

For such reasons, Steinbart felt able to declare the substructure of orthodox Protestant thinking on the atonement to be a relic of a bygone era.

More recently, the idea of guilt – a central aspect of legal approaches to soteriology – has been the subject of much discussion, especially in the light of Freud's views on the origin of guilt in childhood experiences. For some twentieth-century writers, "guilt" is simply a psychosocial projection, whose origins lie not in the holiness of God but in the muddleheadedness of human nature. These psychosocial structures are then, it is argued, projected onto some imaginary screen of "external" reality, and treated as if they are objectively true. While this represents a considerable overstatement of the case, it has the advantage of clarity, and allows us to gain an appreciation of the considerable pressure that this approach to the atonement is currently facing.

Nevertheless, this view continues to find significant representatives. The collapse of the evolutionary moral optimism of liberal Protestantism in the wake of the First World War did much to raise again the question of human guilt, and the need for redemption from outside the human situation. Two significant contributions to this discussion may be regarded as precipitated directly by the credibility crisis faced by liberal Protestantism at this time.

P. T. Forsyth's *Justification of God* (1916), written during the war years, represents an impassioned plea to allow the notion of the "justice of God" to be rediscovered. Forsyth is less concerned than Anselm about the legal and juridical aspects of the cross; his interest centres on the manner in which the cross is inextricably linked with "the whole moral fabric and movement of the universe." The doctrine of the atonement is inseparable from "the rightness of things." God acts to restore this "rightness of things," in that he makes available through the cross a means of moral regeneration – something which the war demonstrated that humanity needed, yet was unable to provide itself.

> The cross is not a theological theme, nor a forensic device, but the crisis of the moral universe on a scale far greater than earthly war. It is the theodicy of the whole God dealing with the whole soul of the whole world in holy love, righteous judgement and redeeming grace.

Through the cross, God aims to restore the rightness of the world through rightful means – a central theme of Anselm's doctrine of atonement, creatively restated.

More significant is the extended discussion of the theme of "atonement" or "reconciliation" (the German term *Versöhnung* can bear both meanings) to be found in Karl Barth's *Church Dogmatics*. The central section (IV/1, §59, 2) addressing the issue is entitled – significantly – "The Judge Judged in Our Place." The title derives from the *Heidelberg Catechism*, which speaks of Christ as the judge who "has represented me before the judgment of God, and has taken away all condemnation from me." The section in question can be regarded as an extended commentary on this classic text of the Reformed tradition, dealing with the manner in which the judgment of God is in the first place made known and enacted; and in the second, is taken upon God himself (a central Anselmian theme, even if Anselm failed to integrate it within a Trinitarian context).

The entire section is steeped in the language and imagery of guilt, judgment and forgiveness. In the cross, we can see God exercising his rightful judgment of sinful humanity (Barth uses the compound term *Sündermensch* to emphasize that "sin" is not a detachable aspect of human nature). The cross exposes human delusions of self-sufficiency and autonomy of judgment, which Barth sees encapsulated in the story of Genesis 3: "the human being wants to be his own judge."

Yet alteration of the situation demands that its inherent wrongness be acknowledged. For Barth, the cross of Christ represents the locus in which the righteous judge makes known his judgment of sinful humanity, and simultaneously takes that judgment upon himself.

> What took place is that the Son of God fulfilled the righteous judgement on us human beings by himself taking our place as a human being, and in our place undergoing the judgement under which we had passed. . . . Because God willed to execute his judgement on us in his Son, it all took place in his person, as *his* accusation and condemnation and destruction. He judged, and it was the judge who was judged, who allowed himself to be judged. . . . Why did God become a human being? So that God as a human being might do and accomplish and achieve and complete all this for us wrongdoers, in order that in this way there might be brought about by him our reconciliation with him, and our conversion to him.

The strongly substitutionary character of this will be evident. God exercises his righteous judgment by exposing our sin, by taking it upon himself, and thus by neutralizing its power. The cross thus both speaks "for us" and "against us." Unless the cross is allowed to reveal the full extent of our sin, it cannot take that sin from us:

> The "for us" of his death on the cross included and encloses this terrible "against us". Without this terrible "against us", it would not be the divine and holy and redemptive and effectively helpful "for us", in which the conversion of humanity and the world to God has become an event.

Exemplarist approaches. A central aspect of the New Testament understanding of the meaning of the cross relates to the demonstration of the love of God for humanity. With the rise of the Enlightenment worldview, increasingly critical approaches were adopted to theories of the atonement which incorporated transcendent elements – such as the idea of a sacrifice which had some impact upon God, or Christ dying in order to pay some penalty or satisfaction which was due for sin. The increasingly skeptical attitude to the resurrection tended to discourage theologians from incorporating this into their theologies of atonement with anything even approaching the enthusiasm of earlier generations. As a result, the emphasis of theologians sympathetic to the Englightenment came to focus upon the cross itself. However, many Enlightenment theologians also had difficulties with the "two natures" doctrine. The form of Christology which perhaps expresses the spirit of the Enlightenment most faithfully is a degree Christology – that is to say, a Christology which recognizes a difference of *degree*, but not of *nature*, between Christ and other human beings. Jesus Christ was recognized as embodying certain qualities which were present, actually or potentially, in all other human beings, the difference lying in the superior extent to which he embodied them.

291

When such considerations are applied to theories of atonement, a consistent pattern begins to emerge. This can be studied from the writings of G. S. Steinbart, I. G. Töllner, G. F. Seiler and K. G. Bretschneider. Its basic features can be summarized as follows.

1   The cross has no transcendent reference or value; its value relates directly to its impact upon humanity. Thus the cross represents a "sacrifice" only in that it represents Christ giving up his life.
2   The person who died upon the cross was a human being, and the impact of that death is upon human beings. That impact takes the form of inspiration and encouragement to model ourselves upon the moral example set us in Jesus himself.
3   The most important aspect of the cross is that it demonstrates the love of God toward us.

This approach became enormously influential in rationalist circles throughout nineteenth-century Europe. The mystery and apparent irrationalism of the cross had been neutralized; what remained was a powerful and dramatic plea for the moral improvement of humanity, modelled on the lifestyle and attitudes of Jesus Christ. The model of a martyr, rather than a savior, describes the attitude increasingly adopted toward Jesus within such circles.

The most significant challenge to this rationalist approach to the cross is due to F. D. E. Schleiermacher, who insisted upon the *religious* value of the death of Christ. Christ did not die to make or endorse a moral system; he came in order that the supremacy of the consciousness of God could be established in humanity. Nevertheless, Schleiermacher was often represented as teaching a view of the atonement as *Lebenserhöhung*, a kind of moral elevation of life (as in the account set forth by Gustaf Aulén). His distinctive ideas proved to be capable of being assimilated to purely exemplarist understandings, rather than posing a coherent challenge to them.

The most significant statement of this approach in England is to be found in the 1915 Bampton Lectures of the noted modernist Hastings Rashdall. In these lectures, Rashdall launched a vigorous attack on traditional approaches to the atonement. The only interpretation of the cross which is adequate for the needs of the modern age is that already associated with the medieval writer Peter Abelard:

> The church's early creed, "There is none other name given among men by which we may be saved", may be translated so as to be something of this kind: "There is none other ideal given among men by which we may be saved, except the moral ideal which Christ taught us by his words, and illustrated by his life and death of love."

Other English writers who adopted similar or related approaches include G. W. H. Lampe and John Hick. In his essay "The Atonement: Law and Love," contributed to the liberal Catholic volume *Soundings*, Lampe launched a fierce attack on legal approaches to his subject, before commending an exemplarist approach based on "the paradox and miracle of love."

The position of John Hick is of especial interest, in that it relates to the place of the work of Christ in inter-faith dialogue. The religious pluralist agenda has certain important theological consequences. Traditional Christian theology does not lend itself particularly well to the homogenizing agenda of religious pluralists. The suggestion that all religions are more or less talking about vaguely the same thing finds itself in difficulty in relation to certain essentially Christian ideas – most notably, the doctrines of the incarnation, atonement and the Trinity. The suggestion that something unique is made possible or available through the death of Christ is held to belittle non-Christian religions. In response to this pressure, a number of major Christological and theological developments may be noted. Doctrines such as the incarnation, which imply a high profile of identification between Jesus Christ and God, are discarded, in favor of various degree Christologies, which are more amenable to the reductionist program of liberalism. A sharp distinction is thus drawn between the historical person of Jesus Christ, and the principles which he is alleged to represent. Paul Knitter is but one of a small galaxy of pluralist writers concerned to drive a wedge between the "Jesus-event" (which is unique to Christianity) and the "Christ-principle" (accessible to all religious traditions, and expressed in their own distinctive, but equally valid, ways). Viewed in this pluralist light, the cross of Christ is thus understood to make known something which is accessible in other manners, and which is a universal religious possibility. Thus Hick argues that the Christ-event is only "one of the points at which God has been and still is creatively at work within human life," his distinctiveness relates solely to his being a "visible story," and not an "additional truth."

The cross: constitutive or illustrative?

In his *Doctrine of Reconciliation* of 1898, Martin Kähler posed the following question concerning theories of the atonement: "Did Christ just make known some insights concerning an unchangeable situation – or did he establish a new situation?" With this question we come to a central aspect of soteriology. Does the cross of Christ illustrate the saving will of God? Or does it make such a salvation possible in the first place? Is it constitutive or illustrative?

The latter approach has been characteristic of much writing inspired by the Enlightenment, which treats the cross as a historical symbol of a timeless truth. John Macquarrie firmly defends this approach in his *Principles of Christian Theology* of 1977:

It is not that, at a given moment, God adds the activity of reconciliation to his previous activities, or that we can set a time when his reconciling activity began. Rather, it is the case that at a given time there was a new and decisive interpretation of an activity that had always been going on, an activity that is equiprimordial with creation itself.

A similar approach is associated with Maurice F. Wiles, who argues in his *Remaking of Christian Doctrine* of 1974 that the Christ-event is "in some way a demonstration of what is true of God's eternal nature." Brian Hebblethwaite concurs: "it needs to be stated quite categorically that God's forgiving love does not depend on the death of Christ, but rather is manifested and enacted in it."

Yet the debate is far from over. In his *Actuality of Atonement* (1988), Colin Gunton suggests that non-constitutive approaches to the atonement run the risk of falling back into exemplarist and subjective doctrines of salvation. Yet it is necessary to say that Christ does not just reveal something of importance to us; he achieves something for us – something without which salvation would not be possible. Raising the question of whether "the real evil of the world is faced and healed *ontologically* in the life, death and resurrection of Jesus," Gunton argues that there must be a sense in which Christ is a "substitute" for us: he does for us something that we ourselves cannot do. To deny this is to revert to some form of Pelagianism, or a purely subjective understanding of salvation.

This theme has been taken up in *Atonement and Incarnation* (1991) by Vernon White, who argues for the constitutive nature of the Christ-event on moral grounds. Real reconciliation demands that something must "happen in response to moral evil." Reconciliation demands that evil be confronted in history – which can only happen through the Christ-event.

> The only adequate "undoing" of past disruption involves the attempted recreation of something new. . . . [This] is exemplified throughout the incarnate life, and pre-eminently in the cross and resurrection. God overcomes evil and achieves reconciliation, first by experiencing the consequences of it, both in terms of his own temptation to live for self, and in terms of the assault of other people's selfishness on him.

White is thus able to ground the constitutive nature of the cross of Christ through God's encounter with human suffering in history – something which had to "happen."

A similar issue underlies the distinction between *objective* and *subjective* approaches to atonement. The former suggests that there is a change in the external situation – that is, that God is in some way affected by the cross of Christ. The latter argues that it is our perception of the situation which is radically altered. It will be clear that the former corresponds broadly to constitutive, and the latter to illustrative, approaches to atonement. The parallel, however, is not exact.

The nature of salvation

What is the salvation that is made known or possible through the death of Christ? "Salvation" is an enormously complex notion, embracing a number of related and mutually interacting ideas. The following major themes may all be discerned in modern discussions of the subject, and are noted simply to indicate the complexity of the subject, as well as to allow the reader to gain an appreciation of some of the characteristic emphases within modern theology.

It must be stressed that a major theological point underlies the various manners in which salvation is interpreted. The growth of Christianity in recent centuries, chiefly through missionary work, has raised the issue of *contextualization*. How should the vocabulary and conceptual framework of the Christian tradition be adapted or refined to meet the new situations into which the Christian faith has expanded? Harvey M. Conn is one writer to raise the importance of this question, noting that salvation is to be *particularized* in terms of the situation addressed by the gospel at any given moment. Historically, this has meant that notions of salvation have varied from one cultural context to another – a point which lends added weight to Wolfhart Pannenberg's plea that Christologies should not be constructed solely on soteriological foundations, but should engage with and be grounded in the history of Jesus of Nazareth. A brief survey will indicate the considerable diversity of concepts of salvation which have gained influence since 1700.

Deification. The motif of deification dominates the soteriology of the early church, as can be seen from the writings of (to note but a few examples) Athanasius and the Cappadocian Fathers. It has remained an integral part of Eastern Orthodox theology in the modern period, and plays a significant role in the theology of modern writers within this tradition such as Vladimir Lossky.

Righteousness before God. The notion of righteousness before God (*coram Deo*) played a major part in the development of Luther's doctrine of justification in the sixteenth century. Lutheran orthodoxy, especially during the eighteenth century, retained this emphasis on justification. Both pietist and Enlightenment writers regarded the notion of "imputed righteousness" with some suspicion, considering it to amount to a legal fiction or moral deception. This led to an increased emphasis upon holiness within the pietist tradition, and upon morality within Enlightenment circles, and an increasing reluctance on the part of mainstream Protestant theologians to make use of the imagery of justification. In part, this is due to the increased use of the imagery of union with Christ within Calvinist theological circles.

Union with Christ. The notion of a personal union between the believer and Christ was a significant element of patristic soteriologies. The notion of a union with Christ was developed by both Luther and Calvin at the time of the Reformation; only in the writings of the latter, however, did it assume a major soteriological role. In later Calvinism, the idea comes to be of central importance. Eighteenth-century Calvinist writers in both Europe and America regarded this emphasis upon union with Christ as by-passing the moral difficulties raised by the Lutheran concept of justification. In that believers were genuinely united to Christ, they were entitled to share in his righteousness.

Moral perfection. The characteristic view of the Enlightenment was that religion, where it could be approved, was concerned with the moral improvement of humanity. In its typical form, this view argues that Jesus is to be regarded as a teacher of the moral life, which is conformity to the will of God. This will, which can be known equally well through reason as through the teaching of Christ, was distorted by New Testament writers, who sought to add various arbitrary or self-serving doctrines to the simple moral religion of Jesus.

In its more developed form, this approach subsequently drew upon the ideas of Immanuel Kant, especialy in his *Religion within the Limits of Reason Alone.* Kant discussed the role of Jesus in relation to the "ideal of moral perfection," and related this to the notion of the "kingdom of God," understood as a realm of ethical values. This approach would have considerable influence within liberal Protestantism, especially the Ritschlian school, which regarded Jesus as "the founder of a universal moral community."

Consciousness of God. F. D. E. Schleiermacher, reacting against purely rational or moral conceptions of Christianity, developed the idea that human salvation was to be discussed in terms of the domination of God-consciousness. This consciousness finds its prototypal expression in Jesus of Nazareth, and is thence made available as a possibility within the community of faith.

Genuine humanity. The rise of existentialism in the twentieth century is widely regarded as linked with a sense of dehumanization in contemporary western culture. A number of writers have therefore argued that salvation is to be understood in terms of the rediscovery and restitution of genuine humanity. Significant contributions here were made by Eberhard Grisebach and Friedrich Gogarten, drawing on the personalism of Martin Buber. Grisebach analyzed the dilemma faced by modern humanity in terms of a quest for authentic human identity. Gogarten argued that soteriology concerns the question of how a human can become a person – a genuine "Thou" in a world which threatens to depersonalize human existence, and reduce it to the level of an "It."

Political liberation. Latin American liberation theology has emphasized the political aspects of the notion of salvation, and may be regarded as a recovery of the social, political and economic aspects of biblical (especially Old Testament) approaches to the theme. This move, which may be regarded as a protest against purely individualist conceptions of salvation (such as those noted immediately above), has met with considerable resistance from those who regard salvation as a privatized matter, divorced from the affairs of this world. Gustavo Gutiérrez's *Theology of Liberation* of 1971 and José Miguel Bonino's *Towards a Christian*

Political Ethics of 1983 represent typical accounts of politicized concepts of salvation, drawn from Roman Catholic and evangelical traditions respectively.

Conclusion

This brief survey of the understandings of salvation in modern Christian thought has touched on the main issues of debate. Inevitably, most have been discussed at only a fraction of the length that they merit. It will, however, be clear that discussion of these issues – including the contextualization of salvation – will remain a perennial task of responsible Christian theology.

Case Study 4.3   The Debate over the Resurrection

The resurrection has been one of the most widely-debated areas of modern Christian theology. In part, this reflects the fact that the important question of the relation of faith and history often comes to focus on the question of the resurrection of Christ. The question of the resurrection of Christ – more specifically, whether Christ was indeed raised from the dead, and, if so, what that event might mean – brings together the central components of the Enlightenment critique of traditional Christianity. In what follows, we shall outline the main positions to have developed during the modern period, and attempt to assess their significance.

The Enlightenment: the resurrection as non-event

The characteristic Enlightenment emphasis on the omnicompetence of reason and the importance of contemporary analogues to past events led to the development of an intensely skeptical attitude toward the resurrection in the eighteenth century. G. E. Lessing provides an excellent example of a writer to adopt this skeptical attitude. Lessing confesses that he does not have first-hand experience of the resurrection of Jesus Christ; so why, he asks, should he be asked to believe in something which he has not seen? The problem of chronological distance, according to Lessing, is made all the more acute on account of his doubts (which he evidently assumes others will share) concerning the reliability of the eyewitness reports. Our faith eventually rests upon the authority of others, rather than the authority of our own experience and rational reflection upon it:

> But since the truths of these miracles has completely ceased to be demonstrable by miracles happening now, since they are no more than reports of miracles . . . I deny that they can and should bind me to the very least faith in the other teachings of Jesus.

297

In other words, as men and women are not raised from the dead now, why should we believe that such a thing happened in the past?

> **Gotthold Ephraim Lessing (1729–81).** A significant representative of the German Enlightenment, noted for his strongly rationalist approach to Christian theology.

As we have seen, rationalist writers such as Reimarus and Lessing denied that human testimony to a past event (such as the resurrection) was sufficient to make it credible if it appeared to be contradicted by present direct experience, no matter how well documented the original event may have been. Similarly, the leading French rationalist Denis Diderot declared that if the entire population of Paris were to assure him that a dead man had just been raised from the dead, he would not believe a word of it. This growing skepticism concerning the "miraculous evidences" of the New Testament forced traditional Christianity to defend the doctrine of the divinity of Christ on grounds other than miracles – which, at the time, it proved singularly incapable of doing. Of course, it must be noted that other religions claiming miraculous evidences were subjected to equally great skeptical criticism by the Enlightenment: Christianity happened to be singled out for particular comment on account of its religious domination of the cultural milieu in which the Enlightenment developed.

At issue here is a central theme of the Enlightenment: human autonomy. Reality is rational, and human beings have the necessary epistemological capacities to uncover this rational ordering of the world. Truth is not something which demands to be accepted on the basis of an external authority; it is to be recognized and accepted by the autonomous thinking person, on the basis of the perception of congruence between what that individual knows to be true, and the alleged "truth" which presents itself for verification. Truth is something that is discerned, not something that is imposed. For Lessing, being obligated to accept the testimony of others is tantamount to the compromising of human intellectual autonomy. There are no contemporary analogues for the resurrection. Resurrection is not an aspect of modern experience. So why trust the New Testament reports? For Lessing, the resurrection is little more than a misunderstood non-event, of no fundamental importance to the moral significance of Jesus.

David Friedrich Strauss: the resurrection as myth

In his *Life of Jesus* (1835), Strauss provided a radical new approach to the question of the resurrection of Christ. Strauss himself notes that the resurrection of Christ is of central importance to Christian faith:

The root of faith in Jesus was the conviction of his resurrection. He who had been put to death, however great during his life, could not, it was thought, be the Messiah: his miraculous restoration of life proved so much the more strongly that he *was* the Messiah. Freed by his resurrection from the kingdom of shades, and at the same time elevated above the sphere of earthly humanity, he was now translated to the heavenly regions, and had taken his place at the right hand of God.

Strauss notes that this understanding of what he terms "the Christology of the orthodox system" has come under considerable attack since the Enlightenment, not least on account of its presupposition that miracles (such as a resurrection) are impossible.

On the basis of this *a priori* assumption, which corresponds neatly to the Enlightenment worldview, Strauss declares his intention to explain "the origin of faith in the resurrection of Jesus without any corresponding miraculous fact." In other words, Strauss was concerned to explain how Christians came to believe in the resurrection, when there was no objective historical basis for this belief. Having excluded the resurrection as a "miraculous objective occurrence," Strauss located the origin of the belief at the purely subjective level. Belief in the resurrection is not to be explained as a response to "a life objectively restored," but is "a subjective conception in the mind." Faith in the resurrection of Jesus is the outcome of an exaggerated "recollection of the personality of Jesus himself," by which a memory has been projected into the idea of a living presence. A dead Jesus is thus transfigured into an imaginary risen Christ – a mythical risen Christ, to use the appropriate term.

Strauss's distinctive contribution to the debate was to introduce the category of "myth" – a reflection of the gospel writers' social conditioning and cultural outlook. To suggest that their writings were partly "mythical" was thus not so much a challenge to their integrity, but simply an acknowledgment of the premodern outlook of the period in which they were written. The gospel writers must be regarded as sharing the mythical worldview of their cultural situation. Strauss distances himself from Reimarus's suggestion that the evangelists distorted their accounts of Jesus of Nazareth, whether unconsciously or deliberately. He argues that mythical language is the natural mode of expression of a primitive group culture which had yet to rise to the level of abstract conceptualization

For Reimarus, the gospel writers were confused or liars – more likely the latter. Strauss moved the discussion away from this by his introduction of the category of "myth." The resurrection was to be viewed as a myth – not a deliberate fabrication, but an interpretation of events (especially the memory and "subjective vision" of Jesus) in terms which made sense in first-century Palestinian culture, dominated by a mythical worldview. Belief in the resurrection as an objective event must be regarded as becoming impossible with the passing of that worldview.

Strauss's *Life of Jesus*, along with other rationalizing works of the same period, such as Ernest Renan's work of the same name (1863), attracted enormous attention. The resurrection, traditionally seen as the basis of Christian faith, was now viewed as its product. Christianity is seen as relating to the memory of a dead Jesus, rather than the celebration of a risen Christ. However, the debate was far from over. In what follows, we shall consider later developments in this intriguing chapter of modern theology. Perhaps Strauss's most acute reinterpreter in the twentieth century has been Rudolf Bultmann, to whose distinctive views on the resurrection we may now turn.

Rudolf Bultmann: the resurrection as an event in the experience of the disciples

Bultmann shared Strauss's basic conviction that, in this scientific age, it is impossible to believe in miracles. As a result, belief in an objective resurrection of Jesus is no longer possible; however, it may well prove to be possible to make sense of it in another manner. History, Bultmann argued, is "a closed continuum of effects in which individual events are connected by the succession of cause and effect." The resurrection, in common with other miracles, would thus disrupt the closed system of nature. Similar points had been made by other thinkers sympathetic to the Enlightenment.

Belief in an objective resurrection of Jesus, although perfectly legitimate and intelligible in the first century, cannot be taken seriously today. "It is impossible to use electric light and radio equipment and, when ill, to claim the assistance of modern medical and clinical discoveries, and at the same time believe in the New Testament world of spirits and miracles." The human understanding of the world and of human existence has changed radically since the first century, with the result that modern humanity finds the mythological worldview of the New Testament unintelligible and unacceptable. A worldview is given to someone with the age in which they live, and they are in no position to alter it. The modern scientific and existential worldview means that that of the New Testament is now discarded and unintelligible.

> **Rudolf Bultmann (1884–1976).** A German Lutheran writer, who was appointed to a chair of theology at Marburg in 1921. He is chiefly noted for his program of "demythologization" of the New Testament, and his use of existential ideas in the exposition of the twentieth-century meaning of the gospel.

For this reason, the resurrection is to be regarded as "a mythical event, pure and simple." The resurrection is something which happened in the subjective experience of the disciples, not something which took place in the public arena of history. For Bultmann, Jesus has indeed been raised – he has been raised up into the *kerygma*. The preaching of Jesus himself has been transformed into the Christian proclamation of Christ. Jesus has become an element of Christian preaching; he has been raised up and taken up into the proclamation of the gospel:

> All speculation concerning the modes of being of the risen Jesus, all the narratives of the empty tomb and all the Easter legends, whatever elements of historical facts they may contain, and as true as they may be in their symbolic form, are of no consequence. To believe in the Christ present in the *kerygma* is the meaning of the Easter faith.

Consistent with his anti-historical approach in general, Bultmann directs attention away from the historical Jesus towards the proclamation of Christ. "Faith in the church as the bearer of the kerygma is the Easter faith which consists in the belief that Jesus Christ is present in the *kerygma*."

Karl Barth: the resurrection as an historical event beyond critical inquiry

Barth wrote a small work entitled *The Resurrection of the Dead* in 1924. However, his mature views on the relation of the resurrection to history date from considerably later, and have clearly been influenced by Bultmann. Barth's essay "Rudolf Bultmann – An Attempt to Understand Him" (1952) set out his misgivings concerning Bultmann's approach. This was followed up by a sustained engagement with the issues at stake in *Church Dogmatics* IV/1 (1953). In what follows, we shall attempt to set out Barth's position, and compare it with that of Bultmann.

> **Karl Barth (1886–1968).** Widely regarded as the most important Protestant theologian of the twentieth century. Originally inclined to support liberal Protestantism, Barth was moved to adopt a more theocentric position through his reflections on the First World War. His early emphasis on the "otherness" of God in his Romans commentary (1919) was continued and modified in his monumental *Church Dogmatics*. Barth's contribution to modern Christian theology has been immense.

In his early writings, Barth argued that the empty tomb was of minimal importance in relation to the resurrection. However, he became increasingly alarmed at Bultmann's existential approach to the resurrection, which seemed to imply that it had no objective historical foundation. For this reason, Barth comes to place considerable emphasis upon the gospel accounts of the empty tomb. The empty tomb is "an indispensable sign" which "obviates all possible misunderstanding." It demonstrates that the resurrection of Christ was not a purely inward, interior or subjective event, but something which left a mark upon history.

This would seem to suggest that Barth regards the resurrection as being open to historical investigation, to clarify its nature and confirm its place in the public history of the world, rather than in the private interior experience of the first believers. Yet this is not so. He consistently refuses to allow the gospel narratives to be subjected to critical historical scrutiny. It is not entirely clear why. The following factor appears to have weighed heavily in his thinking at this point.

Barth emphasizes that Paul and the other apostles are not calling for the "acceptance of a well-attested historical report," but are calling for "a decision of faith." Historical investigation cannot legitimize nor provide security for such faith; nor can faith become dependent upon the provisional results of historical inquiry. In any case, faith is a response to the risen Christ, not to the empty tomb. Barth was quite clear that the empty tomb, taken by itself, was of little value in laying the foundation for faith in the risen Christ. The absence of Christ from his tomb does not necessarily imply his resurrection: "he might, in fact, have been stolen, he might have only appeared to be dead."

As a result, Barth is left in what initially seems to be a highly vulnerable position. Concerned to defend the resurrection as an act in public history against Bultmann's subjectivist approach, he is not prepared to allow that history to be critically studied. In part, this rests upon his passionate belief that historical scholarship cannot lay the basis for faith; in part, it reflects his assumption that the resurrection of Christ is part of a much larger network of ideas and events, which cannot be disclosed or verified by historical inquiry. However much one may sympathize with Barth's theological concerns, it is difficult to avoid the conclusion that he lacks credibility at this point. It is perhaps for this reason that the approach of Wolfhart Pannenberg has been the subject of considerable attention.

Wolfhart Pannenberg: the resurrection as an historical event open to critical inquiry

The most distinctive feature of Pannenberg's theological programme, as it emerged during the 1960s, is the appeal to universal history. Such views are developed and justified in the 1961 volume *Revelation as History*, edited by Pannenberg, in which these ideas are explored at some length. Pannenberg's essay "Dogmatic Theses on the Doctrine of Revelation" opens with a powerful appeal to universal history:

> History is the most comprehensive horizon of Christian theology. All theological questions and answers have meaning only within the framework of the history

which God has with humanity, and through humanity with the whole creation, directed towards a future which is hidden to the world, but which has already been revealed in Jesus Christ.

These crucially important opening sentences sum up the distinctive features of Pannenberg's theological programme at this stage in his career. They immediately distinguish him from the ahistorical theology of Bultmann and his school on the one hand, and the suprahistorical approach of Martin Kähler on the other. Christian theology is based upon an analysis of universal and publicly accessible history. For Pannenberg, revelation was essentially a public and universal historical event which was recognized and interpreted as an "act of God." To his critics, this seemed to reduce faith to insight, and deny any role to the Holy Spirit in the event of revelation.

Wolfhart Pannenberg (born 1928). One of the most influential German Protestant theologians, whose writings on the relation of faith and history, and particularly the foundations of Christology, have had considerable influence.

Pannenberg's argument takes the following form. History, in all its totality, can only be understood when it is viewed from its endpoint. This point alone provides the perspective from which the historical process can be seen in its totality, and thus properly understood. However, where Marx argued that the social sciences, by predicting the goal of history to be the hegemony of socialism, provided the key to the interpretation of history, Pannenberg declared that this was provided only in Jesus Christ. The end of history is disclosed proleptically in the history of Jesus Christ. In other words, the end of history, which has yet to take place, has been disclosed in advance of the event in the person and work of Christ.

This idea of a "proleptic disclosure of the end of history" is grounded in the apocalyptic worldview, which Pannenberg argues provides the key to understanding the New Testament interpretation of the significance and function of Jesus. Whereas Bultmann chose to demythologize the apocalyptic elements of the New Testament, Pannenberg treats them as a hermeneutical grid or framework by which the life, death, and resurrection of Christ may be interpreted.

Perhaps the most distinctive, and certainly the most commented upon, aspect of this work is Pannenberg's insistence that the resurrection of Jesus is an objective historical event, witnessed by all who had access to the evidence. Whereas Bultmann treated the resurrection as an event within the experiential world of the disciples, Pannenberg declares that it belongs to the world of universal public history.

This immediately raised the question of the historicity of the resurrection. As noted earlier, a group of Enlightenment writers had argued that our only knowledge of the alleged resurrection of Jesus was contained in the New Testament. In that there were no contemporary analogues for such a resurrection, the credibility of those reports had to be seriously questioned. In a similar vein, Ernst Troeltsch had argued for the homogeneity of history; in that the resurrection of Jesus appeared to radically disrupt that homogeneity, it was to be regarded as of dubious historicity. Pannenberg initially responded to these difficulties in an essay on "redemptive event and history," and subsequently in *Jesus – God and Man*. His basic argument against this position can be set out as follows.

Ernst Troeltsch (1865–1923). A theologian and sociologist who was closely involved in the founding of the "History of Religions School," which placed an emphasis upon the historical continuity of the religions. His most important theological contributions are thought to lie in the field of Christology, especially his discussion of the relation between faith and history.

Troeltsch, in Pannenberg's view, has a pedantically narrow view of history, which rules out certain events in advance, on the basis of a set of provisional judgments which have improperly come to have the status of absolute laws. Troeltsch's unwarranted "constriction of historico-critical inquiry" was "biased" and "anthropocentric." It presupposed that the human viewpoint is the only acceptable and normative standpoint within history. Analogies, Pannenberg stresses, are always analogies *viewed from the standpoint of the human observer*; that standpoint is radically restricted in its scope, and cannot be allowed to function as the absolutely certain basis of critical inquiry. Pannenberg is too good a historian to suggest that the principle of analogy should be abandoned; it is, after all, a proven and useful tool of historical research. Yet, Pannenberg insists, that is all that it is: it is a working tool, and cannot be allowed to define a fixed view of reality.

If the historian sets out to investigate the New Testament already precommitted to the belief "dead people do not rise again," that conclusion will merely be read back into the New Testament material. The judgment "Jesus did not rise from the dead" will be the presupposition, not the conclusion, of such an investigation. Pannenberg's discussion of this question represents an impassioned and impressive plea for a neutral approach to the resurrection. The historical evidence pointing to the resurrection of Jesus must be investigated without the prior dogmatic presupposition that such a resurrection could not have happened.

Having argued for the historicity of the resurrection, Pannenberg turns to deal with its interpretation within the context of the apocalyptic framework of meaning. The end of history has proleptically taken place in the resurrection of Jesus from the dead. This maxim dominates Pannenberg's interpretation of the event. The resurrection of Jesus anticipates the general resurrection at the end of time, and brings forward into history both that resurrection and the full and final revelation of God. The resurrection of Jesus is thus organically linked with the self-revelation of God in Christ, and establishes Jesus' identity with God, and allows this identity with God to be read back into his pre-Easter ministry. It thus functions as the foundation of a series of central Christological affirmations, including the divinity of Christ (however this is expressed) and the incarnation.

It will be clear that the doctrine of the resurrection of Jesus of Nazareth has been the subject of considerable discussion within the last two centuries. A matter which has been the subject of renewed interest in the twentieth century has been the doctrine of the Trinity, to which we now turn.

Case Study 4.4   The Trinity in Twentieth-century Thought

It is widely agreed that the doctrine of the Trinity was marginalized in nineteenth-century thought. The reasons for this are complex. One factor which is certainly significant is the influence of rationalism, which tended to regard the doctrine of the Trinity as absurd. This view can certainly be found in the writings of Thomas Jefferson, third president of the United States, who regarded the Trinity as an irrational obstacle to proper Christian devotion:

> When we shall have done away with the incomprehensible jargon of the Trinitarian arithmetic, that there are one, and one is three; when we shall have knocked down the artificial scaffolding, reared to mask from view the very simple structure of Jesus; when, in short, we shall have unlearned everything which has been taught since his day, and got back to the pure and simple doctrines he inculcated, we shall then be truly and worthily his disciples.

The German liberal theologian F. D. E. Schleiermacher placed his discussion of the doctrine of the Trinity right at the end of his *Christian Faith*, thus suggesting that he regarded the doctrine as some kind of appendix to Christian theology. In fact, however, Schleiermacher argued that the doctrine of the Trinity brought together a number of critical insights concerning the identity of Jesus and the nature of the Christian faith, without which it would lose its identity. The doctrine acted as a "coping-stone," a final stone added to a complex structure which ensures that all its component parts are secured in their proper places.

4.4.1   F. D. E. Schleiermacher on the Trinity

An essential element of our exposition in this Part has been the doctrine of the union of the Divine Essence with human nature, both in the personality of Christ and in the common Spirit of the Church; therewith the whole view of Christianity set forth in our Church teaching stands and falls. For unless the being of God in
5   Christ is assumed, the idea of redemption could not be thus concentrated in His Person. And unless there were such a union also in the common Spirit of the Church, the Church could not thus be the Bearer and Perpetuator of the redemption through Christ. Now these exactly are the essential elements in the doctrine of the Trinity, which, it is clear, only established itself in defense of the
10   position that in Christ there was present nothing less than the Divine Essence, which also indwells the Christian Church as its common Spirit, and that we take these expressions in no reduced or sheerly artificial sense, and know nothing of any special higher essences, subordinate deities (as it were) present in Christ and the Holy Spirit. The doctrine of the Trinity has no origin but this; and at first it had
15   no other aim than to equate as definitely as possible the Divine Essence considered as thus united to human nature with the Divine Essence in itself. . . . In virtue of this connexion, we rightly regard the doctrine of the Trinity, in so far as it is a deposit of these elements, as the coping-stone of Christian doctrine (*als den Schlußstein der christlichen Lehre*), and thus equating with each other of the divine
20   in each of these two unions, as also of both with the Divine Essence in itself, as what is essential in the doctrine of the Trinity.

However, there has been a remarkable revival of interest in the doctrine of the Trinity in twentieth-century Christian theology. It is generally thought that this trinitarian renaissance is primarily due to the foundational work of Karl Barth. In what follows, we shall explore three major contributions to the modern discussion of the Trinity, reflecting a Reformed (Karl Barth), Roman Catholic (Karl Rahner), and Lutheran (Robert Jenson) perspective.

Karl Barth

Barth sets the doctrine of the Trinity at the opening of his *Church Dogmatics*. This simple observation is important, for he totally inverts the position in which it was placed by his rival, Schleiermacher. For Schleiermacher, as we have seen, the Trinity is perhaps the last word which can be said about God; for Barth, it is the word which must be spoken before revelation is even a possibility. It is thus placed at the opening of the *Church Dogmatics*, because its subject matter makes that dogmatics possible in the first place. The doctrine of the Trinity undergirds and guarantees the actuality of divine revelation to sinful humanity. It is an "explanatory confirmation," as Barth puts it, of revelation. It is an exegesis of the fact of revelation.

> **Karl Barth (1886–1968).** Widely regarded as the most important Protestant theologian of the twentieth century. Originally inclined to support liberal Protestantism, Barth was moved to adopt a more theocentric position through his reflections on the First World War. His early emphasis on the "otherness" of God in his Romans commentary (1919) was continued and modified in his monumental *Church Dogmatics*. Barth's contribution to modern Christian theology has been immense.

"*God* reveals himself. He reveals himself *through himself*. He reveals *himself*." With these words (which I have found to be impossible to translate into inclusive language), Barth sets up the revelational framework which leads to the formulation of the doctrine of the Trinity. *Deus dixit!* God has spoken in revelation – and it is the task of theology to inquire into what this revelation presupposes and implies. For Barth, theology is *Nach-Denken*, a process of "thinking afterwards" about what is contained in God's self-revelation. We have to "inquire carefully into the relation between our knowing of God, and God himself in his being and nature." With such statements, Barth sets up the context of the doctrine of the Trinity: given that God's self-revelation has taken place, what must be true of God if this can have happened? What does the actuality of revelation have to tell us about the being of God? Barth's starting point for his discussion of the Trinity is not a doctrine or an idea, but the actuality of God's speaking and God's being heard. For how can God be heard, when sinful humanity is incapable of hearing him?

The above paragraph is simply a paraphrase of sections of the first half-volume of Barth's *Church Dogmatics*, entitled "The Doctrine of the Word of God," punctuated by occasional quotations. There is an enormous amount being said in this, and it requires unpacking. Two themes need to be carefully noted.

1   Sinful humanity is fundamentally incapable of hearing the Word of God.
2   Nevertheless, sinful humanity has heard the Word of God, in that this word makes its sinfulness known to it.

The very fact that revelation takes place thus requires explanation. For Barth, this implies that humanity is passive in the process of reception; the process of revelation is, from its beginning to its end, subject to the sovereignty of God as Lord. For revelation to be revelation, God must be capable of revelation (which Barth clearly understands as "self-disclosure") to sinful humanity, despite its sinfulness.

Once this paradox has been appreciated, the general structure of Barth's doctrine of the Trinity can be followed. In revelation, Barth argues, God must be in himself what he shows himself to be. There must be a direct correspondence between the Revealer and the Revelation. If "God reveals himself as Lord" (a characteristically Barthian assertion), then he must be Lord "antecedently in himself." Revelation is the reiteration in time of what God is in himself in eternity. There is thus a direct correspondence between:

1 The revealing God
2 The self-revelation of God.

To put this in the language of Trinitarian theology, the Father is revealed in the Son.

So what about the Spirit? Here we come to what is perhaps the most difficult aspect of Barth's doctrine of the Trinity: the idea of "revealedness (*Offenbarsein*)." To explore this, we will have to use an illustration, not used by Barth himself. Imagine two individuals, walking outside Jerusalem on a spring day around the year AD 30. They see three men being crucified, and pause to watch. The first points to the central figure, and says "There is a common criminal being executed." The second, pointing to the same man, replies, "There is the Son of God dying for me." To say that Jesus *is* the self-revelation of God will not do in itself; there must be some means by which Jesus is *recognized* as the self-revelation of God. And it is this recognition of revelation as revelation that constitutes the idea of *Offenbarsein*.

So how is this insight achieved? Barth is quite clear: sinful humanity is not capable of reaching this insight unaided. Barth is not prepared to allow humanity any positive role in the interpretation of revelation, believing that this is to subject divine revelation to human theories of knowledge. Barth has been heavily criticized for this, even by those, such as Emil Brunner, who might otherwise be sympathetic to his aims. The interpretation of revelation as revelation must itself be the work of God – more accurately, the work of the Spirit. Humanity does not become capable of the word of the Lord (*capax verbi domini*), and then hear the word; hearing and capacity to hear are given in the one act by the Spirit.

All this might seem to suggest that Barth is really some kind of modalist, treating the different moments of revelation as different "modes of being" of the same God. It must be conceded immediately that there are those who charge him with precisely this deficiency. Nevertheless, more considered reflection perhaps moves us away from this judgment, although other criticisms can certainly be made. For example, the Spirit fares rather badly in Barth's exposition, which in this respect can be argued to mirror weaknesses in the western tradition as a whole. However, whatever its weaknesses may be, Barth's discussion of the Trinity is generally regarded as having reinstated the doctrine after a period of sustained neglect within dogmatic theology. That process of reinstatement has been further consolidated through the work of the Jesuit theologian Karl Rahner, to which we now turn.

Karl Rahner

Rahner's particular contribution to the development of modern Trinitarian theology is generally agreed to be his analysis of the relation between the "economic" and the "immanent" Trinity. The basic distinction here is between the manner in which God is known through revelation in history ("the economic Trinity"), and the manner in which God exists internally ("the immanent Trinity"). The "economic Trinity" can be thought of as the way in which we experience God's self-disclosure in history, and the "immanent Trinity" as God's diversity and unity as it is within the godhead itself. Rahner's axiom concerning their relationship, which is widely quoted in modern theology, takes the following form: "The economic Trinity is the immanent Trinity, and the immanent Trinity is the economic Trinity." In other words, the way God is revealed and experienced in history corresponds to the way in which God actually is.

Karl Rahner (1904–84). One of the most influential of modern Roman Catholic theologians, whose *Theological Investigations* pioneered the use of the essay as a tool of theological construction and exploration.

Rahner's approach to the Trinity is a powerful corrective to certain tendencies in older Roman Catholic Trinitarian theology, especially the tendency to focus on the "immanent Trinity" in such a way as to marginalize both human experience of God and the biblical witness to salvation. For Rahner, the "economic" Trinity relates to the "biblical statements concerning the economy of salvation and its threefold structure." Ranher's axiom allows him to affirm that the entire work of salvation is the work of one divine person. Despite the complexity of the mystery of salvation, a single divine person can be discerned as its source, origin, and goal. Behind the diversity of the process of salvation there is to be discerned only one God. This fundamental principle of the unity of the economy of salvation can be traced back to Irenaeus, especially in his polemic against the Gnostics (see pp. 40–2), who argued that two divine beings could be distinguished within the economy of salvation.

Rahner therefore insists that the proper starting point of Trinitarian discussion is our experience of salvation history, and its biblical expression. The "mystery of salvation" happens first; then we move on to formulate doctrines concerning it. This "previous knowledge of the economic Trinity, derived from salvation history and the Bible" is the starting point for the process of systematic reflection.

The "immanent Trinity" can therefore be thought of as a "systematic conception of the economic Trinity." Ranher therefore argues that the process of theological reflection which leads to the doctrine of the immanent Trinity has its starting point in our experience and knowledge of salvation in history. The complexity of that salvation history is ultimately grounded in the divine nature itself. In other words, although we experience diversity and unity within the economy of salvation, that diversity and unity correspond to the way God actually is. Rahner expresses this point as follows:

> The differentiation of the self-communication of God in history (of truth) and spirit (of love) must belong to God "in himself," or otherwise this difference, which undoubtedly exists, would do away with God's *self*-communication. For these modalities and their differentiation either are in God himself (although we first experience them from our point of view) or they exist only in us.

In other words, "Father," "Son," and "Holy Spirit" are not simply human ways of making sense of the diversity of our experience of the mystery of salvation. Nor are they roles which God somehow temporarily assumes for the purpose of entering into our history. Rather, they correspond to the way God actually is. The same God who *appears* as a Trinity *is* a Trinity. The way in which God is known in self-revelation corresponds to the way God is internally.

Robert Jenson

Writing from a Lutheran perspective, but deeply versed in the Reformed tradition, the contemporary American theologian Robert Jenson has provided a fresh and creative restatement of the traditional doctrine of the Trinity. In many ways, it is appropriate to regard Jenson as providing a development of Barth's position, with its characteristic emphasis upon the need to remain faithful to God's self-revelation. *The Triune Identity: God According to the Gospel* (1982) provides a fundamental reference point for discussion of the doctrine in a period which has seen fresh interest develop in this hitherto neglected area.

Jenson argues that "Father, Son, and Holy Spirit" is the proper name for the God who Christians know in and through Jesus Christ. It is imperative, he argues, that God should have a proper name. "Trinitarian discourse is Christianity's effort to identify the God who has claimed us. The doctrine of the Trinity comprises both a proper name, 'Father, Son, and Holy Spirit' . . . and an elaborate development and analysis of corresponding identifying descriptions." Jenson points out that ancient Israel was set in a polytheistic context, in which the term "god" conveyed relatively little information. It was necessary to name the god in question. A similar situation was confronted by the writers of the New Testament, who were obliged to identify the god at the heart of their faith, and distinguish this god from the many other gods worshiped and acknowledged in the region, especially in Asia Minor.

The doctrine of the Trinity thus identifies and names the Christian God – but identifies and names this God in a manner consistent with the biblical witness. It is not a name which we have chosen; it is a name which has been chosen for us, and which we are authorized to use. In this way, Jenson defends the priority of God's self-revelation against human constructions of concepts of divinity. "The gospel identifies its God thus: God is the one who raised Israel's Jesus from the dead. The whole task of theology can be described as the unpacking of this sentence in various ways. One of these produces the church's trinitarian language and thought."

Scholars of patristic thought have noted the way in which the early church tended to accidentally confuse distinctively Christian ideas about God with those deriving from the Hellenistic context into which it expanded. The doctrine of the Trinity, Jenson affirms, is and was a necessary defense mechanism against such developments. It allows the church to discover the distinctiveness of its creed, and avoid becoming absorbed by rival conceptions of divinity.

However, the church could not ignore its intellectual context. If on the one hand, its task was to defend the Christian notion of God against rival conceptions of divinity, another of its tasks was to provide "a metaphysical analysis of the gospel's triune identification of God." In other words, it was obliged to use the philosophical categories of its day to explain precisely what Christians believed about their God, and how this distinguished them from alternatives. Paradoxically, the attempt to distinguish Christianity from Hellenism led to the introduction of Hellenistic categories into Trinitarian discourse.

The doctrine of the Trinity thus centers on the recognition that God is named by Scripture, and within the witness of the church. Within the Hebraic tradition, God is identified by historical events. Jenson notes how many Old Testament texts identify God with reference to his acts in history – such as the liberation of Israel from its captivity in Egypt. The same pattern is evident in the New Testament: God is recognized to be identified with reference to historical events, and supremely the resurrection of Jesus Christ. God comes to be identified in relation to Jesus Christ. Who is God? Which god are we talking about? The God who raised Christ from the dead. As Jenson puts it, "the emergence of a semantic pattern in which the uses of 'God' and 'Jesus Christ' are mutually determining" is of fundamental importance within the New Testament.

Jenson thus recovers a personal conception of God from metaphysical speculation. "Father, Son, and Holy Spirit" is a proper name, which we are asked to use in naming and addressing God. "Linguistic means of identification – proper names, identifying descriptions, or both – are a necessity of religion. Prayers, like other requests and praises, must be addressed." The Trinity is thus an instrument of theological precision, which forces us to be precise about the God under discussion.

311

Case Study 4.5   Twentieth-century Discussions of the Doctrine of the Church

The twentieth century has seen renewed interest in the area of ecclesiology, partly on account of the rise of the ecumenical movement (concerned with the promotion of Christian unity), and partly through the enormous stimulus given to this area of theology through the process of renewal and reform initiated by the Second Vatican Council (1962–5), especially the constitution *Lumen Gentium* ("A Light to the Gentiles" – note that authoritative Roman Catholic conciliar and papal statements are generally referred to by their opening words in Latin).

Variations on a Theme: "Wherever Christ is, there is also the Catholic Church"

The first-century writer Ignatius of Antioch declared that "wherever Christ is, there is also the Catholic Church." This memorable aphorism has had a deep impact on ecclesiological reflection – whether Protestant, Catholic, or Orthodox – throughout Christian history. In what follows, we shall explore three different twentieth-century ways of approaching this aphorism.

1 Christ is present sacramentally

One of the most distinctive contributions of the Second Vatican Council to the development of ecclesiology is its assertion of the sacramental character of the church. As *Lumen Gentium* puts it, "the church, in Christ, is a kind of sacrament – a sign and instrument, that is, of communion with God and of unity among all human beings." The Council did not suggest that the church *is* a sacrament; the traditional sevenfold understanding of the sacraments (see pp. 139–43) is retained. Rather, the church is "like a sacrament (*veluti sacramentum*)." In making this statement, the Council seems to have been attempting to bring together the idea of the church as constituted by the word of God on the one hand, and as being a visible entity on the other. This idea is certainly present in Augustine's concept of sacraments as "visible words."

The idea of the church as sacrament has had a major impact on Catholic ecclesiology in the twentieth century. Even before the Council, such ideas were gaining momentum within the church. In part, this reflects the rise of a "theology of retrieval," which sought to reappropriate a series of seminal themes from earlier periods in Christian history, most notably the patristic period, which adopted understandings of the nature of the church that contrasted sharply with the more institutional conceptions which had gained the ascendancy since the sixteenth century.

312

The idea can be seen clearly in the writings of Henri de Lubac, a pre-Vatican II theologian noted for his magisterial grasp of the patristic heritage. In his *Catholicism*, he writes:

> If Christ is the sacrament of God, the church is for us the sacrament of Christ; she represents him, in the full and ancient sense of the term, she really makes him present. She not only carries on his work, but she is his very continuation, in a sense far more real than in which it can be said that any human institution is its founder's continuation.

Although retaining an institutional understanding of the church, de Lubac gave a new sense of identity and purpose to Catholic conceptions of the church: the church is there to make Jesus Christ present to the world. Ignatius' aphorism is therefore given new significance through this sacramental understanding of the role of the church.

In 1953, Otto Semmelroth published a highly influential study entitled *The Church as Primordial Sacrament*, in which he argues for the church as being the "primordial sacrament (*Ursakrament*)," demonstrating God's ability to use the material order to bear witness to the spiritual. The Dominican theologian Edward Schillebeeckx developed related ideas in his *Christ: The Sacrament of the Encounter with God*. The overall effect of this approach is to integrate the fields of Christology, ecclesiology, and sacramentology into a coherent whole. Hans Urs von Balthasar adopts a strongly incarnational approach to his understanding of the church, arguing that the church is the *elongetur Christi* – the prolongation of Christ in time and space. The Jesuit writer Karl Rahner continues this sacramental understanding of the church, declaring that the church is there to make Christ present in the world, in an historical, visible and embodied form.

Rahner's approach has attracted considerable interest. For Rahner, the church "is the continuance, the contemporary presence of that real, eschatologically triumphant and irrevocably established presence in Christ in the world of God's saving will." The church is thus a "concrete manifestation of God's salvation of humanity," the enduring presence of God in the world (an idea anticipated in the sixteenth century in the writings of the Spanish mystic Teresa of Avila). And, on account of its real historical presence in the world, it follows that it requires structures. For this reason, Rahner is able to justify a continuing institutional element in any Catholic understanding of the nature of the church, while at the same time insisting that these particular structures are not necessarily of *defining* importance. Furthermore, Rahner is prepared to concede a degree of flexibility in relation to those structures. What may have been appropriate to the definite historical circumstances of the past may not be appropriate today. The church must be free to achieve its sacramental mission in new historical structures.

Schillebeeckx differs from Rahner at some points of importance, most notably

313

in his rejection of Rahner's argument that the church is the "primal sacrament" (an idea, as we noted above, which can be traced back to Otto Semmelroth). For Schillebeeckx, Christ must be regarded as that primal sacrament; whatever sacramental character the church possesses must be understood to arise through its relation with Christ.

Protestant critics of this approach have expressed anxiety about the relative lack of biblical foundation for the approach, and its relative lack of place for a theology of preaching. In view of the importance of this point, we may move on to consider more Protestant interpretations of Ignatius' axiom, which focus on the presence of Christ resulting from the preaching of the word of God.

2 Christ is present through the Word

A central theme of Protestant understandings of the nature of the church focuses on the presence of Christ resulting from the proclamation of his word, in preaching and the sacraments. For example, consider Calvin's statement on the nature of the church:

> Wherever we see the Word of God purely preached and listened to, and the sacraments administered according to Christ's institution, it is in no way to be doubted that a church of God exists. For his promise cannot fail: "Wherever two or three are gathered in my name, there I am in the midst of them" (Matthew 18: 20). . . . If the ministry has the Word and honors it, if it has the administration of the sacraments, it deserves without doubt to be held and considered a church.

For Calvin, the preaching of the word and right administration of the sacrament are linked with the presence of Christ – and wherever Christ is, there his church is to be found as well.

This kerygmatic (Greek *kerygma*: "herald") theme has continued to be of major importance in the twentieth century, particularly in the writings of Karl Barth. For Barth, the church is the community which comes into being in response to the proclamation of the word of God. The church is seen as a kerygmatic community which proclaims the good news of what God has done for humanity in Christ, and which comes into being wherever the word of God is faithfully proclaimed and accepted. As Barth put it in his 1948 address to the World Council of Churches, the church consists of "the gathering together (*congregatio*) of those men and women (*fidelium*) whom the living Lord Jesus Christ chooses and calls to be witnesses of the victory he has already won, and heralds of its future manifestation." Barth's ecclesiology is thoroughly Trinitarian at this point, involving Father, Son, and Spirit in a dynamic understanding of the nature of the church. For Barth, the church is not an extension of Christ, but is united with Christ, and called and commissioned by him to serve the world, Christ is present within his church, through the Holy Spirit.

The role of the Holy Spirit is particularly important. Although it would not be correct to say that Barth has a "charismatic" understanding of the church, his Christological approach to the identity of the church allocates a definite and distinctive role to the Holy Spirit, which Barth summarized as follows in his *Dogmatics in Outline*:

> *Credo ecclesiam* ["I believe in the church"] means that I believe that here, at this place, in this assembly, the work of the Holy Spirit takes place. By that is not intended a deification of the creature; the church is not the object of faith, we do not believe *in* the church; but we do believe that in this congregation the work of the Holy Spirit becomes an event.

The church is thus seen as an event, rather than as an institution. Barth does not identify the Holy Spirit with the church, nor limit the operation of the Spirit to the bounds of the institution of the church. He argues that the Spirit empowers and renews the church, unites it with Christ's redemptive work on the cross, and is the means by which the risen Christ is made present to the people of God. In this way, the Spirit safeguards the church from lapsing into purely secular ways of understanding its identity and mission.

Rudolf Bultmann also adopts a strongly kerygmatic approach to the nature of the church, linking Barth's emphasis on the foundational role of "proclamation" with the notion of "church as event":

> The word of God and the church are inseparable. The church is constituted by the word of God as the congregation of the elect, and the word of God is not a statement of abstract truths, but a proclamation which is duly authorized and therefore needs bearers with proper credentials (2 Corinthians 5: 18–19). Just as the word of God becomes his word only in event, so the church is really the church only when it too becomes an event.

3 Christ is present through the Spirit

A third major theme in twentieth-century ecclesiology has focused on the role of the Holy Spirit as constitutive of the church. Here, Ignatius' aphorism is interpreted in such a way as to emphasize the necessity of the Spirit in actualizing the presence of Christ. We have already seen the importance of this point in relation to Barth's ecclesiology; however, it is present in more developed forms in writers such as the liberation theologian, Leonardo Boff, and the Orthodox theologian, John Zizioulas. These two writers interpret their pneumatological (Greek: *pneuma* = "spirit") understanding of the church in a different way. Boff remains Christ-centered, despite his emphasis on the Spirit, on account of his strongly western understanding of the Trinity; Zizioulas develops a much more

Orthodox approach, based on a Cappadocian understanding of the role of the Spirit within the godhead.

For Leonardo Boff, the constitutive role of the Holy Spirit in an understanding of the church rests on the fact that it is the Spirit of Jesus Christ. Whereas writers such as Rahner and von Balthasar had defended the view that the church was the physical embodiment or "re-presentation" of Christ in the world, Boff defends the view that the church is primarily the spiritual body of Christ, and is therefore not confined to any specific existing structures. In this respect, Boff can be seen as mounting a criticism of institutionalized understandings of the church, particularly those that flourished before the Second Vatican Council.

In his *Ecclesiogenesis: The Base Communities Reinvent the Church*, Boff provides a definition of the church which shows some parallels with kerygmatic understandings of the church:

> The church comes into being as church when people become aware of the call to salvation in Jesus Christ, come together in community, profess the same faith, celebrate the same eschatological liberation, and seek to live the discipleship of Jesus Christ. We can speak of church *in the proper sense* only when there is question of this ecclesial consciousness.

For Boff, this "ecclesial consciousness" is the result of the work of the Holy Spirit, whose person and work is inseparable from the risen Christ. Boff interprets the creedal doctrine of the procession of the Holy Spirit from the Father *and the Son* as an affirmation of this point.

In the case of Zizioulas, however, the Holy Spirit is allocated a quite distinct role. Zizioulas points out how, especially in 1 Corinthians 12, Paul appears to allocate a constitutive role within the church to the Holy Spirit. Pneumatology is therefore not about "the well-being of the church . . . it is the very essence of the church." Zizioulas' distinctive approach could be summarized as follows: the church may have been *instituted by Jesus Christ*, but it is *constituted by the Holy Spirit*.

Vatican II on the Church

The Second Vatican Council introduced a new vitality into the discussion of the doctrine of the church, partly through its reappropriation of biblical imagery relating to the church. Prior to the Council, Roman Catholic writers tended to think of the church in terms of a "perfect society." This style of imagery dates from the later part of the sixteenth century, and emphasized the institutional credentials of the church, especially in the light of the increasing power of European nation-states. Part of the church's strategy for asserting its independence from the increasing power of the state was to affirm its own identity as a society. Thus Roberto Bellarmine, one of the most important writers of the

Catholic Reformation, argued that the church was as visible and tangible a social reality as "the kingdom of France or the republic of Venice." Thus the standard edition of the pre-conciliar textbook of Adolphe Tanquerey (1854–1932) spends some 64 pages demonstrating that the church is (a) an infallible society, (b) a perfect society, (c) a hierarchical society, and (d) a monarchic society.

Inevitably, this approach to ecclesiology led to the church being defined primarily in terms of its visible aspects, and particularly its visible structures of government and its codes of belief and conduct. The church was, in effect, modeled on social institutions of the late sixteenth century. There has always been an institutional aspect to Christian doctrines of the church, whether Protestant or Catholic. Thus both Luther and Calvin stressed the importance of proper church government. But neither of these reformers regarded the institutional element as being of defining importance. The critical thing was the gospel, not the institution. Similar insights are generally typical of patristic and medieval authors until the fourteenth century. At this point, increasing papal political power and a growing determination to fend off attacks on the institutions of the church (particularly the papacy and hierarchy) led to a growing tendency to defend these institutions by making them integral to a proper understanding of the church.

This tendency is generally thought to have reached its zenith during the nineteenth century. Responding to an increasingly dangerous political situation in Europe, where secularism and anti-Catholicism appeared to be on the increase, the First Vatican Council defined the church in strongly institutionalist terms, insisting that the church has all the marks of a true society. Christ did not leave this society undefined or without a fixed form; rather, he himself gave it existence, determined the form of its existence, and gave it its constitution. This strongly hierarchical conception of the church is perhaps seen most clearly in the rigid distinction between "the pastors and the flock," grounded in the belief that the church of Christ is not a community of equals in which all the faithful have the same rights, but is rather a society of unequals, not only because among the faithful some are clergy and some are laity, but because there is in the church the power from God by which it is given to some to sanctify, teach, and govern, and to others it is not. This point was often expressed in terms of the distinction between *ecclesia docens* ("the teaching church," referring to the hierarchy) and *ecclesia discens* ("the learning church," referring to the laity, whose responsibilities were primarily to obey their superiors).

Yet by the middle of the twentieth century, Catholic scholars and theologians were increasingly expressing misgivings concerning this model. In part, this reflects an awareness of the growing evidence which suggested that the early church did not have a coherent monolithic structure, but had at least a degree of flexibility over its institutions and orders. The emergence of a strongly organized and institutional church increasingly came to be seen as dating from after the apostolic period, and being a response partly to political pressures, such as those resulting from the imperial recognition of Christianity under Constantine. Lucien Cerfaux and others paved the way for a recovery of biblical and patristic insights which had been overlooked on account of the trend towards institutionalization. Others, such as Yves Congar, worked for the recovery of a theology of the laity, concerned over their marginalization in institutional models of the church. The result was that Vatican II was in a position to revitalize Roman Catholic thinking on this vital area of theology, with all its implications for ecumenism and evangelism. The results may be seen in the document *Lumen Gentium* ("A Light to the Gentiles").

We have already explored the Council's teaching on "the church as sacrament" (p. 312), and the manner in which it has been developed by theologians such as Karl Rahner. In what follows, we shall explore three further aspects of the teaching of the Council on the nature of the church.

1 The church as communion

In 1943, the German Catholic writer Ludwig von Hertling published a study entitled *Communio: Church and Papacy in Early Christianity*, which dealt with the importance of the theme of "communion" (often referred to by the Greek term *koinonia*) for a proper understanding of the nature of the church. This work had a deep influence on the Council's reflections, and its distinctive themes can be found in the final statement on the church. On account of the overtones which the term "communion" now possesses, it is perhaps useful to employ the older English word "fellowship" to bring out the point at issue. The basic biblical theme which is expressed by this term is that of sharing in a common life, whether this life is thought of as the life of the Trinity itself, or the common life of believers within the church. The term possesses both vertical and horizontal aspects, the former referring to the relation between the believer and God, and the latter to the relationship between individual believers.

The recovery of this biblical idea proved to be a powerful corrective to the purely institutional conceptions of the church which had gained the ascendancy during the nineteenth century. The regulatory enforcement of fellowship was now seen to be one aspect of the more fundamental idea of the fellowship between the believer and God, established through the death and resurrection of Christ, and lived out in the life of the church.

2 The church as the people of God

Of the various models of the church set forth by Vatican II, the most important is that of the church as the "people of God." This is a strongly biblical idea, with deep roots in both Old and New Testaments. Vatican II is careful to avoid the direct identification of "the people of God" with "the Roman Catholic church," or the suggestion that the church has somehow displaced Israel as the people of God. Indeed, the second chapter of the Council's text on the inner life of the church describes the church as the "new people of God," continuous with Israel. The election of the church as the people of God does not entail the rejection of Israel, but rather the extension of God's kingdom. This point is made particularly clearly in the Council's Declaration on Non-Christian Religions, which recognizes a special continuing place for Jews in God's purposes of salvation:

> The Church of Christ acknowledges that in God's plan of salvation the beginning of her faith and election is to be found in the patriarchs, Moses and the prophets. She professes that all Christ's faithful, who as men of faith are sons of Abraham (cf. Galatians 3: 7), are included in the same patriarch's call and that the salvation of the Church is mystically prefigured in the exodus of God's chosen people from the land of bondage. On this account the Church cannot forget that she received the revelation of the Old Testament by way of that people with whom God in his inexpressible mercy established the ancient covenant. Nor can she forget that she draws nourishment from that good olive tree onto which the wild olive branches of the Gentiles have been grafted (cf. Romans 11: 17–24). The Church believes that Christ who is our peace has through his cross reconciled Jews and Gentiles and made them one in himself (cf. Ephesians 2: 14–16).

3 The church as a charismatic community

The Second Vatican Council took place at the time during which there was widespread interest in the charismatic movement (see pp. 252–3). The impact of this development was felt strongly within some quarters of the Catholic church. It led to the Belgian Cardinal Leo-Josef Suenens delivering a powerful appeal to the Council to include reference to this development in its reflections on the nature of the church. *Lumen Gentium* responded by explicitly recognizing the importance of charismatic gifts within the life of the church. The Council used the term "charism" (Greek: *charisma* = gift) to refer to such gifts or abilities bestowed upon individuals to fulfill some specific service. This term has a long history of use, and does not necessarily imply the kind of "spiritual gifts" (such as speaking in tongues or the gift of healing) specifically associated with the charismatic movement. Nevertheless, the Pauline use of the Greek term *charisma* clearly includes such gifts, suggesting that the Council was allowing a significant degree of openness to this increasingly important aspect of the twentieth-century Christian experience.

Case Study 4.6   The Attributes of God in Process Theology

It is widely agreed that process theology is one of the most significant theological movements to emerge from North America during the twentieth century. The origins of process thought are generally agreed to lie in the writings of the Anglo-American philosopher Alfred North Whitehead (1861–1947), especially his *Process and Reality* (1929). Reacting against the rather static view of the world associated with traditional metaphysics (expressed in ideas such as "substance" and "essence"), Whitehead conceived reality as a process. The world, as an organic whole, is something dynamic, not static; something which *happens*. Reality is made up of building blocks of "actual entities" or "actual occasions," and is thus characterized by becoming, change, and event.

All these "entities" or "occasions" (to use Whitehead's original terms) possess a degree of freedom to develop, and to be influenced by their surroundings. It is perhaps at this point that the influence of biological evolutionary theories can be discerned: like the later writer Pierre Teilhard de Chardin, Whitehead is concerned to allow for development within creation, subject to some overall direction and guidance. This process of development is thus set against a permanent background of order, which is seen as an organizing principle essential to growth. Whitehead argues that God may be identified with this background of order within the process. Whitehead treats God as an "entity," but distinguishes God from other entities on the grounds of imperishability. Other entities exist for a finite period; God exists permanently. Each entity thus receives influence (Whitehead uses the term "prehend" to describe this act of appropriating experience) from two main sources: previous entities and God.

Causation is thus not a matter of an entity being coerced to act in a given manner: it is a matter of *influence* and *persuasion*. Entities influence each other in a "dipolar" manner – mentally and physically. Precisely the same is true of limits of the process itself. God "keeps the rules" of the process. Just as God influences other entities, so God is also influenced by them. God, to use Whitehead's famous phrase, is "a fellow-sufferer who understands." God is thus affected and influenced by the world.

Process thought thus redefines God's omnipotence in terms of persuasion or influence within the overall world-process. This is an important development, as it explains the attraction of this way of understanding God's relation to the world in relation to the problem of evil. Where the traditional free will defense of moral evil argues that human beings are free to disobey or ignore God, process theology argues that the individual components of the world are likewise free to ignore divine attempts to influence or persuade them. They are not bound to respond to God. God is thus absolved of responsibility for both moral and natural evil.

The traditional free will defense of God in the face of evil is persuasive (although the extent of that persuasion is contested) in the case of moral evil –

Table 4.1   A Comparison of Classical and Process Theologies

The classical view (e.g., Aquinas)	Charles Hartshorne
Creation takes place *ex nihilo* by a free act of will. There is no necessary reason for anything other than God existing. Creation depends on God's decision to create; God could have decided not to create anything.	Both God and the creation exist necessarily. The world does not depend on any action of God for its existence, although the fine details of the nature of its existence are a matter of contingency.
God has the power to do anything that God wills to do, provided that a logical contradiction is not involved (e.g., God cannot create a square triangle).	God is one agent among many within the world, and has as much power as any such agent. This power is not absolute, but is limited.
God is incorporeal, and is radically distinct from the created order.	The world is to be seen as the body of God.
God stands outside time, and is not involved in the temporal order. It is therefore inappropriate to think of God "changing" or being affected by any involvement in or experience of the world.	God is involved in the temporal order. God is continually achieving richer syntheses of experience through this involvement.
God exists in a state of absolute perfection, and cannot be conceived to exist in a state of higher perfection.	At any point in time, God is more perfect than any other agent in the world. However, God is capable of achieving higher levels of perfection at a later stage of development on account of God's involvement in the world.

in other words, evil resulting from human decisions and actions. But what of natural evil? What of earthquakes, famines, and other natural disasters? Process thought argues that God cannot force nature to obey the divine will or purpose for it. God can only attempt to influence the process from within, by persuasion and attraction. Each entity enjoys a degree of freedom and creativity, which God cannot override.

While this understanding of the persuasive nature of God's activity has obvious merits, not least in the way in which it offers a response to the problem of evil (as God is not in control, God cannot be blamed for the way things have turned out), critics of process thought have suggested that too high a price is paid. The traditional idea of the transcendence of God appears to have been abandoned, or radically reinterpreted in terms of the primacy and permanency of God as an entity within the process. In other words, the divine transcendence is understood to mean little more than that God outlives and surpasses other entities.

Whitehead's basic ideas have been developed by a number of writers, most notably Charles Hartshorne (1897–), Schubert Ogden (1928–) and John B. Cobb (1925–). Hartshorne modified Whitehead's notion of God in a number of directions, perhaps most significantly by suggesting that the God of process thought should be thought of more as a person than an entity. This allows him to meet one of the more significant criticisms of process thought: that it compromises the idea of divine perfection. If God is perfect, how can he change? Is not change tantamount to an admission of imperfection? Hartshorne redefines perfection in terms of a receptivity to change which does not compromise God's superiority. In other words, God's ability to be influenced by other entities does not mean that God is reduced to their level. God surpasses other entities, even though he is affected by them.

One of the most influential early statements of process theology is to be found in Charles Hartshorne's *Man's Vision of God* (1941), which includes a detailed comparison of "classical" and "neoclassical" understandings of God. The former term is used to refer to the understanding of the nature and attributes of God found in the writings of Thomas Aquinas, and the latter to refer to the ideas developed by Hartshorne. Given the importance of Hartshorne to the formulation of process theology, his ideas on the attributes of God have been set out in tabular form, to allow easy comparison with the classical views which he criticizes (see table 4.1).

While Hartshorne does not use the fully developed vocabulary of process thought, as this would emerge after the Second World War, it will be clear that the basic ideas are firmly in place in this early work.

With this approach to the divine attributes in mind, let us explore how process thought handles the existence of suffering in the world. The key point to note is the rejection of the classic doctrine of God's omnipotence: God is one agent among many, not the sovereign Lord of all. Process theology thus locates the origins of suffering and evil within the world to a radical limitation upon the power of God. God has set aside (or simply does not possess) the ability to coerce, retaining only the ability to persuade. Persuasion is seen as a means of exercising power in such a manner that the rights and freedom of others are respected. God is obliged to persuade every aspect of the process to act in the best possible manner. There is, however, no guarantee that God's benevolent persuasion will lead to a favorable outcome. The process is under no obligation to obey God.

God intends good for the creation, and acts in its best interests. However, the option of coercing everything to do the divine will cannot be exercised. As a result, God is unable to prevent certain things happening. Wars, famines, and holocausts are not things which God desires; they are, however, not things which God can prevent, on account of the radical limitations placed upon the divine power. God is thus not responsible for evil; nor can it be said, in any way, that God desires or tacitly accepts its existence. The metaphysical limits placed upon God are such as to prevent any interference in the natural order of things.

Although process theology is now waning as a theological presence in North America, it is clear that its distinctive ideas have played a highly significant role in theological development in the region. The same can be said of the feminist critique of traditional theology, to which we now turn.

Case Study 4.7   The Feminist Critique of Traditional Christian Theology

Both Old and New Testaments use male language about God. The Greek word *theos* is unquestionably masculine, and most of the analogies used for God throughout Scripture – such as father, king, and shepherd – are male. Does this mean that God is male? Anne Carr expresses such concerns (and notes potential feminist solutions) as follows:

> The fundamental feminist question about the maleness of God in the imagery, symbolism and concepts of traditional Christian thought and prayer leads to new reflection on the doctrine of God. In spite of theological denials of sexuality (or any materiality) in God, the persistent use of masculine pronouns for God and the reaction of many Christians against reference to God as "she" would appear to affirm the "maleness" attributed to God. Yet it is also logical that "she" is not only as appropriate as "he," but is perhaps necessary to reorient Christian imagination from the idolatrous implications of exclusively masculine God-language and the dominant effects of the father image in the churches and Christian practice. A new theory of the thoroughly metaphorical character of religious language has emerged in the light of feminist discussion of the doctrine of God. This theory argues that traditional analogical understanding has tended to stress the similarity between human concepts and God's own selfhood while a metaphorical theology should focus rather on the God–human relationship and on the unlikeness of all religious language in reference to God even as it affirms some similarity

This is an example of the type of question which feminist writers have asked concerning the traditional language and imagery of the Christian tradition. In this case study, we shall explore some aspects of the feminist critique of traditional Christian theology, noting its implications and the possible future directions which the discussion might take.

We may begin by considering the question of the alleged "maleness" of God.

It can be shown that certain persons or social roles, largely drawn from the rural world of the Ancient Near East, were seen by biblical writers to be suitable models for the divine activity or personality. One such analogy is that of a father. Yet the statement that "a father in ancient Israelite society is a suitable model for God" is not equivalent to saying that "God is male," or that "God is confined to the cultural parameters of ancient Israel." Mary Hayter, reflecting on such issues in her work *New Eve in Christ* (1987), writes:

> It would appear that certain "motherly prerogatives" in ancient Hebrew society – such as carrying and comforting small children – became metaphors for Yahweh's activity vis-à-vis his children Israel. Likewise, various "fatherly prerogatives" – such as disciplining a son – became vehicles for divine imagery. Different cultures and ages have different ideas about which roles are proper to the mother and which to the father.

To speak of God as father is to say that the role of the father in ancient Israel allows us insights into the nature of God. It is not to say that God is a male human being. Neither male nor female sexuality is to be attributed to God. For sexuality is an attribute of the created order, which cannot be assumed to correspond directly to any such polarity within the creator God himself.

Indeed, the Old Testament avoids attributing sexual functions to God, on account of the strongly pagan overtones of such associations. The Canaanite fertility cults emphasized the sexual functions of both gods and goddesses; the Old Testament refuses to endorse the idea that the gender or the sexuality of God is a significant matter. As Mary Hayter puts it:

> Today a growing number of feminists teach that the God/ess combines male and female characteristics. They, like those who assume that God is exclusively male, should remember that any attribution of sexuality to God is a reversion to paganism.

There is no need to revert to pagan ideas of gods and goddesses to recover the idea that God is neither masculine or feminine; those ideas are already potentially present, if neglected, in Christian theology. Wolfhart Pannenberg develops this point further in his *Systematic Theology*:

> The aspect of fatherly care in particular is taken over in what the Old Testament has to say about God's fatherly care for Israel. The sexual definition of the father's role plays no part. . . . To bring sexual differentiation into the understanding of God would mean polytheism; it was thus ruled out for the God of Israel. . . . The fact that God's care for Israel can also be expressed in terms of a mother's love shows clearly enough how little there is any sense of sexual distinction in the understanding of God as Father.

In an attempt to bring out the fact that God is not male, a number of recent writers have explored the idea of God as "mother" (which brings out the female aspects of God), or as "friend" (which brings out the more gender-neutral aspects of God). An excellent example of this is provided by Sallie McFague, in her *Models of God* (1987). Recognizing that speaking of "God as father" does not mean that God is male, she writes:

> God as mother does not mean that God is mother (or father). We imagine God as both mother and father, but we realize how inadequate these and any other metaphors are to express the creative love of God. . . . Nevertheless, we speak of this love in language that is familiar and dear to us, the language of mothers and fathers who give us life, from whose bodies we come, and upon whose care we depend.

Anne Carr argues that this metaphor is both illuminating and helpful:

> The metaphor of God as friend corresponds to the feminist ideal of "communal personhood," an ideal that entails non-competitive relationships among persons and groups that are characterized by mutuality and reciprocity rather than dualism and hierarchy. It responds to feminist concerns for expressions of divine–human relation that overcome the images of religious self-denial that have shaped women's experience in patterns of low self esteem, passivity and irresponsibility.

The new interest in the issues raised by the maleness of most of the biblical images of God has led to a careful reading of the spiritual literature of early periods in Christian history, resulting in an increased appreciation of the use of female imagery during these earlier periods. An excellent example of this is provided by the *Revelations of Divine Love*, an account of sixteen visions which appeared to the female English writer Julian of Norwich in May 1373. The visions are notable for their distinctive tendency to refer to both God and Jesus Christ in strongly maternal terms:

> I saw that God rejoices to be our Father, and also that he rejoices to be our Mother; and yet again, that he rejoices to be our true Husband, with our soul as his beloved bride. . . . He is the foundation, substance and the thing itself, what it is by nature. He is the true Father and Mother of what things are by nature.

The feminist critique extends beyond the question of the "maleness" of God; it also extends to other areas of theology. Three additional areas may be noted:

1   The doctrine of the Trinity traditionally involves the terms "Father, Son, and Holy Spirit." The first two are clearly male, raising issues for feminist writers. It is argued by some feminist writers that this difficulty can be overcome by using the phrase "creator, redeemer, and sustainer," which are devoid of gender. Critics have responded that this involves defining the persons of the Trinity in

purely functional terms, which represents a lapse into a form of modalism. Paul Jewett explores the issue of non-inclusive language within the doctrine of the Trinity in his *God, Creation and Revelation* (1991) by suggesting that it is at least hypothetically possible to speak of God in female terms:

> To speak of God as a mother who discloses herself to us in a daughter, though it is a hypothetical way of speaking, is not a heretical way of speaking. Given the realities of salvation history, we grant that it is a way of speaking with no prospects of being other than hypothetical. God the Creator, as we have observed, has given us our humanity in a sexual polarity and God the Savior has assumed that humanity as a male rather than a female. Yet the need to speak in this hypothetical way comes from the fact that women are justified in their complaint that the traditional understanding of our traditional language about God has made them second-class citizens both as members of the human race and as members of the family of God.

2 Jesus of Nazareth was male, and might therefore be argued to lack experience of being female, or potential relevance to females. This point is made forcefully by a post-Christian feminist writer, Daphne Hampson:

> The question of the compatibility of feminism and Christianity then is that of whether there can be a way of speaking of Christ's uniqueness which is not incompatible with feminism. (Let us take also a minimalist definition of feminism, as meaning the proclaimed equality of women and men.) The problem of course with Christology for feminists is that Jesus was a male human being and that thus as a symbol, as the Christ, or as the Second Person of the trinity, it would seem that "God" becomes in some way "male." It should be noted at the outset what is the nature of the problem with which we are concerned. It is not a question of whether feminists have something against "men." Whether or not that is the case, the problem here is not that Jesus was a man, but that this man has been considered unique, symbolic of God, God Himself – or whatever else may be the case within Christianity. The Godhead, or at least Christology, then appears to be biased against women. Feminists have been very aware of the power of symbolism and ideology. It is no small matter then to suggest that western religious thought, which has been so fundamental to western culture, has been ideologically loaded against women.

3 Traditional concepts of sin are often framed in terms of power and domination, which are (at least in the view of some feminist writers) especially associated with men. Women, it is argued, suffer from other shortcomings – such as a lack of self-esteem – which are not properly addressed by traditional Christian theology. Again, Daphne Hampson draws attention to this point, focusing on the concept of sin set out in the writings of Reinholt Niebuhr:

> The feminist criticism is not simply that Niebuhr has described what have been behaviour patterns of men rather than of women. It has seemed to feminist

theologians, that in his sense of the individual as highly individuated and "atomic" rather than in relationship to others, Niebuhr has described what is peculiarly a male propensity. When (as I have discovered) it is said by feminists that Niebuhr fails to have a social conception of the human, this may well be misunderstood. For – the response comes back – no theologian more than he has considered the human in society. Of course this is the case. What is being referred to here however is a different level of the word social. Niebuhr sees the human being as monadic rather than as having an essential relationality. In this he is very different from much feminist thought. Very fine work here has been accomplished by Judith Vaughan. Vaughan, in work originally undertaken with Rosemary Ruether, compares Niebuhr's ethics with Ruether's ethics. She shows that their different ethical and political stance relates to a different understanding of the human being. Vaughan, and Ruether, hold what I earlier designated a Marxist–Hegelian perspective. They see persons as caught up in social relationships and believe that the external relations of the self form the understanding which a person has of him or herself. It is from such a position that Vaughan mounts a critique of Niebuhr.

It will be clear that the feminist agenda thus has considerable implications for traditional Christian theology, at least in the West. Although the merits of some of the lines of criticism of traditional patterns of thought are contested, both inside and outside feminist circles, a significant debate is under way. The same may be said of the issues arising from the existence of religions other than Christianity in the world, to which we now turn.

Case Study 4.8   Christian Approaches to Other Religions

Christianity is but one world religious tradition among a host of others. So how does it relate to other religious traditions? The question is not modern; it has been asked throughout Christian history. Initially the question concerned Christianity's relationship with Judaism, the matrix from which it emerged in the period AD 30–60. And as it expanded, it encountered other religious beliefs and practices, such as classical paganism. As it became established in India in the fifth century, it encountered the diverse native Indian cultural movements which western scholars of religion have misleadingly grouped together, and termed "Hinduism." Arab Christianity has long since learned to coexist with Islam in the eastern Mediterranean.

In the modern period, the question of the relation of Christianity has assumed a new importance in western academic theology, partly on account of the rise of multiculturalism in western society. As will become clear, three main approaches have gained currency. However, it will be helpful to begin by considering the idea of "religion" itself.

A naïve view of religion might be that it is an outlook on life which believes in, or worships, a Supreme Being. This outlook, characteristic of Deism and

327

Enlightenment rationalism, is easily shown to be inadequate. Buddhism is classified as a religion by most people; yet here a belief in some supreme being is conspicuously absent. The same problem persists, no matter what definition of "religion" is offered. No unambiguously common features can be identified among the religions, in matters of faith or practice. Thus Edward Conze, the great scholar of Buddhism, recalled that he "once read through a collection of the lives of Roman Catholic saints, and there was not one of whom a Buddhist could fully approve. . . . They were bad Buddhists though good Christians."

There is a growing consensus that it is seriously misleading to regard the various religious traditions of the world as variations on a single theme. "There is no single essence, no one content of enlightenment or revelation, no one way of emancipation or liberation, to be found in all that plurality" (David Tracy). John B. Cobb, Jr also notes the enormous difficulties confronting anyone wishing to argue that there is an "essence of religion":

> Arguments about what religion truly is are pointless. There is no such thing as religion. There are only traditions, movements, communities, peoples, beliefs, and practices that have features that are associated by many people with what they mean by religion.

Cobb stresses that the assumption that religion has an essence has bedeviled and seriously misled recent discussion of the relation of the religious traditions of the world. For example, he points out that both Buddhism and Confucianism have "religious" elements – but that does not necessarily mean that they can be categorized as "religions." Many "religions" are better understood as cultural movements with religious components.

The idea of some universal notion of religion, of which individual religions are subsets, appears to have emerged at the time of the Enlightenment. To use a biological analogy, the assumption that there is a genus of religion, of which individual religions are species, is a very western idea, without any real parallel outside western culture – except on the part of those who have been educated in the West, and have uncritically absorbed its presuppositions.

What, then, of Christian approaches to understanding the relation between Christianity and other religious traditions? In what way can such traditions be understood, within the context of the Christian belief in the universal saving will of God, made known through Jesus Christ? It must be stressed that Christian theology is concerned with evaluating other religious traditions from the perspective of Christianity itself. Such reflection is not addressed to, or intended to gain approval from, members of other religious traditions, or their secular observers.

Three broad approaches can be identified:

1   *Particularism*, which holds that only those who hear and respond to the Christian gospel may be saved.
2   *Inclusivism*, which argues that, although Christianity represents the normative revelation of God, salvation is nonetheless possible for those who belong to other religious traditions.
3   *Pluralism*, which holds that all the religious traditions of humanity are equally valid paths to the same core of religious reality. We shall consider these individually.

We will explore each of these approaches in what follows.

The particularist approach

Perhaps the most influential statement of this position may be found in the writings of Hendrik Kraemer (1888–1965), especially his *Christian Message in a Non-Christian World* (1938). Kraemer emphasizes that "God has revealed *the* Way and *the* Truth and *the* Life in Jesus Christ, and wills this to be known throughout the world." This revelation is *sui generis*; it is in a category of its own, and cannot be set alongside the ideas of revelation found in other religious traditions.

At this point, a certain breadth of opinion can be discerned within this approach. Kraemer himself seems to suggest that there is real knowledge of God outside Christ when he speaks of God shining through "in a broken, troubled way, in reason, in nature and in history." The question is whether such knowledge is only available through Christ, or whether Christ provides the only framework by which such knowledge may be discerned and interpreted elsewhere.

Some particularists (such as Karl Barth) adopt the position that there is no knowledge of God to be had apart from through Christ; others (such as Kraemer) allow that God reveals himself in many ways and places – but insist that this revelation can only be interpreted correctly, and known for what it really is, in the light of the definitive revelation of God in Christ. (There are important parallels here with the debate over natural and revealed knowledge of God.)

What, then, of those who have not heard the gospel of Christ? What happens to them? Are not particularists denying salvation to those who have not heard of Christ – or who, having heard of him, choose to reject him? This criticism is frequently leveled at particularism by its critics. Thus John Hick, arguing from a pluralist perspective, suggests that the doctrine that salvation is only possible through Christ is inconsistent with belief in the universal saving will of God. That this is not in fact the case is easily demonstrated by considering the view of Karl Barth, easily the most sophisticated of twentieth-century defenders of this position.

Barth declares that salvation is only possible through Christ. He nevertheless insists on the ultimate eschatological victory of grace over unbelief – that is, at the end of history. Eventually, God's grace will triumph completely, and all will come to faith in Christ. This is the only way to salvation – but it is a way that, through the grace of God, is effective for all. For Barth, the particularity of God's revelation through Christ is not contradicted by the universality of salvation.

The inclusivist approach

The most significant advocate of this model is the leading Jesuit writer Karl Rahner. In the fifth volume of his *Theological Investigations*, Rahner develops four theses, setting out the view, not merely that individual non-Christians may be saved, but that the non-Christian religious traditions in general may have access to the saving grace of God in Christ.

1   Christianity is the absolute religion, founded on the unique event of the self-revelation of God in Christ. But this revelation took place at a specific point in history. Those who lived before this point, or who have yet to hear about this event, would thus seem to be excluded from salvation – which is contrary to the saving will of God.

2   For this reason, despite their errors and shortcomings, non-Christian religious traditions are valid and capable of mediating the saving grace of God, until the gospel is made known to their members. After the gospel has been proclaimed to the adherents of such non-Christian religious traditions, they are no longer legitimate, from the standpoint of Christian theology.

3   The faithful adherent of a non-Christian religious tradition is thus to be regarded as an "anonymous Christian."

4   Other religious traditions will not be displaced by Christianity. Religious pluralism will continue to be a feature of human existence.

We may explore the first three theses in more detail. It will be clear that Rahner strongly affirms the principle that salvation may only be had through Christ, as he is interpreted by the Christian tradition. "Christianity understands itself as the absolute religion, intended for all people, which cannot recognize any other religion beside itself as of equal right." Yet Rahner supplements this with an emphasis upon the universal saving will of God; God wishes that all shall be saved, even though not all know Christ: "Somehow all people must be able to be members of the church."

For this reason, Rahner argues that saving grace must be available outside the bounds of the church – and hence in other religious traditions. He vigorously opposes those who adopt too neat solutions, insisting either that a religious tradition comes from God or that it is an inauthentic and purely human invention. Where Kraemer argues that non-Christian religious traditions were little more than self-justifying human constructions, Rahner argues that such traditions may well include elements of truth.

Rahner justifies this suggestion by considering the relation between the Old and New Testaments. Although the Old Testament, strictly speaking, represents the outlook of a non-Christian religion (Judaism), Christians are able to read it and discern within it elements which continue to be valid. The Old Testament is evaluated in the light of the New, and as a result, certain practices (such as food laws) are discarded as unacceptable, while others are retained (such as the moral law). The same approach can and should, Rahner argues, be adopted in the case of other religions.

The saving grace of God is thus available through non-Christian religious traditions, despite their shortcomings. Many of their adherents, Rahner argues, have thus accepted that grace, without being fully aware of what it is. It is for this reason that Rahner introduces the term "anonymous Christians," to refer to those who have experienced divine grace without necessarily knowing it.

This term has been heavily criticized. For example, John Hick has suggested that it is paternalist, offering "honorary status granted unilaterally to people who have not expressed any desire for it." Nevertheless, Rahner's intention is to allow for the real effects of divine grace in the lives of those who belong to non-Christian traditions. Full access to truth about God (as it is understood within the Christian tradition) is not a necessary precondition for access to the saving grace of God.

Rahner does not allow that Christianity and other religious traditions may be treated as equal, or that they are particular instances of a common encounter with God. For Rahner, Christianity and Christ have an exclusive status, denied to other religious traditions. The question is: can other religious traditions give access to the same saving grace as that offered by Christianity? Rahner's approach allows him to suggest that the beliefs of non-Christian religious traditions are not necessarily true, while allowing that they may, nevertheless, mediate the grace of God by the lifestyles which they evoke – such as a selfless love of one's neighbor.

The pluralist approach

The most significant exponent of a pluralist approach to religious traditions is John Hick (b. 1922). In his *God and the Universe of Faiths* (1973), Hick argues for a need to move away from a Christ-centered to a God-centered approach. Describing this change as a "Copernican Revolution," Hick declared that it was necessary to move away from "the dogma that Christianity is at the centre to the realization that it is *God* who is at the centre, and that all religions . . . including our own, serve and revolve around him."

Developing this approach, Hick suggests that the characteristic of God's nature which is of central importance to the question of other faiths is his universal saving will. If God wishes everyone to be saved, it is inconceivable that he should reveal himself in such a way that only a small portion of humanity could be saved. In fact, as we have seen, this is not a necessary feature of either particularist or inclusivist approaches. However, Hick draws the conclusion that it is necessary to recognize that all religions lead to the same God. Christians have no special access to God, who is universally available through all religious traditions.

This suggestion is not without its problems. For example, it is fairly clear that the religious traditions of the world are radically different in their beliefs and practices. Hick deals with this point by suggesting that such differences must be interpreted in terms of a "both–and" rather than an "either–or." They should be understood as complementary, rather than contradictory, insights into the one divine reality. This reality lies at the heart of all the religions; yet "their differing experiences of that reality, interacting over the centuries with the different thought-forms of different cultures, have led to increasing differentiation and contrasting elaboration." (This idea is very similar to the "universal rational religion of nature" propounded by Deist writers, which became corrupted through time.) Equally, Hick has difficulties with those non-theistic religious traditions, such as Advaitin Hinduism or Theravada Buddhism, which have no place for a god.

These difficulties relate to observed features of religious traditions. In other words, the beliefs of non-Christian religions make it difficult to accept that they are all speaking of the same God. But a more fundamental theological worry remains: is Hick actually talking about the Christian God at all? A central Christian conviction – that God reveals himself definitively in Jesus Christ – has to be set to one side to allow Hick to proceed. Hick argues that he is merely adopting a *theo*centric, rather than a *Christo*centric approach. Yet the Christian insistence that God is known normatively through Christ implies that authentically Christian knowledge of God is derived through Christ. For a number of critics, Hick's desertion of Christ as a reference point means abandoning any claim to speak from a Christian perspective.

The debate over the Christian understanding of the relation of Christianity to other religious traditions is likely continue for some considerable time, fueled by the rise of multiculturalism in western society. The three viewpoints outlined above are likely to continue to be reflected in Christian writing on the matter for some time to come.

Case Study 4.9   Theological Method in the Modern Period

The question of the proper starting point for theology has been a subject of considerable interest in the modern period. "Theological method" could be described as "an understanding of where you start your theology from, and what tools you need to construct it." Classic approaches to theology – for example, those found in the writings of Augustine, Aquinas, and Calvin – often rest on assumptions about the nature of revelation and human nature which some modern writers find problematical. Not all modern writers, it should be noted, feel this difficulty: there are many modern theological writers who regard it as perfectly possible to use the basic methods and approaches found in these earlier writers. In what follows, we shall explore a number of approaches to theological method which are sensitive to the concerns of the modern period.

The appeal to experience: Schleiermacher and Tillich

The Enlightenment (see pp. 219–26) was seen by many writers to raise some fundamental problems for Christian theology. Jesus of Nazareth was viewed simply as a good religious teacher, who taught some ideas which were consistent with human reason. There was no need for Jesus to have taught these, as they could have been established by any rational person. The Enlightenment thus called into question the distinctiveness of Jesus of Nazareth. If Jesus merely taught what could be known from reason, what distinct role did he possess?

The leading German theologian F. D. E. Schleiermacher provided what is often regarded as one of the most significant responses to this challenge. He sought to preserve the distinct identity of Christianity by arguing that it mediates an experience or feeling of "absolute dependence" on God. This experience was mediated though Jesus of Nazareth, and could be traced back to him from the contemporary experience of Christian piety. Schleiermacher's theological method thus involves an appeal to the present experience of Christian community, and an interpretation of this experience in terms of the mediating role of Jesus.

F. D. E. Schleiermacher (1768–1834). One of the most influential German Protestant writers since the Reformation. Noted especially for his emphasis on the role of "feeling" in theology in reaction against the rationalism of the Enlightenment. His most important work is *Der christliche Glaube* ("The Christian Faith").

The first statement of Schleiermacher's distinctive theological method can be found in his *On Religion: Speeches to its Cultured Despisers*, published anonymously in 1799. The work develops a defense of Christianity, based partly on the

333

argument that religion is a vivid sense or consciousness of a greater whole, of which the individual is but part and upon which he or she is totally dependent. The essence of religion is declared to lie in a "fundamental, distinct and integrative element of human life and culture." Schleiermacher identifies this as a feeling of being totally and utterly dependent upon something infinite, which is nevertheless made known in and through finite things. Religion in general (rather than Christianity in particular) is commended as the necessary context of science and art, without which human culture is needlessly impoverished.

In his later work *The Christian Faith*, Schleiermacher emphasizes that the Christian faith is not primarily conceptual; rather, doctrines are to be seen as second-order expressions of its primary religious truth, the experience of redemption. Christian piety may be regarded as the fundamental basis of Christian theology; however, this should not be understood to mean the piety of the individual, but the corporate piety of the church. The essence of this piety is not some rational or moral principle, but "feeling." The general human consciousness of being dependent is, according to Schleiermacher, recognized and interpreted within the context of the Christian faith as a sense of total dependence upon God. This "feeling of absolute dependence" constitutes the starting point for Christian theology. As A. E. Biedermann later commented, Schleiermacher's theology may be regarded as the subjection of the deep inner feelings of humanity to critical inquiry. The human intellect reflects upon human feeling, and by doing so, interprets it. Critical introspection reveals that human subjectivity is dipolar, centering around consciousness of oneself, and consciousness of another, coexisting. For Schleiermacher, Christian doctrine provided a means of making sense of this experience.

Paul Tillich (1886–1965). A German Lutheran theologian who was forced to leave Germany during the Nazi period. He settled in the United States and held teaching positions at Union Theological Seminary, New York, Harvard Divinity School, and the University of Chicago. His most significant theological writing is the three-volume *Systematic Theology* (1951–64).

This appeal to experience was developed in the twentieth century by Paul Tillich, whose "principle of correlation" can be seen as an extension of Schleiermacher's approach. Tillich's concern was to make Christianity meaningful in a period in western culture in which it seemed to be losing its public credibility. Like schleiermacher before him, he was concerned to make Christianity acceptable to "its cultured despisers." For Tillich, human culture raises questions which Christian theology is able to answer.

4.9.1   Paul Tillich on Correlation

In using the method of correlation, systematic theology proceeds in the following
way: it makes an analysis of the human situation out of which the existential
questions arise, and it demonstrates that the symbols used in the Christian message
are the answers to these questions. . . . The analysis of the human situation employs
5   materials made available by man's creative self-interpretation in all realms of
culture. Philosophy contributes, but so do poetry, drama, the novel, therapeutic
psychology, and sociology. The theologian organizes these materials in relation to
the answer given by the Christian message. In the light of this message he may
make an analysis of existence which is more penetrating than that of most
10   philosophers. Nevertheless, it remains a philosophical analysis. The analysis of
existence, including the development of the questions implicit in existence, is a
philosophical task, even if it is performed by a theologian, and even if the
theologian is a reformer like Calvin. The difference between the philosopher who
is not a theologian and the theologian who works as a philosopher in analyzing
15   human existence is only that the former tries to give an analysis which will be part
of a broader philosophical world, while the latter tries to correlate the material of
his analysis with the theological concepts he derives from the Christian faith. . . .
The Christian message provides the answers to the questions implied in human
existence. These answers are contained in the revelatory events on which Christi-
20   anity is based and are taken by systematic theology *from* the sources, *through* the
medium, *under* the norm. Their content cannot be derived from the questions,
that is, from an analysis of human existence. They are "spoken" to human existence
from beyond it. Otherwise they would not be answers, for the question is human
existence itself. But the relation is more involved than this, since it is correlation.
25   There is a mutual dependence between question and answer. In respect to content
the Christian answers are dependent on the revelatory events in which they appear;
in respect to form they are dependent on the structure of the questions which they
answer. God is the answer to the question implied in human finitude.

Note especially Tillich's emphasis on the importance of the study of human
culture and experience. A right understanding of human culture allows the
theologian to identify the questions to which Christianity provides the answers.
Although it will be clear that Tillich does not intend human culture to determine
the answers which are given (see especially his comments at lines 19–22), his
critics often argue that Tillich offers an apologetic which lacks any rigorous
theological foundation, and thus ends up by allowing culture the upper hand.
However, this does not appear to have been Tillich's intention.

Karl Rahner: transcendental phenomenology

A significant new development in modern Roman Catholic theology began with Joseph Maréchal, a Belgian Jesuit theologian. In his *Point of Departure for Metaphysics*, Maréchal argues that the basic ideas of Aquinas need to be related to modern philosophical movements, especially Kant's transcendent metaphysics. Rahner built upon this foundation, and developed the "transcendental phenomenology" which is linked with his name. It is not easy to explain this approach. However, it has been so important that it would be unacceptable to ignore it, despite its difficulty. What follows is a simplified account of Rahner's approach.

Karl Rahner (1904–84). One of the most influential of modern Roman Catholic theologians, whose *Theological Investigations* pioneered the use of the essay as a tool of theological construction and exploration.

Rahner drew attention to the importance of the basic human urge to transcend – that is, to go beyond – the limitations of human nature. Human beings are aware of a sense of being made for *more* than they now are, or *more* than they can ever hope to achieve by their own abilities. The Christian revelation supplies this "more," to which human experience points. In his *Foundations of the Christian Faith* (1978), Rahner lists several ways in which this "transcendence" shows itself; we shall note two:

1   The act of knowing an object or willing some individual action leads us to realize that knowing and willing are not limited to one object, but are actually unlimited. In knowing or willing one specific and limited thing, we come to be aware of the unlimited possibilities that lie beyond this. Yet this awareness of a lack of limits is mediated through a limited situation.
2   The human search for meaning presents us with a paradox, in that we realize that we are radically finite on the one hand, and yet on the other we have unlimited questions. Even though we are finite and limited, we experience the hope for an absolute fullness of meaning.

In the end, Rahner's concern is to bring out clearly that, even though we are limited and finite, we possess a strong sense of something that is transcendent – something that surpasses our personal and situational limitations. For Rahner, this awareness has considerable theological significance and potential, and leads to the realization that the Christian concept of God relates easily and naturally to this understanding of the human situation. Rahner thus makes anthropology of fundamental importance, and sets a discussion of human nature (including the human awareness of a transcendent longing) at the beginning of his *Foundations of the Christian Faith*. The human quest for ultimate meaning raises the question of God, and is only satisfied when that God is found. Although Rahner's starting point is thus anthropocentric, his intention is fundamentally theocentric. This may be contrasted with the early writings of Karl Barth, who totally rejects any anthropocentric starting point for theology. We shall explore these early ideas in what follows.

Karl Barth: responding to revelation

The origins of one of the great turning points in modern theology are generally agreed to lie in Karl Barth's commentary on Romans, first published in 1919. Perhaps the work may be regarded as a midwife to a new theological trend rather than its cause; there is considerable evidence for the cumulation of considerable dissatisfaction with liberal theology over the period culminating in the First World War, and Barth's work may simply have triggered off a looming anti-liberal reaction. The Romans commentary is often regarded as a work of prophecy rather than theology. Although its main impact appears to date from the publication of its heavily rewritten second edition (1922), even the first edition caused a mild sensation.

Karl Barth (1886–1968). Widely regarded as the most important Protestant theologian of the twentieth century. Originally inclined to support liberal Protestantism, Barth was moved to adopt a more theocentric position through his reflections on the First World War. His early emphasis on the "otherness" of God in his Romans commentary (1919) was continued and modified in his monumental *Church Dogmatics*. Barth's contribution to modern Christian theology has been immense.

Throughout this work, drawing on insights from the Danish philosopher Søren Kierkegaard, Barth stresses the "infinite qualitative distinction" between God and human beings. Barth emphasizes God's total holiness, and God's remoteness from humanity in general, and from human culture and religion in particular. God "stands over and against humanity and everything human in an infinite qualitative distinction, and is never to be thought of as identical with anything which we name, experience, conceive or worship as God." God cannot and must not be constructed or conceived in human terms, as if God were some kind of projection of human culture, reason, or emotion. Time and time again Barth emphasizes the vastness of the gulf fixed between God and humanity, and the impossibility of bridging this gulf from our side. Barth modifies G. E. Lessing's famous reference to the "ugly great ditch" of history (see p. 297), the

Alpine image of a "crevasse" between time and eternity. God is *totaliter aliter*, wholly and absolutely different from us. How, then, may mediation between God and humanity take place? Barth's answer, stated in the preface to the second edition of the Romans commentary (1922), is significant:

> If I have any system, it is restricted to bearing in mind, as much as possible, what Kierkegaard called the "infinite qualitative distinction" between time and eternity, in its negative and positive aspects. "God is in heaven, and you are on earth." For me, the relation of this God and this person, the relation of this person and this God, is, in a nutshell, the theme of the Bible and the totality of philosophy. The philosophers term this crisis of human knowledge the prime cause; the Bible sees Jesus Christ at this cross-roads.

This is radically different from the approach adopted by Schleiermacher and his successors. Any possibility of interpreting Jesus' relationship to God in terms such as those of liberal Protestantism (e.g., in culture or human experience) is rejected. Human religious consciousness can only be the consciousness of our abandonment by God. God remains unknown and unknowable, and all that may be seen of the reality of this unknown God in the history of the world or of Jesus of Nazareth are his effects, rather than that reality itself.

This approach is often referred to as "dialectical," in that it stresses the radical discontinuity between the divine and human. Barth himself would modify his position in later writings, such as the *Church Dogmatics*. Nevertheless, his radical writings of this early period are widely regarded as being intensely significant for the development of theological method in the twentieth century. Theology, for the early Barth, is about responding to a revelation over which we have no control, rather than exploring human experience or culture.

Postliberalism: community and theology

A major development in North American theology since about 1980 has been the emergence of the "Yale school," or "postliberalism." Whereas older liberal writers, standing in the tradition of Schleiermacher and Tillich, argued that theology could be grounded in the universal realities of human experience, postliberalism stresses the importance of specific communities. There is no common human experience, in that experience is shaped by the beliefs and expectations of a community. To do theology is thus to be part of a Christian community, and learn the distinctive language and ethos of that community. Among the leading representatives of this school of thought, particular attention should be paid to George Lindbeck and Stanley Hauerwas. In what follows, we shall note Lindbeck's emphasis on what he terms a "linguistic–cultural" approach to theology, which recognizes the importance of a community for theological reflection.

4.9.2   George Lindbeck on Community and Theology

Stated more technically, a religion can be viewed as a kind of cultural and/or linguistic framework or medium that shapes the entirety of life and thought. It functions somewhat like a Kantian a priori although in this case the a priori is a set of acquired skills that could be different. It is not primarily an array of beliefs about
5   the true and the good (though it may involve these), or a symbolism expressive of basic attitudes, feelings, or sentiments (though these will be generated). Rather, it is similar to an idiom that makes possible the description of realities, the formulation of beliefs, and the experiencing of inner attitudes, feelings, and sentiments. Like a culture or language, it is a communal phenomenon that shapes
10   the subjectivities of individuals rather than being primarily a manifestation of those subjectivities. . . . Thus the linguistic–cultural model is part of an outlook that stresses the degree to which human experience is shaped, molded, and in a sense constituted by cultural and linguistic forms. There are numberless thoughts we cannot think, sentiments we cannot have, and realities we cannot perceive unless
15   we learn to use the appropriate symbol systems. It seems, as the cases of Helen Keller and of supposed wolf children vividly illustrate, that unless we acquire language of some kind, we cannot actualize our specifically human capacities for thought, action, and feeling. Similarly, so the argument goes, to become religious involves becoming skilled in the language, the symbol system of a given religion.
20   To become a Christian involves learning the story of Israel and of Jesus well enough to interpret and experience oneself and one's world in its terms.

Notice especially the importance which Lindbeck attaches to tradition. The way in which anyone thinks is determined by the tradition within which she stands. This contrasts sharply with Kant's idea of the isolated thinking subject, which has been heavily criticized by writers such as Alasdair MacIntyre. For Lindbeck, "human experience is shaped, molded, and in a sense constituted by cultural and linguistic forms" (lines 12–13). These cultural and linguistic forms are one aspect of the community tradition within which all human beings are located. The Christian tradition is one distinct tradition, with its own understanding of its norms, sources, and values. For Lindbeck, Christian theology is therefore carried out within the Christian tradition. It involves "learning the story of Israel and of Jesus well enough to interpret and experience oneself and one's world in its terms" (lines 20–21). Where Schleiermacher appealed to experience, and Tillich to culture, Lindbeck argues that the proper starting point of theology is the Christian tradition itself.

Liberation theology: theology as praxis

One of the most distinctive features of Latin American liberation theology is its insistence that the starting point for authentically Christian theology must be an analysis of a concrete socio-political situation. The object of theological analysis is to identify patterns of oppression, exploitation, and alienation which results from economic and social inequality. But not all are equally well placed to undertake this analysis. One of the most distinctive features of Latin American liberation theology is its *prioritization of the poor.*

The history of Christianity from the closing of the New Testament shows evidence of distortion of critical Christian insights, on account of the economic and social situation of its interpreters. To restore Christian theology to a state of authenticity, the Christian theological tradition must be read from the perspective of the experience of the oppressed.

Liberation theology places considerable emphasis on the notion of *praxis.* This term, which has its origins in Marxist theory, denotes the idea of a "way of life," a "practice," which is to be contrasted sharply with *theoria*, an abstract and theoretical way of understanding Christian theology. Christian theology is about defining and enabling a way of living, not merely changing the ways in which people think. Theology must engage with ideas – but it must also transform individual lives and societies.

4.9.3 Gustavo Gutiérrez on Theology as Praxis

Theology must be critical reflection on humankind, on basic human principles. Only with this approach will theology be a serious discourse, aware of itself, in full possession of its conceptual elements. But we are not referring exclusively to this epistemological aspect when we talk about theology as critical reflection. We also
5   refer to a clear and critical attitude regarding economic and socio-cultural issues in the life and reflection of the Christian community. To disregard these is to deceive both oneself and others. But above all, we intend this term to express the theory of a definite practice. Theological reflection would then necessarily be a criticism of society and the Church, insofar as they are called and addressed by the
10   Word of God; it would be a critical theory, worked out in the light of the Word accepted in faith and inspired by a practical purpose – and therefore indissolubly linked to historical praxis. . . . This critical task is indispensable. Reflection in the light of faith must constantly accompany the pastoral action of the Church. By keeping historical events in their proper perspective, theology helps safeguard
15   society and the Church from regarding as permanent what is only temporary. Critical reflection thus always plays the inverse role of an ideology which rationalizes and justifies a given social and ecclesial order. On the other hand,

20 theology, by pointing to the sources of revelation, helps to orient pastoral activity; it puts it in a wider context and so helps it to avoid activism and immediatism. Theology as critical reflection thus fulfills a liberating function for humankind and the Christian community, preserving them from fetishism and idolatry, as well as from a pernicious and belittling narcissism. Understood in this way theology has a necessary and permanent role in liberation from every form of religious alienation – which is often fostered by the ecclesiastical institution itself when it impedes an
25 authentic approach to the Word of the Lord.

Notice especially that way in which theology is seen as leading to engagement with "economic and socio-cultural issues in the life and reflection of the Christian community." Theology is not simply about ideas; it is about engagement with social, economic, and political issues inside and outside the life of the church. *Theoria* and *praxis* are indissolubly linked, although there seems to be some divergence amongst liberation theologians as to whether *theoria* merely informs *praxis*, or whether *praxis* determines *theoria*. For Gutiérrez, theology enables the church to avoid becoming trapped in transient or alienating ways of thinking and living, and allows it to offer an informed and justified criticism of the society in which it finds itself. Ecclesial identity and action thus rest on critical theological reflection; yet that reflection must lead to some such action.

From the brief analysis presented in this case study, it will be clear that a number of different approaches to theological method can be found in modern Christian thought. Some place an emphasis on individual experience, where others stress the importance of tradition-mediated ideas and values. Some assume that theology concerns right ways of thinking; others that it defines a way of life. Such diversity is frustrating, not least for anyone trying to teach theology: it is very difficult to be able to describe and explain the diversity in modern theology at this point. However, it is hoped that this brief survey of some of the approaches will enable the reader to get at least some idea of the issues involved.

WHERE NEXT?

Having completed this introductory overview of the history of Christian thought, you may find yourself wondering where you go from here. This brief concluding section is intended to make some suggestions about how you can develop your interest in this fascinating subject.

1 You may find that you are attracted to a particular theologian. As you worked your way through the volume, it is possible *that one individual writer* has stood out as being of especial interest. If so, you might find it worth your while developing a special interest in that writer. Among those writers who are known to repay careful study, the following may be noted in particular: Irenaeus of Lyons, Athanasius, Augustine of Hippo, Anselm of Canterbury, Thomas Aquinas, Martin Luther, John Calvin, Jonathan Edwards, Karl Barth, Karl Rahner, and Hans Urs von Balthasar. Engaging with a particular writer allows you to explore the writer's personal biographical details and the cultural context against which those writings are to be set, as well as to engage with the writer's distinctive ideas.

2 In much the same way, you may find yourself attracted *to a particular period* in the history of Christian thought. Many find the patristic period especially fascinating (with some choosing to specialize in the Greek-speaking East, and others in the Latin-speaking West); others find more tightly-defined periods fascinating – for example, nineteenth-century English religious thought. Among those periods which are known to repay study, the following may be noted (in addition to those just mentioned): early medieval theology (*c*.1000–1300); the Reformation; sixteenth-century Spanish religious thought; eighteenth-century American theology; English mystical writers of the fourteenth century. This kind of study allows you to gain a deep understanding of a specific period in history, and a number of writers who contributed to its theological enrichment.

3 In a similar way, you may find that you become interested in a specific area of Christian thought – for example, the doctrine of the person of Christ, or the Trinity. Exploring the development of one general doctrinal area throughout Christian history is fascinating, and allows you to explore the impact of philosophical and cultural factors upon theology, as well as to interact with some landmark theologians. In my own case, I began my study of historical theology with a detailed engagement with the history of the doctrine of justification. This provided a "window" onto historical theology in general, as well as offering me particular insights into the way in which theology and legal theories have interacted. The following doctrinal themes (in addition to the two just noted) are known to be especially interesting: the work of Christ; the doctrine of grace; the relation of faith and reason; and the doctrine of the church.

4 You may find a particular theological or ecclesiological tradition worth exploring – for example, a denomination (such as Anglicanism, Lutheranism, Greek Orthodoxy, or Roman Catholicism), or a trend within the denominations (such as modernism, liberalism or evangelicalism). Once more, all the above mentioned are known to repay study, and will open doors to further reflection and engagement.

These are simply suggestions for further exploration; you will find suitable resources identified in the "For Further Reading" section.

A GLOSSARY OF THEOLOGICAL TERMS

What follows is a brief discussion of a series of terms that the reader is likely to encounter in the course of reading works dealing with historical theology, such as the present volume.

Adiaphora
Literally, "matters of indifference." Beliefs or practices which the sixteenth-century Reformers regarded as being tolerable, in that they were neither explicitly rejected nor stipulated by Scripture.

Alexandrian school
A patristic school of thought, especially associated with the city of Alexandria in Egypt, noted for its Christology (which placed emphasis upon the divinity of Christ) and its method of biblical interpretation (which employed allegorical methods of exegesis). A rival approach in both areas was associated with Antioch.

Anabaptism
A term derived from the Greek word for "re-baptizer," and used to refer to the radical wing of the sixteenth-century Reformation, based on thinkers such as Menno Simons or Balthasar Hubmaier.

Analogy of being (*analogia entis*)
The theory, especially associated with Thomas Aquinas, that there exists a correspondence or analogy between the created order and God, as a result of the divine creatorship. The idea gives theoretical justification to the practice of drawing conclusions from the known objects and relationships of the natural order concerning God.

Analogy of faith (*analogia fidei*)
The theory, especially associated with Karl Barth, which holds that any correspondence between the created order and God is only established on the basis of the self-revelation of God.

Anhypostasis
A doctrine with its roots in the patristic period, but especially associated with later Protestant writers, which denies the independent existence of the humanity of Jesus Christ. According to this view, the humanity of Jesus Christ results from the decision of the second person of the Trinity to adopt and be united with human nature. It is to be contrasted with the doctrine of *enhypostasis*, which affirms the independent existence of the humanity of Christ.

Anthropomorphism

The tendency to ascribe human features (such as hands or arms) or other human characteristics to God.

Antinomianism

The school of thought which denies any continuing role for the Old Testament Law (Greek: *nomos*) in the Christian life. Views of this nature have been found throughout Christian history, although they were of particular importance at the time of the Reformation.

Antiochene school

A patristic school of thought, especially associated with the city of Antioch (in modern Turkey), noted for its Christology (which placed emphasis upon the humanity of Christ) and its method of biblical interpretation (which employed literal methods of exegesis). A rival approach in both areas was associated with Alexandria.

Anti-Pelagian writings

The writings of Augustine relating to the Pelagian controversy, in which he defended his views on grace and justification. *See* **Pelagianism**.

Apocalyptic

A type of writing or religious outlook in general which focuses on the last things and the end of the world, often taking the form of visions with complex symbolism. The book of Daniel (Old Testament) and Revelation (New Testament) are examples of this type of writing.

Apologetics

The area of Christian theology which focuses on the defense of the Christian faith, particularly through the rational justification of Christian belief and doctrines.

Apophatic

A term used to refer to a particular style of theology, which stressed that God cannot be known in terms of human categories. Apophatic (Greek: *apophasis*, "negation" or "denial") approaches to theology are especially associated with the monastic tradition of the Eastern Orthodox church.

Apostolic era

The period of the Christian church, regarded as definitive by many, bounded by the resurrection of Jesus Christ (*c.* AD 35) and the death of the last apostle (*c.* AD 90?). The ideas and practices of this period were widely regarded as normative, at least in some sense or to some degree, in many church circles.

Appropriation

A term relating to the doctrine of the Trinity, which affirms that while all three persons of the Trinity are active in all the outward actions of the Trinity, it is appropriate to think of those actions as being the particular work of one of the persons. Thus it is appropriate to think of creation as the work of the Father, or redemption as the work of the Son, despite the fact that all three persons are present and active in both these works.

Arianism

A major early Christological heresy, which treated Jesus Christ as supreme amongst God's creatures, and denied his divine status. The Arian controversy was of major importance in the development of Christology during the fourth century.

Atonement

An English term originally coined by William Tyndale to translate the Latin term *reconciliatio*, which has since come to have the developed meaning of "the work of

Christ" or "the benefits of Christ gained for believers by his death and resurrection." The phrase "theories of the atonement" thus means "way of understanding the saving work of Christ."

Barthian

An adjective used to describe the theological outlook of the Swiss theologian Karl Barth (1886–1968), and noted chiefly for its emphasis upon the priority of revelation and its focus upon Jesus Christ. The terms "neo-orthodoxy" and "dialectical theology" are also used in this connection.

Beatific Vision

A term used, especially in Roman Catholic theology, to refer to the full vision of God, which is allowed only to the elect after death. However, some writers, including Thomas Aquinas, taught that certain favored individuals – such as Moses and Paul – were allowed this vision in the present life.

Calvinism

An ambiguous term, used with two quite distinct meanings. First, it refers to the religious ideas of religious bodies (such as the Reformed church) and individuals (such as Theodore Beza) who were profoundly influenced by John Calvin, or by documents written by him. Second, it refers to the religious ideas of John Calvin himself. Although the first sense is by far the more common, there is a growing recognition that the term is misleading.

Cappadocian Fathers

A term used to refer collectively to three major Greek-speaking writers of the patristic period: Basil of Caesarea, Gregory of Nazianzen, and Gregory of Nyssa, all of whom date from the late fourth century.

"Cappadocia" designates an area in Asia Minor (modern Turkey), in which these writers were based.

Cartesianism

The philosophical outlook especially associated with René Descartes (1596–1650), particularly in relation to its emphasis on the separation of the knower from the known, and its insistence that the existence of the individual thinking self is the proper starting point for philosophical reflection.

Catechism

A popular manual of Christian doctrine, usually in the form of question and answer, intended for religious instruction.

Catholic

An adjective which is used to refer both to the universality of the church in space and time, and also to a particular church body (sometime also known as the Roman Catholic Church) which lays emphasis upon this point.

Chalcedonian definition

The formal declaration at the Council of Chalcedon that Jesus Christ was to be regarded as having two natures, one human and one divine.

Charisma; charismatic

A set of terms especially associated with the gifts of the Holy Spirit. In medieval theology, the term "charisma" is used to designate a spiritual gift, conferred upon individuals by the grace of God. Since the early twentieth century, the term "charismatic" has come to refer to styles of theology and worship which place particular emphasis upon the immediate presence and experience of the Holy Spirit.

Christology
The section of Christian theology dealing with the identity of Jesus Christ, particularly the question of the relation of his human and divine natures.

Circumincession *see* **Perichoresis**.

Conciliarism
An understanding of ecclesiastical or theological authority which places an emphasis on the role of ecumenical councils.

Confession
Although the term refers primarily to the admission of sin, it acquired a rather different technical sense in the sixteenth century – that of a document which embodies the principles of faith of a Protestant church, such as the Lutheran Augsburg Confession (1530), which embodies the ideas of early Lutheranism, and the Reformed First Helvetic Confession (1536).

Consubstantial
A Latin term, deriving from the Greek term *homoousios*, literally meaning "of the same substance." The term is used to affirm the full divinity of Jesus Christ, particularly in opposition to Arianism.

Consubstantiation
A term used to refer to the theory of the real presence, especially associated with Martin Luther, which holds that the substance of the eucharistic bread and wine are given together with the substance of the body and blood of Christ.

Correlation, method of
An approach to theology especially associated with Paul Tillich (1886–1965), which attempts to relate the questions of modern western culture to the answers of the Christian tradition.

Creed
A formal definition or summary of the Christian faith, held in common by all Christians. The most important are those generally known as the "Apostles Creed" and the "Nicene Creed."

Deism
A term used to refer to the views of a group of English writers, especially during the seventeenth century, the rationalism of which anticipated many of the ideas of the Enlightenment. The term is often used to refer to a view of God which recognizes the divine creatorship, yet which rejects the notion of a continuing divine involvement with the world.

Demythologization
An approach to theology especially associated with the German theologian Ruldolf Bultmann (1884–1976) and his followers, which rests upon the belief that the New Testament worldview is "mythological." In order for it to be understood within, or applied to, the modern situation, it is necessary that the mythological elements should be eliminated.

Dialectical theology
A term used to refer to the early views of the Swiss theologian Karl Barth (1886–1968), which emphasized the "dialectic between God and humanity."

Docetism
An early Christological heresy, which treated Jesus Christ as a purely divine being who only had the "appearance of being human."

Donatism
A movement, centering upon Roman North Africa in the fourth century, which developed a rigorist view of the church and sacraments.

347

Doxology

A form of praise, especially associated with formal Christian worship. A "doxological" approach to theology stresses the importance of praise and worship in theological reflection.

Ebionitism

An early Christological heresy, which treated Jesus Christ as a purely human figure, although recognizing that he was endowed with particular charismatic gifts which distinguished him from other humans.

Ecclesiology

The section of Christian theology dealing with the theory of the church (Greek: *ekklesia*).

Enhypostasis *see* **Anhypostasis**

Enlightenment, the

A term used since the nineteenth century to refer to the emphasis upon human reason and autonomy, characteristic of much of western European and North American thought during the eighteenth century.

Eschatology

The section of Christian theology dealing with the "end things," especially the ideas of resurrection, hell, and eternal life.

Eucharist

The term used in the present volume to refer to the sacrament variously known as "the Mass," "the Lord's Supper" and "Holy Communion."

Evangelical

A term initially used to refer to the nascent reforming movements, especially in Germany and Switzerland, in the 1510s and 1520s, but now used of the movement, especially in English-language theology,

which places especial emphasis upon the supreme authority of Scripture and the atoning death of Christ.

Ex opere operantis; ex opere operato

Two different ways of understanding the way in which sacraments are effective. The differences between them can be summarized as follows. To affirm that the sacraments are efficacious *ex opere operantis* – literally, "on account of the work of the one who works" – is to say that sacraments work on account of the personal moral qualities of the minister. The view that sacraments are efficacious *ex opere operato* – literally, "on account of the work which is worked" – sees the efficacy of the sacraments depending upon the grace of Christ, which the sacraments represent and convey, so that the personal qualities of the person ministering the sacrament are not of decisive importance. This distinction became of major importance during the Donatist controversy.

Exclusivism

A term once used to refer to the Christian approach to other religions which stressed the uniqueness of the Christian revelation. The term "particularism" is now more widely used.

Exegesis

The science of textual interpretation, usually referring specifically to the Bible. The term "biblical exegesis" basically means "the process of interpreting the Bible." The specific techniques employed in the exegesis of Scripture are usually referred to as "hermeneutics."

Exemplarism

A particular approach to the meaning of the death of Christ, which stresses the moral or religious example set to believers by Jesus Christ.

Existentialism
A movement which places emphasis on the subjectivity of individual existence, and the way in which this is affected by one's environment. The theological development of this approach is especially associated with Rudolf Bultmann and Paul Tillich.

Fathers
An alternative term for "patristic writers."

Feminism
A major movement in western theology since the 1960s, which lays particular emphasis upon the importance of women's experience, and has directed criticism against the patriarchalism of Christianity.

Fideism
An understanding of Christian theology which refuses to accept the need for (or sometimes the possibility of) criticism or evaluation from sources outside the Christian faith itself.

Fides qua creditur; fides quae creditur
Christian theology has always recognized a distinction between the act and content of Christian faith. Two Latin terms are used to express this distinction, as follows. The term *fides qua creditur* (literally, "the faith by which it is believed") refers to the act of trust and assent which lies at the heart of Christian belief. Yet Christian faith has a content, in that it knows what it believes, and believes what it knows. The term *fides quae creditur* ("the faith which is believed") refers to the specific content of Christian faith, expressed in various creeds, confessions, doctrines, and other statements of faith.

Five Ways, the
A standard term for the five arguments for the existence of God associated with Thomas Aquinas.

Fourth Gospel
A term used to refer to the Gospel according to John. The term highlights the distinctive literary and theological character of this gospel, which sets it apart from the common structures of the first three gospels, usually known as the "Synoptic Gospels."

Fundamentalism
A form of American Protestant Christianity, which lays especial emphasis upon the authority of an inerrant Bible, and is noted for its tendency to reject critical biblical scholarship and to withdraw from society as a whole.

Hermeneutics
The principles underlying the interpretation, or exegesis, of a text, particularly of Scripture, particularly in relation to its present-day application.

Hesychasm
A tradition, especially associated with the eastern church, which places considerable emphasis upon the idea of "inner quietness" (Greek: *hesychia*) as a means of achieving a vision of God. It is particularly associated with writers such as Simeon the New Theologian and Gregory Palamas.

Historical Jesus
A term used, especially during the nineteenth century, to refer to the real historical person of Jesus of Nazareth, as opposed to the Christian interpretation of that person, as presented in the New Testament and the creeds.

Historico-critical Method
An approach to historical texts, including the Bible, which argues that proper meaning must be determined only on the basis of the specific historical conditions under which it was written.

History of Religions School
The approach to religious history, and Christian origins in particular, which treats Old and New Testament developments as responses to encounters with other religions, such as Gnosticism.

Homoousion
A Greek term, literally meaning "of the same substance," which came to be used extensively during the fourth century to designate the main-stream Christological belief that Jesus Christ was "of the same substance as God." The term was polemical, being directed against the Arian view that Christ was "of similar substance" (*homoiousios*) to God. *See also* **Consubstantial**.

Humanism
In the strict sense of the word, an intellectual movement linked with the European Renaissance. At the heart of the movement lay, not (as the modern sense of the word might suggest) a set of secular or secularizing ideas, but a new interest in the cultural achievements of antiquity. These were seen as a major resource for the renewal of European culture and Christianity during the period of the Renaissance.

Hypostatic union
The doctrine of the union of divine and human natures in Jesus Christ, without confusion of their respective substances.

Ideology
A group of beliefs and values, usually secular, which govern the actions and outlooks of a society or group of people.

Incarnation
A term used to refer to the assumption of human nature by God, in the person of Jesus Christ. The term "incarnationalism" is often used to refer to theological approaches which lay particular emphasis upon God's becoming human.

Inclusivism
The way of understanding the relation between Christianity and other faiths which affirms that the Christian truth or salvation are, at least to some extent, accessible through other faiths.

Justification by faith, doctrine of
The section of Christian theology dealing with how the individual sinner is able to enter into fellowship with God. The doctrine was to prove to be of major significance at the time of the Reformation.

Kenoticism
A form of Christology which lays emphasis upon Christ's "laying aside" of certain divine attributes in the incarnation, or his "emptying himself" of at least some divine attributes, especially omniscience or omnipotence.

Kerygma
A term used, especially by Rudolf Bultmann (1884–1976) and his followers, to refer to the essential message or proclamation of the New Testament concerning the significance of Jesus Christ.

Liberal Protestantism
A movement, notably associated with nineteenth-century Germany, which stressed the continuity between religion and culture, flourishing between the time of F.D.E. Schleiermacher and Paul Tillich.

Liberation theology
Although this term designates any theological movement laying emphasis upon the liberating impact of the gospel, the term has come to refer to a movement which devel-

oped in Latin America in the late 1960s, which stressed the role of political action and oriented itself toward the goal of political liberation from poverty and oppression.

Liturgy
The written text of public services, especially of the eucharist.

Logos
A Greek term meaning "word," which played a crucial role in the development of patristic Christology. Jesus Christ was recognized as the "word of God"; the question concerned the implications of this recognition, and especially the way in which the divine "logos" in Jesus Christ related to his human nature.

Lutheranism
The religious ideas associated with Martin Luther, particularly as expressed in the Lesser Catechism (1529) and the Augsburg Confession (1530).

Manicheism
A strongly fatalist position associated with the Manichees, to which Augustine of Hippo attached himself during his early period. A distinction is drawn between two different divinities, one of which is regarded as evil, and the other good. Evil is thus seen as the direct result of the influence of the evil god.

Modalism
A Trinitarian heresy, which treats the three persons of the Trinity as different "modes" of the Godhead. A typical modalist approach is to regard God as active as Father in creation, as Son in redemption, and as Spirit in sanctification.

Monophysitism
The doctrine that there is only one nature in Christ, which is divine (from the Greek words *monos*, "only one," and *physis*, "nature"). This view differed from the orthodox view, upheld by the Council of Chalcedon (451), that Christ had two natures, one divine and one human.

Neo-orthodoxy
A term used to designate the general position of Karl Barth (1886–1968), especially the manner in which he drew upon the theological concerns of the period of Reformed orthodoxy.

Ontological Argument
A term used to refer to the type of argument for the existence of God especially associated with the scholastic theologian Anselm of Canterbury.

Orthodoxy
A term used in a number of senses, of which the following are the most important: orthodoxy in the sense of "right belief," as opposed to heresy; Orthodoxy in the sense of the forms of Christianity which are dominant in Russia and Greece; orthodoxy in the sense of a movement within Protestantism, especially in the late sixteenth and early seventeenth centuries, which laid emphasis upon the need for doctrinal definition.

Parousia
A Greek term, which literally means "coming" or "arrival," used to refer to the second coming of Christ. The notion of the *parousia* is an important aspect of Christian understandings of the "last things."

Particularism
The understanding of the relation between Christianity and other faiths which affirms the distinctiveness of Christian truth and salvation.

Patripassianism

A theological heresy which arose during the third century, associated with writers such as Noetus, Praxeas, and Sabellius, focusing on the belief that the Father suffered as the Son. In other words, the suffering of Christ on the cross is to be regarded as the suffering of the Father. According to these writers, the only distinction within the Godhead was a succession of modes or operations, so that Father, Son, and Spirit were just different modes of being, or expressions, of the same basic divine entity.

Patristic

An adjective used to refer to the first centuries in the history of the church, following the writing of the New Testament (the "patristic period"), or thinkers writing during this period (the "patristic writers"). For many writers, the period thus designated seems to be *c*.100–451 (in other words, the period between the completion of the last of the New Testament writings and the landmark Council of Chalcedon).

Pelagianism

An understanding of how humans are able to merit their salvation which is diametrically opposed to that of Augustine of Hippo, placing considerable emphasis upon the role of human works and playing down the idea of divine grace.

Perichoresis

A term relating to the doctrine of the Trinity, often also referred to by the Latin term *circumincessio*. The basic notion is that all three persons of the Trinity mutually share in the life of the others, so that none is isolated or detached from the actions of the others.

Pietism

An approach to Christianity, especially as-

sociated with German writers in the seventeenth century, which places an emphasis upon the personal appropriation of faith, and the need for holiness in Christian living. The movement is perhaps best known within the English-language world in the form of Methodism.

Pluralism

An approach to the relation of Christianity and other faiths which regards the world's religions as equally valid manifestations or representations of the same fundamental spiritual reality.

Postliberalism

A theological movement, especially associated with Duke University and Yale Divinity School in the 1980s, which criticized the liberal reliance upon human experience, and reclaimed the notion of community tradition as a controlling influence in theology.

Postmodernism

A general cultural development, especially in North America, which resulted from the general collapse in confidence of the universal rational principles of the Enlightenment.

Praxis

A Greek term, literally meaning "action," adopted by Karl Marx to emphasize the importance of action in relation to thinking. This emphasis on "praxis" has had considerable impact within Latin American liberation theology.

Protestantism

A term used in the aftermath of the Diet of Speyer (1529) to designate those who "protested" against the practices and beliefs of the Roman Catholic church. Prior to 1529, such individuals and groups had referred to themselves as "evangelicals."

Quadriga

The Latin term used to refer to the "four-fold" interpretation of Scripture according to its literal, allegorical, tropological/moral, and analogical senses.

Radical Reformation

A term used with increasing frequency to refer to the Anabaptist movement – in other words, the wing of the Reformation which went beyond what Luther and Zwingli envisaged, particularly in relation to the doctrine of the church.

Reformed

A term used to refer to a tradition of theology which draws inspiration from the writings of John Calvin (1510–64) and his successors. The term is now generally used in preference to "Calvinist."

Sabellianism

An early trinitarian heresy, which treated the three persons of the Trinity as different historical manifestations of the one God. It is generally regarded as a form of modalism.

Sacrament

In purely historical terms, a church service or rite which was held to have been instituted by Jesus Christ himself. Although Roman Catholic theology and church practice recognize seven such sacraments (baptism, confirmation, eucharist, marriage, ordination, penance, and unction), Protestant theologians generally argue that only two (baptism and eucharist) were to be found in the New Testament itself.

Schism

A deliberate break with the unity of the church, condemned vigorously by influential writers of the early church, such as Cyprian and Augustine.

Scholasticism

A particular approach to Christian theology, associated especially with the Middle Ages, which lays emphasis upon the rational justification and systematic presentation of Christian theology.

Scripture principle

The theory, especially associated with Reformed theologians, that the practices and beliefs of the church should be grounded in Scripture. Nothing that could not be demonstrated to be grounded in Scripture could be regarded as binding upon the believer. The phrase *sola scriptura*, "by Scripture alone," summarizes this principle.

Soteriology

The section of Christian theology dealing with the doctrine of salvation (Greek: *soteria*).

Synoptic gospels

A term used to refer to the first three gospels (Matthew, Mark, and Luke). The term (derived from the Greek word *synopsis.* "summary") refers to the way in which the three gospels can be seen as providing similar "summaries" of the life, death, and resurrection of Jesus Christ.

Synoptic problem

The scholarly question of how the three synoptic gospels relate to each other. Perhaps the most common approach to the relation of the three synoptic gospels is the "two-source theory," which claims that Matthew and Luke used Mark as a source, while also drawing upon a second source (usually known as "Q"). Other possibilities exist: for example, the Griesbach hypothesis, which treats Matthew as having been written first, followed by Luke and then Mark.

353

Theodicy

A term coined by Leibniz to refer to a theoretical justification of the goodness of God in the face of the presence of evil in the world.

Theopaschitism

A disputed teaching, regarded by some as a heresy, which arose during the sixth century, associated with writers such as John Maxentius and the slogan "one of the Trinity was crucified." The formula can be interpreted in a perfectly orthodox sense and was defended as such by Leontius of Byzantium. However, it was regarded as potentially misleading and confusing by more cautious writers, including Pope Hormisdas (died 523), and the formula gradually fell into disuse.

Theotokos

Literally, "the bearer of God." A Greek term used to refer to Mary, the mother of Jesus Christ, with the intention of reinforcing the central insight of the doctrine of the incarnation – that is, that Jesus Christ is none other than God. The term was extensively used by writers of the eastern church, especially around the time of the Nestorian controversy, to articulate both the divinity of Christ and the reality of the incarnation.

Third Quest

A phrase used to describe the historical investigation of the life of Jesus initiated during the 1970s.

Transubstantiation

The doctrine according to which the bread and the wine are transformed into the body and blood of Christ in the eucharist, while retaining their outward appearance.

Trinity

The distinctively Christian doctrine of God, which reflects the complexity of the Christian experience of God. The doctrine is usually summarized in maxims such as "three persons, one God."

Two Natures, doctrine of

A term generally used to refer to the doctrine of the two natures, human and divine, of Jesus Christ. Related terms include "Chalcedonian definition" and "hypostatic union."

Vulgate

The Latin translation of the Bible, largely deriving from Jerome, upon which medieval theology was largely based.

Zwinglianism

The term is used generally to refer to the thought of Huldrych Zwingli, but is often used to refer specifically to his views on the sacraments, especially on the "real presence" (which for Zwingli was more of a "real absence").

FOR FURTHER READING

1 The Patristic Period

Henry Bettenson, *Documents of the Christian Church*, 2nd edn (Oxford: Oxford University Press, 1963).

Henry Chadwick, *The Early Church* (London/New York: Pelican, 1964).

Jean Comby, *How to Read Church History*, vol. 1 (London: SCM Press, 1985).

Jean Daniélou and Henri Marrou, *The Christian Centuries*, vol. 1 (London: Darton, Longman and Todd, 1964).

W. H. C. Frend, *The Rise of Christianity* (Philadelphia: Fortress Press, 1984).

Ian Hazlett (ed.), *Early Christianity: Origins and Evolution to* AD 600 (London: SPCK, 1991).

Niels Hydahl, *The History of Early Christianity* (Frankfurt/New York: Peter Lang, 1997).

Herbert Jedin and John Dolan (eds), *A Handbook of Church History*, vol. 1 (London: Burns & Oates, 1965).

J. N. D. Kelly, *Early Christian Doctrines*, 4th edn (London: A. & C. Black, 1968).

F. van der Meer and Christine Mohrmann, *Atlas of the Early Christian World* (London: Nelson, 1959).

J. Stevenson, *A New Eusebius: Documents Illustrating the History of the Church to* AD 337, rev. edn (London: SPCK, 1987).

———, *Creeds, Councils and Controversies: Documents Illustrating the History of the Church, 337–461*, rev. edn (London: SPCK, 1987).

Frances M. Young, *From Nicea to Chalcedon* (London: SCM Press, 1983).

Individual Theologians

L. W. Barnard, *Justin Martyr: His Life and Thought* (Cambridge: Cambridge University Press, 1967).

Timothy D. Barnes, *Athanasius and Constantius: Theology and Politics in the Constantinian Empire* (Cambridge, MA: Harvard University Press, 1993).

Gerald Bonner, *Augustine: Life and Controversies*, rev. edn (Norwich: Canterbury Press, 1986).

Peter Brown, *Augustine of Hippo* (London: Faber & Faber, 1967).

Hans von Campenhausen, *The Fathers of the Greek Church* (London: A. & C. Black, 1963).

———, *The Fathers of the Latin Church* (London: A. & C. Black, 1964).

Henry Chadwick, *Augustine* (Oxford: Oxford University Press, 1986).

Mary T. Clark, *Augustine* (London: Geoffrey Chapman, 1994).

Henri Crouzel, *Origen* (Edinburgh: T. & T. Clark, 1989).

Robert M. Grant, *Greek Apologists of the Second Century* (Philadelphia: Westminster Press, 1988).

J. N. D. Kelly, *Jerome* (London: Duckworth, 1975).

Denis Minns, *Irenaeus* (London: Geoffrey Chapman, 1994).

Johannes Quasten, *Patrology*, 4 vols (Westminster, MD: Christian Classics, 1986). A definitive study of the life and writings of the theologians of the patristic period to 451.

John M. Rist, *Augustine: Ancient Thought Baptized* (Cambridge: Cambridge University Press, 1994).

William G. Rusch, *The Later Latin Fathers* (London: Duckworth, 1977).

Simon Tugwell, *The Apostolic Fathers* (London: Geoffrey Chapman, 1989).

Joseph Wilson Trigg, *Origen: The Bible and Philosophy in the Third-Century Church* (Atlanta, GA: John Knox Press, 1983).

2 The Middle Ages and Renaissance

Peter Burke, *The Italian Renaissance: Culture and Society in Italy*, rev. edn (Cambridge: Polity Press, 1986).

Frederick Copleston, *A History of Christian Philosophy in the Middle Ages* (London: Sheed & Ward, 1978).

Manfred P. Fleischer (ed.), *The Harvest of Humanism in Central Europe* (St Louis, MO: Concordia Publishing House, 1992).

Etienne Gilson, *The Spirit of Medieval Philosophy* (London: Sheed & Ward, 1936).

Ernesto Grassi, *Rhetoric as Philosophy: The Humanist Tradition* (University Park, PA: University of Pennsylvania Press, 1980).

Maria Grossmann, *Humanism at Wittenberg 1485–1517* (Nieuwkoop: Nijhoff, 1975).

Judith Herrin, *The Formation of Christendom* (Princeton: Princeton University Press, 1987).

David Knowles, *The Evolution of Medieval Thought*, 2nd edn (London/New York, 1988).

A. H. T. Levi, "The Breakdown of Scholasticism and the Significance of Evangelical Humanism," in *The Philosophical Assessment of Theology*, ed. G. R. Hughes (London: Burns & Oates, 1987), pp. 101–28.

Alister E. McGrath, *The Intellectual Foundations of the European Reformation* (Oxford: Blackwell, 1987), pp. 32–121.

John Meyendorff, *Byzantine Theology: Historical Trends and Doctrinal Themes* (New York: Fordham University Press, 1979).

Charles G. Nauert, "The Clash of Humanists and Scholastics: An Approach to Pre-Reformation Controversies," *Sixteenth Century Journal*, 4 (1973), pp. 1–18.

Heiko A. Oberman, *The Harvest of Medieval Theology* (Cambridge, MA: Harvard University Press, 1963).

——, *Masters of the Reformation* (Cambridge: Cambridge University Press, 1981).

——, *The Dawn of the Reformation: Essays in Late Medieval and Early Reformation Thought* (Edinburgh: T. & T. Clark, 1986).

John W. O'Malley, Thomas M. Izbicki, and Gerald Christianson (eds), *Humanity and Divinity in Renaissance and Reformation* (Leiden: Brill, 1993).

J. H. Overfeld, *Humanism and Scholasticism in Late Medieval Germany* (Princeton, NJ: Princeton University Press, 1984).

Steven E. Ozment, *The Age of Reform 1250–1550: An Intellectual and Religious History of Late Medieval and Reformation Europe* (New Haven: Yale University Press, 1973).

Josef Pieper, *Scholasticism: Personalities and Problems of Medieval Philosophy* (London: Faber & Faber, 1961).

Roy Porter and Mikuláš Teich (eds), *The Renaissance in National Context* (Cambridge: Cambridge University Press, 1992).

B. B. Price, *Medieval Thought: An Introduction* (Oxford/Cambridge, MA: Blackwell, 1992).

Lewis W. Spitz, *The Religious Renaissance of the German Humanists* (Cambridge, MA: Harvard University Press, 1963).

Individual Theologians

Frederick Copleston, *Aquinas* (London: Pelican, 1975).

Brian Davies, *The Thought of Thomas Aquinas* (Oxford: Clarendon Press, 1992).

Leo Elders, *The Philosophical Theology of St Thomas Aquinas* (Leiden: Brill, 1990).

Gillian R. Evans, *Anselm* (London: Geoffrey Chapman, 1989).

Gordon Leff, *William of Ockham* (Manchester: Manchester University Press, 1975).

Andrew Louth, *Denys the Areopagite* (London: Geoffrey Chapman, 1989).

James McConica, *Erasmus* (Oxford: Oxford University Press, 1991).

John Meyendorff, *A Study of Gregory Palamas*, 2nd edn (Crestwood, NY: St Vladimir Seminary Press, 1974).

R. J. Schoeck, *Erasmus of Europe: The Making of a Humanist 1467–1500* (Edinburgh: Edinburgh University Press, 1990).

James A. Weisheipl, *Friar Thomas d'Aquino: His Life, Thought and Work* (Garden City, NY: Doubleday, 1972).

Allan B. Wolter and Marilyn McCord Adams (eds), *The Philosophical Theology of John Duns Scotus* (Ithaca, NY: Cornell University Press, 1990).

3 The Reformation and Post-Reformation Periods

John Bossy, *Christianity in the West* (Oxford: Oxford University Press, 1985).

Euan Cameron, *The European Reformation* (Oxford: Oxford University Press, 1991).

Owen Chadwick, *The Reformation* (London/New York: Pelican, 1976).

G. R. Elton (ed.), *The Reformation 1520–1559*, 2nd edn (Cambridge: Cambridge University Press, 1990).

Timothy George, *The Theology of the Reformers* (Nashville, TN: Abingdon, 1988).

Alister E. McGrath, *Reformation Thought: An Introduction*, 2nd edn (Oxford/Cambridge, MA: Blackwell Publishers, 1993).

Richard A. Muller, *Post-Reformation Reformed Dogmatics* (Grand Rapids: Baker, 1987).

Mark A. Noll, *Confessions and Catechisms of the Reformation* (Grand Rapids: Eerdmans, 1991).

John W. O'Malley, Thomas M. Izbicki, and Gerald Christianson (eds), *Humanity and Divinity in Renaissance and Reformation* (Leiden: Brill, 1993).

B. M. G. Reardon, *Religious Thought in the Reformation* (London: Longmans 1981).

Robert P. Scharlemann, *Thomas Aquinas and John Gerhard* (New Haven: Yale University Press, 1964).

Lewis W. Spitz, *The Protestant Reformation 1517–1559* (New York: Scribner's, 1986).

Individual Theologians

Roland H. Bainton, *Here I Stand: A Life of Martin Luther* (New York: Mentor Books, 1955).

W. J. Bouwsma, *John Calvin: A Sixteenth-Century Portrait* (New York: Oxford University Press, 1988).

E. J. Furcha and H. W. Pipkin (eds), *Prophet, Pastor, Protestant: The Work of Huldrych Zwingli* (Allison Park, PA: Pickwick Publications, 1984).

Alexandre Ganoczy, *The Young Calvin* (Edinburgh: T. & T. Clark, 1988).

James M. Kittelson, *Luther the Reformer: The Story of the Man and His Career* (Leicester: InterVarsity Press, 1989).

Walter von Loewenich, *Martin Luther: The Man and His Work* (Minneapolis: Augsburg, 1986).

Bernhard Lohse, *Martin Luther: An Introduction to His Life and Work* (Philadelphia: Fortress Press, 1986).

Alister E. McGrath, *Luther's Theology of the Cross: Martin Luther's Theological Breakthrough* (Oxford: Blackwell, 1985).

——, *A Life of John Calvin* (Oxford/Cambridge, MA: Blackwell, 1990).

Perry Miller, *Jonathan Edwards* (New York: Sloane Associates, 1949).

T. H. L. Parker, *John Calvin* (London: Dent, 1975).

Harold P. Simonson, *Jonathan Edwards: Theology of the Heart* (Grand Rapids: Eerdmans, 1974).

John E. Smith, *Jonathan Edwards: Puritan, Preacher, Philosopher* (London: Chapman, 1993).

W. P. Stephens, *The Theology of Huldrych Zwingli* (Oxford: Oxford University Press, 1986).

François Wendel, *Calvin* (New York: Harper & Row, 1963).

D. F. Wright (ed.), *Martin Bucer: Reforming Church and Community* (Cambridge: Cambridge University Press, 1994).

4 The Modern Period

The bibliography which follows is more detailed than normal, given the particular interest many students have in the more recent aspects of Christian theology. The material to be presented is categorized under "Individual Theologians" and "Theological Movements since the Enlightenment."

Individual Theologians

There are numerous study aids available for those wishing to pursue details of individual theologians during the modern period. The following works are of fundamental importance.

For a survey of Christian thought and thinkers since the Enlightenment, see Alister E. McGrath (ed.), *Blackwell Encyclopaedia of Modern Christian Thought* (Oxford/Cambridge, MA: Blackwell Publishers, 1993).

For specialist studies of nineteenth-century Christian theology and theologians, see:

Ninian Smart, John Clayton, Patrick Sherry, and Steven T. Katz (eds), *Nineteenth-Century Religious Thought in the West*, 3 vols (Cambridge: Cambridge University Press, 1985).

Claude Welch, *Protestant Thought in the Nineteenth Century*, 2 vols (New Haven: Yale University Press, 1972–85).

For valuable surveys of twentieth-century writers, see:

David F. Ford (ed.), *The Modern Theologians*, 2nd edn (Oxford/Cambridge, MA: Blackwell Publishers, 1997).

Stanley J. Grenz and Roger E. Olson, *Twentieth-Century Theology: God and the World in a Transitional Age* (Downers Grove, IL: InterVarsity Press, 1992).

For further details of many theologians active in the nineteenth and twentieth centuries, see Martin E. Marty and Dean G. Peerman, *A Handbook of Christian Theologians* (Nashville: Abingdon Press, 1984).

Theological Movements since the Enlightenment

Black Theology
A. B. Cleage, *The Black Messiah* (New York: Sheed & Ward, 1969).

James H. Cone, *A Black Theology of Liberation* (Philadelphia: Lippincott, 1970).

——, *For My People* (Maryknoll, NY: Orbis, 1986).

Dwight N. Hopkins, *Black Theology, USA and South Africa* (Maryknoll, NY: Orbis, 1989).

Patrick A. Kalilombe, "Black Theology," in D. F. Ford (ed.), *The Modern Theologians*, 2 vols (Oxford/Cambridge, MA: Blackwell Publishers, 1990), vol. 2, pp. 193–216.

Joseph R. Washington, *Black Religion* (Boston: Beacon Press, 1966).

——, *The Politics of God: The Future of the Black Churches* (Boston: Beacon Press, 1967).

Gayraud S. Wilmore and James H. Cone (eds), *Black Theology: A Documentary History 1966–79* (Maryknoll, NY: Orbis, 1979).

The Charismatic Movement and Pentecostalism
R. M. Anderson, *Vision of the Disinherited: The Making of American Pentecostalism* (Oxford: Oxford University Press, 1980).

Stanley M. Burgess, Gary B. McGee, and Patrick H. Alexander (eds), *Dictionary of Pentecostal and Charismatic Movements* (Grand Rapids: Zondervan, 1988).

Walter Hollenweger, *The Pentecostals* (London: SCM Press, 1972).

Killiam McDonnell, *The Charismatic Movement and Ecumenism* (New York: Paulist Press, 1978).

David Martin, *Tongues of Fire: The Explosion of Protestantism in Latin America* (Oxford: Blackwell, 1990).

Richard Quebedeaux, *The New Charismatics: The Origins, Development and Significance of Neo-Pentecostalism* (Garden City, NY: Doubleday, 1976).

Thomas A. Smail, Andrew Walker and Nigel Wright, *Charismatic Renewal: The Search for a Theology* (London: SPCK, 1993).

Russell P. Spitler (ed.), *Perspectives on the New Pentecostalism* (Grand Rapids: Baker Book House, 1976).

C. Peter Wagner, *The Third Wave of the Holy Spirit: Encountering the Power of Signs and Wonders Today* (Ann Arbor, MI: Servant, 1988).

J. Rodman Williams, *Renewal Theology*, 3 vols (Grand Rapids: Zondervan, 1988–92).

Eastern Orthodoxy
Frank Gavin, *Some Aspects of Contemporary Greek Orthodox Thought* (Milwaukee: Morehouse, 1923).

Aidan Nichols, *Theology in the Russian Diaspora* (Cambridge: Cambridge University Press, 1989).

Christos Yannaras, "Theology in Present-Day Greece," *St Vladimir's Theological Quarterly*, 16/4 (1972), pp. 1–20.

Nicolas Zernov, *The Russian Religious Renaissance of the Twentieth Century* (London: Darton, Longman and Todd, 1963).

Evangelicalism

David W. Bebbington, *Evangelicalism in Modern Britain* (London: Unwin Hyman, 1989).

Donald G. Bloesch, *The Essentials of Evangelical Theology*, 2 vols (San Francisco: Harper & Row, 1978–9).

Judith L. Blumhofer and Joel A. Carpenter, *Twentieth Century Evangelicalism: A Guide to the Sources* (New York: Garland Publishing, 1990).

Walter A. Elwell (ed.), *Handbook of Evangelical Theologians* (Grand Rapids: Baker, 1993).

Kenneth S. Kantzer and Carl F. H. Henry, *Evangelical Affirmations* (Grand Rapids: Zondervan, 1990), pp. 27–38.

Alister E. McGrath, *Evangelicalism and the Future of Christianity* (Downers Grove, IL: InterVarsity, 1995, and London: Hodder & Stoughton, 1994).

——, *Evangelical Theology: A Reader* (London: SPCK, 1996).

Mark Noll, *The Scandal of the Evangelical Mind* (Grand Rapids: Eerdmans, 1994).

David F. Wells and John D. Woodbridge (eds), *The Evangelicals* (Nashville: Abingdon, 1975).

Feminism

Marga Bührig, *Woman Invisible* (London: Burns & Oates, 1993).

Anne Carr, "Feminist Theology," in A. E. McGrath (ed.), *The Blackwell Encyclopaedia of Modern Christian Thought* (Oxford/Cambridge, MA: Blackwell Publishers, 1993), pp. 220–8.

Elisabeth Schüssler Fiorenza, *In Memory of Her: A Feminist Reconstruction of Christian Origins* (New York: Crossroad, 1983).

Jacquelyn Grant, *White Women's Christ and Black Women's Jesus: Feminist Christology and Womanist Response* (Atlanta, GA: Scholars Press, 1989).

Daphne Hampson, *Theology and Feminism* (Oxford: Blackwell, 1990).

Mary Hayter, *New Eve in Christ* (London: SPCK, 1987).

Chung Hyun Kyung, *Struggle to be the Sun Again: Introducing Asian Women's Theology* (London: SCM Press, 1991).

Ann Loades, *Feminist Theology: A Reader* (London: SPCK, 1990).

——, "Feminist Theology," in D. F. Ford (ed.), *The Modern Theologians*, 2 vols (Oxford/Cambridge, MA: Blackwell, 1990), vol. 2, pp. 235–52.

Francis Martin, *The Feminist Question: Feminist Theology in the Light of Christian Tradition* (Grand Rapids: Eerdmans, 1994).

Judith Plaskow, *Sex, Sin and Grace: Women's Experience and the Theologies of Reinhold Niebuhr amd Paul Tillich* (Washington, DC: Catholic University of America Press, 1980).

Rosemary Radford Ruether, *Sexism and God-Talk: Towards a Feminist Christology* (Boston: Beacon Press, 1983).

Letty M. Russell, *Household of Freedom: Authority in Feminist Theology* (Philadelphia: Westminster Press, 1987).

——, and J. Shannon, *Dictionary of Feminist Theologies* (Louisville, KY: Westminster/John Knox Press, 1996).

Susan Thistlethwaite, *Sex, Race and God: Christian Feminism in Black and White* (London: Chapman, 1990).

Pamela Dickey Young, *Feminist Theology/Christian Theology: In Search of Method* (Minneapolis: Fortress Press, 1990).

Liberalism and Modernism

Kenneth Cauthen, *The Impact of American Religious Liberalism* (Lanham, MD: University Press of America, 1962).

Sheila Greeve Davaney and Delwin Brown, "Liberalism (USA)," in A. E. McGrath (ed.), *The Blackwell Encyclopaedia of Modern Christian Thought* (Oxford/Cambridge, MA: Blackwell Publishers, 1993), pp. 325–30.

William R. Hutchinson (ed.), *American Protestant Thought in the Liberal Era* (Lanham, MD: University Press of America, 1968).

J. Gresham Machen, *Christianity and Liberalism* (1923; reprinted Grand Rapids: Eerdmans, 1994).

Barry Penn Hollar, *On Being the Church in the United States: Contemporary Theological Critiques of Liberalism* (New York/Berne: Peter Lang, 1994).

John Ratté, *Three Modernists: Alfred Loisy, George Tyrrell, William L. Sullivan* (New York: Sheed & Ward, 1967).

Bernard M. G. Reardon, *Roman Catholic Modernism* (Stanford, CA: Stanford University Press, 1970).

——, *Liberal Protestantism* (Stanford: Stanford University Press, 1968).

George Rupp, *Culture Protestantism: German Liberal Theology at the Turn of the Twentieth Century* (Atlanta, GA: Scholars Press, 1977).

A. M. G. Stephenson, *The Rise and Decline of English Modernism* (London: SPCK, 1984).

David Tracy, *Blessed Rage for Order: The New Pluralism in Theology* (New York: Seabury Press, 1975).

Alec R. Vidler, *The Modernist Movement in the Roman Church* (Cambridge: Cambridge University Press, 1934).

Liberation Theology

José Míguez Bonino, *Doing Theology in a Revolutionary Situation* (Philadelphia: Fortress Press, 1975).

Robert McAfee Brown, *Theology in a New Key: Responding to Liberation Theology* (Philadelphia: Westminster Press, 1978).

——, *Gustavo Gutiérrez: An Introduction to Liberation Theology* (Maryknoll, NY: Orbis Books, 1990).

Rebecca S. Chopp, "Latin American Liberation Theology," in D. F. Ford (ed.), *The Modern Theologians*, 2 vols (Oxford/Cambridge, MA: Blackwell, 1989), vol. 2, pp. 173–92.

Samuel Escobar, "Liberation Theology," in A. E. McGrath (ed.), *The Blackwell Encyclopaedia of Modern Christian Thought* (Oxford/Cambridge, MA: Blackwell Publishers, 1993), pp. 330–5.

Gustavo Gutiérrez, *The Theology of Liberation*, rev. edn (Maryknoll, NY: Orbis Books, 1988).

J. Andrew Kirk, *Liberation Theology: An Evangelical View from the Third World* (Atlanta: John Knox Press, 1979).

Narrative Theology

Gary Comstock, "Two Types of Narrative Theology," *Journal of the American Academy of Religion*, 55 (1987), pp. 687–717.

Mark Ellingsen, *The Integrity of Biblical Narrative* (Minneapolis: Fortress Press, 1990).

David F. Ford, *Barth and God's Story* (Frankfurt: Peter Lang, 1985).

Hans Frei, *The Eclipse of Biblical Narrative* (New Haven: Yale University Press, 1974).

Garrett Green (ed.), *Scriptural Authority and Narrative Interpretation* (Philadelphia: Fortress Press, 1986).

Stanley Hauerwas and L. Gregory Jones (eds), *Why Narrative? Readings in Narrative Theology* (Grand Rapids: Eerdmans, 1989).

L. Gregory Jones, "Narrative Theology," in A. E. McGrath (ed.), *The Blackwell Encyclopaedia of Modern Christian Thought* (Oxford/Cambridge, MA: Blackwell Publishers, 1993), pp. 395–8.

James Wm. McClendon, Jr, *Biography as*

Theology (Nashville, TN: Abingdon, 1974).

H. Richard Niebuhr, *The Meaning of Revelation* (New York: Macmillan, 1941).

Dale Patrick, *The Rendering of God in the Old Testament* (Philadelphia: Fortress Press, 1981).

Robert Paul Roth, *The Theater of God: Story in Christian Doctrines* (Philadelpia: Fortress Press, 1985).

Robert Scholes and Robert Kellogg, *The Nature of Narrative* (New York: Oxford University Press, 1966).

Neo-Orthodoxy

Eberhard Busch, *Karl Barth: His Life from Letters and Autobiographical Texts* (London: SCM Press, 1976).

Edward J. Carnell, *The Theology of Reinhold Niebuhr* (Grand Rapids: Eerdmans, 1951).

Kenneth Durkin, *Reinhold Niebuhr* (London: Geoffrey Chapman, 1989).

David F. Ford, "Karl Barth," in A. E. McGrath (ed.), *The Blackwell Encyclopaedia of Modern Christian Thought* (Oxford/Cambridge, MA: Blackwell Publishers, 1993), pp. 30–4.

Stanley J. Grenz and Roger E. Olson, *Twentieth-Century Theology: God and the World in a Transitional Age* (Downers Grove, IL: InterVarsity Press, 1992), pp. 63–112.

Paul King Jewett, *Emil Brunner's Concept of Revelation* (London: James Clarke, 1954).

Gareth Jones, *Bultmann: Towards a Critical Theology* (Cambridge: Polity Press, 1991).

Postliberalism

Sheila Greeve Davaney and Delwin Brown, "Postliberalism," in A. E. McGrath (ed.), *The Blackwell Encyclopaedia of Modern Christian Thought* (Oxford/ Cambridge, MA: Blackwell Publishers, 1993), pp. 453–6.

Hans Frei, *The Identity of Jesus Christ* (Philadelphia: Fortress Press, 1975).

Paul Holmer, *The Grammar of Faith* (New York: Harper & Row, 1978).

David Kelsey, *The Uses of Scripture in Recent Theology* (Philadelphia: Fortress Press, 1975).

George Lindbeck, *The Nature of Doctrine: Religion and Theology in a Postliberal Age* (Philadelphia: Westminster Press, 1984).

William C. Placher, *Unapologetic Theology: A Christian Voice in a Pluralistic Conversation* (Louisville, KY: Westminster/ John Knox Press, 1989).

——, "Postliberal Theology," in D. F. Ford (ed.), *The Modern Theologians*, 2 vols (Oxford/Cambridge, MA: Blackwell, 1989), vol. 2, pp. 115–28.

Ronald E. Thiemann, *Revelation and Theology: The Gospel as Narrated Promise* (Notre Dame: University of Notre Dame, 1985).

Postmodernism

Diogenes Allen, *Christian Belief in a Postmodern World* (Louisville: Westminster/John Knox Press, 1989).

Thomas J. Altizer, *Genesis and Apocalypse: A Theological Voyage Towards Authentic Christianity* (Louisville, KY: Westminster/John Knox Press, 1990).

Robert Detweiler, "Postmodernism," in A. E. McGrath (ed.), *The Blackwell Encyclopaedia of Modern Christian Thought* (Oxford/Cambridge, MA: Blackwell Publishers, 1993), pp. 456–61.

Edgar V. McKnight, *Post-Modern Use of the Bible: The Emergence of Reader-Orientated Criticism* (Nashville: Abingdon, 1988).

Nancey Murphy and James Wm. McClendon, Jr, "Distinguishing Modern and Postmodern Theologies,"

Modern Theology, 5 (1989), pp. 191–214.

Thomas C. Oden, *After Modernity . . . What? Agenda for Theology* (Grand Rapids: Zondervan, 1990).

Gary A. Philips (ed.), *Poststructural Criticism and the Bible* (Atlanta, GA: Scholars Press, 1990).

Mark C. Taylor, *Erring: A Postmodern A/Theology* (Chicago: Univesity of Chicago Press, 1984).

Roman Catholicism

William V. Dych, *Karl Rahner* (London: Geoffrey Chapman, 1992).

Francis F. Fiorenza and John P. Galvin, *Systematic Theology: Roman Catholic Perspectives*, 2 vols (Minneapolis: Fortress Press, 1991); also published as single-volume edition (Dublin: Gill and Macmillan, 1992).

Sheridan Gilley, *Newman and His Age* (London: Darton, Longman and Todd, 1990).

Stanley J. Grenz and Roger E. Olson, *Twentieth-Century Theology* (Downers Grove, IL: InterVarsity Press, 1992), pp. 237–70.

Philip Kennedy, *Schillebeeckx* (London: Geoffrey Chapman, 1993).

Ian Ker, *The Achievement of John Henry Newman* (London: Collins, 1990).

Catherine M. LaCugna, *The Theological Methodology of Hans Küng* (Chico, CA: Scholars Press, 1982).

Gerald A. McCool, *Catholic Theology in the Nineteenth Century: The Quest for a Unitary Method* (New York: Fordham University Press, 1977).

Aidan Nichols, *Yves Congar* (London: Geoffrey Chapman, 1989).

Robert Nowell, *A Passion for Truth: Hans Küng and His Theology* (New York: Crossroad, 1981).

John J. O'Donnell, *Hans Urs von Balthasar* (London: Geoffrey Chapman, 1992).

Thomas F. O'Meara, *Romantic Idealism and Roman Catholicism* (Notre Dame, IN: University of Notre Dame, 1982).

Bernard M. G. Reardon, *Roman Catholic Modernism* (Stanford, CA: Stanford University Press, 1970).

Herbert Vorgrimler, *Understanding Karl Rahner: An Introduction to his Life and Thought* (New York: Crossroad, 1986).

Edward J. Yarnold, "Roman Catholic Theology," in A. E. McGrath (ed.), *The Blackwell Encyclopaedia of Modern Christian Thought* (Oxford/Cambridge, MA: Blackwell Publishers, 1993), pp. 562–73.

Regional Theologies

Kofi Appiah-Kubi and Sergio Torres (eds), *African Theology en route* (Maryknoll, NY: Orbis Books, 1979).

Robin S. H. Boyd, *Introduction to Indian Christian Theology*, 2nd edn (Madras: CLT, 1974).

William A. Dryness (ed.), *Emerging Voices in Global Theology* (Grand Rapids: Zondervan, 1995).

——, *Learning about Theology from the Third World* (Grand Rapids: Zondervan, 1992).

Elizabeth Isichei, *A History of Christianity in Africa* (London: SPCK, 1995).

Jung Young Lee, "Korean Christian Thought," in A. E. McGrath (ed.), *The Blackwell Encyclopaedia of Modern Christian Thought* (Oxford/Cambridge, MA: Blackwell Publishers, 1993), pp. 308–13.

Kosuke Koyama, "Asian Theology," in D. F. Ford (ed.), *The Modern Theologians*, 2 vols (Oxford/Cambridge, MA: Blackwell, 1990), vol. 2, pp. 217–34.

Stephen Charles Neill, *A history of Christianity in India*, 2 vols (Cambridge: Cambridge University Press, 1984–5).

Caleb Oluremi Oladipo, *The Development of the Holy Spirit in the Yoruba (African)*

Indigenous Christian Movement (Frankfurt/New York: Peter Lang, 1996).

John Parratt (ed.), *A Reader in African Christian Theology* (London: SPCK, 1987).

C. S. Song, *Third-Eye Theology: Theology in Formation in Asian Settings*, rev. edn (Maryknoll, NY: Orbis, 1990).

R. S. Sugirtharajah and C. Hargreaves (eds), *Readings in Indian Christian Theology* (London: SPCK, 1993).

Shunici Takayanagi, "Japanese Christian Thought," in A. E. McGrath (ed.), *The Blackwell Encyclopaedia of Modern Christian Thought* (Oxford/Cambridge, MA: Blackwell Publishers, 1993), pp. 280–4.

Carver T. Yu, "Chinese Christian Thought," in A. E. McGrath (ed.), *The Blackwell Encyclopaedia of Modern Christian Thought* (Oxford/Cambridge, MA: Blackwell Publishers, 1993), pp. 71–7.

Getting Started: Preliminaries

For a selection of primary sources of relevance to this section, see Alister E. McGrath, *The Christian Theology Reader* (Oxford/Cambridge, MA: Blackwell Publishers, 1995), pp. 2–38.

The History of Theology as a Discipline

Gillian R. Evans, *Old Arts and New Theology: The Beginnings of Theology as an Academic Discipline* (Oxford: Clarendon Press, 1980).

——, Alister E. McGrath, and Allan D. Galloway, *The Science of Theology* (Grand Rapids: Eerdmans, 1986).

Edward Farley, *Theologia: The Fragmentation and Unity of Theological Education* (Philadelphia: Fortress Press, 1983).

Wolfhart Pannenberg, *Theology and the Philosophy of Science* (London: Darton, Longman and Todd, 1976).

Prolegomena

Carl E. Braaten, "Prolegomena to Christian Dogmatics," in C. E. Braaten and R. W. Jenson (eds), *Christian Dogmatics*, 2 vols (Philadelphia: Fortress Press, 1984), vol. 1, pp. 5–78.

C. Stephen Evans, *Philosophy of Religion: Thinking about Faith* (Downers Grove, IL: InterVarsity Press, 1982).

Basil Mitchell, *The Justification of Religious Belief* (Oxford: Oxford University Press, 1981).

Wolfhart Pannenberg, *Theology and the Philosophy of Science* (London: Darton, Longman and Todd, 1976), pp. 3–22.

Richard G. Swinburne, *Faith and Reason* (Oxford: Clarendon Press, 1981).

Nicolas Wolterstorff, *Reason within the Bounds of Religion*, 2nd edn (Grand Rapids: Eerdmans, 1984).

The Architecture of Theology

Historical Theology
The following work is especially recommended as an introduction to the various aspects of the history of Christian Theology: Jaroslav Pelikan, *The Christian Tradition: A History of the Development of Doctrine*, 5 vols (Chicago: University of Chicago Press, 1989). The five volumes of this excellent study are arranged as follows:

1 The Emergence of the Catholic Tradition (100–600)
2 The Spirit of Eastern Christendom (600–1700)
3 The Growth of Medieval Theology (600–1300)

4 Reformation of Church and Dogma (1300–1700)
5 Christian Doctrine and Modern Culture (since 1700)

The following are also useful:

Justo L. González, *A History of Christian Thought*, 3 vols (Nashville, TN: Abingdon Press, 1975).

Bernhard Lohse, *A Short History of Christian Doctrine* (Philadelphia: Fortress Press, 1966).

William C. Placher, *A History of Christian Theology* (Philadelphia: Westminster Press, 1983).

Pastoral Theology

D. J. Atkinson and D. H. Field (eds), *New Dictionary of Christian Ethics and Pastoral Theology* (Downers Grove, IL: InterVarsity Press, 1995).

D. S. Browning, *A Fundamental Practical Theology* (Philadelphia: Fortress Press, 1991).

David Deeks, *Pastoral Theology: An Inquiry* (London: Epworth Press, 1987).

E. E. Ellis, *Pauline Theology: Ministry and Society* (Grand Rapids: Eerdmans, 1989).

Robert Allen Krupp, *Shepherding the Flock of God: The Pastoral Theology of John Chrysostom* (New York/London: Peter Lang, 1991).

Thomas C. Oden, *Pastoral Theology* (San Francisco: Harper & Row, 1983).

Derek Tidball, *Skillful Shepherds: An Introduction to Pastoral Theology* (Grand Rapids: Eerdmans, 1986).

Systematic Theology

The following are useful as introductions to this general field, and are all worth exploring. The annotations indicate the kind of approach adopted by their authors.

C. E. Braaten and R. W. Jenson (eds), *Christian Dogmatics*, 2 vols (Philadelphia: Fortress Press, 1984). Very demanding, and written from an explicitly Lutheran perspective; however, it is worth the trouble to read, especially its essays relating to revelation and the doctrine of God.

Millard J. Erickson, *Christian Theology* (Grand Rapids: Baker, 1992). Written from a broadly Baptist and evangelical perspective.

Francis F. Fiorenza and John P. Galvin, *Systematic Theology: Roman Catholic Perspectives*, 2 vols (Minneapolis: Fortress Press, 1991); also published as single-volume edition (Dublin: Gill and Macmillan, 1992). An excellent overview of the leading themes of systematic theology from a Roman Catholic perspective.

Wayne Grudem, *Systematic Theology: An Introduction to Biblical Doctrine* (Grand Rapids: Zondervan, 1994). A good statement of a very conservative evangelical approach to theology.

P. Hodgson and R. King (eds), *Christian Theology* (Philadelphia: Fortress Press, 1982); also available in an expanded edition, with two extra essays on theological method and the sacraments respectively. Written from a generally liberal perspective; stronger on more recent discussions of classic questions.

John Macquarrie, *Principles of Christian Theology* (London: SCM Press, 1966), and also in a later revised edition. The existentialist approach adopted in this work seems a little dated now, but it is still useful to provoke your thinking.

Daniel E. Migliore, *Faith Seeking Understanding* (Grand Rapids: Eerdmans, 1991). A useful overview of all the main areas of theology from a generally Reformed perspective by a highly stimulating and engaging writer.

365

Bruce Milne, *Know the Truth: A Handbook of Christian Belief* (Leicester: InterVarsity Press, 1982), many reprints. A standard conservative evangelical introduction to biblical theology.

Philosophical Theology

David Brown, "Philosophical Theology," in A. E. McGrath (ed.), *The Blackwell Encyclopaedia of Modern Christian Thought* (Oxford/Cambridge, MA: Blackwell Publishers, 1993), pp. 434–40.

Leo Elders, *The Philosophical Theology of St Thomas Aquinas* (Leiden: Brill, 1990).

Austin Farrer, *Reflective Faith: Essays in Philosophical Theology* (London: SPCK, 1972).

Hans Küng, *The Incarnation of God: An Introduction to Hegel's Theological Thought* (Edinburgh: T. & T. Clark, 1987).

Sang Hyun Lee, *The Philosophical Theology of Jonathan Edwards* (Princeton, NJ: Princeton University Press, 1988).

Thomas V. Morris, *Our Idea of God: An Introduction to Philosophical Theology* (Notre Dame, IN: University of Notre Dame Press, 1991).

Alvin J. Plantinga (ed.), *The Ontological Argument* (London: Macmillan, 1968).

Carl A. Raschke (ed.), *New Dimensions in Philosophical Theology* (Missoula, MT: American Academy of Religion, 1982).

T. Sheenan, *Karl Rahner: The Philosophical Foundations* (Athens, OH: Ohio University Press, 1987).

Allan B. Wolter and Marilyn McCord Adams (eds), *The Philosophical Theology of John Duns Scotus* (Ithaca, NY: Cornell University Press, 1990).

Religious Language

Ian G. Barbour, *Myths, Models and Paradigms: The Nature of Scientific and Religious Language* (New York: Harper & Row, 1974).

Sallie McFague, *Models of God: Theology for an Ecological Nuclear Age* (Philadelphia: Fortress Press, 1987).

John Macquarrie, *God-Talk* (London: SCM Press, 1967).

Eric L. Mascall, *Words and Images* (London: Longmans, 1957).

Ian T. Ramsey, *Christian Discourse* (London: Oxford University Press, 1965).

Janet Martin Soskice, *Metaphor and Religious Language* (Oxford: Clarendon Press, 1985).

Anthony C. Thiselton, *New Horizons in Hermeneutics* (Grand Rapids: Zondervan, 1992).

Sources and Methods

For a selection of primary sources of relevance, see Alister E. McGrath, *The Christian Theology Reader* (Oxford/Cambridge, MA: Blackwell Publishers, 1995), pp. 40–88.

The Concept of Revelation

John Baillie, *The Idea of Revelation in Recent Thought* (New York: Columbia University Press, 1956).

M. N. A. Bockmuehl, *Revelation and Mystery* (Tübingen: Mohr, 1990).

F. G. Downing, *Has Christianity a Revelation?* (London: SCM Press, 1964).

Avery Dulles, *Models of Revelation* (Dublin: Gill & Macmillan, 1983).

Paul Helm, *The Divine Revelation* (Westchester, IL: Crossway Books, 1982).

Karl Jaspers, *Philosophical Faith and Revelation* (New York: Harper & Row, 1967).

Paul King Jewett, *Emil Brunner's Concept of Revelation* (London: James Clarke, 1954).

René Latourelle, *Theology of Revelation* (Staten Island, NY: Alba House, 1966).

H. D. MacDonald, *Theories of Revelation: An Historical Study, 1860–1960* (Grand Rapids: Baker, 1979).

H. Richard Niebuhr, *The Meaning of Revelation* (New York: Macmillan, 1941).

Wolfhart Pannenberg, "Revelation in Early Christianity," in G. R. Evans (ed.), *Christian Authority* (Oxford: Oxford University Press, 1988), pp. 76–85.

George Stroup, "Revelation," in P. Hodgson and R. King (eds), *Christian Theology* (Philadelphia: Fortress Press, 1982), pp. 88–114.

Ronald E. Thiemann, *Revelation and Theology: The Gospel as Narrated Promise* (Notre Dame, IN: University of Notre Dame, 1985).

Jonathan B. Webster, "Concept of Revelation," in A. E. McGrath (ed.), *The Blackwell Encyclopaedia of Modern Christian Thought* (Oxford/Cambridge, MA: Blackwell Publishers, 1993), pp. 557–61.

Scripture

General Introductions

D. A. Carson, Douglas J. Moo, and Leon Morris, *An Introduction to the New Testament* (Grand Rapids: Zondervan, 1994).

Bruce Chilton, *Beginning New Testament Study* (London: SPCK, 1986).

James D. G. Dunn, *Unity and Diversity in the New Testament*, 2nd edn (London: SCM Press, 1990).

Robert H. Gundry, *A Survey of the New Testament* (Grand Rapids: Zondervan, 1994).

Luke T. Johnson, *The Writings of the New Testament: An Interpretation* (Philadelphia: Fortress Press, 1986).

Otto Kaiser, *Introduction to the Old Testament* (Oxford: Blackwell, 1975).

The Canon of Scripture

Roger T. Beckwith, *The Old Testament Canon of the New Testament Church* (London: SPCK, 1985).

F. F. Bruce, *The Canon of Scripture* (Downers Grove, IL: InterVarsity Press, 1988).

Brevard Childs, *The New Testament as Canon: An Introduction* (Philadelphia: Fortress Press, 1985).

W. D. Davies, "Canon and Christology," in L. D. Hurst and N. T. Wright (eds), *The Glory of Christ in the New Testament* (Oxford: Clarendon Press, 1987), pp. 19–36.

Bruce M. Metzger, *The Canon of the New Testament* (Oxford: Clarendon Press, 1987).

James A. Sanders, *Canon and Community: A Guide to Canonical Criticism* (Philadelphia: Fortress Press, 1984).

Brooke Foss Westcott, *The Bible in the Church* (London: Macmillan, 1901).

The Inspiration and Authority of Scripture

William J. Abraham, *The Divine Inspiration of Holy Scripture* (New York: Oxford University Press, 1981).

P. J. Achtemeier, *The Inspiration of Scripture: Problems and Proposals* (Philadelphia: Westminster, 1980).

James T. Burtchaell, *Catholic Theories of Biblical Inspiration since 1810* (Cambridge: Cambridge University Press, 1969).

Edward Farley and Peter Hodgson, "Scripture and Tradition," in P. Hodgson and R. King (eds), *Christian Theology* (Philadelphia: Fortress Press, 1982), pp. 35–61.

Carl F. H. Henry, *God, Revelation and Authority* (Waco, TX: Word, 1976–83).

Clark H. Pinnock, *The Scripture Principle* (San Francisco: Harper & Row, 1984).

Robert Preus, *The Inspiration of Scripture: A Study of the Seventeenth-Century*

Lutheran Dogmaticians(London: Oliver & Boyd, 1955).

K. R. Tremblath, *Evangelical Theories of Biblical Inspiration* (Oxford: Oxford University Press, 1988).

The Interpretation of Scripture

James Barr, *Semantics of Biblical Language* (London: Oxford University Press, 1961).

R. J. Coggins and J. L. Houlden, *A Dictionary of Biblical Interpretation* (London: SCM Press, 1990).

E. D. Hirsch, Jr, *The Aims of Interpretation* (Chicago: University of Chicago Press, 1976).

Walter C. Kaiser and Moises Silva, *An Introduction to Biblical Hermeneutics* (Grand Rapids: Zondervan, 1992).

Edgar Krentz, *The Historical–Critical Method* (Philadelphia: Fortress Press, 1975).

Robert Morgan, *Biblical Interpretation* (Oxford: Oxford University Press, 1988).

Stephen C. Neill and N. T. Wright, *The Interpretation of the New Testament, 1861–1986* (Oxford: Oxford University Press, 1988).

R. S. Sugirtharajah (ed.), *Voices from the Margin: Interpreting the Bible in the Third World* (London: SPCK, 1991).

Anthony C. Thiselton, *New Horizons in Hermeneutics: The Theory and Practice of Transforming Biblical Reading* (Grand Rapids: Zondervan, 1992).

Reason

Stephen T. Davis, *Logic and the Nature of God* (Grand Rapids: Eerdmans, 1983).

B. A. Brody, *Readings in the Philosophy of Religion* (Englewood Cliffs, NJ: Prentice-Hall, 1974).

C. Stephen Evans, *Philosophy of Religion: Thinking about Faith* (Downers Grove, IL: InterVarsity Press, 1982).

Anthony Kenny, *The Five Ways: St Thomas Aquinas' Proofs of God's Existence* (London: Routledge and Kegan Paul, 1969).

Basil Mitchell, *The Justification of Religious Belief* (Oxford: Oxford University Press, 1973).

Alvin J. Plantinga (ed.), *The Ontological Argument* (London: Macmillan, 1968).

William L. Rowe and William J. Wainwright, *Philosophy of Religion: Selected Readings* (New York: Harcourt Brace Jovanovich, 1973).

Richard Swinburne, *The Existence of God* (Oxford: Clarendon Press, 1979).

——, *Faith and Reason* (Oxford: Clarendon Press, 1981).

Nicholas Wolterstorff, *Reason within the Bounds of Religion*, 2nd edn (Grand Rapids: Eerdmans, 1984).

Keith E. Yandell, *Christianity and Philosophy* (Grand Rapids: Eerdmans, 1984).

Tradition

Günter Biemer, *Newman on Tradition* (New York: Herder & Herder, 1967).

Hans von Campenhausen, *Tradition and Life in the Church* (London: Collins, 1968).

Yves M.-J. Congar, *Tradition and Traditions: An Historical and Theological Essay* (New York: Macmillan, 1967).

Gerhard Ebeling, *The Word of God and Tradition* (London: Collins, 1968).

J. R. Geiselman, *The Meaning of Tradition* (London: Burns & Oates, 1966).

John Meyendorff, *Living Tradition* (Crestwood, NY: St Vladimir Seminary Press, 1978).

Heiko A. Oberman, "Quo vadis, Petre? Tradition from Irenaeus to Humani Generis," *Scottish Journal of Theology*, 16 (1963), pp. 225–55.

Jaroslav Pelikan, *The Vindication of Tradition* (New Haven: Yale University Press, 1984).

Edward J. Yarnold, "Tradition," in A. E. McGrath (ed.), *The Blackwell Encyclopaedia of Modern Christian Thought* (Oxford/Cambridge, MA: Blackwell Publishers, 1993), pp. 643–7.

Experience

William P. Alston, *Perceiving God: The Epistemology of Religious Experience* (London: Cornell University Press, 1991).

Caroline Franks Davis, *The Evidential Force of Religious Experience* (Oxford: Clarendon Press, 1989).

C. Stephen Evans, *Subjectivity and Religious Belief* (Grand Rapids: Christian University Press, 1976).

Nicholas Lash, *Easter in Ordinary: Reflections on Human Experience and the Knowledge of God* (Charlottesville, VA: University Press of Virginia, 1988).

Alister E. McGrath, "Theology and Experience: Reflections on Cognitive and Experiential Approaches to Theology," *European Journal of Theology*, 2 (1993), pp. 65–74.

Wayne Proudfoot, *Religious Experience* (Berkeley: University of California Press, 1985).

Natural Theology

James Barr, *Biblical Faith and Natural Theology* (Oxford: Clarendon Press, 1993).

Karl Barth and Emil Brunner, *Natural Theology* (London: SCM Press, 1947).

E. A. Dowey, *The Knowledge of God in Calvin's Theology* (New York: Columbia University Press, 1952).

Lloyd P. Gerson, *God and Greek Philosophy: Studies in the Early History of Natural Theology* (London: Routledge, 1990).

Charles Hartshorne, *A Natural Theology for Our Time* (La Salle, IL: Open Court, 1967).

Eugene T. Long, *Prospects for Natural Theology* (Washington, DC: Catholic University of America Press, 1992).

John Macquarrie, "Natural Theology," in A. E. McGrath (ed.), *The Blackwell Encyclopaedia of Modern Christian Thought* (Oxford/Cambridge, MA: Blackwell Publishers, 1993), pp. 402–5.

Eric L. Mascall, *He Who Is* (London: Darton, Longman and Todd, 1966).

Joan E. O'Donovan, "Man in the Image of God: The Disagreement between Barth and Brunner Reconsidered," *Scottish Journal of Theology*, 39 (1986), pp. 433–59.

Frederick Robert Tennant, *Philosophical Theology*, 2 vols (Cambridge: Cambridge University Press, 1928).

Ned Wisnefske, *Our Natural Knowledge of God: A Prospect for Natural Theology after Kant and Barth* (New York: Peter Lang, 1990).

The Doctrine of God

For a selection of primary sources of relevance, see Alister E. McGrath, *The Christian Theology Reader* (Oxford/Cambridge, MA: Blackwell Publishers, 1995), pp. 90–132.

Vincent Brümmer, *Speaking of a Personal God: An Essay in Philosophical Theology* (Cambridge: Cambridge University Press, 1992).

Martin Buber, *I and Thou* (New York: Scribner's, 1970).

Langdon Gilkey, "God," in P. Hodgson and R. King (eds), *Christian Theology* (Philadelphia: Fortress Press, 1982), pp. 62–87.

Colin E. Gunton, *The One, The Three and the Many: God, Creation and the Culture of Modernity* (Cambridge: Cambridge University Press, 1993).

R. P. C. Hanson, *The Search for the Christian Doctrine of God* (Edinburgh: T. & T. Clark, 1988).

Paul Helm, *The Providence of God* (Downers Grove, IL: InterVarsity Press, 1994).

Robert W. Jenson, "God," in A. E. McGrath (ed.), *The Blackwell Encyclopaedia of Modern Christian Thought* (Oxford/Cambridge, MA: Blackwell Publishers, 1993), pp. 234–46.

Christopher B. Kaiser, *The Doctrine of God* (Westchester, IL: Crossway Books, 1982).

Walter Kasper, *The God of Jesus Christ* (New York: Crossroad, 1989).

Sallie McFague, *Models of God* (Philadelphia: Fortress Press, 1987), pp. 91–180.

Ronald H. Nash, *The Concept of God* (Grand Rapids: Zondervan, 1983).

G. L. Prestige, *God in Patristic Thought* (London: Heinemann, 1936).

Peter Widdicombe, *The Fatherhood of God from Origen to Athanasius* (Oxford: Clarendon Press, 1994).

God as Creator

Ian S. Barbour, *Religion in the Age of Science* (New York: Harper & Row, 1990).

Julian N. Hartt, "Creation and Providence," in P. Hodgson and R. King (eds), *Christian Theology* (Philadelphia: Fortress Press, 1982), pp. 115–40.

Philip J. Hefner, "Creation," in C. E. Braaten and R. W. Jenson (eds), *Christian Dogmatics*, 2 vols (Philadelphia: Fortress Press, 1984), vol. 1, pp. 269–357.

Rebecca J. Lyman, *Christology and Cosmology: Models of Divine Activity in Origen, Eusebius and Athanasius* (Oxford: Clarendon Press, 1993).

Gerhard May, *Creatio ex nihilo: The Doctrine of "Creation out of Nothing" in*

Early Christian Thought (Edinburgh: T. & T. Clark, 1995).

Jürgen Moltmann, *God in Creation: A New Theology of Creation and the Spirit of God* (San Francisco: Harper & Row, 1985).

Arthur R. Peacocke, *Creation and the World of Science* (Oxford: Clarendon Press, 1979).

Michael Schmaus, *Dogma 2: Creation* (London: Sheed & Ward, 1969).

Lynn White, "The Historical Roots of our Ecological Crisis," *Science*, 155 (1967), pp. 1203–7.

Christian Theology and Natural Science

Ian G. Barbour, *Issues in Science and Religion* (London: SCM Press, 1966).

——, *Religion in the Age of Science* (New York: Harper & Row, 1990).

John Durant (ed.), *Darwinism and Divinity* (Oxford: Blackwell, 1985).

James R. Moore, *The Post-Darwinian Controversies* (Cambridge: Cambridge University Press, 1979).

Henry M. Morris, *Scientific Creationism* (San Diego: Creation–Life Publishers, 1974).

Arthur R. Peacocke (ed.), *The Sciences and Theology in the Twentieth Century* (Notre Dame, IN: University of Notre Dame Press, 1981).

John Polkinghorne, "Physical Science and Christian Thought," in A. E. McGrath (ed.), *The Blackwell Encyclopaedia of Modern Christian Thought* (Oxford/Cambridge, MA: Blackwell Publishers, 1993), pp. 443–8.

Colin A. Russell, "Biological Science and Christian Thought," in A. E. McGrath (ed.), *The Blackwell Encyclopaedia of Modern Christian Thought* (Oxford/Cambridge, MA: Blackwell Publishers, 1993), pp. 50–6.

God in Process Thought

Eulalio R. Baltazar, *God Within Process* (Paramus, NJ: Newman, 1970).

John B. Cobb, *Process Theology: An Introductory Exposition* (Belfast: Christian Journals, 1976).

Paul Fiddes, "Process Theology," in A. E. McGrath (ed.), *The Blackwell Encyclopaedia of Modern Christian Thought* (Oxford/Cambridge, MA: Blackwell Publishers, 1993), pp. 472–6.

David R. Griffin, *God, Power and Evil: A Process Theodicy* (Philadelphia: Westminster Press, 1976).

The Suffering of God

Richard E. Creel, *Divine Impassibility: An Essay in Philosophical Theology* (Cambridge: Cambridge University Press, 1986).

Paul Fiddes, *The Creative Suffering of God* (Oxford: Clarendon Press, 1988).

——, "Suffering, Divine," in A. E. McGrath (ed.), *The Blackwell Encyclopaedia of Modern Christian Thought* (Oxford/Cambridge, MA: Blackwell Publishers, 1993), pp. 633–6.

T. E. Fretheim, *The Suffering of God: An Old Testament Perspective* (Philadelphia: Fortress Press, 1984).

Kazoh Kitamori, *Theology of the Pain of God* (London: SCM Press, 1966).

Jung Young Lee, *God Suffers For Us: A Systematic Inquiry into the Concept of Divine Passibility* (The Hague: Nijhoff, 1974).

W. McWilliams, *The Passion of God: Divine Suffering in Contemporary Protestant Theology* (Macon, GA: Mercer Press, 1985).

J. K. Mozley, *The Impassibility of God* (London: Cambridge University Press, 1926).

G. F. O'Hanlon, *The Immutability of God in the Theology of Hans Urs von Balthasar* (Cambridge: Cambridge University Press, 1990).

H. Wheeler Robinson, *Suffering Human and Divine* (London: SCM Press, 1940).

The Holy Spirit

Hendrikus Berkhof, *The Doctrine of the Holy Spirit* (Atlanta, GA: John Knox Press, 1977).

Frederick Dale Bruner, *A Theology of the Holy Spirit* (Grand Rapids: Eerdmans, 1970).

Gordon D. Fee, *God's Empowering Presence: The Holy Spirit in the Letters of Paul* (Peabody, MA: Hendrickson, 1994).

Timothy Gorringe, "Pneumatology," in A. E. McGrath (ed.), *The Blackwell Encyclopaedia of Modern Christian Thought* (Oxford/Cambridge, MA: Blackwell Publishers, 1993). pp. 448–53.

Jürgen Moltmann, *The Church in the Power of the Spirit* (London: SCM Press, 1977).

C. F. D. Moule, *The Holy Spirit* (Grand Rapids: Eerdmans, 1978).

Clark Pinnock, *Flame of Love: A Theology of the Holy Spirit* (Downers Grove, IL: InterVarsity Press, 1997).

Jean-Jacques Suurmond, *Word and Spirit at Play: Towards a Charismatic Theology* (London: SCM Press, 1991).

H. B. Swete, *The Holy Spirit in the Ancient Church* (Oxford: Oxford University Press, 1912).

Lukas Vischer (ed.), *Spirit of God, Spirit of Christ: Reflections on the Filioque Controversy* (London: SPCK, 1981).

H. Wheeler Robinson, *The Christian Experience of the Holy Spirit* (London: Fontana, 1962).

J. Rodman Williams, *Renewal Theology*, 3 vols (Grand Rapids: Zondervan, 1988–92), vol. 2, pp. 137–207; 237–70.

The Doctrine of the Trinity

For a selection of primary sources of relevance, see Alister E. McGrath, *The Christian Theology Reader* (Oxford/ Cambridge, MA: Blackwell Publishers, 1995), pp. 90–132.

M. R. Barnes and D. H. Williams (eds), *Arianism after Arius: Essays on the Development of the Fourth-Century Trinitarian Conflicts* (Edinburgh: T. & T. Clark, 1993).

Leonardo Boff, *Trinity and Society* (London: Burns & Oates, 1988).

David Brown, *The Divine Trinity* (London: Duckworth, 1988).

Colin E. Gunton, *The Promise of Trinitarian Theology* (Edinburgh: Clark, 1991).

William J. Hill, *The Three-Personed God: The Trinity as a Mystery of Salvation* (Washington, DC: Catholic University of America Press, 1982).

Robert W. Jenson, *The Triune Identity: God according to the Gospel* (Philadelphia: Fortress Press, 1982).

Eberhard Jüngel, *The Doctrine of the Trinity* (Edinburgh: Scottish Academic Press, 1976).

A. K. Kimel (ed.), *Speaking the Christian God: The Holy Trinity and the Challenge of Feminism* (Grand Rapids: Eerdmans, 1992).

Jürgen Moltmann, *The Trinity and the Kingdom of God* (London: SCM Press, 1981).

John J. O'Donnell, *The Mystery of the Triune God* (London: Sheed & Ward, 1988).

Ted Peters, *God as Trinity: Relationality and Temporality in Divine Life* (Louisville, KY: Westminster/John Knox Press, 1993).

Karl Rahner, *The Trinity* (London: Burns and Oates, 1970).

John Thompson, *Modern Trinitarian Perspectives* (Oxford: Oxford University Press, 1994).

Thomas F. Torrance, *The Trinitarian Faith* (Edinburgh: T. & T. Clark, 1988).

Arthur W. Wainwright, *The Trinity in the New Testament* (London: SPCK, 1969).

Thomas G. Weinandy, *The Father's Spirit of Sonship: Reconceiving the Trinity* (Edinburgh: T. & T. Clark, 1995).

Claude Welch, *In This Name: The Trinity in Contemporary Theology* (New York: Charles Scribner's Sons, 1952).

The Person of Christ

For a selection of primary sources of relevance, see Alister E. McGrath, *The Christian Theology Reader* (Oxford/ Cambridge, MA: Blackwell Publishers, 1995), pp. 134–73.

Donald M. Baillie, *God was in Christ: An Essay on Incarnation and Atonement* (London: Faber & Faber, 1956).

Colin Brown, *Jesus in European Thought 1778–1860* (Durham, NC: Labyrinth Press, 1985).

John C. Cavadini, *The Last Christology of the West: Adoptionism in Spain and Gaul, 785–920* (Philadelphia: University of Pennsylvania Press, 1993).

Roberta C. Chesnut, *Three Monophysite Christologies* (Oxford: Oxford University Press, 1976).

Aloys Grillmeier, *Christ in Christian Tradition*, 2nd edn (London: Mowbrays, 1975).

Colin E. Gunton, *Yesterday and Today: A Study of Continuities in Christology* (London: Darton, Longman and Todd, 1983).

Douglas Jacobsen and Frederick Schmidt, "Behind Orthodoxy and Beyond It: Recent Developments in Evangelical

Christology," *Scottish Journal of Theology*, 45 (1993), pp. 515–41.

Hans Küng, *The Incarnation of God: An Introduction to Hegel's Theological Thought as Prolegomena to a Future Christology* (Edinburgh: T. & T. Clark, 1987).

Alister E. McGrath, *The Making of Modern German Christology*, 2nd edn (Grand Rapids: Zondervan, and Leicester, UK: InterVarsity Press, 1993).

John Macquarrie, *Jesus Christ in Modern Thought* (London: SCM Press, Philadelphia: Trinity Press International, 1990).

Bruce D. Marshall, "Christology," in A. E. McGrath (ed.), *The Blackwell Encyclopaedia of Modern Christian Thought* (Oxford/Cambridge, MA: Blackwell Publishers, 1993), pp. 80–93.

I. H. Marshall, *The Origins of New Testament Christology*, 2nd edn (Leicester: InterVarsity Press, 1992).

John Meyendorff, *Christ in Eastern Christian Thought* (Washington, DC: Corpus, 1969).

C. F. D. Moule, *The Origin of Christology* (Cambridge: Cambridge University Press, 1977).

Elisabeth Schüssler Fiorenza, *Jesus: Miriam's Child, Sophia's Prophet. Issues in Feminist Christology* (London: SCM Press, 1991).

Jon Sobrino, *Jesus in Latin America* (Maryknoll, NY: Orbis, 1987).

David F. Wells, *The Person of Christ* (Westchester, IL: Crossway, 1984).

Rowan Williams, *Arius: Heresy and Tradition* (London: Darton, Longman and Todd, 1987).

Ben Witherington III, *The Christology of Jesus* (Philadelphia: Fortress Press, 1990).

Faith and History

For a selection of primary sources of relevance, see Alister E. McGrath, *The Christian Theology Reader* (Oxford/Cambridge, MA: Blackwell Publishers, 1995), pp. 134–73.

Charles C. Anderson, *Critical Quests of Jesus* (Grand Rapids: Eerdmans, 1969).

M. Eugene Boring, "The 'Third Quest' and the Apostolic Faith," *Interpretation*, 50 (1996), pp. 341–54.

Peter Carnley, *The Structure of Resurrection Belief* (Oxford: Clarendon Press, 1987).

Bruce M. Chilton and Craig A. Evans (eds), *Studying the Historical Jesus: Evaluations of the State of Current Research* (Leiden: Brill, 1994).

J. D. G. Dunn, *Christology in the Making* (London: SCM Press, 1980).

Van A. Harvey, *The Historian and the Believer* (New York: Macmillan, 1966).

Joachim Jeremias, *The Problem of the Historical Jesus* (Philadelphia: Fortress Press, 1972).

Luke Timothy Johnson, *The Real Jesus: The Misguided Quest for the Historical Jesus and the Truth of the Traditional Gospels* (San Francisco: HarperCollins, 1996).

Alister E. McGrath, *The Making of Modern German Christology*, 2nd edn (Grand Rapids: Zondervan, and Leicester, UK: InterVarsity Press, 1993).

I. Howard Marshall, *The Origins of New Testament Christology* (Leicester: InterVarsity Press, 1987).

G. E. Michalson, *Lessing's Ugly Ditch: A Study of Theology and History* (University Park: Pennsylvania State University Press, 1985).

C. F. D. Moule, *The Origins of Christology* (Cambridge: Cambridge University Press, 1977).

Pheme Perkins, *Resurrection: New Testament Witness and Contemporary Reflection* (London: Chapman, 1984).

James M. Robinson, *A New Quest of the Historical Jesus* (London: SCM Press, 1959).

Albert Schweitzer, *The Quest of the Historical Jesus*, 3rd edn (London: A. & C. Black, 1954).

William R. Telford, "Major Trends and Interpretative Issues in the Study of Jesus," in B. Chilton and C. A. Evans (eds), *Studying the Historical Jesus: Evaluations of the State of Current Research* (Leiden: Brill, 1994), pp. 57–61.

Gerd Theissen, *The Shadow of the Galilean: The Quest of the Historical Jesus in Narrative Form* (Philadelphia: Fortress Press, 1987).

N. T. Wright, *Who was Jesus?* (Grand Rapids: Eerdmans, 1992).

Salvation in Christ

For a selection of primary sources of relevance, see Alister E. McGrath, *The Christian Theology Reader* (Oxford/Cambridge, MA: Blackwell Publishers, 1995), pp. 174–209.

Gustaf Aulén, *Christus Victor: An Historical Study of the Three Main Types of the Idea of the Atonement* (London: SPCK, 1931).

Donald M. Baillie, *God was in Christ: An Essay in Incarnation and Atonement* (London: Faber & Faber, 1956).

R. J. Daley, *The Origins of the Christian Doctrine of Sacrifice* (London: Darton, Longman and Todd, 1978).

F. W. Dillistone, *The Christian Understanding of Atonement* (London: SCM Press, 1984).

Paul Fiddes, *Past Event and Present Salvation* (London: Darton, Longman and Todd, 1989).

R. S. Franks, *The Work of Christ: A Historical Study* (London/New York: Nelson, 1962).

Colin E. Gunton, *The Actuality of Atonement* (Edinburgh: T & T Clark, 1988).

Martin Hengel, *The Atonement* (London: SCM Press, 1981).

Morna D. Hooker, *Not Ashamed of the Gospel: New Testament Interpretations of the Death of Christ* (Carlisle: Paternoster Press, 1994).

John MacIntyre, *The Shape of Soteriology* (Edinburgh: T. & T. Clark, 1992).

Leon Morris, *The Apostolic Preaching of the Cross* (Leicester: InterVarsity Press, 1965).

J. I. Packer, "What did the Cross Achieve? The Logic of Penal Substitution," *Tyndale Bulletin*, 25 (1974), pp. 3–45.

John R. W. Stott, *The Cross of Christ* (Leicester: InterVarsity Press, 1986).

S. W. Sykes (ed.), *Sacrifice and Redemption* (Cambridge: Cambridge University Press, 1991).

H. E. W. Turner, *The Patristic Doctrine of Redemption* (London: Mowbray, 1952).

Vernon White, *Atonement and Incarnation: An Essay in Universalism and Particularity* (Cambridge: Cambridge University Press, 1991).

Dietrich Wiederkehr, *Belief in Redemption: Concepts of Salvation from the New Testament to the Present Time* (London: SPCK, 1979).

Frances M. Young, *Sacrifice and the Death of Christ* (London: SPCK, 1975).

Human Nature, Sin and Grace

For a selection of primary sources of relevance to this section, see Alister E. McGrath, *The Christian Theology Reader* (Oxford/Cambridge, MA:

Blackwell Publishers, 1995), pp. 210–57.

Ray S. Anderson, *On Being Human: Essays in Theological Anthropology* (Grand Rapids: Eerdmans, 1982).

——, "Christian Anthropology," in A. E. McGrath (ed.), *The Blackwell Encyclopaedia of Modern Christian Thought* (Oxford/Cambridge, MA: Blackwell Publishers, 1993), pp. 5–9.

G. C. Berkouwer, *Man: The Image of God* (Grand Rapids: Eerdmans, 1962).

David Cairns, *The Image of God in Man*, rev. edn (London: Collins, 1973).

Edmund Hill, *Being Human: A Biblical Perspective* (London: Geoffrey Chapman, 1984).

Philip Edgcumbe Hughes, *The True Image: The Origin and Destiny of Man in Christ* (Grand Rapids: Eerdmans, 1989).

Paul K. Jewett, *Man as Male and Female* (Grand Rapids: Eerdmans, 1975).

David H. Kelsey, "Human Being," in P. Hodgson and R. King (eds), *Christian Theology* (Philadelphia: Fortress Press, 1982), pp. 141–67.

Eugene Laver and Joel Mlecko (eds), *A Christian Understanding of the Human Person: Basic Readings* (New York: Paulist Press, 1982).

Alister E. McGrath, *Iustitia Dei: A History of the Christian Doctrine of Justification*, 2 vols (Cambridge: Cambridge University Press, 1986).

John Macquarrie, *In Search of Humanity: A Theological and Philosophical Approach* (London: SCM Press, 1983).

Gerhard May, *Creatio ex nihilo: The Doctrine of "Creation out of Nothing" in Early Christian Thought* (Edinburgh: T. & T. Clark, 1995).

Karl Menninger, *Whatever Became of Sin?* (New York: Hawthorn, 1973).

Jürgen Moltmann, *Man: Christian Anthropology in the Conflicts of the Present* (Philadelphia: Fortress Press, 1974).

Joan E. O'Donovan, "Man in the Image of God: The Disagreement between Barth and Brunner Reconsidered," *Scottish Journal of Theology*, 39 (1986), pp. 433–59.

Wolfhart Pannenberg, *Anthropology in Theological Perspective* (London: SCM Press, 1985).

Ted Peters, *Sin: Radical Evil in Soul and Society* (Grand Rapids: Eerdmans, 1994).

Alvin Plantinga, *God, Freedom and Evil* (New York: Harper & Row, 1974).

Bernard Ramm, *Offense to Reason: The Theology of Sin* (San Francisco: Harper & Row, 1985).

Paul R. Sponheim, "Sin and Evil," in C. E. Braaten and R. W. Jenson (eds), *Christian Dogmatics*, 2 vols (Philadelphia: Fortress Press, 1984), vol. 1, pp. 363–463.

John Edward Sullivan, *The Image of God: The Doctrine of St. Augustine and Its Influence* (Dubuque, IA: Priory Press, 1963).

W. Telfer, "The Birth of Christian Anthropology," *Journal of Theological Studies*, 13 (1962), pp. 347–54.

N. P. Williams, *The Ideas of the Fall and Original Sin* (London: Longman, 1927).

R. R. Williams, "Sin and Evil," in P. Hodgson and R. King (eds), *Christian Theology* (Philadelphia: Fortress Press, 1982), pp. 168–95.

The Church

For a selection of primary sources of relevance, see Alister E. McGrath, *The Christian Theology Reader* (Oxford/Cambridge, MA: Blackwell Publishers, 1995), pp. 258–87.

Paul D. L. Avis, "Ecclesiology," in A. E.

McGrath (ed.), *The Blackwell Encyclopaedia of Modern Christian Thought* (Oxford/Cambridge, MA: Blackwell Publishers, 1993), pp. 127–34.

Yves M.-J. Congar, "The Church: The People of God," *Concilium*, 1 (1965), pp. 7–19.

Avery Dulles, *Models of the Church* (Dublin: Gill & Macmillan, 1976).

Philip J. Hefner, "The Church," in C. E. Braaten and R. W. Jenson (eds), *Christian Dogmatics*, 2 vols (Philadelphia: Fortress Press, 1984), vol. 2, pp. 183–247.

Peter Hodgson, "The Church," in P. Hodgson and R. King (eds), *Christian Theology* (Philadelphia: Fortress Press, 1982), pp. 223–47.

Hans Küng, *The Church* (London: Sheed & Ward, 1968).

K. McNamara (ed.), *Vatican II: The Constitution on the Church. A Theological and Pastoral Commentary* (London: Geoffrey Chapman, 1968).

Colm O'Grady, *The Church in Catholic Theology: Dialogue with Karl Barth* (London: Geoffrey Chapman, 1969).

D. W. B. Robinson, *The Church of God: Its Form and Unity* (Punchbowl, NSW: Jordan Books, 1965).

Michael Schmaus, *Dogma 4: The Church: Its Origins and Structure* (London: Sheed & Ward, 1972).

——, *Dogma 5: The Church as Sacrament* (London: Sheed & Ward, 1975).

E. Schillebeeckx, *The Church: The Human Story of God* (New York: Crossroad, 1990).

Juan Luis Segundo, *The Community Called Church* (Maryknoll, NY: Orbis Books, 1978).

George H. Tavard, *The Church, Community of Salvation: An Ecumenical Christology* (Collegeville, MN: Liturgical Press, 1993).

G. G. Willis, *Saint Augustine and the Donatist Controversy* (London: SPCK, 1950).

John D. Zizioulas, *Being as Communion: Studies in Personhood and the Church* (New York: St Vladimir's Seminary Press, 1985).

Sacraments

For a selection of primary sources of relevance, see Alister E. McGrath, *The Christian Theology Reader* (Oxford/Cambridge, MA: Blackwell Publishers, 1995), pp. 288–317.

Francis Clark, *Eucharistic Sacrifice and the Reformation* (London: Darton, Longman and Todd, 1960).

Regis A. Duffy et al., "Sacraments," in Francis F. Fiorenza and John P. Galvin, *Systematic Theology: Roman Catholic Perspectives*, 2 vols (Minneapolis: Fortress Press, 1991); also published as single-volume edition (Dublin: Gill and Macmillan, 1992); pp. 503–670.

P. Fink (ed.), *New Dictionary of Sacramental Worship* (Collegeville, MN: Liturgical Press, 1990).

Mark R. Francis, "Sacramental Theology," in A. E. McGrath (ed.), *The Blackwell Encyclopaedia of Modern Christian Thought* (Oxford/Cambridge, MA: Blackwell Publishers, 1993), pp. 581–7.

Alexandre Ganoczy, *An Introduction to Catholic Sacramental Theology* (New York: Paulist Press, 1984).

Brian A. Gerrish, *Grace and Gratitude: The Eucharistic Theology of John Calvin* (Philadelphia: Fortress Press, 1993).

Nicholas H. Haring, "Berengar's Definitions of *Sacramentum* and Their Influence on Medieval Sacramentology," *Medieval Studies*, 10 (1948), pp. 109–46.

Robert W. Jenson, *Visible Words* (Philadelphia: Fortress Press, 1978).

Aidan Kavanagh, *The Shape of Baptism* (New York: Pueblo Publishing, 1978).

Bernard Leeming, *Principles of Sacramental Theology* (Westminster, MD: Newman Press, 1960).

Joseph C. McLelland, *The Visible Words of God: An Exposition of the Sacramental Theology of Peter Martyr Vermigli* (Edinburgh: Oliver & Boyd, 1957).

Gary Macy, *The Theologies of the Eucharist in the Early Scholastic Period* (Oxford: Clarendon Press, 1984).

——, *The Banquet's Wisdom: A Short History of the Theologies of the Lord's Supper* (New York: Paulist Press, 1992).

David N. Power, *The Sacrifice We Offer: The Tridentine Dogma and Its Reinterpretation* (Edinburgh: T. & T. Clark, 1987).

Karl Rahner, *The Church and the Sacraments* (New York: Herder & Herder, 1963).

Hugh M. Riley, *Christian Initiation* (Washington, DC: Catholic University of America Press, 1974).

Edward Schillebeeckx, *Christ: The Sacrament of the Encounter with God* (New York: Sheed & Ward, 1963).

Michael Schmaus, *Dogma 5: The Church as Sacrament* (London: Sheed & Ward, 1975).

Alexander Schmemann, *The Eucharist* (Crestwood, NY: St Vladimir's Seminary Press, 1988).

Juan Luis Segundo, *The Sacraments Today* (Maryknoll, NY: Orbis, 1974).

Otto Semmelroth, *Church and Sacraments* (Notre Dame, IN: Fides, 1965).

Daniel A. Tappeiner, "Sacramental Causality in Aquinas and Rahner: Some Critical Thoughts," *Scottish Journal of Theology*, 28 (1975), pp. 243–57.

Herbert Vorgrimler, *Sacramental Theology* (Collegeville, MN: Liturgical Press, 1992).

World Council of Churches, *Baptism, Eucharist and Ministry* (Geneva: World Council of Churches, 1982).

Christianity and the World Religions

For a selection of primary sources of relevance, see Alister E. McGrath, *The Christian Theology Reader* (Oxford/Cambridge, MA: Blackwell Publishers, 1995), pp. 318–51.

J. N. D. Anderson, *Christianity and World Religions* (Downers Grove, IL: InterVarsity Press, 1984).

Arnulf Camps, *Partners in Dialogue: Christianity and Other World Religions* (New York: Orbis, 1983).

John B. Cobb, *Christ in a Pluralistic Age* (Philadelphia: Westminster Press, 1975).

——, "The Religions," in P. Hodgson and R. King (eds), *Christian Theology* (Philadelphia: Fortress Press, 1982), pp. 299–322.

Gavin D'Costa, *Theology and Religious Pluralism* (Oxford: Blackwell, 1986).

—— (ed.), *Christian Uniqueness Reconsidered: The Myth of a Pluralistic Theology of Religions* (Maryknoll, NY: Orbis Books, 1990).

John Hick, *God and the Universe of Faiths* (London: Fount, 1977).

——, *An Interpretation of Religion* (London: Macmillan, 1988).

——, and Paul Knitter (eds), *The Myth of Christian Uniqueness* (Maryknoll, NY: Orbis Books, 1987).

Paul Knitter, *No Other Name? A Critical Survey of Christian Attitudes Towards the World Religions* (Maryknoll, NY: Orbis Books, 1985).

Hendrik Kraemer, *The Christian Message in a Non-Christian World* (London: Harpers, 1938).

Harold A. Netland, *Dissonant Voices: Religious Pluralism and the Question of Truth* (Grand Rapids: Eerdmans, 1991).

Leslie Newbigin, "The Christian Faith and the World Religions," in G. Wainwright (ed.), *Keeping the Faith* (Philadelphia: Fortress Press, 1988), pp. 310–40.

——, *The Gospel in a Pluralist Society* (Grand Rapids: Eerdmans, 1989).

Joseph A. Di Noia, *The Diversity of Religions: A Christian Perspective* (Washington, DC: Catholic University of America Press, 1992).

Clark H. Pinnock, *A Wideness in God's Mercy: The Finality of Jesus Christ in a World of Religions* (Grand Rapids: Zondervan, 1992).

Karl Rahner, "Christianity and the Non-Christian Religions," in *Theological Investigations*, vol. 5 (London: Darton, Longman and Todd, 1966), pp. 115–34.

Kenneth Rose, *Knowing the Real: John Hick on the Cognitivity of Religions and Religious Pluralism* (Frankfurt/New York: Peter Lang, 1996).

Miikka Ruokanen, *The Catholic Doctrine of Non-Christian Religions According to the Second Vatican Council* (Leiden: Brill, 1992).

Wilfrid Cantwell Smith, *Towards a World Theology* (London: Macmillan, 1981).

Robert L. Wilken, "Religious Pluralism and Early Christian Theology," *Interpretation*, 44 (1988), pp. 379–91.

George H. Williams, "Erasmus and the Reformers on Non-Christian Religions and *Salus Extra Ecclesia*," in T. K. Rabb and J. E. Seigel (eds), *Action and Conviction in Early Modern Europe* (Princeton, NJ: Princeton University Press, 1969), pp. 130–48.

Last Things

For a selection of primary sources of relevance, see Alister E. McGrath, *The Christian Theology Reader* (Oxford/Cambridge, MA: Blackwell Publishers, 1995), pp. 352–74.

Philip C. Almond, *Heaven and Hell in Enlightenment England* (Cambridge: Cambridge University Press, 1994).

John M. Baillie, *And the Life Everlasting* (London: Oxford University Press, 1934).

Carl E. Bratten, "The Kingdom of God and the Life Everlasting," in P. Hodgson and R. King (eds), *Christian Theology* (Philadelphia: Fortress Press, 1982), pp. 274–98.

Rudolf Bultmann, *History and Eschatology* (Edinburgh: Edinburgh University Press, 1957).

Richard T. France, "Kingdom of God," in A. E. McGrath (ed.), *The Blackwell Encyclopaedia of Modern Christian Thought* (Oxford/Cambridge, MA: Blackwell Publishers, 1993), pp. 301–4.

Zachary Hayes, *Vision of a Future: A Study of Christian Eschatology* (Wilmington, DE: Michael Glazier, 1989).

Monika Hellwig, *What are They Saying about Death and Christian Hope?* (New York: Paulist Press, 1978).

Jonathan L. Kvanvig, *The Problem of Hell* (Oxford: Oxford University Press, 1994).

Andrew T. Lincoln, *Paradise Now and Not Yet: Studies in the Role of the Heavenly Dimension in Paul's Thought with Special Reference to his Eschatology* (Cambridge: Cambridge University Press, 1981).

J. A. MacCulloch, *The Harrowing of Hell* (Edinburgh: T. & T. Clark, 1930).

James Martin, *The Last Judgement in Protestant Theology* (Edinburgh: Oliver & Boyd, 1963).

Paul Minear, *Christian Hope and the Second Coming* (Philadelphia: Fortress Press, 1974).

Jürgen Moltmann, *Theology of Hope: On the Grounds and Implications of a Christian Eschatology* (London: SCM Press, and New York: Harper & Row, 1968).

H. Richard Niebuhr, *The Kingdom of God in America* (New York: Harper & Row, 1959).

Joseph Ratzinger, *Eschatology* (Washington, DC: Catholic University of America Press, 1989).

J. A. T. Robinson, *In the End God* (London: Collins, 1968).

Christopher C. Rowland, *The Open Heaven: A study of Apocalyptic in Judaism and Early Christianity* (New York: Crossroad, 1982).

John Sanders, *No Other Name: An Investigation into the Destiny of the Unevangelized* (Grand Rapids: Eerdmans, 1992).

Hans Schwarz, *On the Way to the Future: A Christian View of Eschatology* (Minneapolis: Augsburg Publishing House, 1979).

Albert Schweitzer, *The Quest of the Historical Jesus*, 3rd edn (London: A. & C. Black, 1954).

Krister Stendahl (ed.) *Immortality and Resurrection* (New York: Macmillan, 1965).

Johannes Weiss, *Jesus' Proclamation of the Kingdom of God* (London: SCM Press, 1971).

Ben Witherington III, *Jesus, Paul and the End of the World* (Downers Grove, IL: InterVarsity Press, 1992).

Sources of Citations

All substantial citations within the text of the case studies have been sourced, to allow users to read them in their original context and in greater depth. Shorter citations have not generally been sourced. Note that a figure in bold type against a reading indicates that the reading may be studied in greater depth in the companion volume to this introduction, Alister E. McGrath, *The Christian Theology Reader* (Oxford/Cambridge, MA: Blackwell Publishers, 1995). This work includes 280 readings drawn from 161 different sources, covering the entire range of Christian history and theological issues. Thus **[7.4]** refers to the fourth reading in chapter seven of the collection, entitled "Petilian of Citra on the Purity of Ministers," which is to be found on p. 262 of the work.

p. 41
Irenaeus, *adversus haereses*, II.ii.1–iv.1; in *Sources chrétiennes*, vol. 211, ed. A. Rousseau and L. Doutreleau (Paris: Editions du Cerf, 1974), 24.1–32.29; 44.1–7. **[2.2]**

p. 43
Tertullian, *de praescriptione haereticorum*, xx, 4–xxi, 4; xxxii.1; in *Sources chrétiennes*, vol. 46, ed. R. F. Refoulé (Paris: Editions du Cerf, 1957), 112.17–115.15; 130.1–8. **[2.5]**

p. 44
Vincent of Lérins, *Commonitorium*, II, 1–3; in *Florilegium Patristicum 5: Vincentii Lerinensis Commonitoria*, ed. G. Rauschen (Bonn: Hanstein, 1906), pp. 10–12. **[2.10]**

p. 53
Apollinarius of Laodicea, Letter 2; in H. Lietzmann, *Apollinaris von Laodicea und seine Schule* (Tübingen: Mohr, 1904), 256.3–7. **[4.8]**

p. 54
Gregory of Nazianzen, Letter 101; in J. P. Migne, *Patrologia Graeca*, 37:177B–180A; 181C–184A. **[4.9]**

p. 58
Socrates, *Historia Ecclesiastica*, VII, 32; in *Socratis Scholastica: Ecclesiastica Historia*, ed. R. Hussey (Oxford: Clarendon Press, 1853), vol. 2, pp. 804–7. **[4.10]**

p. 60
Cyril of Alexandria, Letter XVII, 12 (Third Letter to Nestorius); in Oxford Early Christian Texts: *Cyril of Alexandria: Select Let-*

ters, ed. L. R. Wickham (Oxford: Clarendon Press, 1983), 28.17–32.16. **[4.11]**

p. 73
Cyprian of Carthage, *de catholicae ecclesiae unitate*, 5–7; in *Corpus Christianorum: Series Latina*, vol. 3, ed. M. Bévenot (Turnholt: Brepols, 1972), 252.117–254.176. **[7.3]**

p. 77
Augustine, *de baptismo*, IV, 16, 18; in *Oeuvres de Saint Augustin*, vol. 29, ed. G. Finaert (Paris: Desclée, 1964), pp. 270–2; 280. **[8.7]**

p. 78
Petilian of Citra, Letter to Augustine, in Augustine, *contra litteras Petiliani* III.Iii.64; in *Corpus Scriptorum Ecclesiasticorum Latinorum*, vol. 52, ed. M. Petschenig (Vienna: Tempsky, 1909), pp. 462–3. **[7.4]**

p. 81
Pelagius, *Letter to Demetrias*, 16; in J. P. Migne, *Patrologia Latina*, 33:1110A–B. **[6.18]**

p. 85
Augustine, *de natura et gratia iii*, 3–iv, 4; in *Corpus Scriptorum Ecclesiasticorum Latinorum*, vol. 60, ed. C. F. Urba and J. Zycha (Vienna: Tempsky, 1913), 235.8–236.6. **[6.13]**

p. 88
Justin Martyr, *Apologia*, I.xl.vi.2–3; II.x.2–3; II.xiii.4–6; in *Saint Justin: Apologies*, ed. A. Wartelle (Paris: Etudes Augustiniennes, 1987), 160.6–9; 210.3–7; 216.11–18. **[1.1]**

p. 89
Clement of Alexandria, *Stromata*, I.v.28; in *Die griechischen christlichen Schriftsteller*

der erste Jahrhunderte. Clemens Alexandrinus: Zweiter Band. Stromata Buch I–VI, ed. O. Stählin and L. Früchtel (Berlin: Akademie Verlag, 1985), pp. 17.31–18.5. **[1.2]**

p. 90
Tertullian, *de praescriptione haereticorum*, 7; in *Sources chrétiennes*, vol. 46 ed. R. F. Refoulé (Paris: Editions du Cerf, 1957), 96.4–99.3. **[1.3]**

p. 92
Augustine, *de doctrina Christiana*, II.xl.60–61; in *Florilegium Patristicum*, vol. 29, ed. H. J. Vogels (Bonn: Peter Hanstein, 1930), 46.7–36. **[1.4]**

p. 128
Anselm of Canterbury, *Proslogion*, 3; in *S. Anselmi Opera Omnia*, vol. 1, ed. F. S. Schmitt (Edinburgh: Nelson, 1946), 102.6–103.9. **[1.7]**

p. 129
Gaunilo, *Responsio Anselmi*, 6; in *S. Anselmi: Opera Omnia*, vol. 1, ed. F. S. Schmitt (Edinburgh: Nelson, 1946), 128.14–32. **[1.8]**

p. 137
Thomas Aquinas, *Summa Theologiae*, IIIa q.48 a.2. **[5.13]**

p. 140
Hugh of St Victor, *de sacramentis*, IX, 2; in J. P. Migne, *Patrologia Latina*, 176.317C–318B. **[8.14]**

p. 142
Peter Lombard, *Sententiarum libri quatuor*, IV.i.4; ii.1; in *Sententiae in IV Libris Distinctae* (Rome: Editiones Collegii S. Bonaventuri, 1981), vol. 2, 233.9–20; 239.18–240.8. **[8.15]**

p. 146
Bernard of Clairvaux, *Sermones super Cantico Canticorum*, XLVI, 2; in *Sancti Bernardi Opera*, ed. J. Leclerc, C. H. Talbot, and H. M. Rochais (Rome: Editiones Cistercienses, 1958), 56.22–57.7. **[2.11]**

p. 185
Martin Luther, Preface to the Latin Works (1545); *D. Martin Luthers Werke: Kritisch Gesamtausgabe*, vol. 54 (Weimar: Böhlau, 1938), 185.12–186.21. **[6.26]**

p. 189
Martin Luther, Lectures on Romans (1515–1516); in *D. Martin Luthers Werke: Kritisch Gesamtausgabe*, vol. 56 (Weimar: Böhlau, 1938), 269.25–30; 272.3–21. **[6.28]**

p. 192
Council of Trent, Session VI, chapter 4; in H. Denzinger (ed.), *Enchiridion Symbolorum*, 24–25 edn (Barcelona: Herder, 1948), pp. 285–6. **[6.33]**

p. 192
Council of Trent, Session VI, chapter 14; in H. Denzinger (ed.), *Enchiridion Symbolorum*, 24–25 edn (Barcelona: Herder, 1948), pp. 285–6.

p. 193
Council of Trent, Session VI, chapter 7; in H. Denzinger (ed.), *Enchiridion Symbolorum*, 24–25 edn (Barcelona: Herder, 1948), 285–6.

p. 195
John Calvin, *Institutes*, III.ii,7;17; in *Joannis Calvini: Opera Selecta*, vol. 4, ed. P. Barth and W. Niesel (Munich: Kaiser, 1931), 16.31–5; 27.25–36. **[1.12]**

p. 196
Council of Trent, Session XIII, chapter 4;

in H. Denzinger (ed.), *Enchiridion Symbolorum*, 24–25 edn (Barcelona: Herder, 1948), p. 306. **[8.28]**

p. 198
Martin Luther, *The Babylonian Captivity of the Church* (1520); in *D. Martin Luthers Werke: Kritische Ausgabe*, vol. 6 (Weimar: Böhlau, 1888), 509.22–512.4. See also 8.16; 8.28. **[8.18]**

p. 202
Martin Luther, *On the Councils and the Church* (1539); in *D. Martin Luthers Werke: Kritische Gesamtausgabe*, vol. 50 (Weimar: Böhlau, 1914), 628.29–630.2. **[7.9]**

p. 203
Sebastian Franck, Letter to John Campanus, 1531; in B. Becker, "Fragment van Francks latijnse brief aan Campanus," *Nederlands Archief voor Kerkgeschiedenis*, 46 (1964–5), pp. 197–205; extract cited at pp. 201–4. **[7.12]**

p. 206
John Calvin, *Institutes*, IV.i.9–10; in *Joannis Calvini: Opera Selecta*, vol. 5, ed. P. Barth and W. Niesel (Munich: Kaiser Verlag, 1936), 13.24–16.31. **[7.14]**

p. 273
Albert Schweitzer, *The Quest of the Historical Jesus* (London: A. & C. Black, 3rd edn, 1954), p. 17.

p. 276
Martin Kähler, *Der sogenannte historische Jesus und der geschichtliche, biblische Christus*, ed. E. Wolf (Munich: Kaiser Verlag, 1953), p. 43. **[4.24]**

p. 278
Rudolf Bultmann, "The Significance of the Historical Jesus for the Theology of Paul,"

in *Faith and Understanding*, pp. 220–46, quote at p. 241.

p. 299
D. F. Strauss, *The Life of Jesus* (Philadelphia: Fortress Press, 1972), p. 758.

p. 302
Wolfhart Pannenberg, "Redemptive Event and History," in *Basic Questions in Theology*, vol. 1 (London: SCM Press, 1970), pp. 15–80; quote at p. 15.

p. 306
F. D. E. Schleiermacher, *The Christian Faith* (Edinburgh: T & T Clark, 1928), pp. 738–9. **[3.27]**

p. 313
Henri de Lubac, *Catholicism*, London: Burns & Oates, 1950, p. 29.

p. 314
John Calvin, *Institutes*, IV.i.9–10; in *Joannis Calvini: Opera Selecta*, ed. P. Barth and W. Niesel, vol. 5 (Munich: Kaiser Verlag, 1936), 13.24–16.31. **[7.14]**

p. 315
Karl Barth, *Dogmatics in Outline* (London: SCM Press, 1949), p. 143.

p. 315
Rudolf Bultmann, *Jesus Christ and Mythology* (London: SCM Press, 1959), pp. 82–3.

p. 316
Leonardo Boff, *Ecclesiogenesis: The Base Communities Reinvent the Church* (Maryknoll, NY: Orbis Books, 1986), p. 11. **[7.21]**

p. 319
Vatican II, *Nostra Aetate*, October 28, 1965; in *Vatican II: Conciliar and Postconciliar Documents*, ed. Austin Flannery, OP (Northport, NY: Costello Publishing Company, and Dublin: Dominican Publications, 1975), pp. 738–42. **[9.6]**

p. 323
Anne Carr, "Feminist Theology," in A. E. McGrath (ed.), *Blackwell Encyclopaedia of Modern Christian Thought* (Oxford: Blackwell Publishers, 1993), pp. 223–4. **[3.35]**

p. 324
Mary Hayter, *The New Eve in Christ* (London: SPCK, 1987), pp. 87–92. **[6.46]**

p. 324
Wolfhart Pannenberg, *Systematic Theology*, vol. 1 (Grand Rapids: Eerdmans, 1991), pp. 260–1.

p. 325
Sallie McFague, *Models of God* (Philadelphia: Fortress Press, 1987), pp. 122–3.

p. 325
Julian of Norwich, *Revelations of Divine Love*, translated by Clifton Wolters (Harmondsworth: Penguin, 1958), pp. 151; 174. **[3.22]**

p. 326
Paul Jewett, *God, Creation and Revelation* (Grand Rapids: Eerdmans, 1991), pp. 323–5. **[3.34]**

p. 326
Daphne Hampson, *Theology and Feminism* (Oxford: Blackwell, 1990), pp. 50–2. **[4.31]**

p. 326
Daphne Hampson, *Theology and Feminism* (Oxford: Blackwell, 1990), pp. 121–4. **[6.45]**

p. 328
John B. Cobb, Jr, "Beyond Pluralism," in G. D'Costa (ed.), *Christian Uniqueness Reconsidered: The Myth of a Pluralistic Theology of Religions* (Maryknoll, NY: Orbis, 1990), pp. 81–95; quote at pp. 81–4. **[9.10]**

p. 335
Paul Tillich, *Systematic Theology*, vol. 1 (Chicago: University of Chicago Press, 1951), pp. 59–64. **[1.24]**

p. 339
George Lindbeck, *The Nature of Doctrine* (Philadelphia: Westminster Press, 1984), pp. 32–5. **[1.28]**

p. 340
Gustavo Gutiérrez, *A Theology of Liberation*, 2nd edn (Maryknoll, NY: Orbis Books, and London: SCM Press, 1978), pp. 9–12. **[1.26]**

INDEX